Michael Meyer

# HENRIK IBSEN

## The Top of a Cold Mountain

1883-1906

Rupert Hart-Davis   London

Granada Publishing Limited
First Published in Great Britain 1971 by Rupert Hart-Davis Ltd
3 Upper James Street London W1R 4BP

Copyright © 1971 by Michael Meyer

ISBN 0 246 64040 5
Printed in Great Britain by C. Tinling & Co. Ltd
London and Prescot

Note
All translations of passages from languages other than English are
original, unless otherwise indicated.

# HENRIK IBSEN

Also by Michael Meyer

*Play*
  The Ortolan

*Biography*
  Henrik Ibsen
    Vol I: The Making of a Dramatist 1828–1864
    Vol II: The Farewell to Poetry 1864–1882

*Translations of Ibsen*
  Brand
  John Gabriel Borkman
  The Lady from the Sea
  When We Dead Awaken
  Little Eyolf
  The Master Builder
  Hedda Gabler
  The Wild Duck
  Ghosts
  The Pillars of Society
  Peer Gynt
  An Enemy of the People
  The Pretenders
  A Doll's House
  Rosmersholm

*Translations of Strindberg*
  The Plays, Volume One
    (The Father, Miss Julie, Creditors,
    The Stronger, Playing with Fire,
    Erik the Fourteenth, Storm, The
    Ghost Sonata)

Henrik Ibsen..

IBSEN in 1889, at the time of his meeting with Emilie Bardach

For Maria and Nora

# Contents

CONTENTS

# List of Illustrations

# ❧ Acknowledgements

My thanks are due to Mrs Reginald Orcutt for permission to quote from her father Basil King's two articles, *Ibsen and Emilie Bardach*, first published in the *Century Magazine* (New York), October-November, 1923; to Messrs Faber & Faber and the Society of Authors for permission to quote the various extracts from James Joyce's writings; to the Hogarth Press Ltd, Sigmund Freud Copyrights Ltd and the Institute of Psychoanalysis for permission to quote from Freud's essay on *Rosmersholm*; to the Hogarth Press Ltd, for permission to quote from John Linton's translation of Rainer Maria Rilke's *The Notebook of Malte Laurids Brigge*; and to Routledge and Kegan Paul Ltd, for permission to quote the extract from Sidney Keyes's poem, *Sour Land*.

I must also repeat my thanks to Mr Tancred Ibsen for granting me access to his grandfather's unpublished account books; to Mr Øyvind Anker and his staff at the University Library of Oslo; and to the staffs of the University Library of Stockholm, the Royal Library of Stockholm, the library of University College, London, the British Museum, the British Drama League and the Victoria and Albert Museum. I should again like to pay particular acknowledgement of my debt to Halvdan Koht's *Henrik Ibsen: eit diktarliv*, and to the Centenary Edition of Ibsen's works edited by Koht, Francis Bull and Didrik Arup Seip, especially the introductions to the various volumes by those three scholars. In discussing Ibsen's work I have sometimes used material previously printed in my introductions to my translations of the plays, published by Rupert Hart-Davis Ltd. My debts to other sources are recorded in the footnotes and bibliography.

Works which appear repeatedly in the footnotes have been given the following short titles after their first appearance:

*C.E.*—Centenary edition of Ibsen's Works (*Henrik Ibsen, Samlede verker, hundreårsutgave*), I–XXI, ed. Halvdan Koht, Francis Bull and Didrik Arup Seip (Oslo, 1928–58).

ACKNOWLEDGEMENTS

Koht—Halvdan Koht, *Henrik Ibsen: eit diktarliv*, I–II (revised edition, Oslo, 1954).

*Brandes Brevveksling*—Edvard og Georg Brandes, *Brevveksling med nordiske Forfattere og Videnskabsmænd*, ed. Morten Borup, Francis Bull and John Landquist, I–VIII (Copenhagen, 1939–42).

The photograph of Herman Bang is reproduced by courtesy of Det Kgl. Bibliotek, Copenhagen; that of Rosa Fitinghoff by courtesy of Fru Viola Wahlstedt-Guillemaut; and all other illustrations by courtesy of Universitetsbiblioteket, Oslo, and Gyldendal Norsk Forlag, Oslo.

All translations of passages from languages other than English are original, except where otherwise indicated.

M.M.

'We can see horribly clear in the works of such a man his whole life, as if we were God's spies.'

John Keats, writing of Robert Burns to John Hamilton Reynolds

# HENRIK IBSEN

# PART ONE
# THE AUTUMN OF A DRAMATIST

ONE

# The Wild Duck

## (1883–1884)

THE YEAR 1883 opened for Ibsen with a series of productions of *An Enemy of the People*, which he had completed the previous June. The premiere took place at Christiania on 13 January; Bergen followed suit on 24 January, Gothenburg and Helsinki in February, and Stockholm and Copenhagen in March. In Germany, strangely considering the success there of *The Pillars of Society* and *A Doll's House*, it had to wait four years before being staged. Its reception was everywhere cordial but nowhere enthusiastic. Carl Georgsson Fleetwood, a young Swedish diplomat, probably hit on the reason for this when, after seeing the Stockholm production, he noted in his diary: 'It is a mirror in which our age *could* see itself, but which it does not really understand. The audience tonight did not grasp what the play was really about . . . From the moment I read it . . . I realised how lonely and uncomprehended a man like Ibsen must be, and tonight confirmed my conviction'.[1] Ibsen's main appeal in every country was to the young, to men like Fleetwood, Otto Brahm and Paul Schlenther, Herman Bang, William Archer, Konstantin Stanislavsky and Aurélien Lugné-Poe, and the views of the young, the ones who are about, in Dr Stockmann's words, to 'ginger up the future', are often unreflected in the columns of established reviewers.[2] 'Ibsen showed us our problems,' recalled a member of the new generation, 'our doubts, the injustices of our age, how dead tradition survived in a living shape, our belief in the future, in a just world built upon truth'.[3] And another remembered how: 'Terrified parents well-meaningly tried to exercise a censorship over both the reading and the seeing of his plays, but just as forbidden fruit tastes sweetest, so there lay an indescribable delight, tinged with fear, in sneaking up to the gallery of a theatre

---

[1] Carl Georgsson Fleetwood, *Från studieår och diplomattjänst* (Stockholm, 1968), I, p. 286.
[2] As witness John Osborne's *Look Back in Anger*, the most influential play of the nineteen-fifties, which, on the occasion of its original production in 1954, was dismissed by nearly all the London critics.
[3] Gurli Linder, *Sällskapsliv i Stockholm under 1880- och 1890-talen* (Stockholm, 1918), p. 160.

against the express commands of parents and schoolteachers . . . Is it to be wondered at that such stage creations as August Lindberg's Peer Gynt, Hjalmar
Ekdal, John Gabriel Borkman, Oswald, etc., were so engraved upon one's
memory that they can never be erased?'[1]

*An Enemy of the People* had scarcely appeared before Ibsen began to think
about its successor, for on 11 January 1883 he wrote to Hegel from Rome that he
was 'already planning a new drama about contemporary life. It will be in four
acts, and I hope to be able to get down to the actual writing within a couple of
months at most. The Italian air, and the pleasant way of life down here, greatly
increase my eagerness to create. I find it much easier to work here than in
Germany'. He seems at first to have been projecting another broadside of sociological criticism, for his preliminary notes include caustic observations on
marriage ('has set the mark of slavery on everyone'), Christianity ('demoralizes
and inhibits both men and women'), modern society ('merely a society of
males'), and one splendid aphorism which deserves to figure in any anthology
of quotations: 'Our best thoughts are thought by our worst scoundrels'. But
instead of dashing off this play at once, like *An Enemy of the People*, he returned
to his old routine of brooding on it for a year, and by the time he got down to
writing the dialogue of *The Wild Duck* social criticism had faded into the background, where it was to remain for the rest of his life.

As a subsidiary occupation and more immediate source of income, he suggested to Hegel that he might revise, and write a preface to, *The Feast at Solhaug*.
'The rewriting of this old play', he assured Hegel on 21 February, 'will not
seriously delay the new work I am planning'. Hegel replied on 1 March
accepting the idea enthusiastically and suggesting an edition of 4,000 copies
against a fee of 225 crowns (£12-10-0) per signature, or 14 crowns (15
shillings) a page. As with his *Poems* thirteen years previously, Ibsen had no
copy of his own to work from, in print or in manuscript, and had to ask Hegel
to try to obtain one for him from a second-hand bookshop. The work went
rapidly (how can he have thought that dull old play worthy of a reprint?), and
he posted off the final instalment on 6 April.

Early in May the actress Lucie Wolf, who had worked under him in Bergen
and Christiania, asked him to write a verse prologue for a jubilee performance
being arranged to celebrate her thirty years on the stage. Any plea to return to
poetry touched him on a sensitive nerve, like a plea to return to Skien, and he
replied on 25 May with a peppery re-statement of his position:

*. . . If only I could accede to your request! Nothing would be dearer to me. But I
cannot; I cannot because of the artistic convictions I hold in this matter. Prologues,*

---

[1] Unspecified article by Arne Randel, quoted by Per Lindberg, *op. cit.*, p. 379.

epilogues and everything of the kind should unconditionally be barred from the stage. Only dramatic art belongs there, and declamation is not dramatic art.

Your prologue must naturally be in verse, for such is the accepted convention. But I cannot conspire to keep this convention alive. Poetry has caused dreadful damage to the art of acting. A theatrical artist who seeks his repertoire in contemporary drama should not willingly let a line of verse pass his lips. Poetry will scarcely find any place worth mentioning in the drama of the immediate future; for the creative intentions of the future will certainly not be reconciled with it. So it will die. Artistic forms die out just as inefficient prehistoric animals died out when their time was up.

A tragedy in iambic pentameters is already as rare a phenomenon as the dodo bird, of which only a few specimens survive on an African island.

I myself have during the past seven or eight years hardly written a single verse, but have devoted myself exclusively to the incomparably more difficult art of writing in the consistently true language of reality. It is through this language that you have become the distinguished artist that you are. Slick verse has never helped you to corrupt anyone's judgment.

But this leads me to what I think is the main point. In a prologue all kinds of pleasantries must be addressed to the public. They must be thanked for their indulgence and their guiding judgment; the artist must belittle himself as only the intricacies of rhymed verse will permit. But is there any truth in such a device? You know as well as I do that there is no truth in it. Quite the contrary. You do not stand in the public's debt; it is the public which owes an immense debt to you for your thirty years of loyal service.

I regard it as the duty of any serious artist to maintain this standpoint, both for his own sake and for that of his profession. You will, I am sure, appreciate that, feeling as I do, I cannot with a good conscience agree to compose a prologue for the occasion in question . . .

But if I cannot serve you in this matter, I hope you will not the less accept the thanks I now send you, thanks for everything you have been and still are to the art of our theatre, and especially thanks for the distinguished share which you have taken in the presentation of so many of my own dramatic works.

In that hope, and with the heartfelt wish that there may still lie ahead of you a long and brilliant career, I sign myself, in old friendship,

Your affectionate
Henrik Ibsen.

The new edition of *The Feast at Solhaug* appeared in June, and at the same time Ibsen learned that a sixth edition of *The Pretenders*, one of his steadiest sellers, was in the press. He also heard from Georg Brandes that the latter's most recent essay on him (later published as the 'Second Impression' in Brandes's

1898 book on Ibsen) was to appear in Germany, which must have gratified him, since he regarded it as the most penetrating and sympathetic study of his work yet to have appeared.

The Ibsens had now begun to hold weekly soirées, and visitors who had been daunted by tales of their prickliness, and of the Webb-like plainness of the fare they had provided in Munich, were often pleasantly surprised. A young Norwegian named Kristian Gloersen who attended these gatherings speaks of Suzannah's 'always ample and tastefully decorated table, at which a relaxed and witty atmosphere invariably prevailed', and praises both her and Ibsen's excellence as hosts, their attention to even the humblest guests and their skill at arranging congenial little groups within a party, not always a Scandinavian, or for that matter an English talent. He also refers to Ibsen's 'personal lovableness', remarking that 'despite his withdrawnness, his *noli me tangere*, his often chilly mask and eruptions of vehement bitterness, there appeared frequent glimpses of a warmth of heart and of a fine and noble character, doubly winning because of his anxiety to conceal it.'[1] Gunnar Heiberg, too, confirms Ibsen's skill as a host: 'It was an especial pleasure to see Ibsen speak with and entertain the many old or aging ladies who came there. He sat down amongst them and talked of his experiences, his books, his travels. One evening, I well recall, he spoke in great detail to three old ladies about his trip to Egypt. He gesticulated and talked vividly. He let himself be carried away. It was as though he were describing the events for the first time, as though the words were only this moment forming on his lips . . . The old ladies' eyes shone with intense gratitude. I remember this sight of Ibsen creeping out of his marble shell in honour of a few old ladies who he thought needed a little sparkle and happiness in their eyes.'[2]

Gloersen, who saw a lot of Ibsen in 1882 and 1883, records how he enjoyed, as of old, provoking people by the Socratic use of paradox, often pushing his listeners' arguments to the point of absurdity. He 'liked to be opposed when he came out with his most audacious paradoxes, which were perhaps directed to that end.' Thus, late one night at the Café Nazionale, after a ball at the Scandinavian Club, he declared: 'They should guillotine the bourgeoisie as a hundred years ago in France they guillotined the aristocrats.' No-one in Norway who called himself a liberal or a republican was prepared to make any personal sacrifices. They would give nothing, sacrifice nothing, to enable the poor to be equal with them. If it came to the crunch, none of them would

---

[1] Kristian Gloersen, *Henrik Ibsen: minder fra mit samvær med ham i utlandet*, in *Kringsjaa*, 1906, xxvii, pp. 342–347.

[2] Gunnar Heiberg, *Salt og sukker*, pp. 55–56.

man the barricades. There must be a revolution, everything existing must come down, down. 'The Right, did you say? My dear fellow, I want nothing to do with them, one can't count them any longer. They don't belong to the saga of the future. The only useful thing they do is undermine their own position and show us the best way through the ruins. In that respect the reactionaries are our best allies.'[1] No wonder the young Bernard Shaw, to whom William Archer was at this time reading Ibsen's plays, translating off the cuff as he went, felt that he had discovered a kindred spirit.

A similar account of Ibsen in provocative mood that year comes from a Dr Undset, who wrote home to a friend:

'Ibsen is interminably radical; I have now got to know him and his opinions better. One evening I went out with him and the writer N.N., who is also here this winter, to a restaurant. Late at night—somewhere around the sixth glass—Ibsen really started talking, and you should have heard him. Poor N.N., who is a Norwegian liberal, a friend of Bjørnson and so forth, has close connections with *Dagbladet* [the liberal daily]; you should have seen him when Ibsen cut loose and started on them! He didn't name B. B[jørnson]. 'Sverdrup? The most contemptible sharper that ever lived! *Dagbladet* and *Verdens Gang* [another progressive newspaper]? Cheap, lying, cowardly rags! How can these wretched people not see that to hold power is a very subordinate position?' And so on for more than an hour, I think, to the amazed and terrified N.N. Ibsen refuses to acknowledge nationalism or anything any more; he is a complete anarchist, wants to wipe everything out—put a torpedo under the ark— mankind must start from the foundations to rebuild the world—and they must begin with the individual! . . . Society and everything else must be wiped out, wherever it in the smallest degree hampers our work; then possibly some kind of insurance companies may be allowed to emerge in place of the present societies and states. Or else—well, that will be society's problem, to decide what is to emerge; the great task of our age is to blow the existing fabric into the air—to destroy . . . He is remarkable, a titanic character! I mentioned the 'sixth glass', but I don't think Ibsen often drinks that much; only, now and then, when he's with someone he likes talking to, he enjoys going into a café and arguing late into the night. But this happens only seldom, and doesn't affect his life or his serious work.'[2]

---

[1] Gloersen, p. 339.
[2] Gran, II, pp. 143–145.

Dr Undset's comment on Ibsen's drinking habits is confirmed by two reliable observers. William Archer wrote: 'The oft-repeated stories of his over-indulgence in stimulants were, to the best of my belief, such gross exaggerations as to be practically falsehoods . . . In Germany, in Denmark, in Norway, I have been with him repeatedly, have seen him evidently pursuing his daily habit in the matter of spirituous liquors, and have always noted the moderation of that habit. On one public occasion when it was afterwards spread abroad that he had conspicuously exceeded, I both walked and talked with him, and can positively assert that there was no truth whatever in the scandal.'[1] Bergliot Ibsen confirms this: 'I have seen him sit for hours on end sipping at a glass of red wine. In the same way, he used to sip at the famous glass of brandy at the Grand, which people transformed into a 'regiment of nips'. People assumed it must always be a new glass, since it always seemed full. When in his old age Ibsen's complexion became ruddy, the gossips found fresh grist for their mill . . . In fact, Ibsen suffered from a nervous eczema . . . When he died his physician, Dr Bull, told me he had never seen a better preserved constitution.'[2] The idea that Ibsen was a semi-alcoholic for most of his life is another of the myths that need to be exploded.

Ibsen was sometimes inclined to hold forth on subjects of which he was largely ignorant. Thus, Gunnar Heiberg records, he liked to expatiate on science, although 'he was ignorant of the most elementary principles thereof . . . He talked of flying machines and electricity with a buoyant enthusiasm which deceived us laymen but shocked professionals, or even people with a sound general education. A Danish engineer, unimpressed by Ibsen's literary renown, told him in round terms that he lacked the most elementary knowledge and was talking plain rubbish. Ibsen did not like this, but continued. It often seemed as though he preferred to acquire the rudiments of knowledge in this way rather than by reading, which he did not much enjoy . . . J. P. Jacobsen often shook his head when Ibsen touched on his particular field of botany; he smiled his wise, gentle smile and said that he knew many small boys who knew more about botany than this ex-apothecary.'[3] Heiberg adds, probably correctly, that he felt that 'scientific phenomena in themselves interested Ibsen less than how the various people present treated them, the temperament and tempo with which they dismissed them'. Gloersen, too, noted Ibsen's analytical interest in people's ways of speech; he would often ask a question à propos of nothing, directed now to a man, now to a woman, to see how they replied. He once

---

[1] *Ibsen as I Knew Him*, pp. 9–10.
[2] Bergliot Ibsen, pp. 215–216.
[3] Gunnar Heiberg, *Salt og sukker*, pp. 46–48.

asked Gloersen: 'Have you ever noticed how in conversation a woman usually ends a remark with a word of two or three syllables, a man with a mono-syllable?' Gloersen thought this absurd, but on testing Ibsen's theory was astonished to find it correct.[1] Ibsen once similarly surprised John Paulsen, before their quarrel, by saying: 'Has it ever occurred to you that the lines in a play should sound different according to whether they are said in the morning or the evening?'[2]

Gloersen noted Ibsen's routine. He liked to take a morning walk up the Via Sistina to Monte Pincio. Between twelve and one he would drop in at the Café Nazionale, where he had a special seat in which he liked to sit, though it was not reserved for him as at the Café Maximilian in Munich and, later, the Grand in Christiania. He was annoyed if he found it occupied. He lunched at two or two-thirty 'since he could not reconcile himself to the custom most followed abroad then of two meals a day, lunch at twelve to one, and dinner at seven to eight.'[3] He often urged Gloersen to settle in Rome, since he knew of nowhere else that was so good for writing. 'Here I can write a book every year', Ibsen said to him in the euphoric mood of *An Enemy of the People.* 'At home there would be a gap of five years. Why go home and let yourself be buttonholed by hundreds of people, scarcely one per cent of whom you have any use for?'[4] He added that (as he had told Laura Kieler) he preferred to live far from Norway when writing a play with a Norwegian setting. 'Life and its phenomena are best viewed by a writer at a distance, in both time and space.'[5] He assured Gloersen that he was quite indifferent to what critics wrote about him, but Suzannah said (in his absence) that this was quite untrue and that he minded a lot.

Sigurd was now in Paris, his father having promised him a holiday there as a reward for having become, the previous summer, at twenty-two and a half, 'the youngest Doctor of Law in Rome' (as Ibsen proudly informed Bjørnson on 4 August 1882). It was the first time the young man had gone anywhere alone. He wrote frequent and vivid letters home about his cultural and gastronomic experiences; on 24 May he told his father that he had been to the theatre between twenty-five and thirty times in three months. He saw Sarah Bernhardt in Sardou's *Feodora* but, as befitted Ibsen's son, had reservations about her performance. 'The modern theatre-goer', he wrote, 'is somewhat

---

[1] Gloersen, pp. 343–344.
[2] John Paulsen, *Samliv med Ibsen*, I, p. 168.
[3] Gloersen, pp. 337–338.
[4] *Ibid.*, pp. 342–343.
[5] *Ibid.*, p. 347.

sceptical about daggers and poisoned goblets, disguised spies and swapped letters as the causes of death and catastrophe. It is also possible that Sarah Bernhardt's own personality hinders the illusion, that she is too unusual a person to be convincing as an actress, that she absorbs the role instead of losing herself in it. But her appearance, manner, movement and voice are something so remarkable that no one who has seen her will easily forget her.' The smartness of Paris audiences impressed him; and he relates one sad occasion when Lorentz Dietrichson addressed a gathering of artists and so bored and angered them that 'they bombarded him with meatbones and bread, broke his glass so that the wine spilled over his clothes, and called him an idiot . . . so that in the end he had to take his hat and go.'[1]

At the end of June Ibsen left with Suzannah for Gossensass, and while he was there *Ghosts* received its first European performance. The main Scandinavian theatres still fought shy, but August Lindberg, the young Swede who had found Ibsen so taciturn in Munich three years earlier, and had unsuccessfully tried to persuade Ludvig Josephson to stage the play in Stockholm, asked Ibsen's permission to set up a production to tour Sweden, Norway and Denmark. Ibsen agreed, asking 400 crowns (£22) for the Swedish provincial rights excluding Stockholm and Gothenburg, another 400 crowns for Stockholm, 500 crowns (£28) for Copenhagen and 500 crowns for Christiania, stipulating only that 'the play be not staged in Christiania before it has been performed in Stockholm and Copenhagen. The reasons for this I shall not go into.' Presumably he thought it more likely to get a fair hearing in the two last-named capitals. He added some advice on the translation, which, though overlapping that given to Rasmus Anderson of Wisconsin the previous year, bears recording. 'The language must sound natural and the mode of expression must be distinctive for every character in the play; one human being does not express himself like another . . . The effect of the play depends greatly on the audience feeling that they are listening to something that is actually happening in real life.' He also stressed (a reminder of the immense length of time that nineteenth-century audiences liked to spend in a theatre) that *Ghosts*, 'although only three acts, fills a whole evening', and that 'nothing else must be acted either before or after the play. I should also like this work of mine to be staged everywhere without the employment of an orchestra, either before the performance or during the intervals.' *Ghosts* runs (if one allows for two ten-minute intervals) for about two and a half hours, nearly half an hour less than *A Doll's House*, which was itself much shorter than any of his previous plays; one of

[1] Bergliot Ibsen, pp. 93–98.

Ibsen's forgotten contributions to the theatre was to remind audiences of a fact forgotten since the Greeks, that a tragedy need not fill five acts. Strindberg, within the decade, was to prove that it need fill no more than one.

Lindberg coaxed a once-famous actress named Hedwig Charlotte Winter-Hjelm out of retirement to play Mrs Alving and, to prepare himself for the role of Oswald, visited a hospital in Copenhagen to study children who were insane as the result of inherited syphilis. 'Down the steps came a procession of the living dead. Small children, lying in their beds and mechanically playing with a little bell which each held in his or her hand. The procession passed on either side of us. Some were carried in nurses' arms, some ran, but most were pushed in their chairs. I bowed to the doctor, ran down the stairs more quickly than I had ascended them, and returned to Hälsingborg. But I never forgot the sight.'[1]

The rehearsals had a deeply disturbing effect on the players. Lindberg himself suffered from repeated nightmares, and when he rehearsed with Fru Winter-Hjelm's understudy the scene in which Oswald tells his mother of his illness, the effect was such that she had to leave the stage.

*Ghosts* opened at Hälsingborg, on the Swedish west coast, on 22 August 1883. The press and audience came expecting to be scandalised; but the play which respectable citizens had refused to have on their shelves proved, in performance, to scandalise no one. Lindberg telegraphed Ludvig Josephson that the atmosphere in the theatre had been like 'a new Oberammergau'. The Danish newspaper *Dagbladet*'s reporter wrote an ecstatic notice and was rewarded with the sack, the editor being of the opinion that no decent theatre ought to perform the play. Six days later Lindberg's production crossed the Sound and played for ten nights at the Folketeater in Copenhagen, where the effect was the same. 'The excitement in the auditorium', Lindberg recalled, 'rose as though in small cyclones. Fru Winter-Hjelm whispered at one stage: "Dare we go on?" ' The audience found themselves unshocked, moved and gripped, and the production played to full houses each night at double the usual prices. '*Ghosts*', wrote Lindberg to Josephson, 'is causing an excitement which spreads from house and home, from street and café, to the box office at the Folketeater.'

Josephson, his fears allayed, signed up the production to visit his theatre in Stockholm in September, where it was so well received that the Royal Theatre, a few hundred yards away, followed with a production of its own within the month. Then, on 17 October, Lindberg's company presented the first per-

---

[1] For this passage and other details surrounding this production, cf. Lindberg, pp. 96–115.

formance of *Ghosts* in Norway at, appropriately, the old Møllergaden Theatre[1] where, a quarter of a century earlier, Ibsen had, as artistic director, suffered his long series of humiliations. William Archer happened to be in Christiania at the time and attended the premiere. 'I was present, and well remember the profound impression it made on the crowded and enthusiastic audience. By this time the reaction in favour of the play had fairly set in. It happened that on the same evening a trivial French farce, *Tête de Linotte* (known in English as *Miss Featherbrain*) was being played at the Christiania Theatre; and the contrast could not but strike people. They saw a masterpiece of Norwegian literature acted by a foreign (Swedish) company at a minor playhouse, while the official theatre of the capital was given over to a piece of Parisian frivolity. The result was that on the following evening, and for some nights afterwards, demonstrations were made at the Christiania Theatre against the policy of the management in rejecting Ibsen's play . . . Fru Winter-Hjelm's performance of Mrs Alving was exceedingly powerful, and Lindberg seemed to me an almost ideal Oswald. In his make-up, I remember, there was a strong suggestion of the portraits of Edgar Allan Poe.'[2]

Lindberg himself has left an interesting impression of the Christiania premiere as it seemed to someone on the other side of the footlights. 'When the curtain was raised, it felt as though the public held its breath. The scenes of the play unfolded in a silence worthy of a spiritual seance. When the final curtain fell, the silence continued for a good while before the ovations started.'[3] The Norwegian Gunnar Heiberg commented: 'Pastor Manders, Engstrand, Helmer and several other gentlemen had leagued together to prevent *Ghosts* from being staged . . . A foreigner had to bring us our own play. What the Swede Lindberg did remains one of the great occasions in the history of the Norwegian theatre.'[4] And Lindberg himself wrote to Ibsen: 'It was high time that *Ghosts* arrived, for the theatres up here have lived for so long on French comedy that we are well on the way to becoming monkeys instead of men. But now we see the truth, and the clowning and smirking are past. Real tears now fall on

---

[1] Despite an appeal by Ibsen to Lindberg (19 August 1883) not to stage it there. 'The place is so cramped and cluttered, the distance between actors and audience so short, that no full effect will be achievable.' One would have supposed such a small theatre to be ideal for *Ghosts*; Ibsen's own bitter memories of Møllergaden may have been the real reason. Lindberg had asked the Christiania Theatre permission to stage it there, but Schrøder refused. The latter went to see the play at Møllergaden, and came away convinced that he had been right. Cf. Carl Just, *Schrøder og Christiania Theater* (Oslo, 1948), pp. 184–185, 190–191.
[2] Archer's introduction to his translation of *Ghosts* (London, 1900), pp. vii–viii.
[3] Lindberg, p. 112.
[4] *Ibid.*, pp. 113–114.

the stage, and that with no sense of shame. It is something new and splendid to assist in the reintroduction of nature to the stage.'[1]

Altogether, Lindberg's company performed *Ghosts* seventy-five times during this tour and he returned with the production to Christiania several times over the next few years. The following year, a Danish company toured the play through the Norwegian provinces (to give them credit, they and another Danish company had applied for permission to stage *Ghosts* before Lindberg had his premiere)[2] but the main Scandinavian theatres (outside Stockholm) still fought shy, and it was not until 1890, nine years after its publication, that *Ghosts* was acted by a Norwegian company, at the Bergen Theatre. Schrøder, the director of the Christiania Theatre, steadfastly refused to let it be performed there as long as he remained in charge, and it was not played by Norwegians in their own capital until 1900 (when the Christiania Theatre had been replaced by the National Theatre), nor at the Royal Theatre in Copenhagen until 1903. In Germany, police censorship prevented any public performance being given for many years, although a number of private performances took place in various cities from 1886. England and France were not to see the play until the nineties (and no public performance was allowed in England before 1914).

In early October Ibsen left Gossensass for Botzen near the Italian frontier, proceeding to Rome at the end of the month. From Rome, on 30 November, he addressed a final appeal through his old friend O. A. Bachke, to the Norwegian Ecclesiastical Department to admit Sigurd into his country's diplomatic service. The way now lay open, he explained, for Sigurd to make a career in the *Italian* foreign service; 'but before this can happen, he will have to be naturalised. And this is the step which we find it so difficult to take. To cut oneself wholly off from one's country—that is a serious matter. I, therefore, on my son's behalf, make this last effort to keep him a Norwegian citizen by asking if you would and could extract a promise from the government that my son will be considered for a post as attaché when one next falls vacant . . . I am reluctant to believe that, as some have suggested, I should be such a *bête noire* to certain members of the government that they will totally refuse to meet me in this matter. I know well what I can expect from the head of the Ecclesiastical Department, but fortunately his voice is not decisive in this case.'

The likelihood of any politician doing Ibsen a favour after *An Enemy of the People* must have seemed more than ever remote; but who can foretell the ways of statesmen? Bachke lost his job as Minister of Justice the following

---

[1] *Ibid.*, p. 115.
[2] Cf. Ibsen's letter to Betty Borchsenius, 15 June 1883.

spring, so Ibsen approached the Prime Minister, Sverdrup, and when the following summer Sigurd called on him in Christiania, he so impressed him that Sverdrup pulled the necessary strings. Thus Sigurd got into the Norwegian consular service and remained a Norwegian. Future Prime Ministers, unfortunately, were less ready than Sverdrup to appreciate Sigurd's qualities.

So 1883 ended. Thanks mainly to the various productions of *An Enemy of the People*, which brought in 8,704 crowns (£483), it had been a better year:

|  | crowns | £ |
|---|---|---|
| Fee for *An Enemy of the People* in Christiania | 4,000 | 222 |
| Fee for *An Enemy of the People* in Bergen | 800 | 44 |
| Fee for *An Enemy of the People* in Gothenburg | 500 | 28 |
| 2nd edition of *The Feast at Solhaug* | 1,575 | 87 |
| 6th edition of *The Pretenders* | 1,125 | 62 |
| Fee for *An Enemy of the People* in Helsinki | 250 | 14 |
| Fee for *An Enemy of the People* at Royal Theatre, Copenhagen (2nd–10th performances) | 2,204 | 123 |
| Fees from German League of Dramatists | 43 | 2 |
| Fee for *An Enemy of the People* at Royal Theatre, Stockholm (2nd–14th performances) | 950 | 53 |
| Scandinavian provincial rights of *The League of Youth* and *Ghosts* (August Lindberg) | 400 | 22 |
| Fee for *Ghosts* in Copenhagen (Lindberg) | 500 | 28 |
| Fee for *Ghosts* in Stockholm (Lindberg) | 400 | 22 |
| Danish provincial rights for *Ghosts* (Otto Petersen) | 500 | 28 |
| Norwegian provincial rights for *Ghosts* (Olaus Olsen) | 600 | 33 |
| 5th edition of *The League of Youth* | 906 | 51 |
|  | 14,753 | 819 |

In the same year Henry Arthur Jones, an indifferent English playwright, who had just achieved his first success with a melodrama called *The Silver King*, (and who that winter was to adapt *A Doll's House* for the English stage) earned £3,398,[1] well over four times as much as Ibsen.

1884 began with a letter from Bjørnson urging Ibsen yet again to return and take over the directorship of the Christiania Theatre. But the offer held even less attraction for him than when it had last been made, and he replied on 9 January:

---

[1] Doris Arthur Jones, *The Life and Letters of Henry Arthur Jones* (London, 1930), p. 58.

*My experiences and memories of the theatre in Norway are not such that I feel any inclination to repeat them. I might, it is true, sense some twinge of duty and responsibility in this connection if I thought I could achieve anything of value for our theatre; but of that I have the gravest doubts. Our actors, etc. are demoralised, they will not accept discipline and unqualified obedience, besides which we have a press which is always ready to champion rebels against their leader. This is the main reason why we, unlike other countries where anarchic tendencies are less developed, can never achieve any real ensemble playing. I don't think I could improve matters in this respect; it is too closely tied up with our whole national attitude towards life; and anyway, my liking for the practicalities of theatre work is too small . . . I am by no means sure how sincerely the Christiania public feels any need for good theatre. The packed houses on which the operettas and equestrian performances at Tivoli can always rely, and the interest with which dilettante productions of students and shop assistants are received there, seem to me to indicate a cultural outlook that is not yet ripe to appreciate dramatic genuine art.*

Ibsen's visits to Norway had not mellowed his attitude towards his compatriots.

His new play, for which he had laid the first plans over six months earlier, had made negligible progress. 'I have had one of those periods', he wrote to Laura Grundtvig on 22 January, 'when I can only with the greatest reluctance sit down at my desk. But today I have been out and bought new paper, new ink and new pens in honour of a new play which I have been turning over in my mind.' Yet he seems to have done nothing for the next three months but make notes; it was 20 April before he began to write any dialogue.

On 8 February 1884 Ibsen was acted in Russian for the first time (though he had been performed in Russia in Polish, and also in Finnish), when *A Doll's House* was staged in St Petersburg. But the play seems to have made less impact there than in other countries, and it was to be eight years before they staged another of his plays.

That spring Ibsen came as near as he ever did to meeting Strindberg. 'Surely I should visit Ibsen in Rome?' wrote Strindberg on 12 February from Ouchy in Switzerland to Bjørnson and Jonas Lie, together in Paris. 'Will you be kind enough to ask him to receive me, for if he shows me the door I shall feel hurt. I want to see the angriest man in Europe before I die!' But although Strindberg set off for Italy on 1 March he got no further than Genoa, where the weather was so bad that he turned in a temper for home. 'All water is blue when the sky is blue', he wrote to his vicar friend Carl Larsson on 8 March. 'Eva [his children's nursemaid] and I have searched in vain for that damned blue in both sky and water. Humbug, Sir! The olive trees are horribly grey. The landscape like a garden and uglier than the oil paintings. Pine trees are the same everywhere. And the people? Moleskin and slouch hats! Not at all picturesque, old chap! The old houses daubed with red, green and yellow! . . . The whole coast here is occupied by factories and wharves so that one can't get to the beach. The hills covered with villas! Nature is dead here! No walks possible! The roads dusty! Oh, how dusty it is here!' At least it does not seem to have rained much; still, it is a sad thought that had the sun shone in north Italy that week, a meeting would probably have taken place between these two extraordinary men, and one suspects that they might have got on rather well, for Strindberg, when his black mood was not on him, was a tremendous charmer, and he was the kind of emotional individualist (like Brandes) whom Ibsen found stimulating. And when Ibsen liked someone and put his own charm forward, there were few who could resist him. Confound that weather; who but Strindberg would have been unlucky enough to spend a spring week in Italy without seeing the sun? By August, sadly, his hostility towards Ibsen as a champion of feminism had become set, and he was describing the latter's writings as 'swinish'.[1]

Meanwhile, on 3 March, Ibsen's name had appeared for the first time (apart from that single matinée of *The Pillars of Society* in 1880) in the West End of London, though scarcely in a manner to cause him joy. Henry Arthur Jones, together with a collaborator named Henry Herman who had helped him with *The Silver King*, had been approached by the Polish actress Helena Modjeska to adapt *A Doll's House* into English. Between them they produced an even freer adaptation than the one seen in America, re-entitled it

## BREAKING A BUTTERFLY
(founded on Ibsen's *Norah*)

and presented it at the Prince's Theatre in Coventry Street (now the Prince of Wales's Theatre). Harley Granville Barker gives an interesting account of their improvements to the text:

The scene is laid in some English town. Nora becomes Flora and, to her husband, rather terribly, Flossie. He is Humphrey Goddard and we find him gifted with a mother (quite unnecessarily) and a sister (wanted for the piano-playing, *vice* Mrs Linde, who disappears). The morbid Dr Rank is replaced by a Charles-his-friend, called, as if to wipe out every trace of his original, Ben Birdseye! He is not in love with Nora-Flora, of course; that would never do. But Dunkley, alias Krogstad, had loved her as a girl,

---

[1] *August Strindbergs brev*, IV, pp. 39, 65 and 302–303. (The words 'Humbug, sir!' are in English; Strindberg, unlike Ibsen, was an accomplished linguist, and mixed up all his languages in his letters.)

when Humphrey Goddard stole her young heart from him; so love has turned to hate and revenge is sweet. Observe the certainty with which our operators in the English market fasten on the flawed streak in Ibsen's play and cheapen it still further. The tarantella episode, of course, will be the making of the whole affair (such was many people's judgment then, and now we find it rather marring), and this is left intact. But the third act sees the parent play stood deliberately on its head, and every ounce of Ibsen emptied out of it. Burlesque could do no more. Torvald-Humphrey behaves like the pasteboard hero of Nora's doll's-house dream; he *does* strike his chest and say: 'I am the guilty one!' And Nora-Flora cries that she is a poor weak foolish girl, '. . . no wife for a man like you. You are a thousand times too good for me', and never wakes up and walks out of her doll's house at all.'[1]

A distinguished cast had been assembled, including Kyrle Bellew as Goddard/Helmer, Beerbohm Tree as Dunkley/Krogstad and Alice Lingard as Nora/Flora. 'The result', noted William Archer, 'was a nice little play, standing to *Et Dukkehjem* somewhat in the relation of Mr Gilbert's *Gretchen* to Goethe's *Faust;* and even so, it did not succeed.'[2]

Such was the introduction of Ibsen to the English theatre—a single matinée of *The Pillars of Society* in 1880, and this scarcely recognisable perversion of *A Doll's House* in 1884, from which, needless to say, Ibsen did not receive a penny. Apart from an amateur charity performance of *A Doll's House* the following year, there were to be no further productions of Ibsen in England before 1889, when the dramatist was sixty-one. Two years after the Prince's Theatre travesty, however, there was a private reading of *A Doll's House* with, in retrospect, though none of the names meant anything then, a distinguished cast. This, according to Bernard Shaw, took place 'on a first floor in a Bloomsbury lodging-house. Karl Marx's youngest daughter played Nora Helmer; and I impersonated Krogstad at her request, with a very vague notion of what it was all about.'[3] The date was 15 January 1886 and the place 55, Great Russell Street, opposite the British Museum.[4] One would like to know whether Eleanor Marx-Aveling, shortly to translate (rather badly) *An Enemy of the People* and *The Wild Duck*, ever mentioned Ibsen to her father before he died in 1883.

On 20 April Ibsen began writing his new play, *The Wild Duck*, and by 28 April (each act of the manuscript is dated) he had completed the first act.

---

[1] Granville Barker, pp. 167–168.
[2] *The Dramatic Review*, 4 April 1885.
[3] Cf. Shaw's preface ('An Aside') to Lillah McCarthy's *Myself and Some Friends* (London, 1933), p. 3.
[4] Chushichi Tsuzuki, *The Life of Eleanor Marx* (Oxford, 1967), p. 165.

C

On 2 May he began Act Two; but when he was half-way through it he stopped, and started to rewrite the play from the beginning. By 24 May he had completed Acts One and Two in their new form. The last three acts took him less than a week each: 25–30 May, 2–8 June and 9–13 June—a measure of how carefully he had worked the play out in his mind before putting pen to paper. On 14 June he wrote to Hegel: 'I am glad to be able to tell you that yesterday I completed the draft of my new play. It comprises five acts and will, as far as I can calculate, occupy some 200 printed pages, perhaps a little more. It still remains for me to make the fair copy, and I shall start on that tomorrow. As usual, however, this will involve not just copying the draft but a comprehensive rewriting of the dialogue. So it will take time. Still, unless some unforeseen obstacle presents itself I reckon the whole manuscript should be in your hands by mid-September. The play doesn't touch on political or social problems, or indeed any matters of public import. It takes place entirely within the confines of family life. I dare say it will arouse some discussion: but it can't offend anyone.' Little did he know.

This 'comprehensive rewriting' he described more precisely in a letter of 27 June to Theodor Caspari, a young poet who had addressed a lyric to him, as 'the more energetic individualising of the characters and of their modes of expression'—a problem which, as we have seen, particularly obsessed him. He added a remark which contains the central theme of The Wild Duck. Caspari had evidently taken Ibsen up on the latter's abandonment of, and apparent condemnation of verse, and Ibsen replied: 'You are quite wrong in supposing that I should wish you to break your lyre . . . I have long ceased to make universal demands of people because I no longer believe that none of us can have any higher aim in life than to realise ourselves in spirit and in truth. That, in my view, is the true meaning of liberalism, and that is why the so-called liberals are in so many ways repugnant to me'.

One of the central characters in The Wild Duck was to be just such a 'so-called liberal', making blind 'universal' demands of people and so destroying their illusions and their happiness. Ibsen concluded his letter:

'To find the necessary peace and solitude for this work I am going in a few days up to Gossensass in the Tyrol. My wife and son will, at the same time, leave for Norway. Would I could have come with them! But it must not be. At my age one must use all one's time for work; one will never finish it all. One "will not find time to finish the last verse";[1] but one wants to get down as much as possible.'

---

[1] A quotation from Holberg's Jacob von Thyboe, the Cyrano-like hero of which play needs only one word, rhyming with 'fool', to finish his letter to his beloved.

Ibsen left Rome on 30 June, and stayed a full four months in Gossensass. It was the longest period for which he had been separated from Suzannah during the twenty-six years of their marriage, and is consequently the best documented, for he wrote to her and Sigurd almost weekly.

*Gossensass, 4 July 1884*

*Dear Suzannah!*

*Thank you for your card from Basel, which I received this noon. Your cards from Rome arrived yesterday, together with a couple of newspapers. Of the last-named I have so far received only one number of* Dagbladet *direct from Christiania, nothing from* Aftenposten, *though I informed them in good time of my change of address. The scoundrels at* Aftenposten *are of course too conservative to change an address,[1] and from their drunken friends at* Dagbladet *one can expect nothing but chaos and Norwegian slovenliness.*

*I am happy that you have reached Basel safely, and I trust that by tomorrow, or perhaps even today, you will reach Copenhagen.*

*As far as I am concerned, all is as it should be. The journey here was as usual; from Modena by night, and as far as Ala I had to keep my overcoat on; thereafter I didn't need it; exceptionally beautiful weather and fresh air all the way up the valley here. The sandwiches proved most useful; they were my only food throughout the journey; I ate the last in Verona, for breakfast, with a cup of black coffee which was brought to me in the compartment; in Florence I had taken only half a bottle of wine, at Ala in the morning nothing; I shall always take sandwiches when I travel; I can eat them with pleasure at any time.*

*I was heartily welcomed here, but they were much surprised at my arriving alone. I chose the isolated room upstairs in the little annexe, similar to the one Sigurd had downstairs in previous years; no verandah outside, as this room does not stretch so far, and no connecting door with the next room, so that no noise is audible; I am excellently contented here.*

*Hitherto I have risen at 6.30, breakfasted in my room half an hour later, gone out while they do the room, and then written from 9–1. Then lunch with a ravenous appetite. In the afternoons, too, I have managed to write a little, or at any rate do groundwork. The second act will be ready in 5–6 days. I am not drinking any beer; which suits me well. But I am drinking milk and a little—not much—white wine, with water. A light evening meal at 7.30. So far I have been in bed each evening by 10, and have been sleeping well.*

*Quite a lot of visitors have already arrived, and everywhere will soon be full. Of those we know from previous years I have seen only Fru Schlesinger and the Vambergs.*

---

[1] *Aftenposten*, originally unpolitical, had recently become right-wing, like *Morgenbladet*. *Dagbladet* and *Verdens Gang* represented the left.

*Grubhofer has not come yet, but has sent me a card of greeting from Munich. Incidentally, the guests I don't know, who are mostly German ladies, seem to know me, and look very gracious and smiling when we meet. Ravnkilde is expected next week. The three horrors haven't booked yet, so will probably not get in if they come, and will then have to go on to Brennerbad, if they can find anything there.*

*It feels rather strange to be alone; but my work will keep me occupied for a good while yet. Let me hear from you both some time. You need not write at length. I won't write long letters either; I am busy with my play and there is nothing much of interest here to write about.*

*But even if I do not write at length or often, I shall be thinking constantly of you and hoping you are having a really good and enjoyable time on your holiday in Norway. Remember of course that you must let me know from time to time where to address my letters. I shall not now repeat my reminders to take care and forethought in everything you do; I hope, though, that you will comply with them as a matter of common sense . . .*

He bade them 'profit from the good, nourishing Norwegian food', and to eat much fish, especially salmon; and announced that he has 'had to give up the white Tyrol wine, which did not suit me, and now drink an excellent Hungarian Carlowitzer which, surprisingly enough, costs exactly the same.' Pedantically, he noted his changes of routine:

*In the morning I drink tea at seven o'clock precisely; rise each day at 6 at the latest, often earlier, and find this suits me excellently, though I do not now retire before 11. For my admirable, isolated and peaceful room I pay this year only 60 kreuzer a day. All my expenses, including tobacco and laundry, come to 50 francs a week. Each Sunday morning I change a 50-lira note, and manage with that until exactly the following Sunday.*[1]

His peace was disturbed by a hailstorm, which he describes in this same letter of 20 July:

*The hail flew straight through the windows of the dining-room as we sat there; such was their force that they did not smash the panes but made round holes in them of their own size. And what a size! Many were larger than the largest hen's eggs I have ever seen; we collected a lot of them; they were of the hardest ice and polished like glass; I made pencil outlines of two of them. At midnight a new storm burst, and a third at 3 a.m. The church bells rang, incessantly, and most of the guests here*

---

[1] In 1884 the Austrian gulden (100 kreuzer) was worth 1s. 8d., so that Ibsen's room cost him only 1s. a night. The exchange rate of the French and Swiss franc and the Italian lira was in each case approximately 25.45 to the £; thus his other expenses (including food) came to under £2 a week.

*stayed up all night; at 3 I too arose; but then went back to bed. The two following days we had heavy rain and yesterday, Saturday, morning there was a real cloudburst; towards noon the Eisach overflowed its banks . . . and threatened Gossensass where, however, in the end all turned out well. Further down things were worse. You remember the little stream which comes from 'Wasserfall' and flows out under the road to Sterzing, just at the curve where there stands a cross to a murdered man. This stream became a mighty, powerful and destructive current, carrying away the highway so that the whole bend is now a great gaping abyss. The railway beneath got covered with mud so that yesterday the trains from the north could not reach here. All the south-bound passengers had to seek refuge in our hotel, where a great disturbance resulted.*

Young Marcus Grønvold, the painter, had joined him, and his appetite worried Ibsen ('I think he must be suffering from some kind of illness'). An English lady fell and broke her leg, a schoolboy from Berlin cut his hand badly. He warned Suzannah and Sigurd not to bathe ('The water is cold and can easily bring on a fatal attack of cramp'), not to stand behind the horses of Trondhjem 'which are well known for their habit of kicking', and, above all, to avoid anyone carrying a gun. 'In almost every Norwegian newspaper I read of accidents caused by the careless use of loaded rifles. I shall be exceedingly displeased if you do not keep well away from people carrying such weapons. Should an accident happen I must be informed immediately by telegram.' His vanity was gratified by his noticing that 'several copies of Passarge's book about me, and of Brandes's essay in *Nord und Süd*, accompanied by an excellent engraving of my likeness, are circulating amongst the guests. Almost all of them, I suppose, know my plays in German.' Ludwig Passarge himself paid a visit with his wife; they 'said they only live and breathe in my books'. Grønvold's appetite continued to worry him. 'It is not just that he eats excessive quantities; everything must be of the best and most expensive, and that for both lunch and dinner; he spends twice as much each day as I do.'

Meanwhile, he worked steadily revising *The Wild Duck*, taking about a fortnight over each act. He completed the first two acts in their final form by 12 July, just a month after he had finished his first draft of the play; Act Three took him from 14 July to 30 July; Act Four was ready by 17 August.

On 27 August he wrote to Sigurd:

*My play is now fast nearing its conclusion. In three to four days it will be ready; then I shall read it through carefully and send it off. I take great joy in working on this play; it grows all the time in little details, and I shall miss it when I have to part from it; though at the same time, I shall be glad. The German sculptor Professor Kopf, from Rome, has with him a thirteen year old daughter who is the most perfect model for my Hedvig that could be imagined; she is pretty, has a serious face and manner, and is a little greedy.'*

Three days later, on 30 August, he wrote to Suzannah:

*Although I don't know when or where my letters reach you while you continue to move from town to town, I must nevertheless send you the good news that I have just finished my manuscript. The play will be very rich in content, and bigger than any other of my recent works. I have said everything I wanted to say; and I don't think it could easily have been said better. Now to the business of reading it through, which will take 2–3 days; then off it goes to Hegel.*

On 2 September he wrote to Hegel:

*I enclose the manuscript of my new play,* The Wild Duck, *which has occupied me daily for the past four months, and from which I cannot now part without a certain feeling of loss. The characters in it have, despite their many failings, grown dear to me as a result of this long daily association. But I cherish the hope that they will also find good friends and well-wishers among the great reading public and, not least, among theatre people; for they all, without exception, offer rewarding opportunities. But the study and representation of them will not be easy . . . This new play occupies in some ways, a unique position among my dramatic works. The method differs in certain respects from that which I have previously employed. However, I don't wish to enlarge on that here. The critics will, I trust, see this for themselves; they will anyway find something to argue about, something to construe. I believe too, that* The Wild Duck *may possibly tempt some of our younger dramatists to explore new territories, and this I regard as a desirable thing.*

In the middle of September, Ibsen received the letter he had been awaiting for so many years; an invitation from Bjørnson to visit him and his wife at Schwaz, where they were holidaying, two or three hours by rail from Gossensass. Bjørnson had got to know Strindberg in Paris the previous December, and had spent the spring raising funds for him as energetically as, twenty years earlier, he had done for Ibsen. Ibsen accepted his invitation eagerly; so, for the first time in nearly twenty years, these two old friends and enemies met, and spent three days together. Ibsen described the occasion in a letter to Suzannah on 17 September:

*I would not for anything have missed this meeting. I will be better able to tell you the details when we meet; here I shall merely mention a few external circumstances. Bjørnson and his son met me at the station; a room was prepared for me at the Gasthaus where they are staying; but I preferred to lodge at another hotel where, likewise, there awaited me for the occasion an enormous room, very handsome and comfortable. At the hotel I of course paid for my board and breakfast; but I ate lunch and dinner with the Bjørnsons and was with them for almost the whole of the rest of the time; they could not do enough for me. Bjørnson has gone grey, but looks strong. Fru B. is like-wise somewhat greyed, and has grown rather deaf, but in other respects is as bright and lively as before and has developed into an excellent person. Both their daughters are uncommonly handsome, well brought up, unaffected and straightforward; I also much like Erling, their son. I did not see Jonas Lie, since he is so far behind with his novel. But this meant that B. and I were able to talk all the more undisturbed, and this we did, about political, literary and many other matters. B. was often much struck by my remarks and frequently returned to them. In one respect I have, by my visit, prevented a true misfortune from befalling our country.[1] But I don't want to put anything on paper about this . . .*

*Here everything is as usual; many of the summer guests have now departed; but there are still a lot here, and newcomers arrive daily for briefer visits. The weather is now as warm and beautiful as one could wish . . . Frøken Schirmer from Munich is occupying herself with spiritism [sic], or whatever it is called. She has the power of being able, by touching another person, to make her do what she wishes. Here she found a very ready medium in a Frøken von Pfeuffer, a nervous young lady, with whom she has undertaken a series of the most unlikely experiments; and subsequently with other people; she has now left.*

This is the first reference in Ibsen's writings to an interest which was becoming widespread in Europe at this time, and which was to manifest itself powerfully in Ibsen's next four plays: the ability of one human being to gain a supernatural power over the mind of another. Sigmund Freud, then a young neurologist of twenty-eight, had already seen hypnotism therapeutically used and probably made his own first experiments with it the following year; and Strindberg was to employ it with terrifying effect in his play *Creditors* three years later.

'Schwaz', continued Ibsen's letter to Suzannah, 'is quite a town, with 6,000 inhabitants. It was generally known there that I was visiting B., and the locals saluted us when we appeared, whether together or singly. One family sent Fru B. a fine haunch of venison, another game, others had sent excellent Moselle, and yet others old rum and other good things. I saw friendly, contented faces in the doors of the shops and in the windows round about. There has been a lot written about me in the newspapers of Innsbruck and other Tyrolean towns this summer.' One of Bjørnson's daughters, Bergliot, aged sixteen, particularly impressed him. When he saw Suzannah he told her:

---

[1] The nature of this national calamity which Ibsen claimed to have averted has never been identified; Halvdan Koht (II, p. 159) thinks it may have been a projected blind attack on the left-wing government.

'Now I have seen Sigurd's future wife',[1] and he was to be proved right.

Bjørnson gave his impressions of their encounter in a letter to Hegel. 'Ibsen', he wrote (21 September), 'is now a good, well-meaning old gentleman, with whom I disagreed on many points regarding ends and means, but with whom it was in the highest degree interesting to exchange views. His intellect, circumspection and wisdom are remarkable. Yet his intelligence is not of the all-round kind, any more than his knowledge.'[2] He expanded this last observation in a letter to Jonas Lie. 'You and I see more, and we see it better. Our intellectualism is incomparably greater. But he so adjusts himself to his that it gives a pretty good dividend.'[3] Bjørnson was not far from the truth; Ibsen's intelligence was, like that of so many creative writers, intuitive and limited; he lacked many of the advantages of a trained mind; on many aspects of life and knowledge he was, as we have seen, almost childishly ignorant. Yet great creative minds are often thus: of Ibsen's contemporaries, Tolstoy, Dickens, Dostoevsky, Herman Melville and Tennyson shared equal areas of ignorance and blindness.

Unfortunately for Bjørnson, no sooner had he become reconciled with Ibsen than he fell out with his new friend Strindberg, who was prosecuted that autumn for alleged blasphemy in his volume of short stories, *Marriage*, resented some fatherly advice which Bjørnson chose to offer him, and poked fun at the latter's new play, *A Gauntlet*, for demanding that men should, like women, stay chaste until marriage—a particularly incongruous suggestion from a man hardly famous for marital fidelity. 'Be immoral, Bjørnson, as you were when you were young!' Strindberg exhorted him on 14 October 1884. 'The virtue which comes when a man is fifty is not worth preaching!'[4] The advice was no better received than Bjørnson's to Strindberg had been.

During their conversations at Schwaz Bjørnson had yet again attempted to persuade Ibsen to return to Norway and take over the general management of the Christiania Theatre, of which Bjørnson's son Bjørn, fresh from his year's training with the Meiningers, had recently been appointed artistic director. Ibsen was evidently interested enough to leave the question open when they parted, and Bjørnson thought he had persuaded him. 'Before I'd been with him a few minutes', Bjørnson wrote to Jonas Lie on 2 October, 'I realised he had the most burning desire to go home and take charge of the theatre, and build a new one . . . He's been playing you up, or you didn't understand him,

---

[1] Bergliot Ibsen, p. 115.

[2] Bjørnstjerne Bjørnson, *Kamp-tid (brev fra aarene 1879–1894)*, ed. Halvdan Koht (Oslo, 1932), II, p. 245.

[3] *Ibid.*, p. 244.

[4] *August Strindbergs brev*, IV, p. 355.

if you thought he didn't want it. *He has no real interest* now other than to get a good theatre going in a new building in Norway.'[1]

But Bjørnson had evidently mistaken Ibsen's desire for a new theatre in a modern building for a willingness to take charge of things himself. Four days earlier Ibsen had in fact written a letter of refusal to Bjørnson, which the latter had not received when he wrote the above lines to Lie:

*When one has had to do with theatre managements for as long as I have, and when one has busied oneself as exclusively with play-writing as I have, the inclination to take a practical hand often asserts itself, inevitably and powerfully. The theatre has something siren-like about it, and the two occasions on which you have thrown this idea at me have filled my mind with unrest and longing. Besides, I can't deny that I sometimes feel the need for a fixed occupation with duties attached. So I would have practical grounds for going home and taking over the theatre, were that practicable.*

*But the tragedy is that for the time being it is absolutely impracticable. The party which holds power in the theatre is certainly no more favourably inclined towards me than towards you. My wife has just written from up there: 'I would have never have believed that we were so much in the black books of the conservatives as has now, by numerous signs, shown itself to be the case.' I do not for a moment doubt that her observation is correct. To offer me the leadership of the theatre would therefore be, for the board, to place itself in a position of hostility towards any well-wishing families and individuals whose support they cannot do without. So it will not happen. I shall never become director of the theatre as long as the present board remains in power.*

*But you will perhaps protest that I could still go home and try in the meantime to work as a private reformer, hasten the building of the new theatre and thereby help to bring about the conditions under which my appointment as director of the theatre might become a possibility. All this might conceivably happen had I sufficient means to live on while this was happening. But I have not. I have still nowhere near saved enough to suffice for me and my family in the event of my abandoning my literary career. And I would have to abandon it if I went to live in Christiania. I am not thinking so much of all the distracting theatre work. No, the fact is I would not be able to write freely and totally uninhibitedly up there. And that is the same as saying that I would not be able to write at all. When ten years ago, after a ten years absence, I sailed up the fjord, I literally felt my chest tighten with a feeling of sickness and unease. I had the same sensation during the whole of my stay there; I was no longer myself with all those cold and uncomprehending Norwegian eyes staring at me from the windows and pavements.*

*So I must wait another year. If the government and the Storthing decide to raise writers' grants to the extent of making me financially independent, then I might, for*

---

[1] *Kamp-tid*, II, pp. 246–247.

*the cause of our theatre, reciprocate by leaving one or two dramatic works unwritten until later . . .*

Fortunately, the government remained true to character. It is a dreadful thought that, had they been more generous, *The Lady from the Sea* or *Rosmersholm* might never have been written.

The renewal of acquaintance between Ibsen and Bjørnson did not lead to a complete reconciliation. Karl Konow, who knew them both, was probably right when he wrote: 'They respected and venerated each other, they met and talked, but never more than that . . . Several times I have heard [Bjørnson] express regret that he could not get closer to him, and I think Ibsen felt the same. But the differences were too great. They could talk together, but not feel together. In a way they enjoyed each other's company, but they did not understand each other.'[1]

As there was an outbreak of cholera in Italy, Ibsen stayed in Gossensass until the end of October. Suzannah and Sigurd joined him there in the middle of the month ('Should the weather be bad, stormy or foggy when you leave Christiania', he had warned them on 24 September, as neurotic about their safety as he was about his own, 'do not take the steamer but go by land via Sweden'). Sigurd had learned on his return to Christiania that his appeal to Sverdrup had been successful, and that he had been appointed to the consular office in Stockholm; he stayed only a few days with his father before returning north. Thoughts of a new play had already begun to crystallise in Ibsen's mind. 'I felt pretty nervous and overstrained when I had finished my manuscript', he wrote to Hegel on 18 October, 'and decided to rest for a year. But this will not happen. I have already worked out plans for a new play in four acts and hope, before long, when I have settled down in Rome, to be able to start work on it.' On 1 November he and Suzannah left Gossensass and, after a few days at Botzen arrived back in Rome on 13 November.

Two days earlier, *The Wild Duck* had been published, in a printing of 8,000 copies, 2,000 less than *Ghosts* and *An Enemy of the People* (but this was probably due to the fact that there had been a recession in the book trade rather than to any fear that it might prove less popular than its predecessors). The reaction among the critics and the reading public was principally one of bewilderment— which, indeed, was to be the general reaction to his remaining seven plays. Modern opinion regards these eight final plays as Ibsen's greatest period, or at any rate greater than the middle period of his 'social dramas' from *The Pillars of Society* to *An Enemy of the People*. His contemporaries in Scandinavia felt otherwise. From now on, we find him repeatedly accused of being a 'riddling

[1] Karl Konow, *Bjørnson og Lie* (Oslo, 1919), p. 72.

Sphinx', of being obscure for obscurity's sake and of concentrating on the sordid. Only his increasing fame abroad saved his reputation from going into a sharp decline at home.

'The public does not know what to make of it', commented the *Christiania Intelligenssedler* on *The Wild Duck*. 'One paper says one thing and the other just the opposite.' *Aftenposten* (18 November) complained: 'One may study and study to find what Ibsen wants to say and not find it.' *Morgenbladet* (16 and 19 November) found the plot 'as queer as it is thin . . . One has an undeniable impression of something artificial and contrived . . . The total impression can hardly be other than a strong sense of emptiness and unpleasantness.' *Bergens Tidende* thought the play proved Ibsen's inferiority to Bjørnson. 'He does not speak from his heart as does Bjørnson. He does not make demands of the individual with the same strength, he has no faith in his ability to ennoble humanity by means of his writings. He states the problems excellently as he sees them, but makes no attempt to show the way beyond them; he chastises as one who has authority, but makes no demand for improvement.' Bjørnson himself wrote to Hegel on 20 November: 'I find Ibsen's new book nauseating.'[1] Ditmar Meidell in *Norsk Maanedsskrift for Litteratur* (1884, pp. 569–574) admitted the technical mastery but concluded that: 'to read plays in which the characters are total idiots and morally dead . . . is no refinement to the spirit.' About the only two Norwegian critics to appreciate the point of the play were Mathilde Schjøtt in *Nyt Tidskrift* (1884, pp. 616 ff.) who called it a masterpiece, and Irgens Hansen, who, in *Dagbladet* (16 November) recognised that Ibsen 'here stands on humanity's ground and speaks humanity's cause, even though it be the cause of a very shabby humanity.'

Nor was the play much better appreciated in Sweden or Denmark. Helena Nyblom, writing in *Ny Svensk Tidskrift* (1885, pp. 65–69) complained that 'not *every* Norwegian is a good-for-nothing, as Ibsen would have us suppose . . . Ibsen has only one feeling for human beings, and that is contempt . . . Once one has slept on them [i.e. Ibsen's plays] one realises that their effect is merely that of theatrical illusion, and after a few years they can usually not be played again, for only those plays which truthfully reflect life can survive for long.' In the same issue (pp. 444–446), Kristofer Randers, writing from Norway, declared: 'It is a very old play, a morose play, a tired play. It is moreover a very incomprehensible play . . . It has not made any lasting impression on the reading public . . . One can only be angry that such a fine technique should be wasted on such ungrateful material.' And C. D. af Wirsén, a great admirer of Ibsen's early plays, though he was to hate almost all the later ones, while

---

[1] Nielsen, II, p. 136.

acknowledging, in *Post- och Inrikes-Tidning*, Ibsen's 'incomparable technical mastery', thought the play 'as cold, hard and implacable as it is gloomy and pessimistic'.[1] Georg Brandes did not review it, but he confidentially told J. P. Jacobsen (23 November 1884) that '*The Wild Duck* was only a half-pleasure', and he never rated it among Ibsen's masterpieces. 'Ibsen's [book] made a glum impression on me', he wrote to Alexander Kielland on 13 November. 'I thought it rather empty. Why bother exclusively with such totally insignificant people? His contempt for humanity seems perpetually on the increase.'[2] Kielland himself wrote to Hegel on 18 November that he found the play bizarre and archaic: 'these eternal symbols and allusions and heavy underlinings are too crude for me'.[3] Strindberg likewise disapproved, though for a peculiarly Strindbergian reason. He was convinced, as he was to state three years later in *A Madman's Defence*, that the character of Hjalmar Ekdal was maliciously based on him; for one thing, he suspected his wife to have been pregnant by another man when he had married her, for another, his *romans à clef* had led critics to describe him as a photographer. Six years later Strindberg was to make a similar accusation in relation to *Hedda Gabler*.

Yet a few people appreciated it. An anonymous reviewer in the Stockholm *Ny Illustrerad Tidning* (possibly J. A. Runström) praised it hugely. 'Now as always', he wrote (7 February 1885), '[Ibsen] knows how to portray characters so as to excite different opinions, be subjects of argument. And to excite different opinions is just what he wants to do ... He can conclude his plays with a question mark, but he never writes a full stop ... His work has always opened up new vistas, always contained something other than what one expected.' And Edvard Brandes, in *Politiken* (16 November 1884), declared that Ibsen 'has no equal in Europe as a master of dialogue' and concluded: 'It is plays like this that educate actors and spiritually liberate those who see them.' Yet even he, nearly forty years later in 1922, expressed the opinion that *The Wild Duck* 'will not survive in the first rank of Ibsen's plays.'[4]

Again, however, we must remember that the young, to whom Ibsen principally appealed, were inadequately (if at all) represented among the critics. Carl Georgsson Fleetwood in Stockholm must have been speaking for many of his generation when he noted in his diary on 7 December 1884 that *The Wild Duck* was all the more exciting ('A new book by Ibsen is always an exciting event') because he had heard it described as inferior 'by the very people

[1] C. D. af Wirsén, *Kritiker* (Stockholm, 1901), p. 62.
[2] *Brandes Brevveksling*, IV, p. 361.
[3] Nielsen, II, p. 465.
[4] *Om Teater*, p. 116.

who sing the praise of "fearless" Ibsen—probably because he has been fearless enough to expose the nakedness of the new gods too!'[1]

Across the North Sea, Ibsen's English admirers were as baffled as their Scandinavian counterparts. Edmund Gosse condemned it four years later in the *Fortnightly Review*[2] as 'a strange, melancholy and pessimistic drama, almost without a ray of light from beginning to end . . . There is really not a character in the book that inspires confidence or liking . . . There can be no doubt that it is by far the most difficult of Ibsen's dramas to comprehend.' William Archer also failed to understand it at first (though he came to admire it greatly once he had seen it staged). Arthur Symons thought it 'a play of inferior quality',[3] and Havelock Ellis dismissed it as 'the least remarkable'[4] of Ibsen's recent plays.

Almost the only British critic (Ireland being then a part of Britain) to see the point of the play during the next ten years was Bernard Shaw, who devoted to it one of his most penetrating passages in *The Quintessence of Ibsenism*: 'After *An Enemy of the People*, Ibsen . . . left the vulgar ideals for dead and set about the exposure of those of the choicer spirits, beginning with the incorrigible idealists who had idealised his very self, and were becoming known as Ibsenites. His first move in this direction was such a tragi-comic slaughtering of sham Ibsenism that his astonished victims plaintively declared that *The Wild Duck*, as the new play was called, was a satire on his former works; while the pious, whom he had disappointed so severely by his interpretation of *Brand* . . . began to hope that he was coming back repentant to the fold.' Shaw concluded with a remark which strikes surely to the heart of the play: 'the busybody [Gregers] finds that people cannot be freed from their failings from without. They must free themselves.'

Despite the general bewilderment, however, the book sold remarkably well in Scandinavia. Four days after publication *Dagbladet* announced that the first edition had sold out, and a second impression of two thousand copies was in the shops by early December. The principal Scandinavian theatres wasted no time in buying the performing rights, and productions were already in rehearsal in Christiania, Bergen, Copenhagen, Stockholm and Helsinki. 'If there is any living dramatist', reported Erik Bøgh, the censor of the Royal Theatre in Copenhagen, to his board on 17 November, 'whose plays the public demand to see performed, whose earlier plays have brought so much honour and profit as to pioneer a path for his successors . . . it must, before all others, be Henrik Ibsen . . . *The Wild Duck* is in all respects executed with his unique mastery';

[1] Fleetwood, I, p. 613.
[2] *Ibsen's Social Dramas*, in the *Fortnightly Review*, 1 January 1889, pp. 107–121.
[3] *Universal Review*, 3, 1889, pp. 567–574.
[4] Havelock Ellis, *The New Spirit* (London, 1890), p. 166.

and he concluded, unfashionably, by declaring that the play had 'a demonstrably healthy moral attitude'.[1]

On 14 November Ibsen addressed a letter to Hans Schrøder, of the Christiania Theatre, which, like his letters to the same correspondent about *An Enemy of the People*, is full of sharp practical observations invaluable to any modern director of the play. Foreseeing the danger that whoever acted Hjalmar Ekdal might be tempted to play him as a figure of fun (a temptation which too few actors have resisted, just as too many have played Gregers as spiteful), Ibsen warned Schrøder:

*Hjalmar must not be acted with any trace of parody. The actor must never for a moment show that he is conscious that there is anything funny in what he says. His voice has, as Relling observes, something endearing about it, and this quality must be clearly brought out. His sentimentality is honest, his melancholy, in its way, attractive; no hint of affectation. Between ourselves, I would suggest you cast your mind towards Kristofer Janson, who still contrives to give an effect of beauty whatever drivel he may be uttering. There is a pointer for whoever plays the part . . . Where can one find a Hedvig? I don't know. And Mrs Sørby? She must be beautiful and witty,* not vulgar . . . *Gregers is the most difficult part in the play, from the acting point of view. Sometimes I think Hammer would be best, sometimes Bjørn B[jørnson]*[2] *. . . I hope you will spare me Isachsen, as he always carries on like some strange actor instead of like an ordinary human being.*[3] *However, I suppose he might possibly make something out of Molvik's few lines. The two servants must not be cast too casually; Petersen might possibly be played by Bucher, and Jensen by Abelsted, if the latter is not required for one of the dinner guests. Yes, those guests! What about them? You can't just use ordinary extras; they'd ruin the whole act . . . The play demands absolute naturalness and truthfulness both in the ensemble work and in the staging. The lighting, too, is important; it is different for each act, and is calculated to establish the peculiar atmos-*

---

[1] Agerholm, p. 280.

[2] Bjørn Bjørnson had joined the Christiania Theatre the previous month. Aged twenty-five, he had acted for a year in the Meiningen company, and had studied music at the Vienna Conservatoire, with Mahler as a fellow-pupil and Bruckner as a teacher. He was to do much towards revivifying the Christiania Theatre, and became chief of the National Theatre when it was founded in 1899. He directed the Christiania premiere of *The Wild Duck*, and records that Johannes Brun, who could imitate any animal or bird, made the sounds of the duck off-stage as well as playing Old Ekdal. (*Fra barndommens dage*, Oslo, 1922, pp. 40–41.)

[3] Schrøder ignored Ibsen's plea regarding Isachsen and cast him as Relling, in which role he proved a disaster. 'I hear from reliable sources', wrote Ibsen to Schrøder on 30 December 1886, 'that by his lunatic conception and dreadful performance . . . he ruined the whole effect of the play.' (Anker, *Henrik Ibsens brevveksling med Christiania Theater, 1878–1899*, p. 46.)

*phere of that act. I just wanted to pass on these random reflections. As regards every-*
*thing else, please do as you think best.*

Wherein does the 'method' of *The Wild Duck* differ, as Ibsen told Hegel,
from that which he had previously employed? At first sight there is no immediately obvious difference; it seems, like *A Doll's House*, *Ghosts* and *An Enemy of
the People*, to be a realistic play about realistic people, and the method seems
to be his old method of raking over apparently dead ashes and exposing the
live embers beneath. The symbolism? But Ibsen had used symbolism at least
as freely in *Brand*.

Nevertheless, I think there is little doubt that it was the symbolism in *The
Wild Duck* to which Ibsen was referring when he spoke of a new method. In
*Brand* the symbols are incidental to the play, or at any rate are not fully
integrated into it. The ice-church and the hawk are left deliberately imprecise;
there is room for intelligent argument about their meanings; perhaps, indeed,
they are intended to mean different things to different people, like the symbols
in Kafka. In *The Wild Duck*, however, there is a single and precise symbol, that
of the bird itself; and, so far from being incidental to the play, it is the hub and
heart of it. *Brand* is a play into which symbols have worked their way; *The
Wild Duck* is a play dependent on, and held together by, a symbol; as though
the wild duck were a magnet and the characters in the play so many iron
filings held together by this centripetal force. This was not a method that Ibsen
was to use invariably in his subsequent plays; *Rosmersholm*, for example, and
*Hedda Gabler*, have more in common (as regards their symbolism) with *Ghosts*
than with *The Wild Duck*. But we find him returning to it in his later plays: the
towers and spires of *The Master Builder* and the crutch in *Little Eyolf* serve a
similar structural purpose to the wild duck. They are images from which the
characters cannot escape, any more than the iron filings can escape the magnet.

Ibsen probably borrowed the image of the wild duck from a poem by
Welhaven called *The Sea-Bird* which describes how a wild duck is wounded
and dives down to die on the sea-bed; and Professor Francis Bull suggests that
he may also have been influenced by Darwin's account in *The Origin of Species*
of how wild ducks degenerate in captivity.[1] Some astonishing theories have
been advanced as to what the bird is intended to stand for. Surely Ibsen makes
it abundantly clear that he intended it as a double symbol with two precise
and obvious references. Firstly, it is, like Hedvig, a by-product of Haakon
Werle's fondness for sport which has been rejected by him and is now cared
for by the Ekdal family (at any rate in Hjalmar's eyes, though we never know,

---

[1] *C.E.*, X, pp. 23–24.

any more than Gina does, which of the two men is the father).[1] Secondly, with a more general application, it represents the refusal of most people, once they have been wounded, to go on living and face reality. Both Hjalmar and his father have sought to hide themselves in the deep blue sea of illusion, and Gregers, like the 'damned clever dog' trained by his father, hauls them back to the surface. The cynics, Relling and Haakon Werle, watch this operation; so do the two sensible, earthbound women, Gina and Mrs Sørby. These women, Ibsen seems to imply, offer the only real refuge: love. Mrs Sørby can save Haakon Werle, despite Gregers's cynicism, just as she could have saved Relling, who had also once loved her; Relling knows this, and it is hinted that the loss of her is partly responsible for his having turned into a drunkard. And Gina, if Gregers had not intervened, could have saved Hjalmar. Yet Ibsen leaves a question mark here: is love simply another illusion, like the Ekdals' loft? And if so, then is not the illusion of the loft justified, just as much as the illusion of love?

At the same time, while the wild duck has these two specific significances within the play, it is possible that, consciously or unconsciously, it reflects Ibsen's impression of himself when he wrote it: one who has forgotten what it means to live wild, and has grown plump and tame and content with his basket, as unlike the author of *Brand* as the duck is unlike the hawk of the earlier play, of which, likewise the climax had been a shot fired at (or supposedly at) a bird by a girl of fourteen. How far, Ibsen must have asked himself—and he was to ask the question again through Allmers in *Little Eyolf* and Rubek in *When We Dead Awaken*—does the artist, like the Ekdals, shut himself off from life? Is his world so very different from their loft with its imitations of reality? Which is the more cowardly refuge, the Ekdals' loft or Brand's ice-church?

Old Ekdal contains many traits of Ibsen's own father who, too, had been a lieutenant in the militia and a notable huntsman before he had gone bankrupt and brought the family name into disgrace. Hedvig seems to have got her name, and probably some of her character, from Ibsen's sister, the only member of his family for whom he retained any real affection; and the loft was probably a memory of the loft (still to be seen) at Venstøp which, like the Ekdals' loft, contained books left by 'The Flying Dutchman', including that book which delighted Hedvig Ekdal as it had delighted the young Ibsen, *Harrison's* (or, as Ibsen spelt it, *Harryson's*) *History of London*, published in 1775. He also borrowed for the play certain details of a trial which had caused a scandal during his

---

[1] Gina's answer to Hjalmar in Act Four ('I don't know . . . I—couldn't tell') is open to several interpretations. I take it to mean that she was irregular in her periods, missed one soon after Werle had slept with her, told him, he introduced her to Hjalmar, they slept together at once or almost at once, and so the child could be either man's.

student days in Christiania, when an army officer, accused of embezzlement, had, like Old Ekdal, tried unsuccessfully to shoot himself (a source to which he was to return for much of his material for *John Gabriel Borkman*). And, perhaps the most significant echo from his own past, there looms the figure which he had compulsively introduced into *The Pretenders, Brand, Peer Gynt, Emperor and Galilean* and *Ghosts*, of the illegitimate child.

Hjalmar seems to have had several models: Kristofer Janson, the writer whom Ibsen had known in Rome; Edward Larssen, a photographer with whom Ibsen had lodged in earlier days; Magnus Bagge, a failed artist from whom he had taken drawing lessons around 1860 and who is said to have had a constant longing to lift himself above everyday prose (when he went to live in Germany he called himself von Bagge): and a sculptor in Rome, C. D. Magelssen, who was always talking of a great invention he was about to perfect which would revolutionise the craft of casting in bronze and also, in some strange way, the manufacture of torpedoes.[1] Gregers Werle was at first (as we know from Ibsen's notes for the play) based on the novelist and playwright Alexander Kielland, whose radicalism Ibsen regarded as bogus, but he gradually developed into a kind of *reductio ad absurdum* of Dr Stockmann, a living illustration of the danger of a single-minded pursuit of truth if not tempered by common sense and an understanding of human limitations. More important, Hjalmar and Gregers both represent different aspects of Ibsen himself: on the one hand the evader of reality, on the other the impractical idealist who pesters mankind with his 'claims of the ideal' because he has a sick conscience and despises himself. How far, one wonders, did Ibsen identify himself with Gregers in that curious episode when the latter, finding that the stove smokes, throws water on it to put out the fire and only makes the stink worse? He had already portrayed these two conflicting aspects of himself in *Brand* and *Peer Gynt*, and the conflict between Gregers and Hjalmar is as though Brand and Peer Gynt had been brought face to face.

There is one other respect in which the method of *The Wild Duck* was, or seemed, new, and that was the way in which tragedy and comedy tread on each other's heels. This was one of the things about the play which so upset its contemporaries, though it delighted Bernard Shaw—'to look on with horror and pity at a profound tragedy, shaking with laughter all the time at an irresistible comedy', as he wrote of the 1897 London production in the *Saturday Review*. Ibsen instinctively knew what Shakespeare and the Greeks knew, and what Brecht was to remind playgoers of, that if you want to make a tragic event really hurt you must precede it with comedy, a Porter jesting as

[1] Francis Bull, *Vildanden, og andre essays* (Oslo, 1966), pp. 13–14.

he leads the night visitors to Duncan's death-chamber, a Grave-Digger who jokes in Ophelia's grave, a Clown to carry the asp to Cleopatra. This was a lesson which had been forgotten by dramatists; and if Ibsen was referring to this when he said it would be easier for him than for younger dramatists to attempt this effect, critical reaction was to prove him right.

As a postcript to *The Wild Duck*, one may remark how, as in almost every play he wrote, Ibsen anticipated one of the main discoveries of modern psychology. 'Liberation', he had noted in his preliminary jottings for the play, 'consists in securing for individuals the right to free themselves, each according to his particular need.' To free *themselves;* how many of Ibsen's contemporaries who regarded themselves as revolutionaries realised that? Ibsen understood that the demand must come from within, and that truth, if it comes from without, is often regarded as an attack on the defensive system which the 'life-lie', as Relling called it, represents.

The good book sales of *The Wild Duck* saved 1884 from being one of Ibsen's worst years financially, for he had made barely £100 from performing rights and had had only one reprint:

| | crowns | £ |
|---|---|---|
| Fee from August Lindberg for *Lady Inger* | 400 | 22 |
| 5th edition of *Love's Comedy* (2,000 copies) | 1,000 | 55 |
| Fee for *The Vikings at Helgeland* at Oldenburg | 100 | 6 |
| 1st edition of *The Wild Duck* | 7,440 | 413 |
| 2nd edition of *The Wild Duck* | 1,860 | 103 |
| Extra fees from Bergen Theatre for various plays | 510 | 28 |
| Fee for *Ghosts* in Helsinki | 150 | 8 |
| Extra fee for *An Enemy of the People* in Stockholm | 182 | 10 |
| Extra fee for *Ghosts* in Stockholm | 767 | 43 |
| | 12,409 | 688 |

Nevertheless, he asked Hegel (23 November) to buy him 'good, sound securities' to the face value of 8,000 crowns (£444), and on 10 January in the New Year gave his agent in Christiania, Nils Lund, instructions that the first 3,000 crowns (£167) of the fees due to him from the Bergen and Christiania Theatres for *The Wild Duck*, 'plus my pension and whatever else may come' should be held and paid out in instalments to Sigurd in Stockholm.

TWO

# ❧ Rosmersholm

## (1885–1886)

BERGEN PROUDLY STAGED the world premiere of *The Wild Duck* on 9 January 1885, Christiania, Helsinki and Stockholm following suit within the month, and Copenhagen in February. The audiences were, for the most part, as bewildered as the critics had been. However unpleasant the messages of *A Doll's House*, *Ghosts* and *An Enemy of the People* may have been at least they contained a 'hero' or 'heroine' with whom one could identify one's sympathy, but the characters of *The Wild Duck*, apart from the child Hedvig, seemed a thoroughly bad lot; and it was difficult to avoid the implication that they mirrored the audience. In Copenhagen the public expressed its disapproval audibly. 'Ibsen', commented Edvard Brandes, reviewing the production in *Politiken* on 23 February, 'is the finest dramatist writing in Scandinavia and . . . because he punches the Tartuffes of the world in their unctuous phizzes, people hissed him yesterday at the Royal Theatre.'

In Stockholm, alone, was the play well received, mainly because August Lindberg, who directed it there, understood the special problems that *The Wild Duck* posed. 'With your new play', he wrote to Ibsen before starting rehearsals, 'we stand on new and unbroken ground . . . These are quite new human beings, and what will it avail to use the common approach of actors—people who have lost touch with nature through spending their lives playing boulevard comedy? I realised this with *Ghosts*, and it is the same with *The Wild Duck*.' 'My mind reels,' he confided in a friend. 'Such unaccustomed problems for us actors! Never before have we been faced with the like.'[1] He cast an unknown actress as Gina and an eighteen-year-old pupil from drama school as Hedvig. At this flouting of the tradition that the best parts went to the most established performers (in Copenhagen Hedvig had been played by Betty Hennings, the Royal Theatre's leading actress, who was over forty) three of the leading members of the Stockholm company held a press conference to protest.

Lindberg's production of *The Wild Duck* was a landmark in theatrical history,

---

[1] Lindberg, pp. 146, 148.

for it anticipated in almost every respect the naturalism which André Antoine was to introduce five years later at his Théâtre Libre in Paris. Lindberg's son tells how his father astonished audiences by making his actors move and talk as though unconscious of the footlights and the audience, not like actors but like human beings such as one might meet outside a theatre, people living in an ordinary room—a room, moreover, which had doors with *handles* that shut with a click instead of the usual canvas flaps, and which even contained a commode. Lindberg's commode became a symbol for this new kind of production, a forerunner of the modern kitchen sink. His own performance as Hjalmar antagonised the conservative critics, probably (reading between the lines of the complaints) because he did not shrink from the contradictions which are so important a part of the character; Gustaf af Geijerstam, praising his performance in *Aftonbladet*, wrote that Lindberg made Hjalmar 'a human being of whom one gradually sees new aspects, now comic, now pathetic, just as in life one gets to know a person intimately so that in the end one sees him rounded and whole'.[1] He was evidently not afraid, as so many actors have been, of the moments of ridiculousness. Later in his career Lindberg was a famous Gregers; the two roles are closely interlocked, as even Othello and Iago are not, and there can have been few productions of the play when the actors playing them have not at some time felt a compulsive desire to change parts.

Germany had to wait three years before seeing the play (as with *An Enemy of the People*); but Ibsen was about to be introduced to a new and important public, for, as he informed Hegel on 11 February, an 'Italian biographer and translator, Alfred Mazza, has made an excellent translation of *A Doll's House*', and was about to try his hand at *The Wild Duck*. This was to have important results, for although he was never to take Italy by storm as he was to take Germany, England and (less permanently) France, he was to find there his greatest female interpreter. Further north, he added to Hegel, *A Doll's House* had been revived in Warsaw, 'with an actress who is having an extraordinary success in the role [Helena Modjeska]. But of payment to the author there is of course no question.'

On 24 March *Brand* was at last staged—in its entirety, moreover—at Ludvig Josephson's Nya Teater in Stockholm, nineteen years almost to the day after the play's publication. Josephson himself directed it, as he had directed the first production of *Peer Gynt*. 'It lasted for six and a half hours, until 12.30 a.m.', recalled August Lindberg. 'Such ladies as survived to the end lay dozing on their escorts' shoulders, with their corsets and bodices unbuttoned.'[2] 'Although its

---

[1] *Ibid.*, p. 150.
[2] Quoted by Gunnar Ollén in *Ibsens dramatik* (Stockholm, 1955), p. 50.

length and difficulty preclude complete success on the stage', wrote *Dagens Nyheter* on 26 March, 'it proved always interesting and at certain moments highly effective', and, although demanding 'a closer attention on the part of the audience than most modern plays', elicited 'frequent and loud applause' from the full house. Ibsen wrote Josephson a grateful letter on 9 April, saying that the event 'has at last erased from my mind the impression of all those cold, uncomprehending eyes which you yourself remember from a certain other place in the high north', and expressing the hope that it would not be the last time that he and Josephson would work together 'since I still have a whole heap of lunacies in my head out of which I think one might make quite good plays'.

The day after the *Brand* premiere, *A Doll's House* received its first English performance in anything approaching the original text. It was not a grand occasion; the performers were an amateur group called the Scribblers, the place the School of Dramatic Art in Argyle Street, London, and it was in aid of the Society for the Prevention of Cruelty to Children. William Archer was there, and wrote about it the following week in the *Dramatic Review*:

'It has been proved of old that amateurs rush in where artists fear to tread, but never was there a more audacious case in point than the late performance of *Et Dukkehjem*, at the School of Dramatic Art. Since I assisted with two or three other barbarians at a Chinese tragedy in San Francisco, I have not seen an audience so hopelessly bewildered as that which stoically sat out Miss Lord's translation of Ibsen's play. The actors themselves had a glimmering idea of the plot and situations, but even this they failed to convey to the spectators; as for the characterisation, the tendency, the satire, had the play been in Chinese they could not have been more completely lost on performers and spectators alike. The whole affair reminded me of the memorable performance of the 1603 Quarto of *Hamlet* at the St George's Hall, with the stage arranged after the Elizabethan manner. Imagine the conception of Shakespeare which a spectator who had never heard of him would have received from this performance of *Hamlet*. As far, or further, from the truth is the conception of Henrik Ibsen conveyed by the Scribblers' travesty to the minds of those who witnessed it. Miss Lord's *Nora* stands in relation to *Et Dukkehjem* somewhat in the relation of the 1603 *Hamlet* to the perfect text, and the Helmer of Mr Addison was to Emil Poulsen's as Mr Poel's *Hamlet* to Mr Irving's; yet I could not but reflect that the best possible translation of Ibsen's drama, played by the best available English actors, would have been scarcely less bewildering to an average English audience ... Miss Lord's translation is clumsy, and though I believe it has attracted attention in one or two narrow circles (the performance at the School of Dramatic Art seems to prove as much), it has been little noticed by the press, and has certainly not reached the general public.'

Despite the 'cold, uncomprehending eyes' of which Ibsen had complained to Bjørnson, he had begun to dwell with increasing earnestness on the possibility of returning to settle in Norway. Rome had begun to lose its magic; and on 25 April he wrote to Hegel that he felt doubtful whether they would return after their summer holiday. 'For several reasons', he explained, 'it would be convenient for me to spend another year in Germany, where I could take better care of a deal of literary business than I can from down here.' This sounds rather a thin excuse; if he had still been really happy in Rome, he could easily have conducted his correspondence with translators and theatre directors from down there. 'Besides,' he continued more convincingly, 'it will bring me somewhat nearer home, and I have lately begun to think seriously of buying a little villa, or rather a cottage, in the neighbourhood of Christiania, by the fjord, where I could live isolated and exclusively occupied with my work. What I most miss here is the sight of the sea, and this longing increases each year. Besides, I have over the years assembled a not so small collection of works of art, mainly paintings, and all these are now in store in an attic in Munich, without our getting any joy from them.' The sea, in Ibsen's work, always stands for the dark, mysterious force within one over which one has no control, and at fifty-seven he was feeling the compulsion, like so many exiles, to spend his old age in the place where he had been born. It is common for writers to react against the place which first spiritually liberated them. The warmth and colour of Italian life and the Italian landscape, which had so excited him as an aesthetically starved man in his middle thirties, seem to have ceased to stimulate him as he approached sixty. He no longer enjoyed presiding over a Socratic symposium at a crowded *osteria*.

He had intended to holiday in the Tyrol or on Lake Constance; but instead, he went to Norway. After a short stop in Copenhagen, he reached Christiania on 6 June. But if he had hoped that his bitter memories would be speedily dispelled, he was to be sharply disillusioned. On 10 June he sat in the gallery of the Storthing to listen to a debate on what came to be known as the 'Kielland affair'. The immediate issue was whether a civil list pension like his own should be awarded to the novelist Alexander Kielland, but the debate turned into a general discussion of the right of freedom of thought in religious matters. Kielland was a professed free-thinker, as Ibsen had been when his application for a pension had been rejected over twenty years earlier; but now, for the first time, there was a liberal government in power headed by a champion of free thought in Johan Sverdrup, and the result would surely be different. It was not. The government failed to take a decisive stand, the progressives were defeated and Kielland's application was rejected. Ibsen was outraged. The government seemed to him, more forcibly than ever before, to have betrayed its principles, and no longer to represent the true feeling of the left. Next day he took the train north to Trondhjem, and was seen off at the station by Bjørnson's son, Bjørn. 'Tell the youth of Norway from me', he said to him, loudly, so that all could hear, 'that I will stand with them as the cornerstone of the left. What may seem madness in the young will conquer in the end. Be sure of that.'[1]

Three days after his arrival in Trondhjem, on 14 June, the local Workers' Association honoured him with a banner procession, and he used the occasion to deliver a speech demanding a new attitude from those in authority, an attitude which he summed up in that word so beloved of Dr Stockmann, and as unfashionable in Norway then as it is in most countries now, aristocracy. 'There is still much to be done in this country', he declared, 'before we can be said to have achieved full freedom. But our present democracy scarcely has the strength to accomplish that task. An element of aristocracy must enter into our political life, our government, our members of parliament and our press. I am of course not thinking of aristocracy of wealth, of learning, or even of ability or talent. I am thinking of aristocracy of character, of mind and of will. That alone can make us free.[2] And this aristocracy, which I hope may be granted to our people, will come to us from two sources, the only two sections of society which have not yet been corrupted by party pressure. It will come to us from our women and from our working men. The reshaping of social conditions which is now being undertaken in Europe is principally concerned with the future status of the workers and of women. That is what I am hoping and waiting for, and what I shall work for with all my might.'

Ibsen and Suzannah remained a full month in Trondhjem, where they were joined by Sigurd, on leave from Stockholm. They then moved down the coast to the pretty little town of Molde, where they stayed for two months at the newly-built Hotel Alexandra. Molde was, he wrote Hegel on 11 July, 'one of the most beautiful places in the world for panorama. There is a lovely fjord,

---

[1] *Dagbladet*, 11 June 1885, reprinted in *C.E.*, XV, p. 422.

[2] The question had evidently been on Ibsen's mind much during the past three years. Apart from *An Enemy of the People*, Ibsen had written in his preliminary notes for *The Wild Duck*, jotted down during the winter of 1882–3: 'A new aristocracy will arise. It will not be the aristocracy of birth or wealth, of talent or knowledge. The aristocracy of the future will be the aristocracy of the mind and of the will.' The thought may not seem particularly relevant to *The Wild Duck*, but it was to be very relevant to *Rosmersholm*.

bounded by an infinity of snow-capped peaks, yet with a rich, almost Mediterranean vegetation. But I would not wish to stay here long; so there will be
nothing of my earlier notion of buying a property up here.' A newspaper
correspondent in the town reported that 'he and his wife keep very quietly to
themselves, associate with no one and seldom speak to anyone. After meals
they return to their rooms.' He noted that Ibsen spent hours each day standing
on the jetty below the hotel staring down into the water. 'He stands there most
of the day.' When he did talk to anyone he preferred, as at Berchtesgaden and
Gossensass, to chat with the common people rather than the bourgeoisie; and
several times he had himself rowed in a boat along the fjord to the open sea.[1]

A fortnight after his arrival, on 24 July, the town held a reception for him;
but he noticed that few people who were not of left-wing sympathies attended,
and when, the following month, civic receptions were given in honour of the
Prince of Wales (26 August) and William Gladstone (27 August), who were
independently touring the Norwegian west coast that summer, Ibsen was not
invited. He would probably have found little in common with the Prince of
Wales, though they could have conversed in German, but one would think
that he might have got on well with Gladstone, who loved Norway and
found its inhabitants 'a small people living happily in a spirit of democracy',[2] a
more charitable verdict than Ibsen would have delivered.

Ibsen's suspicion that he was being ostracised by the conservatives was
deepened by a coolness that he discerned, or thought he discerned, in two old
friends who were in Molde at the time, Ludvig Daae and Lorentz Dietrichson.
He especially sensed that Dietrichson was being stand-offish towards him, he
could only suppose in deference to the latter's fellow-conservatives in the
town. Dietrichson denies this, saying that when he met Ibsen there on 12 July
he found him 'unusually nervous, almost touchy. He had a feeling, which I am
sure was exaggerated, of being hated and looked askance at in Norway.'[3] He
adds that he knew Ibsen was busy with a new work (which he wasn't), and had
no wish to disturb him; also, that Ibsen's radical friends had untruthfully told
Ibsen that Dietrichson had said harsh things of him.[4] One's instinct is to blame
Ibsen's hypersensitivity; but Gerhard Gran, a sober judge in most matters,
thinks that Ibsen may have been right in his suspicions. The hatred between
conservatives and liberals in Norway then was almost pathological. 'A left-
winger', writes Gran, 'was not merely a supporter of the ungodly impeachment

---

[1] Per Amdam, *Ibsen og Molde*, in *Edda*, 1952, pp. 261–277.
[2] Sir Philip Magnus, *Gladstone* (London, 1954), p. 332.
[3] Dietrichson, I, p. 366.
[4] *Ibid.*, IV, p. 294.

but also a naturalist, a materialist, an anti-Christian and a moral anarchist.'[1]

Still, if Ibsen felt slighted by his political adversaries in Molde, he found ample compensation in the company, from 11 to 15 August, of another old acquaintance from Rome, Count Carl Snoilsky. The two had met again in Stockholm in 1869 and 1877, when Ibsen had been disappointed at Snoilsky's apparent movement towards a more conservative outlook (he had taken a post in the Swedish Foreign Office), and at the withering of his creative talent. In his youth Snoilsky had been a fertile and gifted poet; but after he had married and become a civil servant his creative springs had dried up and for ten years he had found himself scarcely able to write a line. 'I have wasted my life', he had noted sadly in 1874, 'and it is too late to change things now.' But in 1879, at the age of thirty-eight, he had left the Foreign Office, divorced his wife, married one of her relatives and gone abroad into voluntary exile. At once he had found himself able to write again, and published one volume after another. But the kind of poetry he was writing now was very different from the charming lyrics that had made his name. He, the refined nobleman, had become absorbed by the class struggle and the spirit of revolution. He longed to enter into contact with the common people; but his own upbringing and aristocratic heritage inhibited him. In 1883, two years before he met Ibsen at Molde, Snoilsky had written: 'Certainly creative literature can have an enormous influence, as Ibsen has shown, in the debating of social problems . . . [But] my powers do not suffice for so lofty a task, and so broad a public. I dare not aim so high. I am, moreover, conscious of my main handicap—that I have not, from childhood, lived the life of the *people*—my education and upbringing in the narrow classical tradition have unfitted me, like the vast majority of our writers, to address the humbler strata of society in a language they understand. Unlike my colleagues, however, I am often painfully conscious of this barrier, this limitation, and do my best to transcend it.'[2]

---

[1] Gran, II, p. 183. The 'impeachment' the previous year had done more than anything to inflame antagonism between the two parties. The Norwegian cabinet was constitutionally independent of the Storthing and acknowledged responsibility only to the King. This had led to an incongruous situation whereby the Storthing was overwhelmingly liberal while the Cabinet, chosen by the King, remained conservative. When the Storthing tried to resolve this situation King Oscar vetoed the bill, whereupon the Storthing took the extreme measure of impeaching the members of the cabinet before the Supreme Court. One by one they were dismissed and fined. The King selected a new and equally Conservative cabinet; the Storthing dug in its heels; the King refused to yield, and was rumoured to be considering a *coup d'état*; but eventually, on 26 June 1884, he sent for Sverdrup and invited him to form a Liberal ministry. The conflict thus ended in complete victory for the Liberals, but left a legacy of deep and lasting bitterness. For a full account of these happenings, see William Archer's article, *Norway Today*, in the *Fortnightly Review*, September 1885.

[2] Cf. Francis Bull's introduction to *Rosmersholm*, C.E., X, pp. 323–326.

Three years after their divorce Snoilsky's first wife had died of consumption, and many people had blamed him for her death. But Ibsen, during the four days he spent with Snoilsky at Molde, took a great liking both to him and to his new wife; he thought her sensitivity and strength of character largely responsible for Snoilsky's regeneration as a human being. He was deeply interested in Snoilsky's conviction that poetry should not merely deal with the 'beautiful' but should be connected with contemporary thought and ideas (he had boldly and outspokenly defended *Ghosts*), and in the temperamental difficulty which Snoilsky found in accepting this intellectual conviction. Snoilsky had already expressed this difficulty in a poem, *The White Lady*, about the sixteenth-century Duke Carl of Sweden, later King Carl IX, the brother and co-deposer of Erik XIV. Snoilsky portrayed Duke Carl as a man nagged by an uneasy conscience, in contrast to his son, the great Gustav II Adolf, who had no such fear of ghosts. Ibsen, in his youth, had depicted a similar contrast in *The Pretenders*, between Earl Skule and Haakon Haakonsson; and Snoilsky found himself in the same predicament as Earl Skule and Duke Carl—he could not shake off his inherited instincts and identify himself with the people. Gradually, Snoilsky had resigned himself to the idea that he really belonged among the mediaeval troubadours rather than among the socially conscious writers of the eighteen-eighties, such as Ibsen and Strindberg. Ibsen was to base the chief character of his new play, John Rosmer, very recognisably on Snoilsky; and Rebecca West in that play bears certain resemblances, though she is not to be identified with her, to Snoilsky's second wife.[1]

Snoilsky found the meeting equally rewarding. 'You know how much I admire Ibsen', he wrote to a friend shortly afterwards. 'For four days we had the pleasure of his company from morning till evening, and I rejoice to have carried away a warm *personal* memory of the great Sphinx. He was most charming towards us, even forthcoming.'[2] Four years later he wrote a poem, *Ibsen at Molde*, a pleasant reminder of how Ibsen appeared to the few people whom he liked and in whose company he felt secure:

> I remember an August evening
> With Ibsen in the town of flowers.
> I remember him as a mountain
> Whose crown is swathed in a cloud.

---

[1] Ibsen later admitted to Gustaf af Geijerstam the connection between the Snoilskys and *Rosmersholm*, and was alarmed that anyone should have guessed it—though one would think that after Bjørnson and *The League of Youth*, and Laura Kieler and *A Doll's House*, he had learned his lesson.

[2] K. M. Kommandantvold, *Ibsen og Sverige* (Oslo, 1956), p. 18.

I see the expanse of that mighty brow
Growing ever more overcast,
As though sensing some dark storm
About to eclipse our century's sun.

But to an old friend or acquaintance
His face could quickly light up,
And over that grim, closed mouth of his
The loveliest smile would run.

I remember that riddling brooder
Among his mountains and his storm-clouds;
But I do not forget how sunnily he smiled
Among the roses in the land of flowers.

A day or two after the Snoilskys left Molde, Ibsen received an unexpected letter from his youngest brother, Ole Paus Ibsen. Ole had been only seven when Ibsen had left home for Grimstad, and they had not met since, except during Ibsen's brief visit home six years later. Ole seems to have inherited both his father's inefficiency and his mother's melancholy ('He is enclosed', wrote his sister to Suzannah nineteen years later, 'shy, likes to hide himself away, and is somewhat sad and inclined to look on the dark side of life'). He was also, like Hedvig, deeply religious, and the enormous missive he now penned to Ibsen could scarcely have been more unfortunately conceived as an effort to bridge the gap between them. It opens with words of comfort that would have been more appropriately addressed to Vilhelm Foldal, the unrecognised clerk-dramatist of *John Gabriel Borkman*, than to the author of *Peer Gynt* and *A Doll's House* ('If you live some years longer the day will surely come when you will reap a rich reward for your work'), and continues amidst much wild mixing of metaphors into reams of religious cant of the kind that Ibsen most abominated ('What most men lack is Knowledge of God and his ways towards Man'). After rambling on for nearly two and a half thousand words he ended by inviting Ibsen to come and stay with him, on an island at the mouth of the Christiania fjord ('This, I often think to myself, would be the place for Henrik').[1] If Ibsen had cherished any faint inclination to renew contact with his family, this letter must surely have dispelled it; what could those two possibly have found to talk about on Ole's island? Whether he replied to Ole we do not know; yet it signifies something that he, who kept so few letters, kept this one.

On 4 September, the day before Ibsen left Molde, the local Choral Society and Horn Group serenaded him outside his hotel room. Ibsen replied with a

---

[1] Francis Bull, *Henrik Ibsen og Skien*, in *Edda*, 1951, pp. 91–96.

brief speech, in which he hinted that the new play he was planning would upset some people since 'the things that he found it vitally necessary to say would not please everyone', and asked that 'those elements of the community whom it disturbed should respect his views, as he respected theirs'. He added that his stay in Molde 'with its charming landscape and calm and peaceful inhabitants' might possibly 'have some mollifying influence on what he felt compelled to say'.[1]

From Molde he sailed down the coast to Bergen. It was his first visit since he had gone there as an alcoholic failure of thirty-five to the Choral Festival twenty-two years earlier, and his first new impression of the town might have been designed by a malicious Providence to revive those melancholy memories. As he came on deck wearing formal dress with decorations, he saw waiting on the quay four of his old drinking companions, two carpenters, a broker and a sexton, who greeted him with cries of: 'Welcome, old Henrik!' Ibsen hastened back to his cabin and did not emerge until assured that they had departed.[2]

Later impressions, however, were more agreeable, and he spent a pleasant week there. His old theatre had arranged a special production of Lady Inger of Østraat, which had been such a failure at its premiere there in 1855, and had persuaded Laura Gundersen, the star of the Christiania Theatre, to return to the stage where she had made her debut to play the lead. They wanted to make the premiere a special performance in Ibsen's honour, but for some reason, courteously but firmly, he refused. He astonished them, however, by agreeing to attend a rehearsal and, yet more amazingly (for his unwillingness to involve himself with any production was famous), made several suggestions regarding the placings and the speaking; he also gently remarked on the 'improvement' of one of his lines by the young director, Gunnar Heiberg, but allowed it to stand. He came, too, to the dress rehearsal; but when, at the premiere, the audience called for the author, they had to be told that he was not present.[3] And when the artisans' guild wanted to honour him with yet another torch-light procession, he refused—partly, perhaps, to save having to prepare another of those speeches which he so disliked writing and delivering.

Among the acquaintances he renewed in Bergen was one which stirred deep memories. His old love, Rikke Holst, now Fru Henrikke Tresselt, came to see him at his hotel with a bouquet of wild flowers. 'I've been gazing at myself all day in the mirror to make sure I looked all right for you', she told

[1] Romsdals Budstikke, nr. 71, 1885, reprinted in C.E., XV, p. 422.

[2] Paulsen, Samliv med Ibsen, I, pp. 122–123.

[3] Skavlan, pp. 147–148; Anker, Henrik Ibsens brevveksling med Christiania Theater, 1878–1899, pp. 36–37.

him. 'I didn't want you to find me too changed.' He asked if she had found any trace of her in his writing, and she said she could only think of Fru Strawman and her flock of children in *Love's Comedy* (for Rikke was now the mother of a large family). He asked: 'What have you been doing all these years?' and she said: 'While you have been writing all these plays that have made you famous I've just been bringing children into the world and mending old pairs of trousers.' He took both her hands and said: 'You'll never change, Rikke— God bless you!'[1] It was on this occasion that, as recorded earlier,[2] he wondered aloud that nothing had come of their relationship, she reminded him that he had run away, and he replied: 'Yes, yes. I never was a brave man face to face.'

Bergen, then, after that unfortunate first episode, had been a success— though he told a young journalist on the ship to Stavanger that he was sad to find his old theatre in debt, and to hear that the citizens of Bergen were willing to pay 80,000 crowns for a statue of Holberg but not the 2,000 crowns that were required to save the theatre from possible closure.[3] Christiania, to which he now returned, was to revive his sense of being unwanted, and in a way that confirmed his darkest suspicions. At a meeting of the Students' Union on 26 September, Fritz Thaulow[4] (son of that battling chemist on whom Ibsen had partly based Dr Stockmann) suggested that they should greet Ibsen with (of course) a torchlight procession. The conservatives in the Union opposed the idea in a tepid kind of way, but not absolutely; the motion was carried, and Lorentz Dietrichson, as Chairman of the Union, went with another committee member to inform Ibsen. Ibsen, mindful of Dietrichson's treatment of him in Molde, rejected the proposal, explaining that he had just refused a similar one from the Workers' Association of the city (as he had done in Bergen), and that he disliked public appearances; but he asked Dietrichson to convey his thanks to the students for the idea. The result was to be a dismal and undignified public row from which none of the principals, including Ibsen, emerged with any credit.

While he was in Christiania he met August Lindberg who, after his productions of *Ghosts* and *The Wild Duck*, could claim to be his most distinguished living interpreter. Lindberg found Ibsen more forthcoming than at their previous meeting in Munich, but in a state of great hatred towards Christiania.

---

[1] Paulsen, *Samliv med Ibsen*, I, pp. 125–126.

[2] Cf. *Henrik Ibsen, The Making of a Dramatist*, p. 130.

[3] P. Rosenkrantz Johnsen, *Om og omkring Henrik Ibsen og Suzannah Ibsen* (Oslo, 1928), p. 16.

[4] Later a distinguished painter, who was to befriend two notable outcasts in Strindberg (during the latter's Inferno crisis) and Oscar Wilde.

'His hair was quite white and standing on end. He said: "Yes, Lindberg, I would give much to see you play Oswald and Hjalmar Ekdal. But not, at any price, in this city." ' Lindberg asked him about the character of the devious Bishop Nicholas, which he was about to rehearse at Nya Teatern in Stockholm, but all Ibsen would say was: 'Well, you can see him any day here in Norway'.[1] The Christiania Theatre might, one would have thought, have arranged a performance of one of his plays during the week he was there; but they did not.

On 29 September Ibsen sailed to Copenhagen, where there were no such problems. The Royal Theatre put on a special performance of *The Wild Duck*, which Ibsen attended, and Frederik Hegel gave a dinner for him at which Georg Brandes delivered the principal speech of welcome. Rasmus B. Anderson, the Professor from Wisconsin who had unsuccessfully tried to arrange the publication of Ibsen's plays in America, was present, and was surprised (though one would think he had heard about it) at Ibsen's taciturnity. 'No one, not even Brandes, could get him to talk, he was as silent as a sphinx.' Brandes concluded his speech by thanking Ibsen 'for laying bare our faults so that we may note them and mend them'. Anderson continues: 'When Brandes sat down all the guests joined in calling for a speech from Ibsen. After much urging he finally rose to state that he was not able to make a speech and so would have to decline; he wished, however, to say in reply to Brandes that it was not the world about him that he had attempted to expose, but that he had only laid himself bare to his readers. Then he sat down.'[2]

On a later occasion during this week, however, Anderson found Ibsen far from taciturn. They met at the Hotel d'Angleterre, where Ibsen was staying. Ibsen took Anderson into a small private dining-room and ordered two bottles of champagne and a box of cigars; he did not smoke himself, but offered them to Anderson. 'He had evidently had a drink or two before I met him. I let him drink most of the champagne while I did the smoking. This man famous for his taciturnity became very communicative. He talked continuously, telling me over and over again how his books henceforth should become more aggressive. What he had done, he said, was hardly a beginning; but he was going to turn society inside out before he got done with it. He talked of all society as rotten and needing a thorough renovation. He continued talking until far into the small hours of the morning. It must have been about 3 o'clock a.m. when Mrs Ibsen came down in her nightrobe, took her husband by the

---

[1] Lindberg, pp. 174 and 178–179.

[2] Rasmus B. Anderson, *My Life Story* (Madison, 1915), pp. 495–496. The badness of the English is not due to translation; Anderson wrote his book in English, and his style is as insufferable as his complacency.

arm, said goodnight to me and to her husband: "Come with me".'[1] It is a pity that Ibsen did not unburden himself to a more appreciative listener than Anderson who, though an admirer of *Brand*, hated all of Ibsen's later works. 'Apart from the improprieties and offence against good morals that are found in them', he concludes, 'they seem to me mere twaddle.'

One meeting during his stay in Copenhagen must have touched Ibsen's conscience. Laura Kieler, now working as a journalist on *Morgenbladet*, came to interview him, and wrote a (disappointingly unoriginal and unrevealing) article on him which was reprinted in several Norwegian papers. They met, she recalled years later, 'like two strangers who had never known each other'.[2] It was not to be their last encounter.

Georg Brandes gave another dinner for him, and persuaded him to attend a meeting on 3 October of the new Radical Students' Union, founded three years earlier as a counter to the old Union which, like that in Christiania, was controlled by conservatives. Ibsen had already refused an invitation to attend this meeting, and only changed his mind at Brandes' urgent request. But he enjoyed himself, and stayed until after one o'clock in the morning. Brandes made an eloquent speech in honour of 'Youth and Henrik Ibsen', calling him 'the hammer and the benefactor of the North'. Ibsen, in his reply, declared: 'I hope to remain a student all my days. When I cease to be one, I shall regard myself as unworthy to live'.[3]

That same evening, Ibsen was the central figure of another and far less harmonious occasion, at the Students' Union in Christiania. A Danish student named Ove Rode, later to become a prominent politician, announced that he had a message from Dr Ibsen to the Union, to the effect that he could not take seriously a greeting conveyed to him by a society whose committee was headed by his old friend, or rather acquaintance, Lorentz Dietrichson, and that if they wanted to please him they should throw out the present committee and elect a new one, in which event he would be happy to accept the Union's greetings. Dietrichson, in the chair, postponed discussion of the matter until the next week's meeting, and wired Ibsen in Copenhagen asking if he had authorised Rode's statement. Ibsen replied that he could indeed not feel sympathy with any body of which Dietrichson was head. It was a petty attitude to take, but rawly sensitive men are often petty when they feel they have been slighted, and Dietrichson's reaction was even less dignified. On 10 October he made a speech at the Christiania Union denouncing Ibsen's attitude and, worse, recited

---

[1] *Ibid.*, p. 484.
[2] Kinck, p. 518.
[3] Georg Brandes, *Levned*, III, p. 146.

a lampoon which he had written against Ibsen and which the meeting, in a fit of undergraduate high spirits, promptly sang to an extemporised tune.

Next day the story was all over the capital. Dietrichson's speech and lampoon were both published in the conservative newspapers. The left-wing papers retorted by violently attacking the Union and Dietrichson; and the left-wing students staged a protest meeting, to which they invited the townspeople. Seven hundred people attended, and they sent Ibsen an apology and a tribute. The Danish poet Holger Drachmann penned an angry attack on Ibsen, which Dietrichson read out at a later meeting; a prominent Norwegian theologian attacked Ibsen as an example of the danger of free thought; the magazine *Samfundsbladet* declared that it was a straight choice, 'Christ or Ibsen'. Ibsen, by now in Munich, wrote an immense, neurotic and boring letter to the Union 'to be read aloud from the spot from which I was . . . insulted by your chairman', which it was. Dietrichson of course replied at equal length. The result was that two weeks later the left-wing students followed the example of their fellows in Copenhagen by breaking away and forming their own Union, of which they forthwith elected Ibsen an honorary member.[1]

It was the kind of trivial and time-wasting business in which no writer of Ibsen's stature should have got embroiled; yet the affair is significant in that it mirrors the exceptional hatred that existed in Norway just then between the rival political factions. As Gerhard Gran observes, the most extraordinary aspect of the matter is not Ibsen's behaviour but that Dietrichson should, first in Molde and then in Christiania, have risked a friendship of such long standing and of which he was so proud on so minimal an issue. Ibsen was to make the bitterness of this political strife in Norway the background of his next play: that, and his disillusionment with Norway's first liberal government, as particularly exemplified by its conduct in the Kielland affair. 'It was a sad moment', he wrote to Georg Brandes on 10 November 1886, 'when Johan Sverdrup came to power and got muzzled and handcuffed.'

On leaving Scandinavia that autumn Ibsen had re-settled in Munich in a new apartment at Maximilianstrasse 32, 'a big corner-house with a bust of mad King Ludwig II as an eighteen-year-old, full of hope, on the stairs. A maid opens the door', reported a journalist from the Swedish paper *Aftonbladet*, 'and we enter a lobby where a great many felt hats and rough natural walking sticks recall Dr Stockmann in *An Enemy of the People*. "Yes, Dr Ibsen is at home," says the maid, and one enters a simple living-room, a little stiff and cold, for the rooms

---

[1] Cf. Gran, II, pp. 188 ff., and Fredrik Wallem, *Det norske studentersamfund gjennem hundrede aar, 1813–1913* (Christiania, 1916), II, pp. 840–866. For a right-wing view of the affair, cf. Bredo Morgenstierne's review of Wallem's book in *Aftenposten*, 12 November 1916, reprinted in Dietrichson, IV, pp. 287–293.

are "furnished". Ibsen does not want a home. He wants to live as a foreigner in a foreign land.' The reporter noted of Ibsen himself that 'he has the enquiring, piercing look of a doctor'; his glance reminded the man of 'an old seaman I saw one night on a steamer off the north coast near Trondhjem, staring at the rudder, peering out into the night'.[1]

Ibsen described his new surroundings rather differently. 'We are now living handsomely and spaciously in the smartest and most aristocratic street in Munich', he told Hegel on 26 October, 'and yet pay only half the rent we had to pay in Rome.' Three weeks later, on 15 November, he informed Gerda Brandes that he was 'now starting on a new dramatic work which I hope to have ready during the winter'. 'We live pleasantly and quietly; almost too quietly', he wrote to Hegel on 4 December. 'We wish travelling Scandinavians would visit us a little more often. I have now almost completed my plans for my new play and shall begin to write it in a few days. It will be in four acts and interests me much.'

There was excellent news for the family that month. After only nine months in Stockholm Sigurd had been appointed attaché to the Legation in Washington, and had won a stipend of 7,200 crowns (£400), which he was to receive annually for three years. For the past year he had been working in Stockholm with no salary at all. 'It has been an expensive time for me', wrote Ibsen to Hegel on 22 December, and it could hardly have come at a worse juncture. His income that year had consisted almost entirely of fees from performances of *The Wild Duck*, which had not run long anywhere, plus reprints of *Brand*, *The Vikings at Helgeland* and *Peer Gynt*, and a little from the Stockholm production of *Brand*. It had been his poorest year financially since 1881:

| | crowns | £ |
|---|---|---|
| Fee for *The Wild Duck* in Christiania | 2,500 | 139 |
| „   „   „   „   „ in Bergen | 500 | 28 |
| „   „   „   „   „ in Danish provinces (Julius Petersen) | 600 | 33 |
| „   „   „   „   „ in Helsinki | 150 | 8 |
| „   „   „   „   „ in Gothenburg and Swedish provinces (L. Lindgren) | 400 | 22 |
| „   „   „   „   „ at Royal Theatre, Copenhagen (2nd–10th performances) | 1,583 | 88 |
| „   „   „   „   „ at Royal Theatre, Stockholm | 1,511 | 83 |
| Extra fees for *The Wild Duck* in Swedish provinces | 200 | 11 |
| 10th edition of *Brand* (1,500 copies) | 1,360 | 76 |
| „       „       „   „ (supplementary fee) | 170 | 9 |

[1] *Aftonbladet* (Stockholm), 12–13 January 1887.

E

| | crowns | £ |
|---|---|---|
| 6th edition of *The Vikings at Helgeland* (1,500 copies) | 720 | 40 |
| 6th edition of *Peer Gynt* (1,500 copies) | 1,320 | 73 |
| Fee for *Brand* at Nya Teatern, Stockholm | 400 | 22 |
| Unspecified German fees | 356 | 20 |
| | 11,770 | 652 |

'I am much happier here than I was last year in Rome', Ibsen wrote to Nils Lund on 16 January 1886. He fell back at once into his old Munich routine. After his frugal breakfast and his morning at his desk, he would spend the afternoons walking the city streets in his tail coat and top hat, his umbrella in his hand, looking closely at the people and stopping wherever there was any small gathering. Each evening at the same precise hour he would enter the Café Maximilian, in the street where he lived, and seat himself at the second or third table on the right of the entrance, opposite the door and facing a large mirror in which he could see the rest of the room. He would order a cognac and seltzer or a glass of dark Munich beer, arm himself with a stack of newspapers (he especially liked to read the comic ones)[1] and sit there, sometimes glancing at people above his newspaper, sometimes motionless as a marble figure, his lips pursed, his hand as though holding a pen, brooding. After an hour he would silently pay the waitress, take up his silk hat and his ever-present umbrella, and walk out with his short, quick steps.[2]

M. G. Conrad, the editor of *Die Gesellschaft*, who made the above observations, also records a conversation from this period in which Ibsen referred to the necessity of knowing a character fully before starting to write about him or her. 'Before I write one word, I must know the character through and through, I must penetrate into the last wrinkle of his soul. I always proceed from the individual; the stage setting, the dramatic ensemble, all of that comes naturally and causes me no worry, as soon as I am certain of the individual in every aspect of his humanity. But I have to have his exterior in mind also, down to the last button, how he stands and walks, how he bears himself, what his voice sounds like. Then I do not let him go until his fate is fulfilled.'[3] He added yet another warning against the tendency of critics to find symbols everywhere. 'The critics ... like to symbolise, because they have no respect for reality. And if one really gives them a symbol, then they reduce it to a triviality or they revile the author.'[4] No doubt he was thinking of the incomprehension

---

[1] Gerard Schjelderup, *Ibsen-anecdoter*, in *Morgenbladet*, 17 February 1906.
[2] M. G. Conrad, quoted by Zucker, p. 222.
[3] *Ibid.*, p. 224.
[4] *Ibid.*, p. 225.

with which they had greeted the simple and clearly explained symbol of the wild duck.

On another occasion, Ibsen explained his method in more detail: 'As a rule, I make three drafts of my plays, which differ greatly from each other—in characterisation, not in plot. When I approach the first working-out of my material, it is as though I knew my characters from a railway journey; one has made a preliminary acquaintance, one has chatted about this and that. At the next draft I already see everything much more clearly, and I know the people roughly as one would after a month spent with them at a spa; I have discovered the fundamentals of their characters and their little peculiarities; but I may still be wrong about certain essentials. Finally, in the last draft, I have reached the limit of my knowledge; I know my characters from close and long acquaintance— they are my intimate friends, who will no longer disappoint me; as I see them now, I shall always see them.'[1]

He once remarked that he 'liked if possible to plan his day's work in the morning when he awoke, for then he felt his imagination to be at its liveliest; whereas his *critical* sense was at its least sharp then, in the half-dreaming hour of dawn. This did not fully awake till he was seated at his desk, when it often rejected all the ideas he had hit upon when lying in bed.' He also kept small guttapercha devils with red tongues on his desk. ' "There must be troll in what I write", he said, and in a tone midway between jest and earnest he spoke of his "super-devil". "He only comes out last, when things are really difficult. Then I lock my door and bring him out. No other human eye has seen him, not even my wife . . . He is a bear playing the violin and beating time with his feet." '[2]

Sigurd visited his parents in January en route to his new post in America; it was to be the last time they were to see him for three years. He wrote to them each week, with vivid descriptions of the New World, especially of people he thought might interest his father. Ibsen waited impatiently for these letters; Georg Brandes tells that he was present when one arrived, and that Ibsen's hand was so shaking with excitement that he could scarcely open the envelope. And when, in 1888, Sigurd was transferred to Vienna and came to see his parents at Munich on the way, Ibsen was waiting for him at the station an hour and a half before the train was due.[3]

---

[1] Gran, II, p. 166. He does not name his source.

[2] P. A. Rosenberg in *Nationaltidende* (Copenhagen), 28 July 1926, reprinted in *C.E.*, XIX, pp. 217–218. William Archer doubted the existence of these devils, as he never saw them in Ibsen's study. One imagines that when not actually working, Ibsen kept them in a drawer.

[3] Bergliot Ibsen, pp. 116–117.

Henrik Jæger was preparing a biographical study of Ibsen, to commemorate the dramatist's sixtieth birthday in 1888, and Hegel, who was to publish it, wrote to Ibsen asking for information about photographs, paintings and busts of him, and about his own paintings. 'The oldest photograph', replied Ibsen on 25 February, 'was taken by the author Edward Larssen [one of the originals of Hjalmar Ekdal] in either 1861 or 1862.' He named eight others, four busts ('the oldest are from 1867') and three paintings, none of which (not even the one by Kronborg, which he owned) he thought really good. 'My own drawings', he concluded, 'have hardly any artistic value. Should they be reproduced, it could only be as curiosities.'

In March he heard that yet another edition of *Peer Gynt* (the seventh) was required, although a new one had been printed the previous year, and that *Love's Comedy* was to be staged by the Royal Theatre in Copenhagen. He had written to them on 20 February suggesting that they might reconsider this play, which they had twice previously rejected, in 1863 and 1874, and had also asked them to think again about *Ghosts*; but despite the success of the latter play on the stages of Sweden and Norway, they remained (like the Christiania Theatre) adamantly opposed to it. Ludvig Josephson staged *The Pretenders* at Nya Teatern in Stockholm, with August Lindberg as Bishop Nicholas; and on Good Friday (of all days), 14 April, Ibsen attended the German premiere of *Ghosts* at Augsburg, where the young poet Felix Philippi had persuaded August Grosse to present it. The police had banned a public performance, so the play was given in private before an invited audience. The cast was young and keen, and despite certain imperfections the evening was a success. The police ban naturally excited curiosity, and people unable to obtain tickets stormed the bookshops in search of copies.

By now Ibsen was working hard on his new play, to which he had given the provisional title of *The White Horses*. 'Ever since my return here', he wrote to Georg Brandes (10 November), 'I have been plagued by a new play which absolutely demanded to be written'; and to Carl Snoilsky (14 February) he mentioned that he had 'made some close studies for it during my trip to Norway during the summer'. As we have seen, he had hoped to complete it during the winter; but it would not come, and on 20 February he had to inform Edvard Fallesen, director of the Royal Theatre in Copenhagen, that 'it cannot be expected before the autumn'. He had made some brief notes and begun a draft, but had completed less than an act. The notes show that he was basing his two main characters recognisably on the Snoilskys:

## WHITE HORSES

*He*, a refined, aristocratic character, who has switched to a liberal viewpoint and been ostracised by all his former friends and acquaintances. A widower; had been unhappily married to a half-mad melancholic who ended by drowning herself.

*She*, the governess of his two daughters, emancipated, hot-blooded, somewhat ruthless beneath a refined exterior. Is regarded by their acquaintances as the evil spirit of the house; an object of suspicion and gossip.

There were also, at this stage, to have been two daughters, one 'in danger of succumbing to inactivity and loneliness', the other 'sharply observant; rich passions beginning to dawn'; but Ibsen eventually removed them from this play and kept them for his next.

But the draft made painful progress, and on 25 May he scrapped it and began an entirely new one. This new draft (still under the title of *The White Horses*) progressed swiftly; he finished the first act by 1 June and the second by 8 June. On 10 June he began the third act; but five days later he scrapped the whole of this second draft and started a third one, re-naming the play *Rosmersholm*—perhaps feeling that *White Horses* was too similar a title to *Ghosts*, especially since Rebecca had been made to say in the second draft that freedom consisted in 'getting rid of one's white horses'. He completed this third draft in a day over seven weeks; Act One took him from 15–28 June, Act Two from 1–12 July, Act Three from 15–24 July and Act Four from 26 July to 4 August. Two days later he began his fair copy but, although the third draft is essentially the play as we know it, he made a number of small revisions and did not finish it until 27 September. 'It cannot', he told Hegel in a letter of 2 October, 'as far as I can surmise, offer grounds for attack from any quarter. I hope, though, that it may provoke a lively debate.'

*Rosmersholm* was published on 23 November 1886, in an edition of 8,000 copies. 'Under better conditions', Hegel had written to him on 7 October, 'I would have suggested a somewhat larger edition';[1] *The Wild Duck* had, despite its mixed reviews, sold out its first edition of the same size very rapidly, but there was a general slump in the book trade in 1886. Even more than *The Wild Duck*, *Rosmersholm* baffled the critics, and, like *The Wild Duck*, won nothing like the acclaim that had greeted his earlier plays, from *Brand* to *A Doll's House*. Indeed, it got the worst notices of any of his mature plays except *Ghosts*. *Aftenposten* knocked it twice within a week. 'No doubt', observed an anonymous reviewer on 24 November, '*Rosmersholm* will find its admirers, who will acclaim this play as a great masterpiece. But equally surely, many will

---

[1] Nielsen, II, p. 375.

find it distasteful. These characters are all artificial and totally unwholesome. They would do better to keep their thoughts to themselves.' On 30 November in the same paper, Bredo Morgenstierne complained: 'What the play is meant to teach us it is impossible to say . . . Many details of motivation are unintelligible . . . The sum impression is duller than that of Ibsen's earlier plays.' He found the minor characters, apart from Brendel, disappointing, the dramatic tension 'not great', and asked: 'Is this decadence and decline, or merely an ebb?' Alfred Sinding-Larsen in *Morgenbladet* (1–2 December) was no more enthusiastic. He too complained of the obscurity, saying that whereas most writers move towards a greater clarity and harmony as they grow older, Ibsen has done the reverse, employing his technical skill 'to disturb and depress, leading us not to clarity but to darkness, not to calm contemplation but to the fruitless pondering of unsolved riddles. Ibsen seems more and more to have withdrawn into himself and turned away from life and its realities . . . devoting himself more and more to pessimistic speculation . . . Will Ibsen ever return to a more wholesome and positive outlook? *Rosmersholm* gives no promise of this.' Sinding-Larsen found the two principal characters 'sickly, distorted and lame . . . Normal people could . . . scarcely act as they do . . . and spiritual abnormalities are no more suited to the theatre than physical abnormalities.' He complained that the play was feebly constructed, relying overmuch on reported action and being deficient in true action: 'Dramatically, *Rosmersholm* is among the weakest of Ibsen's plays.' Even Irgens Hansen in *Dagbladet* (28 November), who as an admirer of Ibsen must have been anxious to champion the play, could be no more than vaguely favourable.

In Sweden and Denmark, however, *Rosmersholm* found admirers. One of his oldest Swedish champions, Urban von Feilitzen (who wrote under the pseudonym of 'Robinson') was disappointed; reviewing the book in *Nordisk Tidskrift* (1887, pp. 20–38), he thought that Ibsen was indulging in an excess of symbolism and superfluous lines which destroyed the naturalism of the dialogue. But Georg Nordensvan, in *Ny Illustrerad Tidning* (4 December 1886), found it 'shattering, highly characteristic of Ibsen, of his prophetic insight, his restless searching inwards and yet further inwards, his obscurity (here more marked than usual), and his tendency to symbolise, sometimes to the point of unintelligibility.' He thought Rebecca one of Ibsen's greatest characters, perceptively observing: 'It is his exploration of depths of the human mind which no man has previously sounded that makes him obscure and riddling.' Even the reactionary C.D. af Wirsén, after complaining that 'scoundrels, rakes, hypocritical boasters, at best clowns, are those who nowadays tread his boards', ended by admitting that 'even in the labyrinths into which Ibsen has allowed his writing to stray in these last years, he has retained the gift of magically conjuring forth fascinating figures . . . and sometimes, as here, they have the power terrifyingly to grip the imagination.'[1]

Georg Brandes was not particularly impressed after a first reading, but Edvard Brandes loved it. 'This profound work', he wrote in *Politiken* on 25 November 1886, 'is brilliantly written, and filled with that mixture of love of and contempt for humanity which forms the core of Ibsen's recent plays.' He thought that the final scene 'equals in tragic imagination the best that Ibsen has written', and that the only modern work with which it could be compared was *Crime and Punishment*. 'They are akin, Dostoevsky and Ibsen', he concluded, 'and there is something about Rebecca West that reminds one of young Russian girls in their revolutionary struggles. *Rosmersholm* is a masterpiece.' 'I kneel before *Rosmersholm*', he wrote to Strindberg a few weeks later; and Strindberg himself, despite his increasing hostility towards Ibsen, wrote an appreciation of the play the following spring in an essay entitled *Soul-Murder*. In this, he declared that *Rosmersholm* was 'unintelligible to the theatre public, mystical to the semi-educated, but crystal-clear to anyone with a knowledge of modern psychology'—one of the very few occasions on which he ever paid public tribute to Ibsen.[2] One can understand the attraction that *Rosmersholm* held for Strindberg, for he, too, was deeply interested in 'magnetism' and hypnosis, the ability of one person to gain control over the mind of another. He had treated this theme himself in *The Father*, which he began only two months after *Rosmersholm* had appeared, and was to do so again the following year in *Creditors*; while the degenerating effect of an aristocratic heritage, Rosmer's tragedy, was to be the theme, also the following year, of *Miss Julie*.

The hostile press that *Rosmersholm* received was reflected in its sales, as had not been the case with *The Wild Duck*. 'Ibsen's *Rosmersholm* seems unlikely to have the unusually large sale that a new book by him usually has', wrote Hegel to Alexander Kielland on 17 December. '*Morgenbladet's* review seems to have sapped people's desire to read it. It looks as though Lie's novel will be the real Christmas book.'[3] Even more damagingly for Ibsen, the Royal Theatre in Copenhagen, which was treating him so generously in the matter of royalties, rejected the play. Nor, as with *Ghosts*, did the play seem more accessible when performed; for years, it was to succeed nowhere. Many even of Ibsen's admirers

[1] Wirsén, pp. 67 and 80–81.

[2] Though, with characteristic inconsistency, he seems to have reacted against the play by the summer. On 11 May he sent Edvard Brandes an article in which he asserted that Ibsen had written no true work of art since *The Pretenders*. Brandes thought the article reactionary and stupid and told Strindberg so; and it was never printed.

[3] Nielsen, II, p. 484.

agreed that the play was hopelessly obscure and that the characters were abstractions rather than human beings.

This reaction is not surprising. If he had been breaking new ground in *The Wild Duck*, Ibsen was breaking much newer and more dangerous ground in *Rosmersholm*. To begin with, the play is about two lovers as potentially passionate as Romeo and Juliet or Antony and Cleopatra; but Rosmer and Rebecca, unlike Shakespeare's couples, are children of the nineteenth century; they are, much as they would like not to be, dominated by bourgeois moral values and, because of forces both outside and within them, they never touch each other until the moment when they clasp hands to walk out and drown themselves. Unless these banked passions are suggested (and how often has one not seen Rebecca played as an intellectual bluestocking and Rosmer as a sexless parson?) there seems no earthly reason why they should commit suicide. The actors must be able, in Bernard Shaw's words, to 'sustain the deep black flood of feeling from the first moment to the last.'[1] It is only Rebecca's enemy, Dr Kroll, who calls her an intellectual. Of course she had an intellect, but that is another thing. Ibsen, like George Eliot, knew well the predicament of the woman of intellect whose passions can find no outlet. Rebecca and Dorothea Brook of *Middlemarch* have a good deal in common.

Moreover, in this play Ibsen was, for the first time not merely in his work but in any play for over two centuries, *overtly* probing the uncharted waters of the unconscious mind. As already remarked, the problem of how one human being can gain control over the mind of another and persuade him or her to act, not against their will, but according to inclinations within them which they repress, was much in the air; yet although we know that it deeply interested Ibsen (his preliminary jottings for *Rosmersholm* contain references to 'the sixth sense' and 'magnetic influence') it was not something of which the ordinary theatregoer was aware, and although readers would have understood it in a novel, where the author can explain and clarify the actions of his characters, they were not sufficiently used to reading between the lines of plays to comprehend what was merely implied (and implied with marvellous subtlety) in the dialogue. One reader who did understand what *Rosmersholm* was about was Sigmund Freud who, in his essay *Character-Types* which he wrote during the 1914 war, made an extraordinarily penetrating analysis of the play and of the secret motives which impel the characters. In the second section of this essay, sub-titled 'Those wrecked by success', Freud deals with the common and disturbing psychological phenomenon of people who, when what they most

---

[1] Letter to Charles Charrington, 28 January 1890 (*Bernard Shaw, Collected Letters, 1874–1897*, ed. Dan H. Laurence, London, 1965, p. 240).

want at last lies within their grasp, find themselves unable to seize hold of it. After an illuminating consideration of Lady Macbeth, Freud moves on to *Rosmersholm*, and writes thus of Rebecca:

'Ibsen has made it clear by small touches of masterly subtlety that Rebecca does not actually tell lies but is never entirely straightforward. Just as, in spite of her freedom from prejudice, she has understated her age by a year, so her confession to the two men [Rosmer and Kroll] is incomplete, and as a result of Kroll's insistence it is supplemented on some important points. Hence it is open to us to suppose that her explanation of her renunciation exposes one motive only to conceal another ... Rosmer's influence may only have been a cloak, which concealed another influence that was operative, and a remarkable indication points in this direction.'

When, Freud continues, in the final scene, after her confession about herself and Beata, Rosmer again asks Rebecca to become his wife, by implication forgiving her:

'She does not answer, as she should, that no forgiveness can rid her of the feeling of guilt she has incurred from her malignant deception of poor Beata; but she charges herself with another reproach which affects us as coming strangely from this free-thinking woman, and is far from deserving the importance which Rebecca attaches to it ... She has had sexual relations with another man; and we do not fail to observe that these relations, which occurred at a time when she was free and accountable to nobody, seem to her a greater hindrance to the union with Rosmer than her truly criminal behaviour to his wife ...

'After she has learnt that she has been the mistress of her own father, she surrenders herself wholly to her now overmastering sense of guilt. She makes the confession to Rosmer and Kroll which stamps her as a murderess; she rejects for ever the happiness to which she has paved the way by crime, and prepares for departure. But the true motive of her sense of guilt, which results in her being wrecked by success, remains a secret. As we have seen, it is something quite other than the atmosphere of Rosmersholm and the refining influence of Rosmer ...

'Rebecca's feeling of guilt has its source in the reproach of incest, even before Kroll, with analytical perspicacity, has made her conscious of it. If we reconstruct her past, expanding and filling in the author's hints, we may feel sure that she cannot have been without some inkling of the intimate relations between her mother and Dr West. It must have made a great impression on her when she became her mother's successor with this man. She stood under the domination of the Oedipus complex, even though she did not know that this universal phantasy had in her case become a reality. When she came to Rosmersholm, the inner force of this first experience drove her into bringing about, by vigorous action, the same situation which had been realised in the original instance through no doing of hers—into getting rid of the wife and mother, so that she might take her place with the husband and father. She describes with a convincing insistence how, against her will, she was obliged to proceed, step by step, to the removal of Beata... Everything that happened to her at Rosmersholm, her falling in love with Rosmer and her hostility to his wife, was from the first a consequence of the Oedipus complex—an inevitable replica of her relations with her mother and Dr West.

'And so the sense of guilt which first causes her to reject Rosmer's proposal is at bottom no different from the greater one which drives her to her confession after Kroll has opened her eyes. But just as under the influence of Dr West she had become a freethinker and despiser of religious morality, so she is transformed by her love for Rosmer into a being of conscience and nobility. This much of the mental process within her she understands, and so she is justified in describing Rosmer's influence as the motive for the change—the motive that had become accessible to her.

'The practising psycho-analytical physician knows how frequently, or how invariably, a girl who enters a household as servant, companion or governess, will consciously or unconsciously weave a daydream, which derives from the Oedipus complex, of the mistress of the house disappearing and the master taking the newcomer as his wife in her place. *Rosmersholm* is the greatest work of art of the class that treats of this common phantasy in girls. What makes it into a tragic drama is the extra circumstance that the heroine's daydream had been preceded in her childhood by a precisely corresponding reality.'[1]

Of all Ibsen's plays, *Rosmersholm* is the most inexhaustible. To a modern reading public or audience, as to Freud, that is cause for admiration and fascination; but can we blame Ibsen's contemporaries for finding it impossibly obscure, when we remember that Freud's own *Interpretation of Dreams*, published fourteen years later, was to take eight years to sell its first edition of six hundred copies?

On the stage, *Rosmersholm* proved even more perplexing than on the page.

---

[1] James Strachey's translation.

The premiere, at Bergen on 17 January 1887, was coolly received, as was the Christiania production on 12 April, which ran for only ten performances—a particular calamity for Ibsen who, in response to a suggestion from Schrøder, had agreed to take ten per cent of the gross instead of his usual flat fee. No more than six further performances of it were given in Christiania during the next two years, and it was not revived there again before 1900. Its first German production, at Augsburg on 6 April 1887, was a disaster, as was the first English production in 1891. It failed in both Gothenburg (March 1887) and Stockholm (April 1887). The Royal Theatre in Copenhagen, as we have seen, rejected it, and it fell, as so often, to August Lindberg to get to the heart of the play. He toured it through the Swedish provinces and Denmark with himself as Rosmer and with an inadequate Rebecca; and in September 1887 he played in Christiania in the previously unsuccessful production by Bjørn Bjørnson. 'Act after act', Lindberg recalled, 'I felt the atmosphere tighten, both on the stage and in the audience . . . The applause rolled up over the stage like waves of heat. The last act is fever and ecstasy. To enter that ecstasy, to feel it rise in one, without losing control over oneself! To feel how Rosmer and Rebecca are gripped by love—it was like being in a trance. It was like exchanging souls. And at last, out from the closed air of that drawing-room, out of human smallness, out to the mill-race.'[1] After the performance the Norwegian actress Laura Gundersen told Lindberg that they had never understood the play before.

Before presenting the original Christiania production of *Rosmersholm*, Hans Schrøder, the head of the Christiania Theatre, had written to Ibsen telling him of his plans for casting. Replying on 2 January 1887, Ibsen delivered himself of some pungent comments on Schrøder's taste and some valuable observations on the play. 'You think Fru Gundersen was born to play Rebecca. I don't agree. Fru Gundersen's strength is for the big declamatory line, and there are none of those in my play. How could she manage these seemingly light but extremely pregnant dialogues? Dual personalities, complex characters, are not her forte. Then you want Gundersen to play Rosmer. Permit me to ask what the effect is likely to be when Rebecca tells how she has been gripped by 'a wild and sensual longing' for him? Or when Brendel calls him 'my boy', etc? Or when Dr Kroll hectors and browbeats him? Is G's personality compatible with this and much else? For Rosmer you must choose the most delicate and sensitive personality that your theatre can lay its hands on . . . That the role of Dr Kroll, that pedagogic autocrat, should be entrusted to Hr. [Bjørn] Bjørnson is, I trust, a joke on which I need waste no further ink. Is it,

---

[1] Lindberg, p. 210.

though, conceivable that this monstrous idea is seriously being harboured? If the artistic direction of the theatre is so totally lacking in critical and self-critical ability, I can await the production only with the direst misgivings.'[1]

Schrøder yielded with a fair grace, and the cast was altered in accordance with Ibsen's wishes. A month later, on 5 February, Ibsen addressed to him some further advice about the characters, including meticulous details regarding their dress:

*Dr Kroll is an authoritarian with a passion for domineering, as is so often the case with headmasters. He is of course of good family; Major Rosmer's son married his sister. The Doctor's manner is therefore that of a well-born government official. Despite a certain asperity which now and then manifests itself, his behaviour in general is friendly and agreeable. He can be amiable when he pleases, or when he is with people he likes. But it is to be noted that he only likes those people who share his opinions. The rest irritate him, and with them he easily becomes ruthless and reveals a tendency towards malice. His appearance is distinguished; he is handsomely dressed, in black. Coat almost down to his knees, but no lower. He wears a white cravat, large and old-fashioned, which goes twice round his neck, i.e. no tie. His dress explains why Ulrik Brendel at first takes him for Pastor Rosmer and then for a 'brother of the cloth'. In Act One Rosmer also wears a black coat, but grey trousers and a tie or cravat of the same colour. In Acts Three and Four, however, he is dressed entirely in black.*

*Rebecca's manner must on no account carry any hint of imperiousness or masculinity. She does not force Rosmer forward. She lures him. A controlled power, a quiet determination, are of the essence of her character.*[2]

During rehearsals for the Christiania production Constance Bruun, the young actress who had been chosen to replace Laura Gundersen as Rebecca, was taken ill, and the part was given to another young actress, Sofie Reimers. She wrote to Ibsen asking his advice; he gave it briefly (25 March 1887), and it still serves as a general warning to any actor or actress attempting any Ibsen role. 'No declamation! No theatricalities! No grand mannerisms! Express every mood in a manner that will seem credible and natural. Never think of this or that actress whom you may have seen. Observe the life that is going on around you, and present a real and living human being.' No wonder Sarah Bernhardt and Henry Irving disliked the demands this awkward dramatist made.[3]

---

[1] Anker, *Henrik Ibsens brevveksling med Christiania Theater, 1878–1899*, pp. 47–48.

[2] *Ibid.*, pp. 56–57.

[3] Irving never acted in Ibsen, though attempts were made to persuade him to play Bishop Nicholas in *The Pretenders* and John Gabriel Borkman, and although Sarah

*Rosmersholm* marks Ibsen's final withdrawal as a playwright from the political field. A year after writing it he was to declare (in a speech at Gothenburg) that his political interests were waning and, with them, his eagerness for battle. He may have based the character of Rosmer principally on Snoilsky, but he put a good deal of himself into it too. Although he enjoyed writing and making speeches on controversial subjects, he disliked embroiling himself; and what he had seen of the results of party strife in Norway in 1885 determined him to withdraw still further from the battle. *Rosmersholm* is the last of his plays which introduces national or local politics as a decisive factor in shaping people's characters and destinies. In *The League of Youth*, *The Pillars of Society*, *Ghosts* and *An Enemy of the People*, such politics had played an important part; the actions of Stensgaard, Bernick, Manders and Peter Stockmann are, at critical moments, influenced by a fear of offending local political opinion. Gregers Werle in *The Wild Duck* is very much a political animal; and *A Doll's House*, though politics do not enter directly into it, struck at the heart of one of the most controversial issues of the day. But in the six plays which follow *Rosmersholm*, the battle is out of earshot. It is the trolls within, not the trolls without, that determine the destinies of Ellida and Hilde Wangel, Hedda Gabler, Halvard Solness, the Allmers, the Borkmans and Arnold Rubek. They are conscious of strange, sick passions which direct their lives; and *Rosmersholm* provides a link between Ibsen's old method and his new. Rosmer is the last of his characters to be caught up and undermined by local politics; and Rebecca is the first of those passionate but inhibited lovers who dominate the dark plays of his final period.

His disillusionment with politics, arising from his experiences in Norway in 1885, was complete. In his speech in Trondhjem that year he had declared his belief that the present age was the end of an era and that a new age was dawning, a third kingdom in which 'current political and social conceptions will cease to exist'. As Professor Francis Bull has put it, in Trondhjem in 1885 he had a programme, in Stockholm in 1887 a dream vision; in 1885 he had identified himself with the age, in 1887 and afterwards he cherished only a vague hope for an unguessable future.[1]

---

Bernhardt tried herself out as Ellida in *The Lady from the Sea* at Sens in 1904 I can find no record that she played any other of his roles. (Cf. *Aftenposten*, 22 September 1904. The report there says that she acted Hilde Wangel in the play, but even Sarah is unlikely to have tried to portray a girl of fourteen when she was approaching fifty-nine.) When Christian Krohg asked Lugné-Poe in the nineties whether Sarah had ever played Ibsen, Lugné-Poe replied: 'She will not. She says contemptuously of him, Strindberg and everything new: "*C'est de la Norderie*".' (Nyholm, pp. 49–50.)

[1] *C.E.*, X, pp. 318–319.

THREE

# ✑ 'All the Women are in Love with Him'

## (1886–1887)

As THE SCANDINAVIAN theatres perplexedly got down to rehearsing *Rosmersholm* during the last weeks of 1886, Duke Georg of Saxe-Meiningen was preparing a production of *Ghosts*. Ibsen had fallen sharply out of fashion in Germany since the heady days of *The Pillars of Society* and *A Doll's House*; indeed, apart from the private production of *Ghosts* at Augsburg in April 1886 there does not seem to have been a new production of any of his plays at a German theatre since 1880, a gap of over five years.[1] *Ghosts* was still forbidden by the censors; *An Enemy of the People* had been translated but not performed, and *The Wild Duck* had not even been translated. But if the German establishment had written Ibsen off, the young still believed in him. In November 1886 Otto Brahm, then thirty-one, published an enthusiastic article about him in *Deutsche Rundschau*; and the Meiningen production of *Ghosts*, and that in Berlin which followed, were to convert many people to Brahm's judgment.

The performance (a single one) at Meiningen was fixed for 22 December, and the Duke invited Ibsen to stay with him as his guest. He travelled on the 19th, and his reception must have exceeded his most sanguine expectations, as his rather Pooterish letter to Suzannah on the afternoon of the 21st shows:

*Dear Suzannah!*

*I write you in all haste. I reached Würzburg at 1.30 a.m. Left the next afternoon at 1.15 p.m. Arrived here at 4.15 p.m. and was received at the station by the Duke's chamberlain with the ducal coach, and driven to the palace, and here received in the heartiest and most affectionate manner by the Duke and his wife, who both accompanied me to the handsome and festively illuminated apartment which has been prepared for me, comprising four immense salons with every possible amenity. A court lackey has been placed at my exclusive service. P. Lindau, R. Voss and Hans Hopfen are also guests here, but they live downstairs and nothing like so magnificently as I. At 5 p.m.*

---

[1] According to Eller, *op. cit.*, pp. 140–141.

*dinner was served. Prince Ernst had come from Munich by another train. In the middle of the meal we were all surprised by the appearance of a young couple in travelling clothes. It was the Crown Prince and Princess of Meiningen, who had travelled from Rome to see Gespenster. They were then placed at the table. The Princess was put beside me, and spoke with great enthusiasm of her journey to the North Cape. She is most amazingly well informed about our literature. After dinner there was a theatrical performance. P. Lindau's translation of a Spanish piece was played. This was a public performance for the paying public, and so will Voss's Alexandra be tomorrow. Only Gespenster is to be limited to an invited audience this evening. A great many interested people have congregated here from all quarters, especially Berlin, for the occasion. After the performance a grand soirée will be given here in the palace. The performance this evening starts at 6 p.m., in consequence of which dinner has been arranged for 2 p.m. I am extremely happy here. The atmosphere is as unforced as one could imagine, and the Duke and his wife do not know how sufficiently to honour me. I shall be back in Munich on Thursday.*

*12.30 p.m.*

*I was interrupted. The Duke came to see me, and stayed a long time. I must therefore hasten to finish this letter if it is to catch the train.*

*I enclose the draft of the telegram for Sigurd, which you must get Lina [their servant] to send on Thursday morning. I may possibly telegraph him from here too.*[1]

*And how is your eye? I trust it is no worse? Be sure not to worry. It cannot be dangerous. But of course unpleasant. I will try to leave by the morning train on Thursday, if possible. I hope you are no longer suffering any pain or inconvenience from the thing in your mouth, but it is doubly unfortunate that this should happen while I am away. But I hope you are well in other respects! Here there is heavy snow. I am not going out, although I have a carriage at my disposal. The Chamberlain has sent his card and I have sent mine to the court functionaries. Personal calls are not required.*

*Well, I will end here for today. Perhaps I shall hear from you. I feel already as though I had been away for a long time. I am excellently contented; but in the long run I am happiest at home.*

*Your affectionate*
*Henrik Ibsen.*

The performance, with Maria Berg as Mrs Alving and Alexander Barthel as Oswald, was a triumph, as great as the same company's production of *The Pretenders* ten and a half years earlier. The following day the Duke gave Ibsen another medal to add to his collection: the Saxon-Ernestine Order, Commander, First Class, with star. The citation read '*als Zeichen seiner Verehrung und Bewunderung*'—'as a token of reverence and admiration'. 'You mustn't

---

[1] 23 December was Sigurd's birthday.

think I tell you this out of vanity' Ibsen wrote to Hegel a fortnight later, on 5 January, 'but I can't deny it pleases me when I remember the foolish denunciations of which the play was for so long the object in our countries.'

This medal was the occasion of a rare breach of protocol by Ibsen. His fellow-guest at Meiningen, Paul Lindau, tells that on receiving it Ibsen pinned it to his breast next to the Knight Cross that he had previously received from the Duke. Lindau pointed out that it was incorrect to wear the two together, 'as though a colonel were to wear his lieutenant's pips'. But Ibsen replied that the Knight Cross was the first German medal he had been awarded. 'It has dear memories for me, and I don't care to be parted from it.' Lindau, who seems not to have been the most tactful of men, also offended Ibsen by making some unappreciated joke about the character of Regina; when he apologised, Ibsen said: 'One doesn't joke about spiritual matters.'[1] Another German guest, a journalist named Gottfried Weisstein, noted that Ibsen 'looks older than his age, with his snow-white hair, and with his stiff silence suggests a small-town German professor, despite his many decorations.' He also remarked acidly that Ibsen said the simplest things with an impressive air, 'as though he wished to inscribe for ever on the tablets of our memories the fact of his having informed us: "Tomorrow I shall take the train to Munich".'[2]

Lindau and Weisstein sound a tedious pair, and Ibsen was never at his best with people who bored him. One is reminded of a remark Georg Brandes once made when a journalist wrote that a conversation he had had with Ibsen had been empty. 'The fool, getting nothing out of a conversation with Ibsen! When we were together just for a few minutes it was a complete experience!'[3]

On his return to Munich, Ibsen made up his accounts for 1886. It had been about the same financially as the two previous years, a little better than the mid-seventies but nothing like as good as the years of *The Pillars of Society*

---

[1] Lindau, pp. 373–377, reprinted in *C.E.*, XIX, pp. 166–169.

[2] G. Weisstein, *Meininger Erinnerungen* (Berlin, 1906), quoted by Zucker, p. 227.

[3] *Brandes Brevveksling*, IV, p. xxxviii. After Ibsen's death Brandes wrote: 'Rarely has he been described as he was in daily life. In his younger days he was animated, brilliant and observing, cordial and at the same time caustic, but never what one might call good-natured even when cordial. If alone with one or two friends he was spontaneous, communicative and frank, an excellent listener as well as a remarkable talker; but at social functions or among many people he was silent, easily embarrassed and slightly peevish. It did not take much to put him out of humour or to arouse his suspicion . . . but how many examples have I not of his cordiality, his thoughtfulness, his gentleness!' (*Century Magazine*, New York, February 1917, pp. 544–545.) And William Archer (*Ibsen as I Knew Him*, p. 9) wrote that he 'always found him not only courteous but genial and even communicative'.

and *A Doll's House*. Performing rights had brought him no more than £161 (2,910 crowns); only the advance on *Rosmersholm* and reprints of *Peer Gynt* and *Poems* had saved it from being a disaster:

| | crowns | £ |
|---|---|---|
| Fee for *Peer Gynt* at Dagmars Theatre, Copenhagen | 1,500 | 83 |
| Fee from the magazine *Norden* for poem, *Light out of Chaos*[1] | 100 | 6 |
| 7th edition of *Peer Gynt* | 1,815 | 101 |
| Fee for *The Pretenders* at Nya Teatern, Stockholm | 400 | 22 |
| Fee for *The Wild Duck* at Royal Theatre, Stockholm (22nd–29th performances) | 366 | 20 |
| „ „ „ „ „ at Royal Theatre, Copenhagen (11th–13th performances) | 444 | 25 |
| 5th edition of *Poems* | 952 | 53 |
| Single performance of *The Feast at Solhaug* at Dagmars Theatre, Copenhagen | 200 | 11 |
| 1st edition of *Rosmersholm* | 6,240 | 347 |
| | 12,017 | 668 |

However, the interest on his shares for the year came to just over 3,000 crowns (£167), he still, of course, had his pension of £110 a year, and Sigurd was now financially independent—very fortunately, for 1887, thanks to the failure of *Rosmersholm* in the theatres of Europe, was to be Ibsen's worst year financially since 1872.

The Meiningen production of *Ghosts* was such a success that the Duke tried to take it to Berlin, as he had done so triumphantly with his production of *The Pretenders* in the previous decade. But *Ghosts* was a different matter. The police censor had not allowed it to be publicly performed anywhere else in Germany and, Duke or no Duke, he was not now prepared to make an exception. However, the Berlin Dramatic Society gave a private performance of the play on 2 January 1887, and such was the interest aroused by this production that Fritz Wallner of the Berlin Residenztheater determined to follow suit, and managed to obtain permission to present *Ghosts* for a single charity matinée on 9 January. Ibsen travelled up from Munich to see it. 'I had scarcely settled down on my return from Meiningen', he explained to Hegel on 5 January, 'and now I must be off again . . . I would rather have stayed at home; but after the many requests I have received I cannot well not accede to them, especially since

---

[1] *Stjerner i lystaage*, a fine short poem, in theme and manner somewhat anticipating Hardy's *The Darkling Thrush*.

F

*Ghosts* has become a burning literary and theatrical talking-point in Germany. In Berlin I am prepared for some opposition from the conservative press. But this, too, is, for me, an additional reason why I should be present.'

Charlotte Frohn played Mrs Alving, Emmanuel Reicher Manders, and Wallner himself Oswald. The result exceeded all expectations. 'I have never experienced anything like it,' recalled Wallner: 'After the first fall of the curtain, silence reigned for several seconds; everyone was held spellbound by the powerful drama. But then a storm, a hurricane, broke forth, such as I had never witnessed in a theatre. The dramatist was acclaimed by all—no-one expressed disapproval—and, willingly, drunk with victory, he appeared repeatedly on the stage, tears of joy running down his cheeks.' The conservative critics, as Ibsen had anticipated, rejected the play; but it was an important occasion for those who were dissatisfied with the existing state of the German theatre. Otto Brahm praised 'the unconditional truth, the relentless, garish if you like, truth in the portrayal of human character . . . human beings, actual, living men and women, fully and completely observed . . . If the aim in the development of literature is to absorb more and more of nature into art, to wrest new poetic fields from life, as Faust obtained land from the sea, then no recent dramatist has gone forward more boldly and more magnificently than the author of *Ghosts*.' Another member of the audience was the twenty-five-year-old Gerhart Hauptmann, already on the way to becoming Ibsen's most distinguished disciple in Germany. Eugen Sierke, in an article in *Unser Zeit*, states that they could have sold fourteen thousand tickets for the performance,[1] and Julius Hoffory records that the book sold out so completely in the city that five thousand fresh copies had to be ordered from Leipzig.[2]

On 11 January there was a banquet for Ibsen at the Hotel Kaiserhof, with representatives from all walks of life seated at a horseshoe table. Otto Brahm made a speech praising Ibsen as 'a great artist who unites a rich and mature technical mastery with the fresh courage of an eternally youthful mind', adding that, just as Lessing had in his day led German literature away from the pattern of French drama by showing them the example of Shakespeare, so 'we too have to fight against the renewed preponderance of French drama and turn our eyes to this writer of German [sic] blood to aid and liberate us'. The Germans were already claiming Ibsen as a German, as they had claimed Shakespeare.[3] At this banquet Ibsen asked Anton Anno, who had directed the

---

[1] Eller, pp. 59–61. The translations of the quoted passages are his.

[2] *Tilskueren* (Copenhagen, 1888), p. 62.

[3] Sigurd Høst tells a story of a German officer who, when asked by the Belgian historian Henri Pirenne, then a prisoner of war, to name a single great German since 1870, answered without blinking: 'Ibsen'. (*Aftenposten*, 14 March 1928.)

production of *Ghosts*, why they had omitted Mrs Alving's line about the fabric of Manders's reasoning coming apart because it was machine-sewn. Anno explained that sewing-machines had by now reached such a state of refinement that sewing could not possibly come apart on its own. 'You can be sure', replied Ibsen, 'that Mrs Alving still had her old-fashioned sewing-machine up at Rosenvold.' When people expressed regret that the play was still banned from public performance, Ibsen said: 'I can wait. I can wait.'[1]

The excitement aroused by these productions of *Ghosts* sharply revived German interest in Ibsen. He informed Hegel on 26 January that *An Enemy of the People* and *Rosmersholm* had both been booked for performance in Berlin that spring, and that two German translations of the latter play were appearing 'almost simultaneously'. *The Wild Duck*, too, was to be belatedly translated this year. 'My visit to Berlin, and everything connected with it,' he wrote to Julius Hoffory on 4 February, 'I regard as a great and genuine stroke of fortune for me. It has had an amazingly refreshing and rejuvenating effect on me, and will pretty surely leave its mark on my future writing'. And indeed, his next play was to approach closer to optimism than anything he had written for years.

Ibsen's new-found success in Germany must have compensated him for the failure of *Rosmersholm* in the Scandinavian theatres. He was particularly annoyed that the Norwegian critics took exception to the portrayal of Kroll and Mortensgaard as representatives of what was narrowest in the conservative and liberal points of view. Writing to Jonas Lie on 27 January of his intention to spend the summer in Denmark, he added: 'I shall not, in any event, go as far as Norway. I find little attraction in the happenings, atmosphere and general tone of things up there. It is in the highest degree painful to see with what a greedy zest they seize on every kind of petty target as if it were an object of the greatest significance.'

On 5 March the Ostend Theatre in Berlin presented the German premiere of *An Enemy of the People*. Despite an under-rehearsed opening performance, the production was greeted with a storm of approbation and, although the theatre was situated in an unfashionable part of the city, an hour's carriage ride from the centre, ran for two weeks at a stretch and even succeeded when revived during the hottest part of the summer.

On 16 April, *Rosmersholm* was performed at Augsburg; but, as in Scandinavia, the play bewildered the public. It was evidently a lamentable performance. Ibsen attended the dress rehearsal, and Julius Elias, who was with him, noted his reaction: 'He witnessed the performance with weeping and gnashing of teeth. Seated in the front of the stalls he winced in pain at every word uttered

[1] Hoffory in *Tilskueren* (1888), pp. 64 ff.; Koht, II, p. 219.

from the stage; with both hands clutching the plush of the orchestra rail, he groaned ceaselessly: "Oh, God! Oh, God!" In the third act John Rosmer conceived the grotesque idea of appearing with elegant *piqué* spats over shining polished calfskin boots. When the man appeared, Ibsen reeled as though struck, and clasped my arm. "Look, look at that!" The Rosmer he had created was wearing bright yellow spats. We were convinced that Ibsen would prohibit the whole performance at the last moment, with some vehement outburst, but then, suddenly, he straightened himself and, with a gesture as though to brush away a bad dream, said: "I must forget my original conception. Then it isn't too bad." And, with quiet resolve, he adopted this attitude. Once he had forgotten his original conception, he found everything satisfactory.'[1]

The following month, on 5 May, *Rosmersholm* was much better staged in Berlin, by Anton Anno at the Residenztheater, with Charlotte Frohn and Emmanuel Reicher, the team that had been responsible for the triumphant performance of *Ghosts*. The conservative critics greeted it with a fierce broadside. Karl Frenzel, Ibsen's old enemy, was still writing in *Deutsche Rundschau*, and predictably he liked the play no better than he had liked *The Pillars of Society* and *A Doll's House*. He complained that it was never genuine tragic guilt nor a powerful destiny that crushed an Ibsen hero, and that the sickness from which Ibsen and his characters suffered was not life, but Norway. If ever his heroes had had the opportunity to walk down the Unter den Linden, or even the Paris boulevards, they would have been cured of their whims. But if the main purpose of dramatic art was to excite a kind of 'moral sea-sickness', then Ibsen was indeed a master of that art. Another critic, H. von Pilgrim, writing in the *Magazin für die Literatur des Auslandes*, asserted: 'Realism . . . is a canker of the time, like the sentimental bias which called forth *Werther* a hundred years ago. At present no physician for the malady is at hand, but I do not for a moment doubt that he will come . . . Such dramas as those of Henrik Ibsen demonstrate by their vogue how little vitality they contain. It has never been the concern of art to offer the repulsive; symmetry and calm, exalted beauty, are the criteria.'[2]

Yet *Rosmersholm*, like *Ghosts*, was appreciated by the young and restless in Germany, who, if they were not represented among the professional theatre critics, found outlets to express their admiration. Following up his November article, Otto Brahm published a seventy-page pamphlet on Ibsen that spring. 'Ibsen's dramas', he wrote, 'are a continued struggle against the lie, and a victory of the spirit of truth. Wherein is their dramatic strength to be found? In the plot? There are hundreds of plays with more significant plots. In the dialogue?

[1] Julius Elias, *Ibsenminne af hans tyske oversetter*, in *Samtiden*, 1940, p. 403.
[2] Eller, p. 63 (his translation).

More elegant, flowing and perspicacious dialogue is to be found. In their effectfulness? The common effects are avoided with almost Puritanical rigour. The victorious strength of the plays lies solely in the idea, in the resolute prosecution of the idea, which is never deflected by bogus effects and ornament, by empty phrases, by superfluous romance. The one idea which constructs the play is so great, so true and staggering, that it carries us away, crushes us—and liberates us.'[1] Although Anno's production of *Rosmersholm* had to contend with an unusually hot spring, it played for twenty-three consecutive performances and was only withdrawn because Charlotte Frohn was contracted to appear at another theatre.

Ibsen did no writing that spring or summer of 1887, and at the end of June he left with Suzannah for what turned out to be a three months holiday in Denmark and Sweden (he ostentatiously avoided Norway). His longing for the sea had by now become almost obsessive. 'Both my wife and I', he wrote to Hegel on 12 June, 'look forward immensely to seeing the sea again', and he added that they felt a strong inclination to settle permanently in the north— 'but it is perhaps best that we should have, at any rate for the present, a fixed point to which we can return outside the boundaries of our homeland.'

They had planned to stay in Frederikshavn, near the northern tip of Jutland, but after ten days he moved to the smaller resort of Sæby, further down the coast. Here he had a visit from William Archer, who described their meeting in a letter dated 25–28 July:

'It was a delightful drive—a perfect summer day, the corn ripe all round, the wild flowers brilliant, and the Cattegat dancing in the sunlight. All the way we could see Sæby Church straight ahead, and at last we rattled over a bridge, past a lovely old watermill, and into the quaint old main street of Sæby—one-storey houses, with great high gables, and all brightly painted or at the very least whitewashed. The moment we were over the bridge, I saw a short, broad figure ahead in an enormously long surtout and a tall hat made of silk looking far too small for his immense head. It was Ibsen, evidently on the lookout for me. I stopped the trap, we greeted each other with effusion, and then he insisted that I should remain in the trap and drive on to the Hotel Harmonien, where he was stopping, he following on foot . . .

'We drove into the courtyard of Hotel Harmonien, and by the time I had settled with my fellow-traveller Ibsen had arrived. He took me up into an enormous, barely-finished, uncarpeted room on the first floor, with four if not five windows, and two bedrooms opening off it at the back. This

---

[1] *Ibid.*, p. 66 (Eller's translation).

formed his *appartement*, and here we sat and talked for about an hour, until Fru Ibsen came in from a walk in Sæby forest . . . After about another hour we had dinner, then coffee and cigars . . .

'Now for a few Ibseniana. I must say in the first place that the old man was really charming throughout—perfectly frank and friendly, without the least assumption of stiffness of any sort. If I only had the art of drawing people out I could have got any amount of ideas out of him. Unfortunately I haven't the art—on the contrary, I have a morbid shrinking from talking to people about their own works; so that our conversation was, on the whole, far too much devoted to mere small talk and (strange to say) politics, Norwegian, Danish and Irish. However, I shall jot down a few of the things that turned up in the course of our talk. He said that Fru Ibsen and he had first come to Frederikshavn, which he himself liked very much —he could knock about all day among the shipping, talking to the sailors and so forth; and besides he found the neighbourhood of the sea favourable to contemplation and constructive thought. Here at Sæby the sea wasn't so come-at-able, but Fru Ibsen didn't like Frederikshavn because of the absence of pleasant walks about it; so Sæby was a sort of compromise between him and her. Fru Ibsen afterwards added that the Norwegian steamers of Frederikshavn were a source of perpetual temptation to her. For the present Ibsen is not writing anything, and hasn't been all last winter, because his time has been greatly taken up with business connected with the production of his plays in Germany . . . Meanwhile the old man is revolving plans, and hopes to have 'noget galskab færdigt til næste aar' [some tomfoolery ready for next year].

'I tried to get at the genesis of a piece in his head, but the fear of seeming to cross-examine him prevented me from getting at anything very explicit. [However] it seems that the idea of a piece generally presents itself before the characters and incidents, though when I put this to him flatly he denied it. It seems to follow, however, from his saying that there is a certain stage in the incubation of a play when it might as easily turn into an essay as a drama; and he has to incarnate the ideas, as it were, in character and incident, before the actual work of creation can be said to have fairly commenced. Different plans and ideas, he admits, often flow together, and the play he ultimately produces is often very different from the intention with which he started. He writes and re-writes, scribbles and destroys an enormous amount before he makes the exquisite fair copy he sends to Copenhagen. As to symbolism, he says that life is full of it, and that therefore his plays are full of it, though critics insist on discovering all sorts of esoteric meanings in his work of which he is entirely innocent. He was particularly amused by a sapient person . . . who had discovered that Manders in *Gjengangere* was a symbol for mankind in general, *l'homme moyen* (not especially *sensuel*), and therefore called *Manders* . . .

'In politics he came out very strong against the 'compact majority', but on this point his thinking is scarcely less crude than U.D.'s for example. This may seem a hard saying, but the fact is I am becoming more and more convinced that as a many-sided thinker, or rather a systematic thinker, Ibsen is nowhere. He is essentially a kindred spirit with Shaw—a paradoxist, a sort of Devil's Advocate, who goes about picking holes in every 'well-known fact' as J. would say; or, as Ibsen himself would put it, looking at the teeth of every 'normally built truth' and proclaiming it too old to pass any longer. And Ibsen is even worse than Shaw, who (in the main) knows himself for what he is and remembers that the exception proves the rule. To Ibsen, on the other hand, his paradoxes are apt to present themselves as the whole truth, and his general idea is that the exception destroys the rule. To say that the minority is always right, as Ibsen did in so many words, is at least as unphilosophical as to proclaim the infallibility of the majority. But this question of Majority v Minority is really one which can only be treated thoroughly in a scientific, one might almost say in a mathematical essay; whereas the minority-paradox is the very thing for enforcement in dramatic form. The upshot of all this is that if Ibsen were not a great poet he would be a rather poor philosopher—but that is in fact what you can say of all the leading spirits of this century; for example of Carlyle and Ruskin; George Eliot is the one exception that occurs to me at the moment. But then Ibsen is Ibsen, and I am the last to complain that he is *not* Herbert Spencer. Of course even as a thinker he is on a totally different plane from men like Tennyson and Browning, who only pretend to think and never get any forra'der.

'Altogether my day at Sæby was an unforgettable experience. You'd better preserve this letter—it may be useful sometime . . . A greater than Shelley is here; at least a greater than Shelley ever *was*, though it is hard to say what he might have been but for that white squall in the Gulf of Spezia. It gives one a strange sensation to sit at a man's table and eat and drink and talk with him on equal terms, and then to think every now and then: This is the man who wrote *Peer Gynt* and the 4th act of *Brand*, and *Et Dukkehjem* [*A Doll's House*] and *Gjengangere* [*Ghosts*]. Except Shakespeare . . . I don't know that there is anyone in all literature whom I would care so much to know as Ibsen. Of course one would like to have seen Goethe or Thackeray or George Eliot, but they have not the enigmatic attraction of Ibsen . . .

'I was glad to find Ibsen and his wife warm in praise of [Bjørnson's] *Over Ævne* [*Beyond Mortal Power*], though there is a suggestion of *Brand* about it which a small-minded man, with any ungenerous sense of rivalry, might have turned to Bjørnson's disadvantage . . .'[1]

'Jutland is a beautiful place to spend the summer in', Ibsen wrote to Hegel on 13 August. 'The people are kind and likeable; we have the open sea practically under our noses, and the weather is as perfect as one could wish'. As at Molde two years earlier, he spent hours each day gazing out to sea. A nineteen-year-old Danish girl named Engelke Wulff, who was also staying there, noticed on the shore 'a little broad-shouldered man with grey side-whiskers and spectacles. He stood staring out across the water, with his hand shading his eyes. He had a stick with him with which he supported himself while he took a book out and wrote something in it. From where I sat and watched him, I supposed him to be drawing the sea.' Ibsen saw her, too, as she sat doing her handiwork, and after a time got into conversation with her. She told him of her longing to see the world, and of her love of the theatre, and he promised he would put her into his next play. One thinks immediately of Bolette; but, as we know, he had already conceived Bolette's character in his early plans for *Rosmersholm*, and when they met by chance in a street in Christiania some years later he called Engelke 'my Hilde'; so one must assume that some of Hilde's lines in *The Lady from the Sea*, if not her character, stemmed from those conversations on the shore at Sæby.[2]

Another young lady from Sæby imprinted herself on Ibsen's memory, though he never met her, for the good reason that since 1883 she had been lying in the town churchyard. Her name was Adda Ravnkilde; she was a talented young writer who had killed herself at the age of twenty-one, leaving behind her several stories and a novel, which was later published with a foreword by Georg Brandes. One theme recurs throughout her writings: the unsuccessful efforts of a young girl to free herself of her obsession for a man she knows is not worthy of her. Ibsen read her writings, and visited her home and her grave.

Her story must have reminded him of an early and similar adventure which had occurred to his mother-in-law, Magdalene Thoresen. In her own words: 'While I was studying in Copenhagen I met a young man, a wild, strange, demented creature. We studied together, and I had to yield before his monstrous and demonic will. With him I could have found passion and fulfilment. I still believe that . . . So I have lived my life oppressed by a feeling of want and

[1] Charles Archer, pp. 152-157.
[2] Francis Bull's introduction to *The Lady from the Sea*, C.E., XI, pp. 23-24.

longing.' She had fled to Norway to escape from this affair and had married a man nearly twice her age; he 'was my friend, my father and my brother, and I was his friend, his child'. And at Molde, two years earlier, the local people had told him two strange legends about the sea, and the power it had over those who lived near it. One was of a Finn who, by means of the troll-power in his eyes, had induced a clergyman's wife to leave husband, children and home and go away with him. The other was of a seaman who left home and stayed away for many years, so that his family believed him dead; suddenly he returned, and found his wife married to another man. These four tales, with their related themes of the power of the sea and the demon lover, were to form the starting-point of Ibsen's next play. 'People in Norway', he said to a German friend the following year, while he was writing *The Lady from the Sea*, 'are spiritually under the domination of the sea. I do not believe other people can fully understand this.'[1]

At the end of August the Ibsens returned to Frederikshavn, where Henrik Jæger, busy preparing his biography of Ibsen, visited them and stayed for three days. He took detailed notes of their conversations, which remained unpublished until 1960:

'Henrik Ibsen's life follows an extraordinarily regular pattern. He rises at 7 in the summer, a little later in the winter; he dresses slowly and carefully, spends an hour at his toilette, then eats a light breakfast. At 9 he sits down at his desk, where he stays till 1. Then he takes a walk before dinner, which in Munich he eats at 3. If anyone wishes to visit him he will be told that he is at home at 2.30. In the afternoon he reads; he takes his evening meal early, at 7. At 9 he drinks a glass of toddy and retires to bed.[2] He eats with a hearty appetite and sleeps well. He spends the winter planning his books, the summer in writing; the summer is his best working time; almost all his books have been written in the summer; of those which he has published since he left Norway in 1864 only two, *The League of Youth* and *Emperor and Galilean*, have been written during the winter. When he begins to write a book he eats and drinks no more than the barest minimum; it inhibits him in his work; a small piece of bread and half a cup of black coffee are all he takes before sitting down to his desk. He smokes a little when working, otherwise not at all.[3] He cannot understand how people

---

[1] *Ibid.*, pp. 24–27; Koht, II, pp. 193–194.

[2] It is interesting that Ibsen apparently omitted to mention to Jæger the fact of his daily visit to the Café Maximilian.

[3] This was untrue; several witnesses (William Archer for one) have testified to his liking for a cigar during conversation.

who have to work can use stimulants; the only thing he can imagine that might be beneficial is a couple of drops of naphtha on a lump of sugar. In this respect he is like the caterpillar which ceases to take nourishment when it has to spin its cocoon.

'In general he is regular to the point of pedantry; his day is divided according to the clock. These three days I have been living in his immediate proximity, slept next door to him and eaten at his side, we have lived by the clock from morning to night to a degree I could never tolerate indefinitely. One small example: each day when we have risen from the dinner-table, he has walked over to the window and looked at the thermometer which hangs outside. To do so before sitting down to table, or to ask the servant what the outside temperature is, seems not to occur to him.

'He needs good air in quantity; lofty, airy rooms are an absolute necessity to him, he told me yesterday when we were discussing where he might lease an apartment in Munich for the winter. He much praises the air up here in northern Jutland because it is so clean and fresh on account of the unceasing wind. It must be for this reason that he has so often spent his summers in the Gulf of Naples or at Gossensass in the Tyrol. To my question why he chooses to settle in so cold and harsh a climate as Munich he replied that the Munich climate suited his temperament excellently; he said he liked it greatly. Although it is already September here and has been very windy these past few days so that we have had to put double fasteners on the open windows, he has kept two windows open all the time, one in each bay, though his desk is set right next to one bay. Each morning and evening he takes a cold rub down.'

Concerning Ibsen's method of work Jæger noted that:

'he likes to meditate what he is writing in the fresh air on long walks, and during the time he takes to dress. Works through the whole thing in his head before starting draft. Likes to stop with several lines ready in his head with which he can start the next day, which helps him to begin work. But if he gets stuck he stays put until he has got the thing moving again. Regards first draft as a means of getting to know his characters, outside and in, the way they talk, etc. Then the rewrite, and finally the fair copy.[1] Feels a great sense of relief as he approaches the end of a work, but

---

[1] Extraordinarily for so meticulous a writer, he never (even after his return to Norway in 1891) read proofs. 'I don't bother about proofs', he once remarked, adding: 'I have never personally read any of my books . . . When I have finished a new book I don't look at it again. I begin at once on something new.' (Interview with Hans Tostrup in Ørebladet, 13 March 1898, reprinted in C.E., XIX, pp. 212–213.)

as he does so new plans start popping up. He has to keep walking when working—he needs 3–4 rooms to move around in while he is working on his books.'

On politics:

'He shares the views of the extreme left, but cannot join their party because it is too dishonest; people don't seek truth but only whether it is a "respectable" person who has said something; if one of these respected gentlemen talks nonsense, nobody dares tell him so . . . Ibsen this evening compared the people at home with tadpoles. Some time they will become fully developed frogs, but they still have black tails hanging down behind, and these black tails which they use to steer their course are obsolete ideas which they ought to have dropped long ago.'

Ibsen spoke much to Jæger of his love of the sea. "There is something extraordinarily fascinating about the sea," he said. "When one stands and stares down into the water it is as though one sees that life that moves on earth, but in another form. Everything is connected; there are resemblances everywhere" . . . He would have liked to have . . . gone to the west coast of Jutland, where the full force of the North Sea tumbles in; but he gave up that idea because he said that here on the north-east Jutland coast he found the same thing on a slightly smaller scale.' He also told Jæger of his hatred of public speaking. 'The worst thing he knew was to address a large gathering, and he greatly admired people who can do it . . . "I could never learn to speak publicly", he said, "however long and assiduously I might practise".'[1]

In the second week of September Ibsen crossed the Sound into Sweden, and spent six days in Gothenburg. On his fourth day there, 12 September, he made a speech at a banquet given for him by a literary society, Gnistan, in which he surprised his listeners by saying that his political interests were waning and, with them, his eagerness for battle. He visited the distinguished Valands Club, founded the previous year, and attended a French Opera, Massenet's *Don César de Bazan*.[2] On 14 September he left for Stockholm by ship along the Göta Canal.

A handsome blonde lady of thirty-eight, named Anne-Charlotte Leffler, accompanied him on the s.s. *Pallas*. She was well known as a dramatist and short story writer, and as an outspoken champion of women's rights; three years earlier she had visited England, where she had met amongst others

[1] Cf. Midbøe, pp. 151 ff.; and *Folkebladet, julenummer* 1887, pp. 23 and 25, reprinted in C.E., XIX, pp. 172–173.
[2] Kommandantvold, pp. 21–22.

Oscar Wilde, whose mother had just written a book about Scandinavia, Jenny Lind, Karl Marx's daughter Eleanor, and Annie Besant. She had met Ibsen in Gothenburg and had got on excellently with him; the night before their departure, he told her, he had dreamed that he was going on a honeymoon with her, but realised in his dream that this was impossible 'for she is married and I am married'. Then, still in his dream, he said: 'Of course—it is a dramatic honeymoon'; and he added to her: 'Perhaps the future will show it to have been so'—which baffled Anne-Charlotte, who assumed it meant that they might co-operate on a play together, but knew he never wrote in collaboration with anyone else. He also spoke cryptically of *The Magic Flute* and the water test which the two characters undergo, and added that 'he thought we had done that, and wondered what it would lead to'.[1]

She was much intrigued by this unfamiliar preoccupation with dreams, and noted in her diary as they sailed along the canal: 'Ibsen is very quiet, but what he says is always interesting. But he is a curiously lonely soul—he seems to read almost nothing—he has certainly read vastly less than I. He associates with almost no one, he just lives and dreams or lives quietly and looks at life without living it himself. He doesn't work much, years go by when he writes nothing—he hasn't written a line since *Rosmersholm*. Thursday night we spent in the saloon with Robinson, Ibsen's great admirer and commentator, whom we telegraphed to join us at Motala . . . Ibsen was very amiable to me and told me repeatedly that it was a great pleasure for him to travel with me. They are of course going to fête him tremendously in Stockholm. We must give a dinner for him too.'[2]

'Robinson' was the pseudonym of the writer Urban von Feilitzen, one of Ibsen's most persistent champions in Sweden (though he had disliked *Rosmersholm*); he described Ibsen after their meeting as a 'sensitive hermit devoured by social sympathies, freezing in his austere prophet's cave'.[3] There was another interesting passenger on the *Pallas*; a young Swedish explorer and author named Sven Hedin, who had returned the previous autumn from an adventurous expedition into the heart of Persia. Ibsen invited Hedin to join them, and questioned him closely about Persia; Hedin showed him drawings he had made of Xerxes's palace at Persepolis and other memorabilia, and was surprised to find Ibsen particularly interested in the great ruins at Ctesiphon, which (he later realised) figures in *Emperor and Galilean*. Ibsen asked him the most minute details about this, including the materials of which it was con-

---

[1] Gustav Näsström, *Ibsen på Götakanalen, september 1887*, in *Svenska Dagbladet*, 6 April 1969.

[2] Anne-Charlotte Leffler, *En självbiografi* (Stockholm, 1922), pp. 108 ff.

[3] Letter to Adolf Noréen, quoted by Näsström.

ALL THE WOMEN ARE IN LOVE WITH HIM'

structed, and Hedin, in turn, questioned him about his trip to Egypt.[1] Hedin, then twenty-two, was to become one of the greatest explorers and orientalists of his time; also, sadly, an enthusiastic Nazi, and a personal friend of Hitler and Himmler. I met him in 1950, shortly before his death, and he expressed to me his amazement that historians were describing these men as cruel. 'I knew them both', he said. 'They were gentle, humble men.' But, as with the Norwegian Nazi, Knut Hamsun, the follies of Hedin's age do not detract from the achievements of his saner years.

Ibsen stayed a week in Stockholm, where reception after reception was given in his honour. The Swedish novelist Gustaf af Geijerstam met him at several of these, and noted his dislike of large gatherings. 'I sensed that he was not in his element. He never once spoke so that his voice could be heard throughout the room, and it was noticeable that he only relaxed when he was in a corner talking *à deux*.'[2] On 22 September Anne-Charlotte Leffler and her husband gave a small dinner for him. She wrote to a friend, Adam Hauch:

'He is so inexplicably kind to me, kisses my hand and gives me the warmest assurances of his affection. Yet he is still a closed book to me. I don't understand him. Although I have been quite a lot together with him, and although I usually read people's characters quickly, I couldn't write a character sketch of him . . . Yesterday I had a very interesting day with Ibsen. Gösta [her husband] gave a stag party. Sonja and I were the only ladies, and it was a select gathering of interesting men, so that Ibsen became quite high-spirited and forthcoming. He isn't anyway nearly as wary and calculating as most people suppose, just a little shy and embarrassed, and needs to be in a special atmosphere to be able to express himself. But he answers quite happily whatever one asks him—how he works, who were his models, etc . . . Ibsen is no public speaker, but when he replied yesterday to Gösta's speech he said something very surprising. "Of all my fatherlands," he said, "Sweden is the one where I have found most understanding" . . . How angry they would be in Norway if they heard that! . . . He can say terribly crushing, cutting things sometimes, and then a glint appears in those cold steel eyes, which fits well with something he often says: "A writer must never be afraid of a little devilry". He evidently loves devilry before all else. The Devil is his god, like Carducci's in his *Inno Satanico*.'[3]

There was in fact a third lady at Anne-Charlotte's party, besides herself and

[1] Sven Hedin, *Stormän och kungar*, I (Stockholm, 1950), pp. 75–79.
[2] Gustaf af Geijerstam, *Två minnen om Henrik Ibsen*, in *Ord och Bild*, 1898, pp. 115–124.
[3] Leffler, pp. 109–112.

her friend Sonja Kowalevski:[1] a remarkable novelist and short-story writer, Victoria Benedictsson, better known under her pseudonym of Ernst Ahlgren, who was to commit suicide the following year at the age of thirty-eight as the result of an unhappy love affair with Georg Brandes. She gave her impressions of Ibsen in a letter to Brandes, then involved in a violent row with Bjørnson as a result of some unkind remarks which Brandes (like Strindberg) had made about Bjørnson's demand for male chastity in *A Gauntlet*.

'Ibsen . . . makes so true and human an impression, he doesn't put on a show. He makes one want to confide in him. He looks as though one could talk to him about anything . . . so composed and sealed, so whole . . .

'Ibsen was in a good mood, with little roguish remarks and pats on the shoulder for the ladies, and was treated like God the Father. I was nauseated by this worship and had kept perversely aloof all evening, thinking I could be equally happy whether I'd talked to Ibsen or not. But somehow it happened that he wandered over to a doorway where there was a group of people chatting, including me. Of course the group spread out with our guest of honour as the central point . . .

' "Has anyone been following the row between Georg Brandes and Bjørnson?" the old boy asked without warning.

'Some said yes, some no. You can guess how wide my eyes and ears grew! People muttered little hypocrisies. Someone said you had been unfair to Miss G. and bitter in your attacks—personal.

'Then a glint came into those small grey Ibsen eyes.

' "He may have been bitter", he said. "And he may have behaved ruthlessly. But one must remember how he has been attacked and how he has been treated. And Denmark ought to know what a man it possesses in him."

'There was some talk of propriety and morality, and I couldn't hold my tongue either—people got quite worked up. And then he smiled with that calm, wise smile of his.

' "I'll tell you all something", he said. "And you remember it. What one must cling to, cling to and defend, is the morality one has within one, within oneself—what the morality of society calls sinful, because it is the new morality, the kind that is germinating and will grow . . ."

'He said more, you can guess what. And they listened, they applauded—they, who all their lives will trample on and stifle everything he talked of,

---

[1] Sonja Kowalevski was Russian-born, and in 1884 became Professor of Mathematics in Stockholm. She wrote a play in collaboration with Anne-Charlotte Leffler, who after Sonja's death wrote a biography of her. Anne-Charlotte herself died shortly afterwards, at the age of forty-three.

about the individual's inner moral code, the free feeling that in *this* case *this* is right—the individual's development from his own self, his own nature, the fulfilment of his biggest and best potentialities! They applauded; and tomorrow they'll go out and trample on it . . . Am I being silly again? Are you laughing?'[1]

But Ibsen, when the occasion arose three years later, did not defend Brandes publicly, any more than in a few years he was to defend Laura Kieler against a spiteful libel by Brandes himself. On 26 September 1890 Brandes wrote to Jonas Lie that he had been continuously vituperated against in the German press, especially in the Munich newspaper *Allgemeine Zeitung*. 'It would only cost Henrik Ibsen', Brandes complained, 'who sees this paper every day and is worshipped in Munich as a demi-god, a two-line letter to the editor to end the matter . . . But you don't for a moment suppose that he'd even turn over in his bed to do any such thing!'[2]

Two days after Anne-Charlotte Leffler's dinner, a grand banquet, of the kind Ibsen disliked most, was given for him at the Grand Hotel. In his reply to the official speech of welcome, Ibsen surprised his listeners by describing himself as an 'optimist', declaring that he believed that the world was entering a new epoch in which old differences would be reconciled and humanity would find happiness. August Lindberg was there, but had difficulty in getting near Ibsen because of the press of grand ladies who surrounded him—so many head-plumes, Lindberg noted, as to make Ibsen look as though he were seated in the royal hearse. Lindberg determined, if possible, to give a party for Ibsen where he could meet the young, and especially the young of the theatre, the actors and actresses who had performed in his plays. He and his wife managed at last to get through to Ibsen and asked if he would attend such an informal lunch gathering the next day; and to their delight, he smiled and accepted, 'as though he sensed that it was a plot by those who had not been able to get near him during the banquet'.[3]

The next day was a Sunday, and they had some difficulty in fixing the food and wine in time; but they managed, and at two o'clock on the dot Ibsen appeared, wearing a top hat but, they were glad to note, no medals or even ribbons.

'It was said that he always liked to sit on a small and uncomfortable chair; he always wanted to appear stiff and correct, and a comfortable chair

---

[1] Letter from Victoria Benedictsson to Georg Brandes, 24 September 1887 (*Brandes Brevveksling*, VI, pp. 247–249).
[2] *Ibid.*, IV, pp. 447–448.
[3] Lindberg, p. 211.

easily causes a man to hunch himself unattractively. Nevertheless, he was
put into a large, high-backed chair with arms, but at least hard, for it was
of oak. He did not protest, and even took our one-year-old daughter on
his knee. Beside him there stood a bottle of wine, and we saw to it that his
glass was always full. 'I don't understand', he said. 'I keep on drinking, and
yet my glass grows no emptier'. He enjoyed himself; his old bohemian
self emerged from the tightly buttoned coat and he sat and told us about his
travels and how *A Doll's House* came to be written. In the end the ladies
took hold of him and—chaired him. And he replied by kissing each of them
on the cheek.'[1]

Gustaf af Geijerstam, who was there, adds:

'I don't doubt that Ibsen, like other mortals, is capable of feeling pride
at being respectfully acclaimed. But this is sure, that he enjoyed it twice as
much when the tribute found expression in a style of unforced gaiety, when
stiff formalities were banished and merriment reigned, when the great
man was allowed to be simply a human being among other human beings.
Pehr Staaff in his speech of welcome at this gathering hailed Ibsen as "no
pessimist, prepared to sign his name to a declaration of mankind's bank-
tuptcy, but an optimist who believes in the ability of humanity . . . to
rise like the Phoenix renewed from its ashes . . . I give you the health of
Henrik Ibsen, optimist!"

'It was very strange to see Henrik Ibsen when this tribute was paid to
him by a group of young people at a private party. The great man suddenly
became communicative, once or twice underlining the speaker's words by
murmuring: "Yes! Exactly!" '

He had an appointment that evening at the theatre, to see *An Enemy of the
People*, and they parted on the warmest terms. Geijerstam continues:

'But when I saw Henrik Ibsen later, he was seated in a box surrounded by
notabilities, and his face wore something of that expression which commonly appears in his photographs.

'It is perfectly true to say that Henrik Ibsen can be uncommunicative
and off-putting, but it is equally true that no-one can be more open-
hearted than he, more freely and unforcedly friendly and kind, more sus-
ceptible to personal affection . . . All that is needed to arouse this feeling is
that he himself should feel unconstrained and know that he is understood
by those with whom he is speaking. That is why Henrik Ibsen is in his
heart an enemy to everything official, and why, when lionised by too

[1] *Ibid.*, p. 212.

many people, he can suddenly become enclosed and buttoned-up . . .
amidst all the cheering which echoes around him he searches for a sympathetic and understanding eye to meet his own.'[1]

Ibsen's visit to Stockholm had been a triumph. 'All the women are in love
with him', wrote Anne-Charlotte Leffler to her friend Adam Hauch, 'especially
Sonja, and one said on Saturday that she wasn't going to wash her hands for a
week now that Ibsen had touched them . . . I was delighted to find that, like
almost all men of genius I have met, he fully and firmly believes in a socialistic
future.' She had been one of Ibsen's companions in the theatre box. 'You
can't imagine', she continued to Hauch, 'how much talk there has been in the
press all week about Ibsen's box in the theatre. All the papers have had something to say about us lucky chosen ones, all the scandal sheets have been joking
about the "bouquet of ladies" with whom he surrounded himself . . . I really
think it's ladies who get the most out of him. He's a ladies' man like all poets.'[2]

On 26 September Ibsen returned to Denmark, and on 5 October he attended a dinner given for him by Hegel. In his address of thanks he said that
this summer, in Denmark, he had discovered the sea; that the smooth and
pleasant Danish sea, which one could come close to without feeling that
mountains cut off the approach, had given his soul rest and peace, and that he
was carrying away memories of the sea which would hold significance for his
life and his writing.

What were the reasons for this sudden mellowing in Ibsen, as exemplified
in his utterances in Gothenburg, Stockholm and Copenhagen? Partly, no
doubt, the acclamation he had received in Meiningen and Berlin at the turn of
the year; partly, perhaps, his discovery of the sea, though one would guess
this to be a reflection rather than a cause of his change of mood. Possibly, too,
as Francis Bull has suggested,[3] those conversations with Henrik Jæger at
Frederikshavn in September may have had a therapeutic effect. In the course of
these conversations, Professor Bull observes, Ibsen had recalled many old
memories to help Jæger with the early chapters of his book. These
memories included some which Ibsen had tried to forget; but now, when he
dragged them out into the daylight, he found that they no longer had the
power to frighten him. Consequently, Ibsen must have felt impelled to ask
himself whether it did not lie within a man's power to drive away 'ghosts' or
'white horses' of whatever kind, provided he had the courage to look his past
in the face and make his choice between the past and the present, a choice
taken (to quote from the play he was about to write) 'in freedom and full

[1] Geijerstam, pp. 115–124.
[2] Leffler, pp. 113–114.
[3] Introduction to *The Lady from the Sea*, C.E., XI, p. 17.

G

responsibility'. In *Rosmersholm* a potentially happy relationship between two people is destroyed by the power of the past; in *The Lady from the Sea*, Wangel and Ellida overcome that power, and it may be that Ibsen's conversations with Jæger gave him a new confidence, if only a temporary one, in man's ability to escape from the terror of his own history.

Yet in certain matters he remained as inflexible as ever, and one was his relationship with his family, always excepting Hedvig. His brother, Ole Paus Ibsen, who seems to have inherited all his father's inability to hold down a job on land, asked Ibsen to support an application he was making for the humble post of lighthouse keeper; this being a state post, Ole, who started his letter 'Dear brother Henrik' and described his circumstances as 'very bad', begged Ibsen to use his personal influence with the Prime Minister. Ibsen's note to Sverdrup on the subject, dated 3 October 1887 from Copenhagen, is as frosty a reference as one brother can ever have written for another:

*Your Excellency!*

*My only surviving brother, Ole Paus Ibsen, domiciled at Tjømø, is applying for a post as lighthouse keeper and asks me to put in a word on his behalf to Your Excellency. May I in this connection ask Your Excellency to be so good as to read the enclosed letters and testimonials. I myself have nothing further to add on the subject.*

*I remain Your Excellency's respectful and most obedient servant,*

*Henrik Ibsen.*

Ole Paus Ibsen got the job and kept it for seventeen years before retiring for the remainder of his long life (he lived until 1917) to a home for retired seamen.

That month, *Ghosts* was publicly performed in both Berne and Basel, arousing, as it did everywhere, violently conflicting reactions. On the other side of the world the German actor Friedrich Mitterwurzer was touring the play, in English, through America under the title of *Phantoms, or The Sins of the Fathers*, and advertised on the posters as 'BANNED IN GERMANY'. Clemens Petersen saw it in Chicago and wrote to Bjørnson that it was excellently performed but that the theatre was 'disagreeably empty', adding the hope that 'Ibsen will write a new *Ghosts*, or *Rosmersholm* or something like them every year, for then I shall live to see this bubble burst.'[1]

Ibsen returned to Munich in the second week of October, and in a letter he wrote on 15 November to a Swedish bookseller named Hans Österling there appears, for the first time in his letters, the name of that former admirer of his to whom his own name was gradually becoming anathema:

*During my visit to Stockholm in September you were so kind as to send me a copy*

---

[1] *Bjørnstjerne Bjørnsons brevveksling med danske, 1875–1910*, ed. Ø. Anker, Francis Bull and Torben Nielsen (Copenhagen and Oslo, 1953), I, pp. 280–281.

*of Strindberg's recently published play* The Father, *and I beg you to accept my sincerest thanks for this most valuable gift.*

*One does not read a new work by a writer such as Strindberg during the restlessness and changing moods of travelling. I have therefore postponed the perusal and study of this work until now, when I have returned to the peace of my home.*

*Strindberg's observations and experiences in the sphere of which* The Father *principally treats do not accord with my own. But this does not prevent me from recognising and being gripped by the author's violent strength, in this as in his earlier works.*

The Father *is soon to be performed in Copenhagen. If it is acted as it needs to be, with merciless realism, the effect will be shattering.*

During the past twelve months, Strindberg's references in his correspondence to Ibsen had become less and less complimentary. In a play *The Robbers*, which he wrote in November 1886, he had appealed: 'Give us back joy, you who preach the joy of life! Give us the cheerful little spirit of compromise, and send the Old Men of the Dovre back to their caves!' On 10 December 1886, replying to his publisher's offer to send him the latest works of Ibsen and Alexander Kielland, he declared: 'Ibsen and Kielland have nothing to teach me, two ignorant women's writers'.[1] Apart from Ibsen's championship, or supposed championship, of the feminist cause, Strindberg disliked him for his praise of aristocrats (though Strindberg himself was secretly attracted to them), and because he, Strindberg, always developed a resentment against anyone who had influenced him. When Edvard Brandes suggested that Strindberg might address himself directly to Edvard's brother Georg, Strindberg replied (3 January 1887): 'Why don't I write myself? Because I am afraid, afraid of him as of all fertilising spirits, afraid as I was of Zola, Bjørnson, Ibsen, of becoming pregnant with other men's seed and bearing other men's offspring.' In *The Father* itself, which he wrote that January, there is a reference to *Ghosts* ('When I sat in the theatre the other evening and heard Mrs Alving orating over her dead husband, I thought to myself: "What a damned shame the fellow's dead and can't defend himself!"'), and on 22 January (his thirty-ninth birthday) he wrote to Edvard Brandes, with reference to his own play, *The Robbers*: 'That I have portrayed a mean and dishonourable woman is not more unjust or unæsthetic than Ibsen's and his sisters' scandalous attacks on men. Woman is, in general, by nature mean and instinctively dishonest, though we ruttish cocks have not been able to see it; so, I have portrayed a typical woman.'[2]

---

[1] *August Strindberg's brev*, VI, p. 123.
[2] *Ibid.*, VI, p. 148. Ibsen's 'sisters' were the feminist writers such as Anne-Charlotte Leffler and Victoria Benedictsson.

In May, Strindberg sent Brandes the article cited above in which he said that Ibsen had written no true work of art since *The Pretenders*, and on 3 June he wrote to August Lindberg, who was preparing to present *Rosmersholm* and other Ibsen plays at Dagmars Theatre in Copenhagen: 'You can't go on with Ibsen, he probably won't write much more, and his *genre* is on the way out. You should read the Germans on *Rosmersholm*! Let him go his way, and we ours!'[1] The fact that he himself had, however reluctantly, admired *Rosmersholm* did not prevent him from rejoicing in the Germans' denigration of it. Strindberg knew that all men are full of contradictions, and never bothered about them in himself.

To digress one generation beyond Strindberg, it is interesting to note that a similar resentment towards supposed literary ancestry was displayed by a writer who is often thought of as one of Strindberg's most gifted disciples. 'I don't want to write like Galsworthy, nor Ibsen, nor Strindberg, nor any of them, even if I could', wrote D. H. Lawrence to Edward Garnett on 1 February 1913. 'We have to hate our immediate predecessors, to get free from their authority.' Three months earlier, on 30 October 1912, he had written to Garnett: 'I hate Strindberg. He seems unnatural, forced, a bit indecent—a bit wooden, like Ibsen, a bit skin-empty'; and on another occasion earlier that month: 'I bet your play will be better than that rotten Strindberg!' But Lawrence's tastes in literature were as unpredictable as Strindberg's. 'My God, what a clumsy *olla putrida* James Joyce is!' he wrote to Aldous Huxley and his wife on 15 August 1928. 'Nothing but old fags and cabbage-stumps of quotations from the Bible and the rest, steeped in the juice of deliberate, journalistic dirty-mindness—what old and hard-worked staleness, masquerading as the all-new!'[2]

Ibsen lost a good friend and counsellor that Christmas of 1887; on 27 December Frederik Hegel died at the age of seventy. Their relationship had never been close, but during the two decades of their acquaintance Ibsen had trusted him as he had trusted few people; Hegel had always been ready to advance Ibsen money when he needed it and, although only eleven years the older man, had been something of a father-figure to Ibsen, as a publisher should be to his authors. His son Jacob, who succeeded him, was a much lesser man—'a decent and well-meaning fellow', wrote Alexander Kielland to his brother, 'but . . . I wonder if he isn't really more interested in horses than writers.'[3] However, Jacob Hegel had an unusually pretty wife, Julie, and continued his father's tradition of hospitality at Skovgaard. Ibsen's relationship

---

[1] *Ibid.*, VI, p. 216.

[2] *The Letters of D. H. Lawrence*, ed. Aldous Huxley (London, 1932), pp. 66, 104, 742.

[3] Harald Grieg, *En dansk forlegger og fire norske diktere* (Oslo, 1955), p. 146.

with him remained cordial, and he continued to ask him, as he had asked his father, for advice on investments.

It was not the best time for Ibsen to have lost his publisher, for 1887 had, financially, been a disastrous year. *Rosmersholm* had failed in the Scandinavian theatres, the flurry of German productions of his plays at the beginning of the year had brought him virtually no money, and he had had no reprints. His experiment of taking ten per cent of the gross for the Christiania production instead of his usual fixed fee had lost him something like 2,000 crowns (£111).

| | crowns | £ |
|---|---|---|
| Fee for *Rosmersholm* at Bergen | 400 | 22 |
| Fees for various unspecified productions of 'Nora' | 400 | 22 |
| Fee for *Rosmersholm* at Gothenburg | 300 | 17 |
| Fee for *An Enemy of the People* at Ostend Theatre, Berlin | 228 | 13 |
| Fee for Danish provincial rights of *Rosmersholm* and *A Doll's House* (C. W. Foght) | 400 | 22 |
| Royalties from *A Doll's House* in Munich (last quarter of 1886) | 215 | 12 |
| Miscellaneous extra payments from Bergen | 320 | 18 |
| Fees for *Rosmersholm* in Berlin and *Ghosts* at Meiningen | 305 | 17 |
| Royalties for *Rosmersholm* in Christiania | 540 | 30 |
| Royalties for *A Doll's House* at Munich Residenztheater | 546 | 30 |
| Royalties for *A Doll's House* at Munich Hoftheater | 59 | 3 |
| Unspecified fees from Royal Theatre, Stockholm | 950 | 53 |
| | 4,663 | 259 |

'Ibsen's plays aren't earning him as much as before, wrote Edvard Brandes (who presumably had the information from someone at Gyldendal) to Jonas Lie on 16 March 1888. 'What will he cook up now? Let's hope he doesn't retreat; we'd be in trouble then; we who dabble in the theatre would lose our standard-bearer.'[1] And indeed Ibsen might have been forgiven if he had made his next play a straight discussion drama of the kind that had proved so popular, a successor to *The Pillars of Society* and *A Doll's House*. It was typical of his courage and integrity as a writer, however Peer Gynt-like he may have been in his private life, that he followed his own stern bent and wrote a play as difficult and psychologically experimental as the one which had just proved so unpopular.

[1] *Brandes Brevveksling*, V, p. 283.

FOUR

 The Lady from the Sea;
and the Breakthrough in England

(1888–1889)

IBSEN'S SIXTIETH BIRTHDAY, on 20 March 1888, was marked by the
publication of Henrik Jæger's biography of him, a sober and intelligent appraisal
containing some carefully censored biographical matter provided by the subject
himself. Among the many telegrams of good wishes was one signed by fifty-
four members of the Storthing, one from the actors at the Christiania Theatre,
and one from Bjørnson which included the sentence: 'Today the world comes
to the recluse.'[1] Many German writers and artists visited him personally to
deliver their greetings. *Aftenposten* printed an anonymous front-page leader (by
Professor Bredo Morgenstierne, who disliked and wrote hostile reviews of most
of Ibsen's mature plays), paying tribute to 'our greatest living writer', stressing
how Norwegian he was and declaring that no foreigners could ever more than
partially appreciate him, words which must have rung somewhat hollowly in
Ibsen's ears. As evidence of his international fame the newspaper proudly published extracts from his early poem *Terje Vigen* in English, German and Polish
translation; one would have thought they might have found something more
recent. Yet, while the left-wing papers joined in saluting him, the leading Tory
paper, *Morgenbladet*, said not a word.

Ibsen's gratitude for the liberals' acclaim of him was tempered by the evidence it gave that he was still the adopted champion of a party in which he no
longer had any real confidence. 'One of the things that has pained me most in
my literary connection with my fatherland', he wrote to Amandus Schibsted,
the editer of *Aftenposten*, on 27 March, 'is the knowledge that, over a number
of years, ever since *The League of Youth* appeared, I have always been claimed
as the possession of one or other of the political parties. I, who have never in
my life concerned myself with politics, but only social questions! And my
presumed opponents refuse to understand this. It is not praise or favour that I
ask for, but understanding. Understanding!'

---

[1] Cf. *Verdens Gang*, 28 March 1888.

Earlier that month *An Enemy of the People* had been staged at Meiningen, 'where [noted William Archer] the fourth act was naturally found to offer a superb opportunity for the Meiningen methods of stage-management.'[1] And indeed one would like to have seen what Duke Georg made of that crowd scene, on which so many productions of the play fall down. Max Grube played Dr Stockmann; but Ibsen, a little surprisingly, did not attend. 'I hardly ever go to the theatre here', he wrote to the Danish playwright Jens Christian Hostrup on 2 April, 'though I like to read a play now and then of an evening, and since I have a strong power of imagination for the dramatic . . . the reading serves almost for a performance.' No doubt it served much better than most of the performances he saw. Productions of his plays in Munich, however, he could hardly help attending, and he was present when the Residenztheater presented *The Wild Duck* on 4 March, a performance which elicited sixteen curtain calls. There would probably have been more productions to mark his birthday had not the old Kaiser Wilhelm died a few days earlier; but there was scarcely a serious German newspaper or periodical which did not commemorate the occasion with a piece about him.

Irgens Hansen wrote a long article on 'Ibsen in Germany' which *Dagbladet* in Christiania published in four instalments on 20, 22, 25 and 28 March. In 1880, Hansen recalls, despite the success of *The Pretenders*, *The Vikings at Helgeland* and *The Pillars of Society*, and the discussion aroused by *A Doll's House*, Ibsen was not on all men's lips in Germany, and was in fact less well known than Bjørnson, thanks to the latter's stories and *A Bankrupt*. Nor had the banning of *Ghosts* helped; but now 'what admirers thought impossible in 1886 has become a reality. German theatres have dared to perform the play, and German audiences have seen it.' So hotly are his plays debated (continued Hansen) that it has even been seriously suggested that 'four young Jews have written his entire works', and the recently published translation of *Emperor and Galilean* was to be seen in every bookshop window.

Hansen quotes from numerous German newspaper and magazine articles about Ibsen published during the preceding twelve months, but expresses surprise that the German theatres stage his plays for so few performances at a time, for 'here is a writer who follows no-one and sets sail for unknown shores'. The first of the four instalments includes a vivid picture of the dramatist in exile: 'In the high rooms at Maximilianstrasse he has hung his beloved paintings. For the third year now one may of an afternoon see his figure, so familiar to the citizens of Munich, in his long Ulster and top hat, slowly walking the streets. Behind the spectacles the eyes smile oftener than the severe features

---

[1] Archer's introduction to his translation of *An Enemy of the People* (London, 1901), p. x.

would have one suspect; for it amuses him to walk among the crowd. He likes to stop where people throng before a window. He knows everything on his routes and notices every little new thing. For an hour to an hour and a half he walks thus in the city, never in the country—"the country is uninteresting" —and soon after 6.30 one will see him at his regular table at the Café Maximilian. There he sits for half an hour, then returns home. Now and then he spends an evening at the Writers' Club when they have a meeting. Otherwise he is not seen.'

Julius Hoffory, the Dane working as a Professor in Berlin, wrote a perceptive appraisal of Ibsen's standing in Germany in the Copenhagen magazine *Tilskueren* that year. The critics, he tells, are divided into two factions, 'some hailing him as a new leader, others denouncing him as an evil messenger of darkness who strives only to destroy everything that one regards as sacred', contrasting his 'gloomy art' with the 'bright and beautiful world of Goethe' (a curious comparison, Hoffory comments, remembering that Goethe was the author of *Götz* and *Werther*). The debate cut across party lines; left-wing papers such as *Berliner Tageblatt* and *Volks-Zeitung* were among Ibsen's bitterest opponents, while others such as *Vossische Zeitung* and *Die Nation* championed him in lengthy articles. *Post* and *Deutsches Tageblatt* attacked him; but other right-wing papers such as *Fremdenblatt* and *Börsen-Zeitung* supported him. The government organ *Norddeutsche Allgemeine Zeitung* violently condemned him, while another government publication, *Deutsche Reichs-Anzeiger*, praised his 'great art and Titanic strength'.

Hoffory concludes: 'It must not be forgotten that the attacks on Ibsen contributed just as much as the eulogies to impress the significance of his work on the German public. It can already be claimed without exaggeration that no living German writer is as well known, as widely read and as earnestly discussed as Henrik Ibsen. In newspapers and books, in brochures and literary magazines, literary historians and essayists, philosophers, lawyers and doctors compete in the interpretation of his work. In the bookshop windows his latest plays are on show by the score, and if one enters, a carefully arranged collection of Ibsen's works is very often the first thing to meet one's eye. His plays are circulated in cheap editions which reach the widest circles and are read and prized by people who are seldom seen with a work of literature in their hand.'[1]

Evidence of the continued increase of Ibsen's reputation in Germany over the next few years appears in an article which Georg Brandes contributed to the same magazine two years later. Brandes declared Ibsen to be a more creative

[1] *Tilskueren* (Copenhagen, 1888), pp. 61–70.

influence in German writing than any other living author, and thought the reason was that he demanded the unusual combination of socialism and individualism—not the individualism of selfishness but the individualism of self-fulfilment. As examples of young German dramatists who were disciples of Ibsen Brandes cites Richard Voss, Hermann Bahr, Wolfgang Kirchbach (who had been born in London of German parents) and Gerhart Hauptmann who, although only twenty-seven when Brandes was writing, had already completed *Vor Sonnenaufgang, Das Friedensfest* and *Die Selicke auf Arno Holz und Johannes Schlef.* All these writers, explained Brandes, admired Ibsen as a realist: 'his name has become a banner, and a whole new generation is rallying to this banner in such magazines as *Freie Bühne, Modern Dichtung,* etc.' The fact that Ibsen never declared his principles or contributed a line himself to these magazines, concludes Brandes, impressed the Germans hugely; and he was very amiable to his young admirers such as Otto Brahm, Paul Schlenther and Hermann Bahr when he met them or they sent him their work.[1]

A new play was due from Ibsen this year, especially after the poor returns of the previous year, and on 5 June he jotted down his first notes, nearly two and a half thousand words:

'The sea's magnetic power. The longing for the sea. Human beings akin to the sea. Bound by the sea. Dependent on the sea. Must return to it. One species of fish is a vital link in the chain of evolution. Do rudiments of it still reside in the human mind? In the minds of certain people?

'Images of the teeming life of the sea and of "what is lost for ever".

'The sea operates a power over one's moods, it works like a will. The sea can hypnotise. Nature in general can ... She has come from the sea ... Became secretly engaged to the young, carefree ship's mate ... At heart, in her instincts—he is the one with whom she is living in marriage ...'

These notes, which include a very detailed synopsis of the first act, provide some interesting revelations of the dramatist's mind at work. At first Ibsen intended to make Wangel, Ellida's husband, a lawyer, 'refined, well-born, bitter. His past stained by a rash affair. In consequence, his future career is blocked.' But he abandoned this conception, and Wangel became instead a kindly and understanding doctor. His wife first appears as Thora (an echo of Magdalene Thoresen?) but Ibsen changed this to Ellida; in the *Saga of Frithiof the Bold* there is a ship named Ellide which (as Halvdan Koht has pointed out) is like a living person fighting against secret troll-powers that try to drag her down beneath the sea.[2] The young ship's mate does not figure in Ibsen's first

---

[1] *Tilskueren,* 1890, pp. 423-450.
[2] Koht, II, p. 193.

cast-list, and Ibsen seems to have intended that he should not appear; there is, though, a Strange Passenger, 'once a lion in the capital', who 'felt a deep attachment to her [Ellida] when she was engaged to the young sailor'. Ibsen later changed this character into Arnholm, the schoolmaster, and introduced the young sailor as the Strange Passenger or, as he finally called him, the Stranger. There was also originally to have been 'an old married clerk. In his youth wrote a play, which was performed once. Is continually touching it up, and lives in the illusion of getting it published and becoming famous.' Ibsen discarded him, but used him four plays later as Vilhelm Foldal in *John Gabriel Borkman*, just as he used here the two young daughters, Bolette and Hilde, whom he had originally conceived as characters for *Rosmersholm*.

Five days after he had made these notes Ibsen began to write Act One, provisionally entitling the play *The Mermaid*, and he completed his first draft in just over seven weeks. Act One is dated 10–16 June; Act Two 21–28 June; Act Three, 2–7 July; Act Four, 12–22 July; and Act Five, 24–31 July. Early in August he began to revise it, and by 18 August he had corrected the first two acts to his satisfaction. Two days later he began to revise the third act, and on 31 August he started on the fourth. On 25 September he was able to send his fair copy to Jacob Hegel. 'The work was finished a little later than I had calculated', he wrote to Hegel the following day, 'but I hope it is still in good time, provided the printing can begin at once. May I ask that the title page be printed last and the title kept secret—as, likewise, I trust that the printers will observe the maximum of discretion . . . I am confident that this play will arouse general interest. In many respects I have struck out in a new direction here.'

He was still as bitter as ever about Norway; despite the birthday tributes, his experiences of the previous summer continued to rankle. 'It would be totally impossible for me to settle for good in Norway', he wrote to Georg Brandes on 30 October. 'There is nowhere where I would feel more homeless than up there. The old conception of a fatherland no longer suffices for anyone intellectually mature. We can no longer rest content with the political community in which we live.' He went on to indulge in a little wishful thinking. 'I believe that national consciousness is on the way towards dying out, and will be replaced by racial consciousness. I at any rate have undergone this evolution. I began by regarding myself as a Norwegian, developed into a Scandinavian and have now arrived at the general idea of Teutonism.' Another of his current preoccupations, his disillusionment with the left, inevitably came in for treatment. 'The leaders of the left are wholly lacking in worldly experience and have consequently been cherishing the most unreasonable illusions. They imagined that a leader of the opposition would and could remain the same man after he had achieved power as he had been before'—a note of disenchantment which has been echoed by many a radical voter since.

Continuing the same letter on 4 November, Ibsen added: 'I see that knave John Paulsen has committed another act of literary villainy as thanks for the kindness I showed him.' Paulsen had just published a new novel, *Fru Cecilia*, a melodramatic but not altogether contemptible romance about a woman who is wrongly supposed to have had a shady past. The young man who loves her daughter is forbidden by his aristocratic mother to involve himself with such a family; there is an extra complication in that he had admired the mother before he fell in love with the daughter. To clear the young couple's path, Fru Cecilia kills herself. None of the characters could possibly be confused with anyone in the Ibsen household, and the only reference to Ibsen is when the young man says to Fru Cecilia: 'I will bring you Ibsen's new play. They say it's full of brilliant paradoxes.'[1] It seems a little hard of Ibsen to have regarded this as villainous or ungrateful.

Ibsen indulged in, for him, an unusual amount of correspondence that November, while awaiting the publication of *The Lady from the Sea* (as he had now re-entitled it). Apart from his long letter to Brandes, he wrote a detailed missive to August Larsen, an editor at Gyldendal, dealing with points of spelling and so forth, and adding the (as events were to turn out) surprising remark: 'I have never had any doubt that my play will be completely understood outside Norway.' He also wrote to Julius Hoffory thanking him for translating the play into German. Henrik Jæger, his biographer, had written from Bergen passing on a suggestion from the theatre there that, instead of paying the usual lump sum, they should give him ten per cent of the gross takings; but this he refused, after his unfortunate experience with *Rosmersholm* in Christiania. 'Our impecunious theatres', he replied on 17 November, 'would be tempted to perform the plays as seldom as possible; whereas if they have paid the author his whole fee it will be in their own interest to get the money back from performances as quickly as possible. I must therefore stick to the old fixed fee system as the only practicable one as long as the present laws concerning literary copyright persist.' He may have sensed that none of his future plays would be popular successes as *The Pillars of Society* and *A Doll's House* had been.

On 20 November he thanked his old Holland friend Ludvig Daae for a long appreciation of Paul Botten Hansen which Daae had recently published in the Danish magazine *Vidar*. 'It gripped me with an extraordinary power to take myself back again so vividly into those times which exercised so decisive

---

[1] John Paulsen, *Fru Cecilia* (Copenhagen, 1888), p. 19.

an influence upon my later development and from which I have never really freed myself—never been able or wanted to free myself.' (It is interesting that he did not reject the Christiania years of humiliation as he rejected Skien.) He ended the letter by asking Daae to 'greet all the survivors' of the Holland circle 'from their, and your, affectionate old friend, Henrik Ibsen', a little surprisingly when one remembers how many of that circle had by now retreated into conservatism. This mellow note is repeated in a letter he wrote the following day to Bredo Morgenstierne thanking him (five months late) for his birthday tribute in *Aftenposten* and assuring him that 'when I return to Christiania—if that ever happens—I will visit the circle where I feel most at home.' And on 25 November, acknowledging to Magdalene Thoresen the repayment of a debt she said she owed him, he wrote that he could not recall having lent her the money and insisted that she take it back. 'Use the money on something that will bring you joy. You must in some way or other celebrate your freedom from debt, on which I congratulate you with all my heart. I know from my own experience what such a liberation means'—a reminder, were one needed, of how this particular subject obsessed him.

Jonas Lie visited Ibsen this month on his way to Paris, and, so Lie wrote to Georg Brandes on 26 November, they 'had as always an unusually pleasant evening. We've been friends since youth, and although we were so different then he often used to choose me to preach to about his dramatic plans.'[1] The next day we find Ibsen expressing an opinion on one of the very few contemporary writers who shared his own stature. Thanking Emmanuel Hansen, a translator who lived in St Petersburg, for sending him a copy of Tolstoy's play *The Power of Darkness* in Danish, he wrote: 'I have read *The Power of Darkness* with much interest. I have no doubt that, carefully and respectfully performed, it must make a considerable effect on the stage. Nevertheless, it seems to me that the author does not possess a complete insight into dramatic technique. The play contains conversations rather than scenes, and the dialogue strikes me in many places as epic rather than dramatic, the work in general as being less of a drama than a narrative in dialogue'—a verdict with which most directors and actors would agree. He added, however, that 'the great writer's genius lives and is revealed there.'

This was, parenthetically, a more charitable judgment than Tolstoy was to pass on Ibsen, for he found all of the latter's plays (except, oddly enough, *Rosmersholm*) repellent. 'Have read *Love's Comedy*', he wrote in his diary on 19 November 1889. 'How bad! Clever German sophistry—terrible!' V. L. Nemirovitch-Dantchenko lent him *An Enemy of the People*, but he disliked that

---

[1] *Brandes Brevveksling*, IV, p. 429.

too, remarking: 'This Dr Stockmann is much too conceited.'[1] On 20 August 1890 he noted: 'Have read Ibsen's *Wilde Ente* [*The Wild Duck*]. Not good'. (As he called the play by its German title he had presumably read it in that language; it was not translated into Russian until 1892). The next day he noted: 'Have read Ibsen's *Rosmer* [*sic*] . . . So far not bad'. But it seems doubtful if he liked the rest of it, for on 14 September 1891 he wrote to Ibsen's Russian translator, P. G. Hansen, that he loved Bjørnson's writing and personality, 'but I cannot say the same of Ibsen. I have read all [*sic*] his plays too, and his poem *Brand*, which I was patient enough to read to the end. Everything is contrived, false and very clumsy—none of his characters is consistent and lived-through. His reputation in Europe merely proves the poverty of European creative writing.' In his essay *What is Art?* written in 1898, Tolstoy made particular mockery of *Little Eyolf* and *The Master Builder*; but Ibsen was in good company, for Tolstoy poured equal scorn on Beethoven, Baudelaire, Wagner, Verlaine and Zola. In his diary of 28 October 1900, citing Ibsen as an example of 'the poetry and art of the cultural mob', Tolstoy linked his name disparagingly with those of Shakespeare and Dante, finding all three immoral and irreligious and, there-fore, bad artists;[2] and, dismissing Chekhov's *The Seagull* as 'utterly worthless', he added that it was written 'just as Ibsen writes his plays'.[3] Chekhov's own attitude towards Ibsen was to be most oddly ambivalent.

On 28 November 1888 *The Lady from the Sea* was published in an edition of 10,000 copies, 2,000 more than *Rosmersholm* or *The Wild Duck*. Ibsen's con-viction that the play would be 'completely understood outside Norway' proved sadly unfounded; it was not even understood inside Norway. The critics were as bewildered by it as they had been by *Rosmersholm*, and although it got a slightly better press on account of the happy, or seemingly-happy ending, such tributes as it received were grudging. 'The play is not free from riddles and problems', wrote an anonymous critic in *Morgenbladet* (5, 8, 11 and 12 December), regarding this as a defect, 'but wholesomeness emerges vic-torious . . . It certainly moves in a cleaner air.' At the same time, he complained, Ellida's story 'is from first to last a story of sickness, a bizarre psychological case-history, the development of which taxes the action of the play . . . There is no real drama in this.' Bredo Morgenstierne, who had been so severe on *The Wild Duck* and *Rosmersholm*, also welcomed (in *Aftenposten*, 5 December) the 'cleaner air' of this play, but found little else to praise, and even Irgens

---

[1] V. L. Nemirovitch-Dantchenko, *My Life in the Russian Theatre*, translated by J. Cournos (London, 2nd edition, 1968), p. 333.

[2] Cf. Martin Nag, *Ibsen i russisk åndsliv* (Oslo, 1967), pp. 99–103.

[3] David Magarshack, *Chekhov the Dramatist* (New York, 1960), p. 16, quoting Alexey Suvorin's diary for 11 February 1897.

Hansen, while praising the truthfulness of the psychology, thought (*Dagbladet*, 30 November) that the subject would have been better treated in a novel. Knut Hamsun dismissed it as an 'insanity',[1] and the historian J. E. Sars doubtless expressed many people's views when he declared: 'It seems to me a proof of how modern aesthetics have strayed that Henrik Ibsen has almost [*sic*] overtaken Bjørnson in public estimation. He is a purely negative spirit . . . Surely this pessimistic problem writing must by now have reached its limit.'[2] Tolstoy would have agreed with that, although it is ironical to reflect that he himself was never to receive the Nobel Prize for Literature, despite the fact that he lived for nine years after its inception, because the Swedish Academy regarded him as insufficiently idealistic.

The Swedish and Danish press were scarcely more favourable. Kristofer Randers, reviewing the play in *Ny Svensk Tidskrift* (1889, pp. 500 ff.), complained that it continued the trend noticeable in Ibsen's work since *The Wild Duck*, in that 'an obscure mysticism and a musing symbolism seem more and more to predominate at the expense of the natural and the immediate.' C. D. af Wirsén, in *Post- och Inrikes-Tidning*, thought it 'doubtful whether this curious play will survive long on the stage. Come back, old Shakespeare, with your wholesome humanity, and dispel these eccentricities.'[3] (He does not seem to have read *Troilus and Cressida*.) P. A. Rosenberg, a Danish admirer, also found it negative.[4] Edvard Brandes welcomed the play enthusiastically in *Politiken*, but found himself almost alone. 'I don't understand', wrote the young Swedish poet Ola Hansson to Strindberg, 'how Edvard Brandes can express himself in such superlatives . . . Of course the end of the play will evoke cries of joy from sheep and rabbits. It might be interpreted as the apotheosis of marital duty.' Strindberg replied (7 December) that Ibsen 'ought now to be repudiated as moralistic and religious',[5] though within a decade he was to become both himself. Erik Bøgh advised the Royal Theatre in Copenhagen to reject it, and in a Scandinavian newspaper on the other side of the world a forgotten enemy took up his pen to denounce it. Clemens Petersen gave it a bad review in the Chicago *Nordisk Folkeblad*.[6]

Almost the only critic apart from Edvard Brandes to acclaim *The Lady from*

---

[1] *Samtiden*, 1890, p. 8.

[2] Letter to John Paulsen, 12 September 1889 (J. E. Sars, *Brev, 1850–1915*, Oslo, 1957, p. 182).

[3] Wirsén, p. 102.

[4] P. A. Rosenberg, *Literatur og Kritik* (Copenhagen, 1888), pp. 444–450.

[5] *August Strindbergs brev*, VII, p. 196.

[6] Petersen never gave up. As late as 1895 he was still protesting to Bjørnson that Ibsen 'is a critic, not a creative writer'. (*Bjørnstjerne Bjørnsons brevveksling med danske, 1875–1910*, II, p. 229.)

*the Sea* whole-heartedly was the Swede J. A. Runström, who had recently taken over the dramatic column of the Stockholm weekly *Ny Illustrerad Tidning*, a task which he was to fulfil with considerable distinction. What other critics had condemned in the play, he welcomed. 'The psychological', he wrote (15 December), 'has always been Ibsen's principal strength, and here it is dominant and undistracted by polemical issues. He has put social criticism aside.[1] A play of rare fulfilment. Not only is the characterisation masterly and enthralling; the brilliant assurance with which the plot is conceived and carried through fills one with an admiration which grows the more one ponders it.'[2]

It was fortunate for Ibsen that Jacob Hegel did not consider printing a smaller impression of *The Lady from the Sea* following the failure of *Rosmersholm*, for otherwise 1888 had been an even worse year financially than 1887. Not only had there been no reprints of his earlier works; he had received no performance fees from Scandinavia at all, apart from 189 crowns (£10) for two performances of *An Enemy of the People* in Stockholm. Luckily for him the German theatres were beginning to pay a little more; even so, his earnings for the year, excluding the advance for *The Lady from the Sea*, totalled only 2,346 crowns (£130).

|  | crowns | £ |
| --- | --- | --- |
| Fees for *The Wild Duck* in Berlin | 195 | 11 |
| Fees for *A Doll's House* in Berlin | 300 | 17 |
| Other unspecified fees from Berlin | 49 | 3 |
| Fee for 24th and 25th performances of *An Enemy of The People* at the Royal Theatre, Stockholm | 189 | 10 |
| Fees from Munich Hoftheater for 13 performances of *The Pillars of Society* and 1 performance of *A Doll's House* | 1,466 | 81 |
| Fee from Cologne Stadttheater for *The Pillars of Society* | 147 | 8 |
| 1st edition of *The Lady from the Sea* | 8,550 | 475 |
|  | 10,896 | 605 |

---

[1] It is significant that Ibsen, as his notes for the play show, originally intended that Ellida should have broken her engagement with the seaman because of social and moral prejudices derived from his upbringing; but he discarded this motive, and the conflict between Wangel and the Stranger became instead a struggle to gain control over the subconscious powers of her soul. (Cf. Koht, II, p. 194.)

[2] Sadly, Runström used *The Lady from the Sea* as a stick with which to belabour Strindberg's *Miss Julie*, which had appeared almost simultaneously, and which Runström reviewed in the same article. 'It goes without saying', he wrote, 'that the play *Miss Julie* bears traces of its author's talent, and contains one or two effective scenes, but . . . it treats a subject . . . which, when expressed as nakedly as it is here, makes a most disagreeable impression even upon reading, and will surely nowhere find a public that could endure to see it.' In this at least Runström was speaking for his fellow-countrymen, for it was to be sixteen years before *Miss Julie* was staged in Sweden.

However, the interest on his investments brought him 3,288 crowns (£183) to add to his pension of 2,000 crowns (£111); and so economically did he live that on 11 December and 20 January he asked Hegel to buy him further securities to a total value of 14,000 crowns (£777), which suggests that, with Sigurd now earning a sufficient salary, Ibsen and Suzannah were living on little more than his pension. The fear that he might find himself incapacitated by illness or a stroke (as eventually happened), or that he might lose his public (as now seemed not impossible), was always in his mind, and he was determined that he and his wife should never find themselves in the situation in which, half a century earlier, his father had left him.

At last there were signs of a belated breakthrough in England. In the closing weeks of 1888, thanks to William Archer's efforts, a publisher bearing the illustrious name of Walter Scott issued a volume, in a series called the Camelot Classics, containing Archer's translation of *The Pillars of Society*, a careful revision by him of Henrietta Frances Lord's version of *A Doll's House*, and a translation by Karl Marx's daughter Eleanor of (as she called it) *An Enemy of Society*. The volume was introduced by a twenty-nine year old ex-medical student named Havelock Ellis, then earning a living as editor of the Mermaid Series of Old Dramatists. Ellis expressed his envy of the Scandinavian countries for having a stage on which 'the burning issues of the day [may] be scenically resolved', and concluded by declaring that Ibsen's ideas 'are of the kind that penetrate men's minds slowly. Yet they penetrate surely, and are proclaimed at length in the market place.' Ellis's own first book, *The New Spirit*, which appeared just over a year later, was to contain a forty-three page section on Ibsen. It is a measure of the impact which Ibsen was about to make on the English scene that the little Camelot volume of his plays sold, during the next five years, no fewer than fourteen thousand copies, a quite unprecedented figure for a volume of plays by a living dramatist, and thereby established a new trend which, in due course, Shaw and Galsworthy were profitably to follow.

On New Year's Day, 1889, Edmund Gosse returned to the Ibsen scene after an absence of five years with a long article in the *Fortnightly Review* entitled *Ibsen's Social Dramas*, dealing with all the prose plays from *The Pillars of Society* to *The Lady from the Sea*. He welcomed the last-named play as possessing 'a glamour of romance, of mystery, of landscape beauty, which has not appeared in Ibsen's work to anything like the same extent since *Peer Gynt*.' And before the year was out Ibsen was to enjoy his first success on the London stage. All in all, 1889 was to prove an important year for him abroad.

*The Lady from the Sea*, however, failed on the stages of Europe as calamitously as *Rosmersholm* had done. It received its premiere on 12 February, simultaneously in Christiania and Weimar.[1] *Aftenposten*, reviewing the Christiania production, dismissed the play as 'one of Ibsen's feeblest', and although it managed twenty-one performances that season it was thought worthy of only two the following season. It failed in Weimar and also, four days later, in Copenhagen when, despite Erik Bøgh's recommendation to the contrary, the Royal Theatre presented it. There was great public curiosity to see how it would fare on the stage, and the first night's takings were the biggest for any Ibsen play at this theatre during the dramatist's lifetime, but it achieved no more than eleven performances. Edvard Brandes thought it a bad production, and wrongly cast in the leading role; Ibsen had wanted Betty Hennings, but the theatre chose their other leading lady, Josephine Eckhardt. 'Who cast the play with such lack of consideration?' asked Brandes in *Politiken* on 20 February. 'But one cannot wholly acquit the dramatist of blame, since the aristocratic indifference with which he treats the Scandinavian theatres extends to his not choosing the casts . . . They have designed no new scenery, but have merely shoved together old pieces . . . They could have played it successfully between three bare walls had they played it well.' In Stockholm, too, the following month, it failed. J. A. Runström, who had so welcomed it on publication, felt bound to admit (*Ny Illustrerad Tidning*, 30 March) that 'the right place for *The Lady from the Sea* is not on the boards. It is a play to be read, and as such is enthralling, but in the theatre it loses a good deal of the magic it exercises on one's imagination. What seems natural and inevitable on the page seems almost unnatural on the stage . . . The central character is too subtle to withstand the brightness of the limelight. She hovers on the frontier between the world of reality and the world of poetry without appearing to have a true foothold in either.'

Like *Rosmersholm*, *The Lady from the Sea* was to fail time and again when staged, with occasional (and memorable) exceptions, and for two reasons. Firstly, like *Rosmersholm*, it delved into depths of the human soul with which both audiences and actors were unfamiliar. Secondly, the part of Ellida needs a very special kind of actress. It is one of those roles, like Lear and Othello, Strindberg's Father and Miss Julie, which demand a particular quality of personality, and the most accomplished actress in the world, if she lacks this quality, cannot succeed. She may get excellent notices for her performance, but the play will fail. But with the right actress, the result is one of the rarest experiences that the theatre can offer, like a great Othello.

The first to encompass the role was Eleonora Duse. James Agate, in a memorable passage, described her in the part: 'This play is a godsend to a great

---

[1] According to Eller (pp. 78–79), four other German theatres applied for the right to stage the first production, but all declined after reading the play.

artist whose forte is not so much doing as suffering that which Fate has done to her. With Duse, speech is silver and silence is golden ... The long second act was a symphony for the voice, but to me the scene of greatest marvel was the third act. In this Duse scaled incredible heights. There was one moment when, drawn by every fibre of her being to the unknown irresistible of the Stranger and the sea, she blotted herself behind her husband and took comfort and courage from his hand. Here terror and ecstasy sweep over her face with that curious effect which this actress alone knows—as though this were not present stress, but havoc remembered of past time. Her features have the placidity of long grief; so many storms have broken over them that nothing can disturb again this sea of calm distress. If there be in acting such a thing as pure passion divorced from the body yet expressed in terms of the body, it is here. Now and again in this strange play Duse would seem to pass beyond our ken, and where she has been there is only a fragrance and a sound in our ears like water flowing under the stars.'[1]

Greta Garbo would have been supremely suited to play Ellida; why did nobody think of making a film of it with her? I once saw a young Irish actress, Jean Robinson, make something extraordinary of the part in a fog-filled theatre at Lancaster in 1967.

At the beginning of March there was an Ibsen week in Berlin, with *The Lady from the Sea* at the Schauspielhaus, *The Wild Duck* at the Residenztheater and *A Doll's House* at the Lessingtheater. Ibsen went up for the occasion, staying at the Hotel du Nord, and was fêted as enthusiastically as he had been two years earlier. Various banquets were given for him, and he himself invited Otto Brahm, Paul Schlenther, Julius Hoffory and Ove Rode, the young Dane who had led the rebellion in the Students' Union in Christiania, to 'a splendid luncheon which lasted almost till evening ... It will be good to have some peace again', he wrote to Suzannah on 5 March, after attending a charity matinée of *The Lady from the Sea* the previous day. 'I already feel quite tired.'[2] But in a letter of thanks on 26 March to Hoffory, whose translation of *The Lady from the Sea* had rapidly gone into a third edition, he described his stay in Berlin as 'the most exciting time of my life. When I look back on it, the whole thing seems like a dream. It makes me almost afraid.' Before returning to Munich he spent a week in Weimar, where he found the production of *The Lady from the Sea* (he told Hoffory in the same letter) 'quite excellent. I could not wish, nor could scarcely imagine, the Stranger better interpreted—a tall,

[1] *Sunday Times*, 10 June 1923, reprinted in Agate's *Red Letter Nights* (London, 1944), pp. 71–72.
[2] *C.E.*, XIX, p. 356. The letter is there dated 1891, but cf. Koht's note on p. 555 of that volume.

lean figure with a long face, black staring eyes and a magnificent, deep, subdued voice.'

In Munich he found a new edition (the seventh) of *The Pretenders* awaiting him, with the news that an eleventh edition of *Brand* was in the press, and that he now had 17,000 crowns (£944) to his credit with Gyldendal, information which he described to Hegel (11 April) as 'a great and joyful surprise'. The idea of spending any of this windfall on luxuries did not occur to him, or if it did it was firmly rejected, for the next day he wrote Hegel that the whole amount was to be invested in gilt-edged securities, 7,000 crowns' worth of it in Russian railways.

*The Pillars of Society* was revived in April at the Deutsches Theatre in Berlin, and the same month he heard from Snoilsky that two of his plays had, at last, been translated into French. The translator was not a Frenchman, any more than Hoffory in Berlin was a German or P. G. Hansen (his Russian translator) a Russian; it was a Lithuanian, Count Moritz Prozor. Married to a niece of Snoilsky, he had, when secretary at the Russian embassy in Stockholm in 1883, seen *Ghosts* performed there; the play had made a deep impression on him, and on moving to the Berne embassy in 1887 he had, with the aid of his wife, turned both *Ghosts* and *A Doll's House* into French. Now, in 1889, he had managed to get both translations published in Paris. (It is typical of the piratical conditions then governing copyright as far as a Norwegian was concerned that Ibsen should not have known even of the translations' existence until after they had appeared in print.) 'I have not yet seen it', he wrote to Snoilsky on 19 April, referring to the *Ghosts* translation, 'but even if I had read it I would be unable to pass any well-founded judgment, since my knowledge of the French language is very inadequate. I am all the happier that you find the translation very well done.' He added that two Frenchmen had been negotiating with his German translators to make version of his plays from the German, a common practice in several countries up to recent times (one of the most frequently performed 'translators' of Ibsen in England during the forties and fifties worked from German texts which were often wildly inaccurate).

On 7 June 1889 Ibsen achieved his first real breakthrough on the English stage. Hitherto, he had been represented only by the single matinée of *The Pillars of Society* in 1880, the dreadful travesty *Breaking a Butterfly* in 1884 and the amateur performance of 'Nora' in 1885. Now, however, a young Irish actor-manager named Charles Charrington produced *A Doll's House* in Archer's revised translation at the Novelty Theatre in Kingsway (later the Kingsway Theatre) with his wife, the twenty-five year old Janet Achurch, as Nora. Before her tragic suicide in 1916 at the age of fifty-two Janet Achurch was to become one of the great actresses of her generation (in 1907 she was a memorable Mrs Alving), and this production established her reputation at the same time that it established Ibsen's. William Archer recorded the occasion in the columns of the *World*, of which he had, since 1884, been dramatic critic, starting at a salary of three guineas a week. At the age of thirty-three, he had already proved himself the best English dramatic critic since William Hazlitt.

'The general public', wrote Archer on 19 June, 'has risen heroically to the occasion. It has come—nay, more, it has paid—to see *A Doll's House*, and that in larger numbers night by night . . . So far from having drunk its fill of Ibsen in a single week, it is crying out for more, and the departure of Miss Achurch and Mr Charrington for Australia has with difficulty been postponed in answer to that demand. If these things had been prophesied six weeks ago, who would have believed them?' Years later, Archer recalled: 'It was this production which really made Ibsen known to the English-speaking peoples. In other words, it marked his second stride towards world-wide, as distinct from merely national renown—if we reckon as the first stride the success of *The Pillars of Society* in Germany . . . The Ibsen controversy, indeed, did not break out in full virulence until 1891, when *Ghosts* and *Hedda Gabler* were produced in London; but from the date of the Novelty production onwards, Ibsen was generally recognised as a potent factor in the intellectual and artistic life of the day.'[1] Harley Granville Barker, in *The Coming of Ibsen*, noted: 'The play was talked of and written about—mainly abusively, it is true—as no play had been for years. The performances were extended from seven to twenty-four. The takings were apt to be between £35 and £45 a night. Charrington lost only £70. This was not bad for an epoch-making venture in the higher drama.'[2]

The newspaper criticisms were, as Barker says, generally unfavourable. 'I never sat out a play more dreary or illogical as a whole, or in its details more feeble or commonplace', complained the *Sporting and Dramatic News*. 'It is as though someone had dramatized the cooking of a Sunday dinner' (no bad subject for a play, one might think nowadays). Bernard Shaw praised it anonymously in the *Manchester Guardian* (8 June); so did R. K. Hervey in *The Theatre* (1 July): 'Those who have not read *A Doll's House* or seen it acted can have no conception with what a master hand the characters are drawn.' But the same issue contained a violent attack on the play by the editor, Clement Scott: 'The atmosphere is hideous . . . it is all self, self, self! . . . a congregation of men and women without one spark of nobility in their nature, men without conscience and women without affection, an unlovable,

---

1 Charles Archer, p. 169.
2 Granville Barker, p. 179 n.

unlovely and detestable crew.' Scott had already written an anonymous attack in the radical organ *Truth* (13 June) on the people who supported this new cult, dismissing them as 'a scant audience of egotists and Positivists assembled to see Ibsen . . . and to gloat over the Ibsen theory of woman's degradation and man's unnatural supremacy.'

Among these despicable characters was W. B. Yeats, then twenty-four, who left an account of the occasion and the impression it made on a young writer in *The Trembling of the Veil*: '. . . somebody had given me a seat for the gallery. In the middle of the first act, while the heroine was asking for macaroons, a middle-aged washerwoman who sat in front of me stood up and said to the little boy at her side: "Tommy, if you promise to go home straight we will go now"; and at the end of the play, as I wandered through the entrance hall, I heard an elderly critic murmur: "A series of conversations terminated by an accident". I was divided in mind. I hated the play; what was it but Carolus Duran, Bastien-Lepage, Huxley and Tindall all over again; I resented being invited to admire dialogue so close to modern educated speech that music and style were impossible. "Art is art because it is not nature", I kept repeating to myself, but how could I take the same side with critic and washerwoman? As time passed Ibsen became in my mind the chosen author of very clever young journalists who, condemned to their treadmill of abstraction, hated music and style; and yet neither I nor my generation could escape him because, though we and he had not the same friends, we had the same enemies.'[1]

Archer, in an essay entitled *The Mausoleum of Ibsen* which he contributed to the *Fortnightly Review* in 1893, listed some of the comments of those 'enemies' on Charrington's production of *A Doll's House*:

'By the new school of theorists the *genre ennuyeux* is assigned a place of distinction; for *A Doll's House* with its almost total lack of dramatic action is certainly not an enlivening spectacle.'

*The Times*

'It would be a misfortune were such a morbid and unwholesome play to gain the favour of the public.'

*Standard*

'Such a starting point has dramatic possibilities. A Sardou might conceivably turn it to excellent account on the stage . . . It is simply as a mild picture of domestic life in Christiania that the piece has any interest at all. It is a little bit of genre painting, with here and there an effective touch.'

*Daily News*

[1] W. B. Yeats, *Autobiographies* (London, 1955), p. 279.

'Of no use—as far as England's stage is concerned.'

*Referee*

'Unnatural, immoral and, in its concluding scene, essentially undramatic.'

*People*

'Ibsen . . . is too faddy and too obstinately unsympathetic to please English playgoers.'

*Sunday Times*

'Strained deductions, lack of wholesome human nature. Pretentious inconclusiveness . . . Cannot be allowed to pass without a word of protest against the dreary and sterilizing principle which it seeks to embody.'

*Observer*

'The works of the Norwegian playwright are not suitable for dramatic representation—at any rate on the English stage.'

*St James's Gazette*

Among those who made the production possible was, of all people, Henry Irving, who remained until his death in 1906 an implacable opponent of Ibsen. Janet Achurch, relates Irving's grandson, 'had asked him for money to sustain her and her husband . . . in a comedy, *Clever Alice* . . . He had sent her £100, only to discover that she and Eleanor Marx-Aveling were conspiring to produce Ibsen. She asked him to come and see *A Doll's House*. He went. "If that's the sort of thing she wants to play she'd better play it somewhere else," was the only comment he made.'[1]

Ibsen was delighted with the success of Charrington's production. 'The movement in London', he wrote to Archer on 26 June, enclosing a signed photograph for Janet Achurch, 'marks a shining epoch in my life, far surpassing anything I had ever dreamed of.'[2] The interest in *A Doll's House* stimulated a brief revival of *The Pillars of Society* the following month for a single matinée at the Opera Comique in the Strand. R. K. Hervey, despite his editor's views on the playwright, again wrote enthusiastically in *The Theatre* ('It is impossible in a short article to do justice to this remarkable play') and Austin Brereton in *The Stage* thought that 'the piece . . . would in all probability succeed for a time in an evening bill, more particularly after the excitement and controversy

---

[1] Laurence Irving, *Henry Irving* (London, 1951), p. 535.

[2] Cf. Charles Archer, pp. 183–184, and Bjørn Tysdahl, *Ibsen-brev i Brittisk Museums Archer-samling* in *Edda*, 1966, pp. 246–259. Tysdahl notes that the British Museum collection contains seventeen letters written by Ibsen to Archer between 1889 and 1900, only two of which (plus a third not in the British Museum) are printed in the Collected Edition of Ibsen's Works.

the production of *A Doll's House* created.' An American actress named Elizabeth Robins made her first appearance in an Ibsen part, in the role of Martha; she was to do much to pioneer his work on the English stage during the coming decade.

The Charringtons took their production of *A Doll's House* to Australia that year; also to New Zealand and, in due course, to Egypt, India and America. It was well received everywhere except in Sydney, where 'an indignant and outraged audience greeted Nora's exodus with howls and hisses.'[1]

Ibsen had spent the previous summer in Munich, working on *The Lady from the Sea*, but this year he decided to take a holiday. 'In the beginning of next month', he wrote to Nils Lund on 29 June, 'we shall be going to the Tyrol to spend the rest of the summer there. We shall probably choose Gossensass, where we have so often stayed before.' It was a fateful decision. That summer in Gossensass in 1889 was to throw Ibsen sharply out of the mood of mellow optimism which had found expression in *The Lady from the Sea*, and was to leave its mark on all his future work.

[1] Miriam Franc, *Ibsen in England* (Boston, 1919), p. 83.

# PART TWO
## THE SUMMER IN GOSSENSASS

# FIVE

 The Summer in Gossensass

## (1889)

IT WAS IBSEN's first visit to Gossensass for five years, since he had spent the summer of 1884 alone there finishing *The Wild Duck*. Sigurd, now transferred from Washington to the embassy in Vienna, joined his parents there; they stayed, as before, at the Gröbner family hotel, and a sister of the proprietor remembered how Ibsen 'lived like a clock', just as in Munich. Each day he took a walk along the river Eisach, standing for a long while on the bridge and staring broodingly into the water. The locals, indeed, nicknamed him 'Der Wassermann', which might not unfairly be translated as Old Man River. Fräulein Gröbner recalled how *soigné* he was in his dress, even on his country walks, and, from his weekly bills, how simply and modestly he lived.[1]

The little town had decided to celebrate his return by naming his old lookout on the hill the Ibsenplatz, and on 21 July the ceremony took place. There was a grand procession and Ibsen, despite the steep ascent, climbed at the head of it and received with friendliness and dignity the homage accorded him. A concert followed, and after the concert he met a young Viennese girl named Emilie Bardach. As she remembered seventeen years later, this happened at a crowded reception; but if we are to believe an American's transcription of her diary (the original has disappeared),[2] they first really got to know each other

---

[1] Bergliot Ibsen, p. 90.

[2] Basil King printed extracts from Emilie's diary, in English translation, in two articles entitled *Ibsen and Emilie Bardach* in the *Century Magazine*, New York, October 1923 (pp. 803–815) and November 1923 (pp. 83–92). André Rouveyre published some of the same extracts, in French, in *Le mémorial inédit d'une amie d'Ibsen*, in *Mercure de France*, 15 July 1928, pp. 257–270. There are discrepancies between the two versions and, as Emilie's journal has disappeared, it is impossible to say which is correct. King's daughter, Mrs Reginald Orcutt, tells me that her father returned the journal to Emilie and that after her death her effects went to a female cousin, whom I have been unable to trace, and who is now almost certainly dead. Emilie's account of the party meeting occurs in *Meine Freundschaft mit Ibsen*, an article she wrote for the Vienna newspaper *Neue Freie Presse*, 31 March 1907. Much fuss has been made about the discrepancy between King's version of her diary and her own reminiscence, but if, in King's translation of her diary extract for 5 August, one substitutes 'got to know him' for 'made his acquaintance', the problem disappears.

123

when he came on her seated alone on a bench, reading a book, in a valley named the Pflerschtal on the outskirts of the town. He seated himself beside her and, questioning her closely as was his wont, learned her age (eighteen), details of her home and family, and the fact that they lived so near each other in Gossensass that his windows looked into hers. A few days later she ran into him at a dull birthday party. 'It is a pity', she noted in her journal, 'that German gives him so much difficulty, as apart from that we understand each other so well.'

She fell ill, and a few days later Ibsen came to see her, climbing over the garden gate to do so. 'He remained with me a long while, and was both kind and sympathetic.' A little later: 'We talk a great deal together. His ardour ought to make me feel proud.' He asked her endless questions, and seemed particularly anxious to catch her in a lie.[1] Then:

> 'Ibsen has begun to talk to me quite seriously about myself. He stayed a long time with me on Saturday, and also again this evening. Our being so much together cannot but have some painful influence over me. He puts such strong feeling into what he says to me. His words often give me a sensation of terror and cold. He talks about the most serious things in life, and believes in me so much. He expects from me much, much, much more than I am afraid he will ever find. Never in his whole life, he says, has he felt so much joy in knowing anyone. He never admired anyone as he admires me. But all in him is truly good and noble! What a pity it is that I cannot remember all his words! He begs me so intensely to talk freely to him, to be absolutely frank with him, so that we may become fellow-workers together.'

Next she writes:

> 'Mamma has just gone out, so that I have the room to myself. At last I am free to put down the incredible things of these recent days. How poor and insufficient are words! Tears say these things better. Passion has come when it cannot lead to anything, when both of us are bound by so many ties. Eternal obstacles! Are they in my will? Or are they in the circumstances? . . . How could I compare anything else that has happened to an outpouring like this? It could never go so far, and yet—!'

She swings off to Baron A., the only lover who offered a standard of comparison.

> 'But how much calmer *he* was, how inarticulate, beside this volcano, so terribly beautiful! Yesterday afternoon, we were alone together at last!

---

[1] So she told A. E. Zucker in 1927; cf. Zucker, *op. cit.*, p. 242.

Oh, the words! If only they could have stamped themselves on my heart more deeply and distinctly! All that has been offered me before was only the pretence at love. This is the true love, the ideal, he says, to which unknowingly he gave himself in his art. At last he is a true poet through pain and renunciation. And yet he is glad of having known me—the most beautiful! the wonderful! Too late! How small I seem to myself that I cannot spring to him!'

Neither Suzannah nor Emilie's mother seem to have suspected what was afoot. But:

'The obstacles! How they grow more numerous, the more I think of them! The difference of age!—his wife!—his son!—all that there is to keep us apart! Did this have to happen? Could I have foreseen it? Could I have prevented it? When he talks to me as he does, I often feel that I must go far away from here—far away!—and yet I suffer at the thought of leaving him. I suffer most from his impatience, his restlessness. I begin to feel it now, even when we are in the salon, quite apart from each other . . .

'It all came to me so suddenly! I noticed for the first time how he began to change his regular ways of life, but I didn't know what it meant. Of course I was flattered at his sympathy, and at being distinguished among the many who surround him, eager for a word . . .'

An early snowstorm came, and the guests at Gossensass began to leave. Emilie realised they would soon have to part.

'And I have nothing to give him, not even my picture, when he is giving me so much. But we both feel it is best outwardly to remain as strangers . . . His wife shows me much attention. Yesterday I had a long talk with his son . . .

'I am reading Love's Comedy, but if anyone comes I am seen holding Beaconsfield's Endymion in my hands. Nearly everyone has gone. The days we have still to spend can now be counted. I don't think about the future. The present is too much. We had a long talk together in the morning, and after lunch he came again and sat with me. What am I to think? He says it is to be my life's aim to work with him. We are to write to each other; but what am I to write?'

Ibsen (according to King) confided his feelings to two ladies. One fainted; another described the scene to Emilie as 'beautiful and terrible as a thunderstorm. She wonders that I do not lose my head. She says that she herself would have been absolutely overcome. This consoles me. I do not seem so weak.'

Did something happen between Ibsen and Emilie on 19 September, and if so was it anything like what Hilde Wangel in *The Master Builder* describes as having happened on another 19 September?

HILDE: Was it just a little detail that I happened to be alone in the room when you came in?

SOLNESS: Were you?

HILDE: You didn't call me a little devil then.

SOLNESS: No, I don't suppose I did.

HILDE: You said I looked beautiful in my white dress. Like a little princess.

SOLNESS: So you did, Miss Wangel. And besides—I felt so happy and free that evening—

HILDE: And then you said that when I grew up, I would be your princess.

SOLNESS: (*with a short laugh*): Well, well! Did I say that, too? . . .

HILDE: It sounded as though you were making fun of me.

SOLNESS: I'm sure I didn't mean that.

HILDE: I can well believe you didn't. Considering what you did next—

SOLNESS: And what on earth did I do next? . . .

HILDE: You took me in your arms and kissed me, Mr Solness.

SOLNESS: (*gets up from his chair, his mouth open*). *I* did?

HILDE: Yes, you did. You took me in both your arms and bent me backwards and kissed me. Many, many times.

SOLNESS: Oh, but my dear, good Miss Wangel—

HILDE: (*gets up*): You're not going to deny it?

SOLNESS: I certainly am! . . . All this that you've told me must have been something you've dreamed . . . No, there's more to it than that . . . I must have thought all this. I must have wanted it—wished it—desired it. So that— Couldn't that be an explanation? . . .

HILDE: Perhaps you've also forgotten what day it was? . . .

SOLNESS: Hm—I've forgotten the actual day, I must confess . . .

HILDE: It was . . . the nineteenth of September.

Nearly forty years later, in 1927, Emilie told A. E. Zucker that Ibsen had never kissed her;[1] perhaps with Ibsen, as with Solness, these things only happened in his mind. Next day, 20 September, he wrote in Emilie's album a line from *Faust*: 'Hohes, schmerzliches Glück—um das Unerreichbare zu ringen!'—'Oh, high and painful joy—to struggle for the unattainable!'

---

[1] Zucker, p. 242.

The following day, 21 September, another young girl, a German painter named Helene Raff, who was staying at Gossensass and had met Ibsen for the first time four days earlier, wrote in her diary: 'The B[ardach] completely crazy about Ibsen'; and the day after, she noted: 'Miss B. broken-hearted'.[1]

On 27 September Emilie wrote in her diary:

'Our last day at Gossensass. Then nothing but memory will remain. Two weeks ago, memory seemed to Ibsen so beautiful, and now— He says that tomorrow he will stand on the ruins of his happiness. These last two months are more important in his life than anything that has gone before. Am I unnatural in being so terribly quiet and normal? . . . Last evening, when Mamma went to talk to his wife, he came over and sat at our table. We were quite alone. He talked about his plans. I alone am in them—I, and I again. I feel quieter because he is quieter, though yesterday he was terrible.'

That night, at 3 a.m., the express from Verona to Vienna passed through Gossensass, and Emilie left on it. A few hours earlier she had confided to her diary:

'He means to possess me. That is his absolute will. He intends to overcome all obstacles. I do what I can to keep him from feeling this, and yet I listen as he describes what is to lie before us—going from one country to another—I with him—enjoying his triumphs together . . . Our parting was easier than I had feared.'

Emilie told Zucker in 1927 that Ibsen had, in Gossensass, 'spoken to her of the possibility of a divorce and of a subsequent union with her, in the course of which they were to travel widely and see the world'.[2] Once back in Munich, however, Ibsen seemed to resign himself to the impossibility of going through with such a plan. Perhaps he feared the scandal; perhaps he felt a duty towards his sickly and aging wife, who had stood so firmly behind him during the long years of failure; perhaps he reflected that the difference of forty-three years between their ages was too great; perhaps, away from Gossensass, he felt old. At any rate, his letters from Munich to Emilie in Vienna are no more than those of an affectionate old man to a charming schoolgirl (though we must bear in mind that he was writing in a foreign language that 'gives him . . . much difficulty', that he was always an extremely inhibited letter-

---

[1] Extracts from Helene's diaries are given in C.E., XIX, pp. 173–181, and in J. W. McFarlane's Oxford Ibsen, VII, pp. 562 ff.

[2] Zucker, p. 292.

writer, and that he must have been very careful not to commit himself on paper):[1]

*Munich, Maximilianstrasse 32,*
*7 October 1889*

*With my whole heart I thank you, my beloved Fräulein, for the dear and delightful letter which I received on the last day of my stay at Gossensass, and have read over and over again.*

*There the last autumn week was a very sad one, or it was so to me. No more sunshine. Everything—gone. The few remaining guests could give me no compensation for the brief and beautiful end-of-summer life. I went to walk in the Pflerschtal. There there is a bench where two can commune together. But the bench was empty and I went by without sitting down. So, too, the big salon was waste and desolate . . . Do you remember the big, deep bay-window on the right from the verandah? What a charming niche! The flowers and plants are still there, smelling so sweetly—but how empty!—how lonely!—how forsaken!*

*We are back here at home—and you in Vienna. You write that you feel surer of yourself, more independent, happier. How glad I am of these words! I shall say no more.*

*A new poem begins to dawn in me. I want to work on it this winter, transmuting into it the glowing inspiration of the summer. But the end may be disappointment. I feel it. It is my way. I told you once that I only correspond by telegraph. So take this letter as it is. You will know what it means. A thousand greetings from*

*Your devoted*
*H.I.*

The 'poem' (the Norwegian word *digt* means, like the Greek *poema*, not merely something in verse but a 'thing of creation') may have been *Hedda Gabler*, which he was to write the following year, or it may have been *The Master Builder*, which he did not write until three years later but may have conceived at this stage and then deliberately put aside until he could consider it with more detachment.[2] On receiving this letter, Emilie, the following day, noted in her diary:

'A few words before I go to bed. I have good news. Today, at last, came Ibsen's long-expected letter. He wants me to read between the lines. But do not the lines themselves say enough? This evening I paid Grandmamma a quite unpleasant visit. The weather is hot and stuffy and so is Pappa's

---

[1] I quote these letters in Basil King's translation, with a few emendations.
[2] Or it may, as Else Høst argues (*Hedda Gabler, en monografi*, Oslo, 1958, pp. 80–81), have been a play that never got written.

mood. In other days, this would have depressed me; but now I have something to keep me up.'

We do not know how she replied to Ibsen, for he did not preserve her letter.
On 15 October, however, he writes again:

*I receive your letter with a thousand thanks—and have read it, and read it again.
Here I sit as usual at my desk, and would gladly work, but cannot do so.*

*My imagination is ragingly at work, but is always straying to where in working
hours it should not. I cannot keep down the memories of the summer, neither do I
want to. The things we have lived through I live again and again—and still again. To
make of them a poem is for the time being impossible.*

*For the time being?*

*Shall I ever succeed in the future? And do I really wish that I could and would so
succeed?*

*For the moment, at any rate, I cannot—or so I believe. That I feel—that I know.
And yet it must come. Decidedly it must come. But will it? Or can it?*

*Ah, dear Fräulein—but forgive me!—you wrote so charmingly in your last—no,
no! God forbid! in your previous letter you wrote so charmingly: 'I am not Fräulein
for you.'—So, dear Child—for that you surely are for me—tell me—do you remember
that once we talked about Stupidity and Madness—or, more correctly, I talked about
it—and you took up the role of teacher, and remarked, in your soft, musical voice,
and with your far-away look, that there is always a difference between Stupidity and
Madness . . . Well, then, I keep thinking over and over again: Was it a Stupidity or
was it Madness that we should have come together? Or was it both Stupidity and
Madness? Or was it neither?*

*I believe the last is the only supposition that would stand the test. It was a simple
necessity of nature. It was equally our fate . . .*

*Your always devoted*
*H.I.*

Of this letter, Emilie wrote in her diary:

'I left it unopened until I had finished everything, and could read it
quietly. But I was not quiet after reading it. Why does he not tell me of
something to read which would feed my mind instead of writing in a way
to inflame my already excited imagination? I shall answer very soberly.'

Before he wrote to her again, he had started up a close acquaintance (it was
never to be anything more, with any of the young girls who henceforth
successively seized and filled his imagination) with his other youthful admirer
from Gossensass, Helene Raff. Determined to meet him again when he had no

I

Emilie to dazzle him, Helene spent several days walking up and down Maximilianstrasse until at last, on 19 October, she was successful. The next morning she ran into him again at an art exhibition; and later that day, they saw each other again. Five days later, having meanwhile primed herself by reading Otto Brahm's pamphlet on him, she waylaid Ibsen in Maximilianstrasse, accompanied him to his apartment and spent an hour with him, which she found 'very interesting, but rather upsetting'. He spoke about hypnosis and the power of the will. 'He underlined that women's will in particular tends to remain undeveloped; we dream and wait for something unknown that will give our lives meaning. As a result of this women's emotional lives are unhealthy, and they fall victims to disappointment.' The words precisely enshrine the theme of the play he was about to write, *Hedda Gabler*. When Helene left he saw her down to the courtyard, and there they kissed.

They do not seem to have met for a fortnight after this, and in the meantime, on 29 October, four days after that meeting with Helene, he wrote again to Emilie:

*I have been meaning every day to write you a few words, but I wanted to enclose the photograph. This is still not ready, and my letter must go off without it . . .*

*How charmingly you write! Please keep sending me a few lines, whenever you have a half hour not good for anything else.*

*So you leave my letters unopened till you are alone and quite undisturbed! Dear child! I shall not try to thank you. That would be superfluous. You know what I mean.*

*Don't be uneasy because just now I cannot work. In the back of my mind I am working all the time. I am dreaming over something which, when it has ripened, will become a poem.*

*Someone is coming. Can write no further. Next time a longer letter. Your truly devoted.*

*H.I.*

Emilie's diary:

'I wrote to him on Monday, very late at night. Though I was tired, I did not want to put off doing so, because I had to thank him for the books I received on Sunday. The same evening I had read *Rosmersholm*, parts of which are very fine. I have had to make so many duty calls, but this and a great many other things I can stand better than I used to. They are only the outward things, my inner world is something very different. Oh, the terror and beauty of having him care about me as he never cared about anyone else! But when he is suffering he calls it *hohes, schmerzliches Glück*—high and painful joy!'

Helene noted in her diary for 7 November: 'Painted in afternoon, then went in vain to Maximilianstr.' But the next day she was luckier, and was 'touched by his pleasure at my coming'. The day after that: 'Visited Frau Ibsen, he also present. Extraordinary situation!' Suzannah told her how at the time of their marriage Ibsen 'had an easel and wanted to paint; but I did not like that; I thought a dramatist should not divide himself.' Three days later: 'Met Ibsen in evening, he wants to visit me—I was much relieved. He accompanied me home; tender parting.' It pleased him when she told him she had been educated at home, not at school or in church (her father was a composer).[1] 'Well, then', he declared, 'you are a little heathen!' Then, becoming serious, he said: 'That is the education of the future, without state, school or church', and suddenly seized her hands as though in triumph and cried: 'Yes, yes, child, the future is ours!' And then: 'Only when one is free of the mass of inherited opinions which school and church hand down can one become outwardly and inwardly strong like you, who are like a child of the forest.'

Six days later, on 18 November, he visited her in her studio, bringing a copy of Jæger's biography with him. Helene asked him why he liked her and what he saw in her.

'He replied: "You are youth, child, youth personified—and I need that—for my work, my writing." I was troubled that he used certain phrases which reminded me of what Fräulein Bardach had told me. I asked him not to speak to me as he had to her, to which he naïvely answered: "Oh, that was in the country. In town one is more in earnest." '

Helene was clearly displacing Emilie as the object of his affections, for two reasons: she was in Munich while Emilie was in Vienna and (it is a fair assumption) she was less emotionally demanding. He had, in Solness's phrase, offered Emilie a kingdom, and she, like Hilde, did not regard the offer as a joke. Helene, much cooler and harder-headed, seems to have wanted no more from Ibsen than he was giving her, admiration and flattering companionship. The day after this last meeting with Helene he wrote to Emilie in a noticeably cooler (though still affectionate) mood:

*At last I can send you the new picture. I hope you may find it a better likeness than the one you have already. A German sketch of my life will appear within a few days, and you will receive it at once. Read it when you have time. It will tell you my story to the end of last year.*

*Heartfelt thanks for your dear letter; but what do you think of me for not having*

[1] Joachim Raff, well known in his time. Amongst other things he was the author of a popular tarantella.

*answered it earlier? And yet—you know it well—you are always in my thoughts, and will remain there. An active exchange of letters is on my side an impossibility. I have already said so. Take me as I am.*

*I am greatly preoccupied with the preparations for my new play. Sit tight at my desk the whole day. Go out only towards evening. I dream and remember and write. To dream is fine; but the reality at times can still be finer.*

*Your most devoted*

*H.I.*

On the back of the photograph Ibsen had inscribed: '*An die Maisonne eines Septemberlebens*'—'To the May sun of a September life'.

On 28 November Ibsen and Suzannah both visited Helene at her studio; the next day she went to them, and that same evening he wrote her a letter:

*Dear Child!*

*How beautiful, how lovable of you to visit us yesterday! My wife is so deeply fond of you. And I—too. As you sat there in the dusk and spoke to us so sensibly, so understandingly, do you know what I thought and wished? No, you cannot. I wished: ah, if only I had such a sweet and lovely daughter.*

*Come and visit us again very soon. But in the meantime keep working hard in your studio. You must not let yourself be distracted.*

*Blessings on your dear head.*

*Your devoted*

*H.I.*

Helene was baffled at the way Ibsen was drawing Suzannah into their relationship. When, one evening, a couple of weeks later, she hovered on Maximilianstrasse in the hope of seeing him, and was successful, 'he towed me off to his wife; I was confused and vexed.' Helene did not yet comprehend, any more than Emilie ever would, that, as she phrased it nearly forty years later: 'Ibsen's relations with young girls had in them nothing whatever of infidelity in the usual sense of the term, but arose solely from the needs of his imagination; as he himself said, he sought out youth because he needed it for his poetic production.'[1] Some fanciful theories have been advanced to explain Ibsen's unwillingness to attempt to develop any of his infatuations into a full sexual relationship, when his plays show him to have been (to borrow Emilie's metaphor) a volcanically passionate man. But there are many passionate men who are terrified by the reality of sex, even to the point of impotence when offered it, and Dr Edvard Bull's evidence about Ibsen's unwillingness to

---

[1] Letter from Helene Raff to A. E. Zucker, 8 December 1927, quoted by Zucker, p. 242.

THE SUMMER IN GOSSENSASS

expose his sexual organ even during medical examination suggests that this may well have been Ibsen's tragedy. Neither Solness, Borkman nor Rubek, the three most obvious self-portraits among Ibsen's characters, suffered from this inhibition (or did Rubek? He never touched Irene, and his wife was unsatisfied). But John Rosmer and Alfred Allmers (in *Little Eyolf*) were both sexually shy; and so was the chief character of the play which he was now planning, 'tight at my desk', and which he might well have sub-titled: *Portrait of the Dramatist as a Young Woman*. 'The great tragedy of life', he wrote in his notes for *Hedda Gabler*, 'is that so many people have nothing to do but yearn for happiness without ever being able to find it'; and 'It is a great delusion that one only loves one person.'

A psychiatrist's view of Ibsen may be noted here. On reading the first volume of this biography a distinguished member of that profession, and a distinguished author in his field, Dr Anthony Storr, wrote to me:

'Ibsen appears to have been what psychiatrists call an obsessional character. This type of person is generally meticulous about cleanliness, disturbed by disorder, punctilious, punctual and polite. He is often tied to routine—for example, may feel compelled to take his clothes off and put them on in a particular order. If he becomes neurotic, he may be plagued by irrational thoughts which he cannot banish; parsons fear that swear-words may interrupt their sermons, etc. Ritual cleanliness—compulsive hand-washing, for example—attains a symbolic significance. This kind of character is built upon a fear of letting instincts or emotional forces loose. Emotions must be controlled, for spontaneity is dangerous. Such people find it difficult to 'let go' physically or emotionally. They are often constipated and may also have difficulty in reaching orgasm. As a colleague has put it: "the obsessional defence leads to antagonism to emotion as such and feelings come to be regarded as intruders which disturb the orderliness of the world of which the obsessional has made himself master".[1] Creative people of this temperament may be led into creativity because they (a) want to create an imaginary world in which everything can be controlled, and (b) want to avoid the unpredictability and spontaneity of real relationships with real people.'

A week after leaving Helene 'confused and vexed', on 6 December, Ibsen wrote in a warmer manner than of late to Emilie:

*Two dear, dear letters have I had from you, and answered neither till now. What do you think of me? But I cannot find the quiet necessary to writing you anything*

---

[1] Dr Charles Rycroft, *Anxiety and Neurosis* (London, 1968).

*orderly or straightforward. This evening I must go to the theatre to see* An Enemy of the People. *The mere thought of it is torture. Then, too, I must give up for the time being the hope of getting your photograph. But better so than to have an unfavourable picture. Besides, how vividly your dear, serene features remain with me in my memory! The same enigmatic princess stands behind them. But the enigma itself? One can dream of it, and write about it—and that I do. It is some little compensation for the unattainable —for the unfathomable reality.*

*In my imagination I always see you wearing the pearls you love so much. In this taste for pearls I see something deeper, something hidden. I often think of it. Sometimes I think I have found the interpretation—and then again not. Next time I shall try to answer some of your questions, but I myself have so many questions to ask you. I am always doing it—inwardly—inaudibly.*

*Your devoted*

*H.I.*

In her diary, Emilie repeated his words: 'It is some little compensation for the unattainable, for the unfathomable reality.' She wrote to him and he replied, again warmly and affectionately, on 22 December:

*How shall I thank you for your dear and delightful letter? I simply am not able to, at least not as I should like. The writing of letters is always hard for me. I think I have told you so already, and you will in any case have noticed it for yourself.*

*I read your letter over and over, for through it the voice of the summer awakens so clearly. I see—I experience again—the things we lived together. As a lovely creature of the summer, dear Princess, I have known you, as a being of the season of butterflies and wild flowers. How I should like to see you as you are in winter! I am always with you in spirit. I see you in the Ring Strasse, light, quick, poised like a bird, gracious in velvet and furs. In soirées, in society, I also see you, and especially at the theatre, leaning back, a tired look in your mysterious eyes. I should like, too, to see you at home, but here I don't succeed, as I haven't the data. You told me so little of your home-life— hardly anything definite. As a matter of fact, dear Princess, in many important details we are strangers to each other . . .*

*More than anything I should like to see you on Christmas night at home, where I suppose you will be. As to what happens to you there, I have no clear idea. I only imagine—to myself.*

*And then I have a strange feeling that you and Christmas don't go well together. But who knows? Perhaps you do. In any case accept my heartfelt wishes and a thousand greetings.*

*Your ever devoted*

*H.I.*

That same day, 22 December 1889, Emilie wrote to him from Vienna, enclosing at last her photograph. It is one of the only two letters from her which have survived:

> Sunday.
>
> Here is the photograph—very unlike the original—to wish you a happy Christmas. Are you satisfied with it? Do you think it a good one? I don't think any better picture of me can be expected, but I hope it may give you some small pleasure. Now I must confess that I have had this proof for a fortnight—I kept it back so long in order to send it to you as a Christmas greeting. It was hard to keep it a secret from you for so long, but I wanted to have some little thing to contribute to the lovely holiday.
>
> Should I play no role at all in that? It's bad enough that I am not able to do more. In spite of my '*Nicht Rönnaug*' a few weeks ago I painted a trifle for you which would have been altogether pointless if it did not recall Gossensass. I used to buy little deer bells there, and since I so often met you on my way home from my study trip to the Strassberg ruins I perpetuated the picture on one of these bells. Then I waited for your son to come here as I would have liked to give it to him to take to you—but he didn't come and it seemed too small a thing to make a business of sending it. I will be silent for a while, then I will be able to tell you better about that. How much longer are you going to make me wait? This detailed letter which is to tell me so much—but no don't think this is a reproach—I don't mean it like that. I will send a Christmas greeting to your wife—I must write a few words just to her.
>
> Well, once more many tender wishes and regards.
>
> > Sincerely
> > Emilie.

On Christmas Day Helene paid an afternoon visit to the Ibsens but saw only Suzannah and Sigurd there—'she very kind, the son very dull'. Four days later she went again to Maximilianstrasse in the hope of seeing him, but 'in vain'. On New Year's Eve: 'With Aunt again to Maximilianstr., where we met Ibsen . . . He promises I may paint him . . . To bed contented.' The previous day, he had written to Emilie:

> *Your lovely and charming picture, so eloquently like you, has given me a wholly indescribable joy. I thank you for it a thousand times, and straight from the heart. How you have brought back, now in midwinter, those brief, sunny summer days!*
>
> *So, too, I thank you from the heart for your dear, dear letter. From me you must expect no more than a few words. I lack the time, and the necessary quiet and solitude, to write to you as I should like . . .*

Shortly before Christmas Ibsen fell a victim to the influenza epidemic which swept Europe that winter (this, presumably, was why Helene did not see him on her Christmas visit to Maximilianstrasse). It was the first time he had been ill for twenty-eight years; but with his iron constitution he threw it off. Emilie, in Vienna, caught it too. 'How sorry I am', Ibsen wrote to her on 16 January, 'to learn that you, too, have been ill. But what do you think? I had a strong presentiment that it was so. In my imagination I saw you lying in bed, pale, feverish, but sweet and lovely as ever . . . How thankful I am that I have your charming picture!'

But he had made the decision to break off their correspondence. Her next letter to him has not survived; but on 6 February he wrote to her:

*Long, very long, have I left your last, dear letter—read and read again—without an answer. Take today my heartfelt thanks for it, though given in very few words. Henceforth, till we see each other face to face, you will hear little from me, and very seldom. Believe me, it is better so. It is the only right thing. It is a matter of conscience with me to end our correspondence, or at least to limit it. You yourself should have as little to do with me as possible. With your young life you have other aims to follow, other tasks to fulfil. And I—I have told you so already—can never be content with a mere exchange of letters. For me it is only half the thing; it is a false situation. Not to give myself wholly and unreservedly makes me unhappy. It is my nature. I cannot change it. You are so delicately subtle, so instinctively penetrating, that you will easily see what I mean. When we are together again, I shall be able to explain it more fully. Till then, and always, you will be in my thoughts. You will be so even more when we no longer have to stop at this wearisome halfway house of correspondence. A thousand greetings.*

*Your*

*H.I.*

'Till we see each other face to face'—'When we are together again'—such words must have excited Emilie's most passionate hopes. And yet he wished to break off their correspondence. She replied to his letter of 6 February the following day:

Please forgive me for writing again so soon. All these days I have been intending to write to you, for it is part of my nature to feel anxious about persons to whom I am deeply attached if I do not hear from them for a longish while. Possibly this is a petty characteristic, but it is impossible to control one's feelings. Nevertheless, I mean to control mine, and since I know how sensitive you are in this respect I came halfway to meet you. Yes, I knew very well that you are an unwilling letter-writer, and from time to time I even felt that you might find my letters a nuisance. All the same, your last letter has shaken me badly, and I have needed all my self-control to conceal my feelings. But I don't want this to prevent you from carrying out your intentions. I certainly do not wish you to write to me frequently, and since you wish it I shall also refrain. However, I cannot allow myself to prescribe the problems and the moods to which, as you say, I should surrender myself in my young life. What I have so often told you remains unaltered and I can never forget it. Unfortunately the fact remains that I cannot surrender myself completely, nor taste unalloyed enjoyment. Forgive me for drawing you into a conflict with fate. That is ungrateful of me, seeing that you have so often said to me that whatever happens we shall remain good friends, and that I must hold fast to that. And is it friendship not to know if the other is ill or well, happy or wretched? And then can I prevent the thought coming to me that *you* want to avoid seeing me again, and anyhow, if you do not write, how am I to know where we can find each other again? Well, I'll be very, very patient; I can wait, but I shall suffer very much if I don't get a line or a book from you from time to time, or some other proof that you think of me. I am not noble enough to dispense with such little proofs of your interest.

Ought I to be ashamed of my frankness? Will you think less of me for not wishing to give up what has made me so happy and more contented through all these months? I know you a little and that is why I understand so much that is in you, but I am sure that *your conscience* should never hinder you from continuing to write to me. By so doing you only show your kindness. I will try to understand all other reasons that may prevent you from writing and certainly I don't want you to act against your feelings. What a multitude of things there are to write about, but you do not wish me to write, even though I should not expect an answer.

Tonight I have an invitation to a ball—with friends; I never go out in public. When I am there I shall allow myself to think a little about you because I often find parties like these extremely uninspiring, unless I have something of my own to fall back on. Anyhow, I mean to go, if I can.

> With love
> Emilie.

Emilie made no entries in her diary for four days after receiving the news that Ibsen wished to break off their correspondence. Then she writes of balls, singing lessons, domestic duties. Then suddenly: 'What is my inner life after Ibsen's letter? I wrote at once and henceforth will be silent.' Ten days later: 'Will he never write any more? I cannot think about it. Who could? And yet, not to do so is in his nature. In his very kindness there is often cruelty.'

For seven months he did not write to her. In September he broke his silence to send her a short letter of sympathy on the death of her father, with some news of himself and his family, but no more. On 30 December he wrote, again briefly, to thank her for a Christmas present:

*I have duly received your dear letter, as well as the bell with the beautiful picture. I thank you for them, straight from the heart. My wife finds the picture very pretty. But I beg you, for the time being, not to write to me again. When conditions have changed, I will let you know. I shall soon send you my new play. Accept it in friendship—but in silence. How I should love to see you and talk with you again! A Happy New Year to you and to Madame your mother.*

*Your always devoted*

*H.I.*

She did not write to him again, nor did the meeting to which they had both looked forward so eagerly ever take place. For seven years there was no contact between them. Then, for his seventieth birthday, she sent him a telegram of congratulation. His letter of reply was the last message that passed between them:

*Christiania, 13 March 1898*

*Herzlich liebes Fräulein!*

*Accept my most deeply felt thanks for your message. The summer in Gossensass was the happiest, the most beautiful in my whole life.*

*I scarcely dare to think of it—and yet I must think of it always. Always!*

*Your truly devoted*

*H.I.*

Only once, as far as is known, did Ibsen ever comment on his relationship with Emilie. The German literary historian Julius Elias (later to become one of Ibsen's executors) tells that in February 1891, less than two months after Ibsen had made the final break with Emilie, he and Ibsen were lunching together in Berlin: 'An expansive mood came over Ibsen and, chuckling over his champagne glass, he said: "Do you know, my next play [*The Master Builder*] is already hovering before me—in general outline, of course. One thing I can see clearly, though—an experience I once had myself—a female character. Very interesting—very interesting." Then he related how he had met in the Tyrol, where she was staying with her mother, a Viennese girl of very remarkable character, who had at once made him her confidant. The gist of it was that she was not interested in the idea of marrying some decently brought-up young man; most likely she would never marry. What tempted, fascinated and delighted her was to lure other women's husbands away from them. She was a demonic little wrecker; she often seemed to him like a little bird of prey, who would gladly have included him among her victims. He had studied her very, very closely. But she had had no great success with him. "She did not get hold of me, but I got hold of her—for my play. Then I fancy she consoled herself with someone else." '[1]

This account by Ibsen of his relationship with Emilie is impossible to reconcile either with Emilie's diary extracts and letters to him, or with his letters to her. It reveals him at his most cowardly; and it came especially ill from one who preached the importance of responsibility. The girl he described to Elias was not Emilie Bardach but the Hilde Wangel he was about to create in *The Master Builder*; but from the time Elias published this account (just after Georg Brandes had published Ibsen's letters to Emilie) people identified the unfortunate Emilie with Hilde, just as they had identified Bjørnson with Stensgaard and Laura Kieler with Nora.

The change which Ibsen's relationship with Emilie wrought on him was immediate and drastic. For years he had deliberately suppressed his own emotional life; but his encounter with Emilie had awoken him to the realisation that, as Mr Graham Greene has somewhere remarked, fame is a powerful aphrodisiac. 'All the women are in love with him', Anne-Charlotte Leffler had written during his visit to Stockholm in 1887; but it had happened too late for him to gain any joy from it. Throughout his plays he had preached that whatever a man turns his back on gets him in the end; and now the chickens were to come home to roost with a vengeance. In 1887 he had startled his audience in Stockholm by describing himself as an 'optimist', and *The Lady from the Sea*, written the following year, had reflected this optimism. 'It is in some respects', Edmund Gosse had written on its appearance, 'the reverse of *Rosmersholm*, the bitterness of restrained and balked individuality, which ends in death, being contrasted with the sweetness of emancipated and gratified individuality, which leads to health and peace.'[2] But none of his five subsequent plays could by any stretch of the imagination be described as comedies. The mood of *Hedda Gabler*, *The Master Builder*, *Little Eyolf*, *John Gabriel Borkman* and *When We Dead Awaken* is, like that of *Rosmersholm*, 'restrained and balked individuality', and I do not think there can be much doubt that this stems from the realisation that for various reasons (fear of scandal, sense of duty towards Suzannah, consciousness of old age, perhaps the consciousness

[1] Julius Elias, *Christiania-fahrt: Erinnerungen*, in *Neue Deutsche Rundschau*, 1906, Vol. 17, p. 1462.
[2] Edmund Gosse, *Ibsen's Social Dramas*, in the *Fortnightly Review*, 1 January, 1889, p. 121.

or fear of physical impotence), he, who had suppressed his longings for so long, now had the opportunities to fulfil them but was unable to do so. As a result of his meeting with Emilie Bardach a new glory, but also a new darkness, entered into his work.

# SIX

## Portrait of the Dramatist as a Young Woman

## (1889–1890)

IBSEN'S NAME HAD come before the readers and audiences of various countries a considerable amount that autumn. In September August Lindberg, visiting Christiania with his company, gave a special performance of *Ghosts* for members of the city Workers' Association; the play had still not been performed in the capital in Norwegian. On the twenty-ninth of the month Otto Brahm and Paul Schlenther opened their Freie Bühne in Berlin (a private theatre modelled on Antoine's Théâtre Libre in Paris and likewise limited to members in order to escape the shackles of censorship) with a production of *Ghosts*. The cast included a promising young actress named Agnes Sorma as Regina. The Freie Bühne was to last only three seasons, but its effect on the German theatre was incalculable. On 25 October we find Ibsen writing to Moritz Prozor thanking him for his efforts in France, and on 3 November he addressed a similar letter to William Archer, thanking him especially for the 'handsome edition' (limited to 115 copies) of *A Doll's House* which Fisher Unwin had brought out, bound in vellum and illustrated with photographs of the Charrington-Achurch production. 'I have the book always on my table and it excites the lively admiration of everyone who sees it and who knows anything of the art of typography. I cannot deny that I am somewhat proud that a work of mine should have appeared in great England in such a dress.'

The previous day, 2 November, the *Academy* magazine had reported: 'Ibsen's vogue seems to be spreading through all parts of the world. A Dutch translation of *The Wild Duck*, one of the least known[!] of Ibsen's plays, has been acted this week in Amsterdam and in the Hague. A Russian version of *The Pillars of Society* is appearing on the stage of one of the St Petersburg theatres. *A Doll's House*, *Ghosts* and *The Young Men's League* are all being played in different cities of Germany. An English version of *The Lady from the Sea* will be published next week by Mr Fisher Unwin [translated by Eleanor Marx-Aveling with an introduction by Gosse], and we hear of more than one translation of *Rosmersholm* as ready to appear. Finally, there is a rumour of a complete edition of Ibsen's works, to be published first in New York, under the joint supervision of Mr Archer and Mr Gosse.'[1]

A few days earlier there had occurred the first respectable production (in English, at any rate) of Ibsen in the United States. On 30 October Beatrice Cameron presented *A Doll's House* in Boston, playing Nora herself, and toured it with fair success through several other large cities. But Ibsen's progress in the New World was slow, and it was not until the middle nineties that he was to gain any kind of foothold in the American theatre (and then thanks principally to visiting actors from Europe such as the Charringtons, Gabrielle Réjane and Herbert Beerbohm Tree).

On 7 November *Love's Comedy* received its Swedish premiere, at Gothenburg under August Lindberg's direction, with Lindberg himself as Guldstad and a new star, Julia Håkonsson, as Svanhild. The performance was a splendid success; the audience, Lindberg records, sat 'pale with astonishment' as the play, hitherto regarded as a literary pleasantry, turned out to be full of dramatic life.[2] *Göteborgs Handels- och Sjöfarts-Tidning* described it as the production of the season; and, as when Lindberg had taken the initiative in staging *Ghosts*, the Royal Theatre in Stockholm, which had twice rejected him as an actor, was quick to seize on the play's success and arrange its own production. Lindberg followed up the success of *Love's Comedy* by reviving *A Doll's House* in Gothenburg, where it went as well as ever.

Sigurd, after his promising start in the diplomatic service, had run into difficulties; he was still prevented from advancing further by the fact of his not having taken the Norwegian law examinations, and his proud assertion of his Norwegianness was a constant source of irritation to his Swedish superiors. Although his Swedish was as good as his Norwegian, he wrote his reports from Vienna, which the ambassador had to sign, in Norwegian, and thus they

---

[1] This last statement was not quite correct. There were two projects under way. Archer had been negotiating with the London publisher Walter Scott, who, encouraged by the success of the Havelock Ellis volume, agreed to bring out a collection of eleven Ibsen plays in four volumes (later expanded to thirteen plays in five volumes). Archer wrote to Ibsen on 1 November asking his permission, and Ibsen replied on 3 November accepting gratefully—'and I am particularly obliged to you for the terms offered in regard to the author's fee.' These terms do not seem to have been very generous, for only very small sums appear in Ibsen's account books and, as stated, the first volume alone sold 14,000 copies in five years. Archer did his work so energetically that the first four volumes appeared within a year, in November 1890. Gosse had meanwhile arranged with the New York house of John W. Lovell to edit a three-volume edition of the plays, which appeared in 1890–1891. The only translations common to the series were Archer's versions of *The Pillars of Society*, *A Doll's House*, *Ghosts* and *Hedda Gabler*.

[2] Lindberg, p. 270.

appeared on the Foreign Minister's desk in Stockholm. He caused further vexation by stating that he did not wish to serve in the Swedish Foreign Office; and when it was made clear to him that unless he agreed to do so he would not receive promotion he announced that in such a case he would resign. On 11 December Ibsen wrote to Emil Stang, who had succeeded Sverdrup as Prime Minister, asking him to intercede on Sigurd's behalf and reminding him that twenty-five years earlier he (Stang) had acted as intermediary in obtaining for Ibsen the travel stipend which had enabled him to go to Rome. But neither Sigurd nor the Swedes would yield, and that month he implemented his threat, to the considerable annoyance of his by now (in Norwegian eyes) embarrassingly pro-Swedish father. Sigurd's future wife Bergliot tells us that this was probably the first time Ibsen and Sigurd had disagreed as adults.[1]

Sigurd returned to Christiania and wrote a series of articles in *Dagbladet* attacking the conditions under which Norwegians serving in the diplomatic service were forced to work, and indicting his fellow-countrymen for their willingness to truckle to the senior partner in the Union. Henceforth, he was to be as lone a wolf in the sphere of politics as his father was in the theatre.

Thanks mainly to the productions (albeit unsuccessful) in Christiania, Stockholm and Copenhagen of *The Lady from the Sea*, the reprints of *The Pretenders* and *Brand*, and a number of small German payments, 1889 had been a rather better year financially:

|  | crowns | £ |
|---|---|---|
| Royalties for *The Wild Duck* and *Rosmersholm* at Residenztheater, Berlin, and Thalia Theatre, Hamburg | 411 | 23 |
| Royalties for *The Pillars of Society* at Cologne Stadttheater | 51 | 3 |
| Royalties for *The Pillars of Society* at Munich Residenztheater (from 1888) | 492 | 27 |
| Fee for *The Lady from the Sea* at Christiania Theatre | 2,500 | 139 |
| Fee for *The Vikings at Helgeland* at Darmstadt (2 pfs) | 116 | 6 |
| 7th edition of *The Pretenders* | 1,125 | 62 |
| Royalties for *The Wild Duck* in Breslau (7 pfs) and Berlin (1 pf), and *Rosmersholm* in Hanau (2 pfs) | 117 | 6 |
| Royalties for *The Pillars of Society* in Mannheim (4 pfs) | 169 | 9 |
| Royalties for *The Pillars of Society* in Munich (1 pf) | 61 | 3 |
| Royalties for *The Lady from the Sea* in Kassel, Halle and Berlin | 702 | 39 |
| Fee for *Rosmersholm* in Christiania | 405 | 22 |

[1] Bergliot Ibsen, p. 118.

|                                                                                                                                                                                   | crowns  | £   |
| --------------------------------------------------------------------------------------------------------------------------------------------------------------------------------- | ------- | --- |
| Fees from Royal Theatre, Stockholm, for *The Lady from The Sea* (5 pfs), *A Doll's House* (5 pfs), *The Wild Duck* (3 pfs)                                                        | 1,244   | 69  |
| 11th edition of *Brand*                                                                                                                                                            | 1,360   | 76  |
| Fees from Bergen for *A Doll's House*, *The Wild Duck*, *The Feast at Solhaug* and *The League of Youth*                                                                           | 640     | 36  |
| Extra fee for 7th edition of *The Pretenders*                                                                                                                                      | 75      | 4   |
| Fee from Royal Theatre, Copenhagen, for *The Lady from The Sea* (1st–11th pfs)                                                                                                     | 1,962   | 109 |
| Misc. German royalties                                                                                                                                                            | 893     | 50  |
| 50 per cent of French book sales from Count Prozor                                                                                                                               | 104     | 5   |
| Royalties for *The Pillars of Society*, *A Doll's House* and *An Enemy of the People* at Munich Hoftheater                                                                         | 607     | 34  |
| Fee for *The Lady from the Sea* at Svenska Teatern, Helsinki                                                                                                                       | 300     | 17  |
|                                                                                                                                                                                   | 13,334  | 739 |

Ibsen had told Emilie, in his letter of 19 November, that he was 'greatly preoccupied with the preparations for my new play. Sit tight at my desk the whole day'; but (as stated) it is unsure whether he was yet working on *Hedda Gabler*. Some notes which would appear to date from that October or November seem to refer to an idea he later abandoned; of two women friends who make a suicide pact, which only one of them carries out. There is a mass of notes and jottings dating (presumably) from this autumn, winter and spring, some in a notebook, others on odd sheets of paper, a jotting pad and even a visiting card; even the notebook entries may not necessarily have been written in chronological order, and we cannot be sure that he decided definitely on the theme of *Hedda Gabler* before the spring.[1]

Meanwhile, having severed his connection with Emilie, he was seeing even more of Helene, who made avid notes of their conversations. He told her that he needed very little sleep; 'four hours is enough for me', and defended his reticence. 'You must never tell everything to people', he warned her. 'To keep things to oneself is the most valuable thing in life ... I don't write letters willingly or well, mostly in a shorthand style. I can only speak freely through the mouths of characters in a play.' And even plays 'are always better while still unwritten than when they have become reality. So one prefers the unwritten to the finished work.' On another occasion he said: 'My plays make

---

[1] Cf. *C.E.*, XI, pp. 397 ff., and McFarlane, VII, pp. 474 ff.

people uncomfortable because when they see them they have to think, and most people want to be effortlessly entertained, not to be told unpleasant truths . . . People who are afraid of being alone with themselves, thinking about themselves, go to the theatre as they go to the beach or to parties—they go to be amused. But I find that people's eyes can be opened as well from the stage as from a pulpit. Especially as so many people no longer go to church.' He complained how badly his plays were usually acted, especially by 'actresses who declaim instead of speaking', but confessed that he did not interfere at rehearsals. On the subject of fame he said: 'I haven't written to become famous. But of course fame has served me in so far as it has created interest in my ideas and my writing.'

He inveighed vehemently against indolence, as people who need little sleep often do. Once, he told Helene, on a train journey from Rome to Gossensass, he had shared a compartment with a lady who had slept the whole way without once looking out through the window. Even the memory of her made him angry again. 'What a *lazy* woman! To sleep the whole way! How can anyone be so lazy?' On another occasion he remarked: 'Most people die without ever having lived. Luckily for them, they don't realise it.' He disappointed Helene by his almost (not complete, as John Paulsen and the New England lady in Rome supposed) lack of interest in music; he admitted to her that he had once 'positively wallowed' in Hans von Bülow's concerts—'and that says a lot, for music usually only makes me nervous'.

He spoke to her of Suzannah; and those who have assumed that, because he loved the company of young girls and longed for what she had never been able to give him, his relationship with his wife was now dead, should note his words. He admired (wrote Helene in her diary) Suzannah's 'intellectual quickness', and the way she maintained her own individuality. Despite her almost passionate belief in him, she would not hesitate to speak her own mind when her view differed from his. He praised her 'inner freedom and completeness of personality', a compliment, he added, which he could not pay to many people. Yet, while he admired strength of character, 'strength and subtlety must always go together. Brutal strength is something unbearable.'

We have seen how he admired, in Michelangelo, Bernini and the architect of Milan cathedral, those artists who had the courage to depart from accepted standards of taste, to 'commit a madness', as he himself was never afraid to do; and this, too, he discussed with Helene. He said he thought it was a longing that everyone possessed, though few yielded to it. As a schoolboy, he remembered, he had often yearned to hit his teacher over the nose with a ruler, without feeling any hatred for the man. 'This longing to commit a madness stays with us throughout our lives. Who has not, when standing with some-

K

one by an abyss or high up on a tower, had a sudden impulse to push the other over? And how is it that we hurt those we love although we know that remorse will follow?' (a thought that must have been much in his mind at that time). 'Our whole being', he added, 'is nothing but a fight against the dark forces within ourselves.' Those last eight words sum up the theme of *Rosmersholm* and *The Lady from the Sea*, and of the two plays he was to write next, *Hedda Gabler* and *The Master Builder*.

He told her of his dislike and distrust of abstract thought. 'Philosophical theories, unless put into practice, seem worthless to me.' On the subject of suffering, he remarked: 'It is not what we experience that matters, but how we understand it.' He spoke much of the importance of will-power. 'To me will is always the most important thing. Few people have strong wills. It always strikes me as comical when people tell me that something they wanted didn't work out. They have merely desired or longed for something, not willed it. He who really wills something attains his goal.' He had dramatised this theory in *Emperor and Galilean*. 'Self-realisation', he declared, 'is man's highest task and greatest happiness.' One of the tragedies of women, he thought, was that their will-power tended to remain undeveloped. 'They spend their lives inactively, dreaming and waiting for something unknown that will give their lives meaning. Their emotional lives are unhealthy as a consequence, and they become a prey to disillusion.' This was to be very much the theme of *Hedda Gabler*. 'What is healthy is the happiness one acquires through one's own will.'

On 19 March Helene took a small oil-painting she had done, apparently an imaginary portrait of Solveig in *Peer Gynt*, to Suzannah and asked her to give it to Ibsen on the following day (his birthday), as she herself would be away then. Suzannah thanked her but did not want to unwrap the present, saying: 'He must do that himself.' Helene feared the paper might stick to the paint, which was not yet quite dry, so Suzannah unwrapped it, liked the painting greatly, and said: 'I am quite sad to have seen it first—that pleasure should have been his.' She repeated this several times. When, on 31 March, Helene saw Ibsen and told him of Suzannah's remark, 'he seemed quite surprised, and said: "Oh. She doesn't say such things to *me*." Then he was silent for a long time.'[1]

His new play, *Hedda* (as he at first entitled it) was making the most painful progress. The character he was attempting to portray was of a complexity unprecedented even in Ibsen's work; it was a curious amalgam of himself and the young girl in Vienna to whom he had made such extravagant and unkept promises, and it involved the most searching and agonising self-analysis.

Promising news reached him in April from Moritz Prozor, his French trans-

---

[1] Letter from Helene Raff to Julius Elias, 26 June 1907 (*C.E.*, XIX, p. 534).

lator, who wrote that his version of *A Doll's House* was to be performed at the Théâtre de l'Odéon; also, less enthusiastically, that André Antoine was proposing to stage *Ghosts* at his Théâtre Libre, but in another version by Rodolphe Darzens. Since Ibsen had granted Prozor the French rights to the two plays, the latter asked Ibsen to intervene; but this he refused to do. Antoine later told Halvdan Koht that Prozor's translation was not sufficiently speakable,[1] and word of this may have reached Ibsen. He knew from experience how much his plays could be crippled by bad translation, and it is remarkable, considering the quality of most of the versions used, that they achieved the success they did.

The *Doll's House* project came to nothing (the play had to wait another four years before its first French production), but *Ghosts* was duly staged by Antoine at the tiny Théâtre des Menus Plaisirs—'a dark corner, deep hidden in a passage, and beyond this passage some ten feet of gallery', as George Moore described it—for two performances, on 29 and 30 May. Moore, who managed to get in ('Once the doors are opened, a thousand pounds would fail to procure you a seat. But M. Antoine is always anxious to oblige a *confrère*'), thought Mlle Barny excellent as Mrs Alving and Antoine himself 'wonderful' as Oswald, and declared the production to be the Théâtre Libre's greatest triumph since they had presented Tolstoy's *The Power of Darkness* two years previously, six years before it was allowed to be performed in Russia. Of the final scene of *Ghosts*, Moore wrote: 'Most assuredly nothing finer was ever written by man or god. Its blank simplicity strikes upon the brain, until the brain reels, even as poor Oswald's brain is reeling.'[2] The young Aurélien Lugné-Poe, shortly to establish himself as Ibsen's most assiduous champion in France, wrote of the occasion that it was 'a thunderbolt in French theatrical history. It can never be described how stunned and shaken we were that day.'[3] Antoine toured his production around France, presenting it for over two hundred performances.

As if Ibsen had not enough guilt on his conscience concerning women that summer, Laura Kieler now dramatically re-entered his life. Two years earlier she had sent him a play she had written called *Men of Honour*. As he had shown in the case of her autobiographical novel, he could be severe on work he did not like, but of this play he had written to her (23 July 1888) that he had read it 'with *keen* interest, and I think that *all* our theatres should *hasten* to perform it'. Poor Laura's luck had, however, continued. Dagmars Theatre in Copenhagen accepted it but went bankrupt before they could stage it, and although the Casino Theatre in Copenhagen put it on in 1890 and the Christiania

---

[1] Loc. cit.
[2] George Moore, *Impressions and Opinions* (London, 1914), pp. 162–167.
[3] Lugné-Poe, *Ibsen* (Paris, 1936), p. 11.

Theatre in 1891, it failed on both occasions. It was keenly and eloquently defended by Bjørnson, and brought her a number of grateful letters from young people; but the pleasure this gave her was more than countered by a vicious article from the pen of (alas) Georg Brandes who, reviewing J. B. Halvorsen's *Biographical Lexicon* (which contained a long section on Ibsen), went out of his way to assert that the original of Nora had committed her crime for reasons much less idealistic than those which had inspired Ibsen's heroine.[1] Laura wrote to Ibsen's friend in Stockholm, Fredrika Limnell, begging her to ask Ibsen to deny this and the other rumours that were circulating about her; and Fru Limnell wrote to Ibsen on 10 June, enclosing various press cuttings to show that Laura's complaints were justified.[2]

Ibsen refused; and his reply to Fru Limnell of 1 July is difficult to defend. 'I don't quite understand', he wrote, 'what Laura Kieler really has in mind in trying to drag *me* into these squabbles. A statement from me such as she proposes, to the effect that "she is not Nora", would be both meaningless and absurd, since I have never suggested that she is. If untrue rumours have been spread in Copenhagen that something happened earlier in her life which bears a certain similarity to the business of the forged document in *A Doll's House*, then she herself or her husband, preferably both, are the only people able to kill these rumours by an open and emphatic denial. I cannot understand why Herr Kieler has not long since taken this course, which would immediately put an end to the gossip. I am genuinely sad that I cannot accede to your request to intervene. But I think that on considering the matter more closely . . . you will agree that I can best serve our mutual friend by remaining silent and not intervening.'

Ibsen's attitude in this matter was as cowardly and hypocritical as his account to Julius Elias of his relationship with Emilie Bardach. Whether or not he had suggested that Laura was the original of Nora, she was, and many people knew it; and he could easily have written an open letter to a newspaper stating truthfully that her conduct had been deserving only of praise and flatly contradicting Brandes's assertion. Such an action would have established her as what she was, a figure no whit less heroic than Nora. Bjørnson would have done it; and was Ibsen so afraid of offending Brandes? But there was something of Pontius Pilate in him, as in Peer Gynt.

On 18 July there occurred in London an event that was ultimately to prove of great importance in the establishment of Ibsen's reputation. Bernard Shaw,

---

[1] As late as 1917 Brandes was still asserting that Laura got the money 'not in order to save her husband's life, but to beautify her home'. (Georg Brandes, *Henrik Ibsen: Personal Reminiscences and Remarks about his Plays*, in *Century Magazine*, New York, February, 1917, p. 543.)
[2] Kinck, p. 527.

then an unsuccessful novelist of thirty-four who had yet to complete his first play,[1] delivered a lecture on Ibsen to the Fabian Society at a restaurant in Regent Street. Since it was from this lecture (mainly devoted to *A Doll's House*)[2] that *The Quintessence of Ibsenism* grew, it is worth recalling the particular terms of reference within which it was written. As Shaw states in his original preface to the *Quintessence*, the Fabian Society had arranged a series of lectures under the general heading of Socialism in Contemporary Literature. 'Sydney Olivier consented to "take Zola"; I consented to "take Ibsen" . . . and . . . purposely couched it in the most provocative terms'. *The Quintessence of Ibsenism*, Shaw's first important book, was to perform a great service for Ibsen in drawing attention to his work; but it was one of the most misleading books about a great writer that can ever have been written. Had it been entitled *Ibsen considered as a Socialist*, or *The Quintessence of Shavianism* (not that the word Shavianism had been coined then), one would have no quarrel with it.

As a result of Shaw's lecture, a correspondent of the London *Daily Chronicle* questioned Ibsen on 12 August concerning his views on socialism, and next day the *Chronicle* printed the following report:

'In consequence of the continuous efforts of the Social Democrats to represent Henrik Ibsen as one of their party, and specially on account of the abuse of Ibsen's name by certain moral philosophers in England ever since *A Doll's House* was performed in London, I interviewed Ibsen, who since his return from Italy resides with his family permanently in Munich. Ibsen was very pleased to receive me, and glad to converse on the subject I had called to see him about. He declared that he had never at any time belonged to the Social Democratic Party. He never had studied the Social Democratic question, nor does he intend to join the Social Democratic Party at a future date. In fact, he declared he never was nor ever would be a Social Democrat. He was surprised to find his name used as a means for the propagation of Social Democratic dogmas. If a mere accidental coincidence of certain tendencies or principles involved in his book *Nora* with regard to the matrimonial and woman question are [sic] identical with or cover certain planks of the Social Democratic platform, his *Nora* is not, he explained, an abstract hypothesis conceived to demonstrate certain party dogmas, but was taken from life. Nora existed; but he never intended to lay down a hard and fast rule that all women in a similar position to Nora should or must act like Nora.'

---

[1] He had begun *Widowers' Houses* (at Archer's instigation) in 1884, but did not finish it until 1892.

[2] Cf. Bernard Shaw: *Collected Letters, 1874–1897*, ed. Dan H. Laurence (London, 1965), pp. 257–258.

This report grossly distorted what Ibsen had in fact said to the reporter. He had no intention of being used as a stick to beat the socialists in any country, and on 18 August he addressed the following letter to H. L. Brækstad, that Norwegian bookseller who had first introduced his works to Edmund Gosse in Trondhjem seventeen years earlier, and who had for the past ten years been living in London, where he was Norwegian consul:

*Dear Herr Brækstad,*

*Since an article from Berlin concerning me in the* Daily Chronicle *of 13 August strikes me as likely to be misinterpreted in several respects, as has already happened in Norwegian newspapers, I should like, for your sake and that of my other British friends, to correct some of the remarks attributed to me. I feel that what I said was not in all instances reported quite clearly or fully.*

*I did not say that I have never studied the question of Social Democracy. On the contrary, I have, as far as I was able and could spare the time, sought with keen curiosity to understand it. What I said was that I have never found time to study the great mass of literature on the subject dealing with the different socialist systems.*

*When the reporter quotes me as saying that I did not belong to the Social Democrat Party I would prefer that he had not omitted to mention what I added on the subject, namely, that I had never belonged and probably never would belong to any party.*

*In other words, it has become a necessity for me to operate as a complete independent.*

*The reporter's statement that I was astonished at seeing my name used as a means of spreading Social Democratic doctrines is likely to be especially misleading.*

*What I in fact expressed was my surprise that I, who had made it my principal task to portray human characters and human destinies, had, on certain issues—without having consciously or deliberately so intended—arrived at the same conclusion as that reached by the Social Democrat moral philosophers through scientific research.*

*This surprise—and, I may add, pleasure—I expressed as the result of the reporter telling me how someone, or some people, had given lectures in London which, according to his account, had been largely devoted to* A Doll's House . . .

*Your affectionate and bounden*

*Henrik Ibsen.*

This letter was published in the *Daily Chronicle* on 28 August, and must have given considerable satisfaction to all good socialists.

A few days after Ibsen had written the above, William Archer visited him, en route for Oberammergau. He described the meeting in a letter to his brother:

'His fame in England is, as he says, "a fairy tale" to him . . . He is obviously older, but looks very well and is quite alert and cheerful. He trotted me round a vast exhibition of modern pictures, where there is a portrait of himself by a Norwegian named Smith—a vivid enough but far from flattering one. He won't go into the room where it hangs, but waited round the corner. Just as I discovered it, an Englishman and his wife were standing before it. The man looked up his catalogue and said: "Oh, that's Ibsen, the Norwegian poet", to which the lady replied with the greatest interest: "Oh, is it? Well, now, that's just what I would have expected him to look like." I was tempted to tell them that they need only step into the next room to see the original; but instead, I reported their conversation to the "Old Man", who was amused . . .

'You would see from Shaw's letter which I sent you that Ibsen was supposed to be infuriated at being classed as a Socialist by G.B.S. He explained to me, however, that his rage existed only in the imagination of the *Daily Chronicle* interviewer. What he really said was that he never had belonged, and probably never would belong, to any party whatsoever; but he expressed himself as pleasantly surprised that English Socialists, working on scientific lines, had arrived at conclusions similar to his. This the *Chronicle* interviewer . . . twisted into an expression of unpleasant surprise that anyone should have the audacity to make use of his name in Socialist propaganda. The Old Man was quite put out about this, for the thing had got into the German and Danish papers too. While I was with him he received a letter from Wollmar, one of the Socialist leaders in the Reichstag, asking him what the devil he meant by this seemingly contemptuous disclaimer, not only of Socialism but of all sympathy with Socialism. Ibsen had already written a letter to Brækstad, intended for the English papers; and he forthwith sat down to write a German translation of this letter for Wollmar.

'Fru Ibsen and he had an amusing little scene apropos of this incident. She said: "I warned you when that man came from Berlin that you would put your foot in it. You should have let me see him; women are much more cautious than men in what they say." Whereupon the Old Man smiled grimly and said that wasn't generally supposed to be the strong point of the sex; adding that since the interviewer was going to lie about what he said, it didn't much matter whether he was cautious or not. Then Fru Ibsen suggested that he ought not to have seen him at all, and I closed the discussion by assuring her that in that case he would have made up the interview entirely from his own consciousness.'[1]

Archer found the rooms in Maximilianstrasse no more homely than the

---

[1] William Archer, *Ibsen as I Knew Him*, pp. 14–15.

apartment in the Capo le Case: 'lofty and handsome, but still, to my thinking, unattractive'.

Ibsen's unwillingness to commit himself to any political party has often been criticised; but he was not the only man of progressive sympathies who has felt unable to identify himself with the left-wing party in his country. He once said to Laura Kieler: 'I sympathise with all my heart with the cause of the left, in both Norway and Denmark. I am a man of the left, in so far as the left fights against what is conservative. But if they do not also make the workers' cause their own, then the left has shirked its task; I am no longer one of them.'[1]

The cause of the controversy in the *Daily Chronicle* himself almost met Ibsen that summer. Bernard Shaw was in Munich at the beginning of August, on a trip with Sidney Webb to see (like Archer) the Passion Play at Oberammergau; but 'my total ignorance of Norwegian' (he wrote to Archer on 17 August) 'prevented my calling on him during my stay . . . to explain his plays to him.'[2] The two could have conversed in German, and one wonders why Shaw did not make the effort; perhaps he felt he would make a dull impression on his hero in any language but his own. The two were never to meet.

Meanwhile, Ibsen had continued to make heavy weather of *Hedda Gabler*. On 29 June he had written to Snoilsky that he would probably have to sacrifice his summer holiday since 'I shan't leave Munich before I have completed the first draft, and there is little or no prospect that I shall get that far during July.' He did not even begin his first draft of Act Two until 13 August, and in the next three weeks he wrote only the opening stage directions (the scene was to take place in Hedda's garden) and three lines of dialogue; or if he wrote more, he destroyed it). There was obviously some deep technical or, more probably, psychological block. 'I am not likely to get out into the country this summer', he wrote sadly to Nils Lund on 24 August. 'I sit here fully occupied with my new work, and anyway the weather this year is not inviting for a country holiday. It is cold and rainy, with occasional days of intolerable heat and closeness.' On 6 September he started a new draft of Act Two, and at last the play began to move. Nine days later, the act was ready; the third act took him only twelve days, and the fourth and final act a week.

The play was at this stage still entitled simply *Hedda*; and the differences between this draft and the play as we know it are numerous and revealing. Apart from changing Tesman from an ordinary bourgeois husband into a ninny spoiled (like Hjalmar Ekdal) by loving aunts, he improved him morally, for he originally intended that Tesman should suggest hiding Løvborg's manuscript 'to frighten him'; then Hedda tells him to burn it 'to see if I have

[1] Laura Kieler, *Silhouetter* (Odense, 1887), p. 13.
[2] Shaw: *Collected Letters, 1874–1897*, p. 258.

any power over you . . . I know I have over him'. Miss Tesman's important account to Bertha in Act One of Hedda's life with her father was an after-thought; so were Mademoiselle Danielle, Mrs Elvsted's abundant hair and Hedda's jealousy of it, the image of the vine-leaves, and Hedda's threat (before the play opens) to shoot Løvborg. Thea knows that the 'other woman' who stands between her and Løvborg is Hedda; and Act One ends much less strongly than in the final version, with no mention of Hedda's disappointed hopes (the bay mare, etc.), or of the pistols. Tesman, like Thea, knows of Hedda's former close relationship with Løvborg; and Miss Tesman's role is much less rich than in the final version—she does not realise in Act One that Hedda is going to have a baby, and has a far less effective scene with Hedda in Act Four. Indeed, there is no clear suggestion that Hedda is pregnant at all. The conversation between Hedda, Løvborg and Tesman over the photograph album about the honeymoon contains a direct reference to Gossensass, sub-sequently deleted (no doubt for reasons private to Ibsen). And Brack, in a passage which one is rather sorry to lose, describes sadly to Hedda how three 'triangles' of which he was a part have been broken up during the past six months—not, as Hedda guesses, by other bachelors, but by intruders far more destructive to extra-marital relationships: children. Finally, one may note two remarks which Ibsen originally put into Hedda's mouth but subsequently deleted: (1) 'I can't understand how anyone could fall in love with a man who isn't married—or engaged—or at least in love with someone else' (2) 'To take someone from someone else—I think that must be so wonderful!' He saved these thoughts for a character, already created in miniature in *The Lady from the Sea*, to whom he was to allot the principal female role in his next play two years later—Hilde Wangel in *The Master Builder*.

On 18 September, while wrestling with his draft, he had briefly broken his silence towards Emilie to write her a letter of commiseration on the death of her father; but, apart from some news of himself and his family, he said nothing more, avoiding the emotionally evocative tone of his earlier letters to her. All this time he was continuing his meetings with Helene. While fair-copying his final draft, on 30 October, he took time off to write an affectionate note to an old acquaintance from his student days. Karl Hals had, with his brother, started a piano factory in Christiania in 1847, three years before Ibsen's arrival there. The factory was about to celebrate the manufacture of its ten-thousandth piano, and Hals invited Ibsen, for old friendship's sake, to attend the cele-brations. The invitation obviously stirred warm memories, for Ibsen (though unable to accept) sent an unusually affectionate reply:

*. . . I should like to send you my warmest congratulations for the occasion. I dare not*

*claim that I saw you working on piano no. 1. But one of the first of the long line must have been that on which you and your brother Peter were busy when we first met. It was in the autumn of 1850, and it was Ole Schulerud who brought me along. You and your brother were then living in the Cappelin building, where you had a little workshop. I remember well that you both actively partook in the work. As an assistant you had Thorman, who later appeared as an actor at the Christiania Theatre.*

*I was very fond of your brother Peter. He died, of course, many years ago. But I still remember vividly what a fine man he was.*

*So it is now forty years since we first met. Neither of us had much of the good things of life then. Not I, anyway. But since then the two of us have both done quite well, each in his own way.*

*You learned to love work early in life. The joy of work was not revealed to me until later. But then I learned to prize it richly and with a vengeance.*

*Now I sit down here, buried in a new play. I have not had a free hour for several months. For I receive an overwhelming mass of correspondence, and that has to be taken care of too. But none of this shall prevent my thoughts from being with you in your festive circle on the evening of 3 November.*

*Yours in sincere friendship*
*Henrik Ibsen.*

On 16 November, after nearly six weeks of revision, he at last finished fair-copying *Hedda Gabler* (as he had re-entitled it, as though to underline the fact that, though officially Hedda Tesman, she was her father's child, a General's daughter who should have been born a boy). Two days later, late indeed for a Christmas book (and how badly he needed those Christmas sales), he posted the manuscript to Copenhagen. 'It leaves me with a strange feeling of emptiness', he wrote to Moritz Prozor on 20 November. 'But I am glad to be done with it. Living incessantly with these imagined characters was beginning to make me more than a little nervous.'

That month the increasing English interest in Ibsen was marked by the publication of Clara Bell's translation of Jæger's biography; and he received sad news from Georg Brandes, of the death of the latter's small daughter. 'Your little girl lives in my memory in song', he wrote to Brandes on 26 November. 'The last time we were at your home she sang for us. I think I still hear that beautiful child's voice, and I shall always remember it.'

The next day he himself had sad tidings to convey to Julius Elias about their mutual friend Julius Hoffory, who had been living up to the character of Ejlert Løvborg which Ibsen had just modelled on him:

*He came here from Weimar about two weeks ago and settled in at the Hotel Roth, where he still is. Almost as soon as he arrived it struck me that his thought and speech were impaired. He had difficulty in finding words, and particularly in remembering the names of various people, even those close to him.*

*This condition of his has worsened daily. Dr Brahm saw him and spoke with him several days ago and will be able to tell you about that. I can only add that since Brahm's departure things have continued to go downhill with Hoffory. Yesterday I tried earnestly to persuade him to return at once to Berlin. But unhappily in vain. He made a pathetic pretext about some love affair which kept him here and which he had to settle before he could leave. I think his will is so broken that he cannot take the decision to pack his bag, ask for his hotel bill or go to the railway station. I think too that he is quite incapable of looking after his money. Both last night and the night before I saw him at the Café Maximilian try repeatedly to pay his bill after he had already done so.*

*Under these circumstances it seems to me obvious that he must get away from here. But how this is to be done I don't quite know. I beg you to discuss this with Eric Schmidt, who lives quite near you and for whom Hoffory has especial respect. Possibly an earnest insistence from him might persuade H. to return and put himself in the care of doctors who know the history of his illness. That is absolutely essential. Here he has no one whose advice he can, or will, ask. So he gets worse and worse every day.*

*I know from my own experience how ready you are to sacrifice your time and endeavours in the cause of friendship. That is why, in this sad history, I am turning to you. A man's life, or at least his future, is at stake.*

Hoffory, who was only thirty five, was removed to a sanatorium before the end of the month. He was later released, but never fully recovered. The following year he sent Ibsen a deed of gift bequeathing to him all his possessions —a dreadfully ironic situation to arise between Løvborg and his creator. He was to die insane at the age of forty-two.

On 4 December Ibsen asked Hegel to invest as much as 12,000 crowns (£667) in securities for him; and the same day he stressed in a letter to Moritz Prozor: 'I have not tried in this play to deal with so-called problems. My main object was to portray human beings, human moods and human destinies, as conditioned by certain relevant social conditions and attitudes.' Though happy to be reckoned a Socialist, he was tired of being branded as a sociologist, a reputation which Bernard Shaw's lecture, and the controversy it had aroused, had considerably fostered.

The English publisher William Heinemann, impressed by the constant publicity that was now being accorded to Ibsen in England—apart from the *Doll's House* production and Shaw's lecture, the first four volumes of the collected edition under Archer's editorship had appeared that November— had offered Ibsen £150 for the rights of *Hedda Gabler*, provided the proof-sheets could be sent direct from Gyldendal to Edmund Gosse (who was to translate it) as they came off the press. Ibsen happily accepted this windfall, telling Gosse (29 November) that he felt 'much bounden to Mr Heinemann for so liberal an honorarium' and expressing his 'deep joy and satisfaction at seeing how my writings increasingly win an entry into the immense territory of the English-speaking peoples, in which a foreign author generally has such difficulty in establishing a foothold.'[1] To secure his copyright Heinemann, then only twenty-seven and in his first year as a publisher, issued an edition of twelve copies of the play in Norwegian on 11 December, five days before the Gyldendal edition—a procedure he was to adopt with Ibsen's subsequent plays. On 16 December the Gyldendal edition appeared, in a printing of 10,000 copies.

*Hedda Gabler* received the worst press notices of any of Ibsen's mature plays, not excluding *Rosmersholm*. Bredo Morgenstierne, who had written a front-page tribute to Ibsen on his sixtieth birthday, regretted in *Aftenposten* (20 and 21 December) that, after the 'cleaner air and brighter perspectives of *The Lady from the Sea*', Ibsen had now reverted to the unpleasant thematic matter of *Ghosts* and *Rosmersholm*—'and the obscurity, the eccentric and abnormal psychology, the empty and desolate impression which that whole way of life leaves, is here stronger than ever . . . With the best will in the world one has difficulty in following the master's thought. We do not understand Hedda Gabler, nor believe in her. She is not related to anyone we know.' Alfred Sinding-Larsen in *Morgenbladet* (21 December) described Hedda as 'a horrid miscarriage of the imagination, a monster in female form to whom no parallel can be found in real life . . . far from likely to cause any joy or much admiration.' Harald Hansen, reviewing the year's drama in *Samtiden* (1891, p. 312), dismissed it in a sentence as 'an ungrateful play which hardly any of the participants will remember with real satisfaction'.

Even some of Ibsen's warmest supporters were disappointed. Gerhard Gran wrote sadly in *Samtiden* (1891, pp. 75–77) that the play 'awoke my curiosity without capturing my interest . . . It is a law, or anyway has until now been a law, that drama, in its present state of technical development, can only present comparatively simple characters . . . Everything that should make this curious being intelligible to us, her development, her secret thoughts, her half-sensed misgivings and all that vast region of the human mind which lies between the conscious and the unconscious—all this the dramatist can no more than indicate. For that reason, I think a novel about Hedda Gabler could be extremely interesting, while the play leaves us with a sense of emptiness and betrayal.' Gran's remarks explain why people who accepted Emma Bovary, Anna

<hr/>

[1] This letter, not in the Centenary Edition, was first published in Bredsdorff, pp. 43–44.

Karenina and Dorothea Brooke were baffled by Ellida Wangel, Rebecca West and Hedda Gabler. Neither actors nor audiences, nor even those who bought the play in book form, were able to read between the lines of dialogue as we can today.

Nor did the Swedes and Danes appreciate it. *Fædrelandet* thought the book should not be found on the table of any decent family. C. D. af Wirsén wrote in *Post- och Inrikes-Tidning*: 'One doubts whether reality can provide an example of Hedda Gabler. Certain traits are perhaps truthfully portrayed, but the psychological combination of these traits is without logic. And a dramatist should make his play intelligible as a whole, not unintelligible . . . Here and there things appear which strike us as very true, but they do not add up to anything which, taken as a whole, gives us the impress of truth. Still . . . we have no doubt that even with this play there will be many who will praise the Emperor's non-existent new clothes, and will pretend to discover in this *camera obscura* an infinitude of subtleties that do not exist.'[1] Georg Göthe in *Nordisk Tidskrift* (1891, pp. 171–175) complained: 'The whole characterisation of the play is obscure . . . They are alive, but only to a degree; deep inside them there is something abstract, cold, dead.'

Some of the critics were embarrassed that the first Norwegian author to gain widespread international recognition should give such a gloomy picture of their country's way of life and morals. Alfred Sinding-Larsen, in the *Morgenbladet* review quoted above, suspected him of pandering to contemporary European fashion. 'Ibsen is *fin-de-siècle*', he declared. '. . . As long as his works were healthy they remained unnoticed [abroad]. But . . . once his plays had the right tinge of darkness and comfortlessness, the right undertone of pessimism, Godlessness and despair, they were fitted to satisfy the contemporary craving for sensation and titillation . . . The fact that Ibsen has become fashionable does not mean that the works with which he has achieved this will have any real permanence or significance . . . Ibsen's modern drama is the drama of abnormality. His main characters have nothing human about them save the flesh in which they are clothed.'

Almost the only critics to appreciate what Ibsen was trying to do in *Hedda Gabler* were Henrik Jæger in Norway and Edvard Brandes in Denmark. Jæger, who had come a long way since he had stumped the country lecturing against *Ghosts*, wrote a late review in *Dagbladet* on 4 February, and after lambasting the other critics for their treatment of the play, he declared: 'Bigness and pettiness are so blended in Hedda's character that she belongs neither to hell nor to heaven but to earth. She is neither a monster nor a saint . . .

---

[1] Wirsén, p. 108.

simply a tragic character who is destroyed by the unharmonious and irrecon-
ciliable contrasts in her own character . . . Tragedy is not very popular in
Norway just now. People do not want to see tragedies on the stage . . . So
naturally the play is "foul", "contemptible" and "immoral".' And Edvard
Brandes, reviewing the Copenhagen premiere in *Politiken* on 26 February,
declared: 'Ibsen's latest play is being debated round the world. There are
today two or three writers who set people's minds in motion when a work
leaves their desk—Tolstoy, Zola—but a novel does not nag at the mind and
*demand* an answer like a play. Whether *Hedda Gabler* is in the top rank of Ibsen's
work is difficult to decide. For people who are interested in things of the
mind, Ibsen's plays are milestones in their development; people have *thought*
differently in Scandinavia since *Ghosts* and *Rosmersholm* . . . *The Lady from
the Sea* did not have quite the same impact, and *Hedda Gabler* too will scarcely
have a significance comparable to that of *Ghosts*. Many will rejoice that the
supernatural element is absent from *Hedda Gabler*. No white horses ride here,
no Stranger rides to Hedda Gabler by night.' He found Hedda like the heroines
of Russian novels—cold, scornful, ambitious to win men and oust other women,
*blasée* and eager for excitement. Though doubtful whether she would have
killed herself, he found the play 'gripping and powerful', and concluded:
'One may read it again and again and find new things to marvel at.'

One suspects, too, that, as with *Ghosts* (and, for that matter, *Rosmersholm*
and *The Lady from the Sea*) there were many young men and women whose
views were inadequately represented by the main body of printed criticism.
Carl Georgsson Fleetwood was probably speaking for many of his generation
when he noted in his diary his amazement that anyone should be puzzled by
the psychology of Hedda or think her unreal.[1] Herman Bang, one of Ibsen's
most eloquent Danish admirers, also saw the point.'Most of Ibsen's plays',
he declared perceptively in a lecture delivered in Christiania on 14 November
1891,[2] 'had been about egotistical men and selfless women; but here was a
play about an egotistical *woman*, and whereas a man's egotism may at least often
cause him to accomplish much, a woman's merely drives her into isolation and
self-adoration. Hedda has no source of richness in herself and must constantly
seek it in others, so that her life becomes a pursuit of sensation and experiment;
and her hatred of bearing a child is the ultimate expression of her egotism, the
sickness that brings death.'

*Hedda Gabler* is, today, perhaps the most universally admired of Ibsen's
plays, the most frequently performed (in England, at any rate), and certainly

---

[1] Fleetwood, II, pp. 1127 ff. and 1217.
[2] Printed in *Tilskueren*, October-November 1892, pp. 827–838.

one of the easiest for an average audience to appreciate. Why did it so baffle its contemporaries? Partly because, as stated, people who could comprehend a complex character in a novel, with the aid of narrative explanation and the character's reflections, were often helpless when faced with the same character expressed only through dialogue. And partly, too, because Ibsen was using a new technique, though it has since become so much a part of common practice in playwriting that it is difficult for us to realise that it can ever have been new. Several times in contemporary criticism of *Hedda Gabler* one comes across the comment that here, for the first time, Ibsen has virtually dispensed with long speeches, that he has written the play almost entirely in short exchanges of two or three sentences per character, a kind of dramatic shorthand. 'No concession is made to the general public to help it to understand', wrote Henrik Jæger in his review quoted above. 'No explanations by other characters, no self-characterisation to excuse or defend herself, even a minimum of information about events that have gone before—Ibsen has scorned all this as the quackery of salesmanship. Nor is that all. He has so striven to make the dialogue natural and lifelike that everything is chiselled out in very short lines, usually no more than a few words, seldom more than one or two lines.'

Edmund Gosse, reviewing the play in the *Fortnightly* on 1 January 1891, remarked: 'In the whole of the new play there is not one speech which would require thirty seconds for its enunciation, I will dare to say that I think in this instance Ibsen has gone perilously far in his desire for rapid and concise expression. The *sticomythia* of the Greek and French tragedians was lengthy in comparison with this unceasing display of hissing conversational fireworks, fragments of sentences without verbs, clauses that come to nothing, adverbial exclamations and cryptic interrogations. It would add, I cannot but think, to the lucidity of the play if some one character were permitted occasionally to express himself at moderate length, as Nora does in *A Doll's House*, and as Mrs Alving in *Ghosts* . . . On the stage, no doubt, this rigid broken utterance will give an extraordinary sense of reality.' But with actors and actresses looking less for reality than for big theatrical moments, it didn't.

As with most of Ibsen's plays, certain elements in *Hedda Gabler* can be traced to incidents in the lives of people whom he knew personally or had heard or read about. On his visit to Norway in 1885 he must have heard of the marriage the previous winter between a famous beauty named Sophie Magelssen and the philologist Peter Groth. Groth had married her on a research grant which he had won in competition with Hjalmar Falk, whom many thought the better scholar of the two (and who gets a consolatory mention in the play as the dead Cabinet Minister who had previously owned the Tesmans' villa). Neither Tesman nor Løvborg, however, was modelled on either of these two.

Ibsen told his son Sigurd[1] that he had based Tesman on Julius Elias, the young German literary historian whom he had got to know in Munich. Elias's great passion was for 'putting other people's papers in order' (which Tesman describes as his speciality); later he became a distinguished man of letters, and ironically it fell to him to put Ibsen's own papers in order when he shared with Halvdan Koht the task of editing the dramatist's literary remains.[2]

Løvborg was, as previously stated, closely modelled on Julius Hoffory, the Dane who had translated *The Lady from the Sea* into German and was Professor of Scandinavian Philology and Phonetics in Berlin; he mixed freely with women of low repute and had once lost the manuscript of a book during a nocturnal orgy. He recognised himself delightedly when *Hedda Gabler* appeared, and thereafter adopted Løvborg as his pseudonym.

At the same time, it has been convincingly argued[3] that Løvborg and Tesman both represent aspects of Ibsen's own self: Løvborg an idealised portrait of himself as he had been in the wild days of his youth, Tesman a *reductio ad absurdum* of what he had chosen to become; that Løvborg stands for his emotional self, Tesman for his intellectual self. Ibsen was haunted throughout the latter half of his life by the feeling that he had stifled his emotional self and that only his bourgeois and slightly ludicrous intellectual self had lived on; and although he had persuaded himself to accept this state of affairs, the encounter with Emilie must have reminded him forcibly of his self-betrayal.

Miss Tesman, George's aunt, was based on an old lady from Trondhjem named Elise Holck. Ibsen had met her a number of times during the early seventies in Dresden, where she tended a sick sister for three years until the latter died. He wrote a charming poem in tribute to her in 1874. She is the only character, as far as is known, who was based on a Norwegian original, and this may have influenced early critics who wrote that *Hedda Gabler* was the least Norwegian of Ibsen's plays and that the town (unnamed as usual) in which the action takes place was less suggestive of Christiania than of a Continental capital (though William Archer, who knew Christiania well, felt sure that Ibsen had that city in mind).

Three further incidents which came to Ibsen's notice found their way into the play. While he was actually working on it, a young married couple came to seek his advice; their happiness, they said, had been ruined because the husband had been hypnotised by another woman. Then there was the unfortunate case

---

[1] Cf. Halvdan Koht's introduction to *Hedda Gabler* in C.E., XI, p. 279.

[2] In fairness to Elias, one should add that Tesman is a much less ridiculous character in the draft of the play than Ibsen subsequently made him. His maddening repetition of nursery phrases such as 'Fancy that!' was added during revision.

[3] Arne Duve, *Symbolikken i Henrik Ibsens skuespill* (Oslo, 1945), pp. 315–326.

of the Norwegian composer Johan Svendsen, whose wife Sally, in a fit of rage at discovering a letter from another woman hidden in a bouquet of flowers, had burned the score of a symphony which he had just composed. Finally, he heard of the even more unfortunate incident of the Norwegian lady whose husband had cured himself of drink and had resolved never to touch it again. To see how much power she had over him, she rolled a keg of brandy into his room as a birthday present, and before the day was over he was dead drunk. All these episodes are reflected in *Hedda Gabler*.

What of Hedda herself? She has been rather glibly assumed by some critics to be a portrait of Emilie, on the grounds that both were beautiful and aristocratic and did not know what to do with their lives, and that Ibsen's description of Hedda (aristocratic face, fine complexion, veiled expression in the eyes, etc.) corresponds to early photographs of Emilie. The same characteristics could, however, be found in the photograph of almost any well-born young lady of the period (the description would apply equally to Queen Alexandra), and few women of Ibsen's time, let alone girls of eighteen, knew what to do with their lives. In any case, the idea of creating such a character had been at the back of Ibsen's mind long before he met Emilie, for his rough notes for *Rosmersholm* in 1886 contain a sketch of a girl, intended as Rosmer's elder daughter (though he finally decided not to include her in the play), who 'is in danger of succumbing to inactivity and loneliness. She has rich talents which are lying unused.' On the other hand, Emilie must certainly have been at the back of his mind when he was writing *Hedda Gabler*, and it is possible that Hedda may be a portrait, conscious or unconscious, of what Ibsen felt Emilie might become in ten years if she did not marry the right man or find a fixed purpose in life. If so, it was a prophecy that came uncomfortably near the truth, for Emilie, though she lived to be eighty-three—she died on 1 November 1955—accomplished nothing and never married.

But a Norwegian psychologist, Dr Arne Duve, has persuasively argued that Hedda is in fact a self-portrait, and that she represents his own repressed and crippled emotional life. Hedda longs to be like Løvborg, but lacks the courage; she is repelled by the reality of sex, as (can we doubt?) Ibsen was (what man not frightened of sex would be shy about exposing his sexual organs to his own doctor?); she prefers to experience it vicariously by encouraging Løvborg to describe his experiences to her. Two emotions are dominant in her, the fear of scandal and the fear of ridicule, and we know that Ibsen, though willing to trail his coat in print, was privately dominated by these emotions. But if Hedda is a self-portrait, it is almost certainly an unconscious one—not that that makes it any the less truthful; rather the reverse.

One contemporary who particularly hated *Hedda Gabler* was August

Strindberg, now fast approaching his 'Inferno' crisis when he hovered on, if he did not indeed cross, the brink of madness. He was convinced that Ibsen had based Ejlert Løvborg on him, as, six years previously, he had believed himself to be the original of Hjalmar Ekdal in *The Wild Duck*. He had, he explained to Karl Nordström on 4 March 1891, revealed some secrets about his private life to friends, and: '*Hedda Gabler* is based on this! And it's obvious that Ibsen has just patched this together from gossip, not observed it at first-hand . . . How can a man of talent be "destroyed" because he gets drunk, whores and fights with the police? It seems to me that Ibsen realises that I shall inherit the crown when he's finished. (He hates me mortally and had the impertinence to refuse to contribute to Jacobsen's tombstone unless my name was struck off the list.) And now the decrepit old troll seems to hand me the revolver a second time! But his shit will rebound on him. For I shall survive him and many others, and the day *The Father* kills *Hedda Gabler* I shall stick that gun in the old troll's neck!'[1]

Strindberg repeated the accusation in another letter four days later, to the poet Ola Hansson, adding the charge that 'Hedda Gabler is a bastard of Laura in *The Father* and Tekla in *Creditors*'; and, querying whether Løvborg could have been destroyed by a night's drinking, he added irrelevantly: 'For my part, I have always felt refreshed by a good debauch!'[2] On 10 March, he wrote to Birger Mörner: 'Do you now see that my seed has fallen into Ibsen's brainpan—and fertilised! Now he carries my seed and is my uterus!'[3]

The German publisher S. Fischer had bought the German rights of *Hedda Gabler* for the ungenerous sum of 300 marks (270 crowns, £15), exactly one-tenth of what William Heinemann had paid. He also wanted to serialise the play in one of his magazines, but Ibsen refused him permission. 'If Herr Fischer really believes that my play will mean so much to his magazine', he wrote to Julius Elias on 17 December, 'he need only print a much bigger edition of the book and advertise that he will give a free copy as a Christmas present to every subscriber.' He added that he had promised his German translator, Emma Klingenfeld, half of any fees he might get from German productions of the play, an extraordinarily generous arrangement, adding that 'on my table lies a mass of written requests from German theatre directors, including several from Berlin, begging for copies of the play so that they may stage it.' Ibsen was having a little trouble with Fischer. 'A few days ago', he wrote to Elias the next day, 'he explained in a letter that he could not possibly have the book out

---

[1] *August Strindbergs brev*, VIII, pp. 198–199. The accusation about Ibsen and the tombstone was, of course, completely untrue.

[2] *Ibid.*, VIII, p. 201.

[3] *Ibid.*, VIII, p. 205.

before the New Year. Now he thinks he can have it ready by Monday. A few days ago he assured me that I need not worry about competition. Now he seems almost distraught at the thought of Fru v. Borch. But never mind.' Fischer printed an edition of 3,000 copies, Ibsen's return from which works out at about a penny-farthing a copy.

Still, 1890 had been quite a good year financially, by Ibsen's standards. German payments totalled 3,386 crowns (£188), not much, but something; and even England had provided £75 (Heinemann's fee for *Hedda Gabler* did not arrive until he published the English edition in January, and then only after two sharp letters from Ibsen asking why he had not fulfilled his contract). But he must, as he looked down his list of earnings for the year, have noted sombrely how little his earlier plays were bringing him. He had received nothing at all from Norway or Denmark, apart from Gyldendal's fee for *Hedda Gabler*—there had been no performances of his plays in either country, and no reprints. No wonder that, although he had 110,310 crowns (£6,128) locked away in securities, he invested a further 15,000 crowns (£833) during the next three months.

| | crowns | £ |
|---|---|---|
| Fee for one performance of *The Pillars of Society* at Mannheim | 27 | 1 |
| Misc. royalties from Berlin from previous year, via Felix Bloch (agent) | 305 | 17 |
| Misc. royalties from Munich Hoftheater for previous year (*The Pillars of Society, A Doll's House, An Enemy of the People*) | 528 | 29 |
| Fee from Walter Scott (London) for collected edition | 906 | 50 |
| Royalties from Bloch for unspecified German performances of *The Vikings at Helgeland, The Pillars of Society, A Doll's House* and *An Enemy of the People* | 627 | 35 |
| Fee from August Lindberg for Swedish rights of *Love's Comedy* | 250 | 14 |
| Misc. German royalties for *The Pillars of Society* and *A Doll's House* | 228 | 13 |
| Fee from Royal Theatre, Stockholm, for *Love's Comedy* | 250 | 14 |
| Fee from Royal Theatre, Stockholm, for two performances of *A Doll's House* | 24 | 1(!) |
| Royalties from Bloch for German performances of *The Vikings at Helgeland* and *The Pillars of Society* | 96 | 5 |

|                                                                                      | crowns | £   |
| ------------------------------------------------------------------------------------ | ------ | --- |
| Royalties from Munich Hoftheater for *The Pillars of Society*                        | 167    | 9   |
| Misc. unspecified royalties from Munich Hoftheater                                   | 252    | 14  |
| Fee from Philippe Reclam, Leipzig publisher, for various of Ibsen's plays published by him | 889    | 49  |
| Fee from Walter Scott and William Archer for *Emperor and Galilean* and *Hedda Gabler* | 450    | 25  |
| Fee from Gyldendal for 1st edition of *Hedda Gabler*                                 | 9,000  | 500 |
| Fee from S. Fischer for German edition of *Hedda Gabler*                             | 267    | 15  |
|                                                                                      | 14,266 | 791 |

SEVEN

# ❧ The End of an Exile

## (1891)

1891 OPENED WITH A tremendous row between Ibsen's two British
champions, Edmund Gosse and William Archer, in which Ibsen found himself
an unwilling and embarrassed participant.

William Heinemann, as we have seen, had offered Ibsen £150 for (as Ibsen
supposed) first publication rights of *Hedda Gabler*. But Gosse did not send Ibsen
the formal contract until 2 January, and it then became clear that Heinemann
was demanding not merely the first, but the exclusive English rights, which
would debar Archer from publishing his translation of the play in the collected
edition which he was editing for Walter Scott. Archer, who had waived his
rights in the matter to oblige Gosse, not unnaturally complained to Ibsen, and
on 8 January Ibsen wrote to Gosse expressing the hope that Heinemann would
withdraw his veto and regretting that 'through an excess of trust I may have
helped to frustrate Mr Archer's intentions—something that his gentlemanly
conduct towards me has in no way deserved, and which lay very far from my
own intentions. The fee which Mr. Archer has sent me from Walter Scott for
*Hedda Gabler* I have of course returned. But the great collected edition will thus
be incomplete, and this I deeply regret.'[1]

This request was ignored. Gosse's translation of *Hedda Gabler* appeared on
20 January, and was the subject, three days later, of an uncharacteristically
violent attack in the *Pall Mall Gazette* by Archer, normally the mildest of men.
Archer described it as 'one of the very worst translations on record', which
'reproduces the terse and nervous original about as faithfully as a fourth form
schoolboy, translating at sight, might be expected to reproduce a page of
Tacitus'. Pointing out that 'some months ago I waived in Mr Gosse's favour a
position of advantage which I held in regard to *Hedda Gabler* . . . on the explicit
understanding that the privilege I thus transferred to him could not and would
not be used to impede Mr Walter Scott in completing his edition of Ibsen's
Prose Dramas under my editorship', Archer concluded: 'To find a parallel for

---

[1] Cf. Bredsdorff, pp. 44–45.

Mr Gosse's conduct in this matter, I need go no further than the play itself. Yet the parallel is not exact. It was by chance, not through an act of courtesy, that Hedda became possessed of Løvborg's manuscript; and having become possessed of it, she did not deface, stultify and publish it—and then claim copyright. She did a much less cruel thing—she burned it.'

Could any friendship survive such a betrayal on the one side, and such a public denunciation on the other? Amazingly, it did. Not only did Archer's translation of *Hedda* appear later that year, both independently and as Volume 5 of the Walter Scott Collected Edition; Gosse even included it, in preference to his own, in the Collected Ibsen which he himself was editing for Lovell's of New York. Indeed, as Archer's brother points out, 'the incident had the happy result of bringing Archer into relations with the firm [Heinemann] which was eventually to publish, under his editorship, the complete standard edition of the poet's works.'[1]

So that unpleasant matter was settled; and the first six months of 1891 saw an unprecedented number of productions of Ibsen's plays, as the following list shows:

| | |
|---|---|
| 27 January | *A Doll's House* in London (single matinée) |
| 31 January | World premiere of *Hedda Gabler* in Munich |
| 6 February | *Hedda Gabler* in Helsinki |
| 9 February | *A Doll's House* in Milan |
| 10 February | *Hedda Gabler* in Berlin |
| 19 February | *Hedda Gabler* in Stockholm |
| 23 February | *Rosmersholm* in London |
| 25 February | *Hedda Gabler* in Copenhagen |
| 26 February | *Hedda Gabler* in Christiania |
| 13 March | *Ghosts* in London |
| 31 March | *Hedda Gabler* in Gothenburg |
| 11 April | *The Pretenders* in Vienna |
| 15 April | *An Enemy of the People* in Vienna |
| 16 April | *The Wild Duck* in Vienna |
| 20 April | *Hedda Gabler* in London / *A Doll's House* in Budapest |
| 28 April | *The Wild Duck* in Paris |
| 10 May | *The Pretenders* in Berlin |
| 11 May | *The Lady from the Sea* in London |
| late May | *A Doll's House* in Paris (private performance) |
| 2 June | *A Doll's House* in London (new production). |

[1] Charles Archer, p. 175. Two years later, Gosse and Archer translated *The Master Builder* together!

Before January was out, *A Doll's House* was published in Italian, in a Rome theatrical magazine, *Carra di Tespi* (surprisingly, it did not appear in book form in Italy before 1895); and on 27 January it was performed in a new production in London, albeit only for a single performance. An actress named Marie Fraser, who had played the part a few months earlier in Edinburgh, acted Nora; Bernard Shaw thought her 'desperately in earnest and desperately bad',[1] but the *Athenaeum* (31 January) observed: 'Whatever may be the character of Ibsen's work . . . that its influence is growing day by day is one of the things that he who runs may read.' *Dagbladet* in Christiania (2 February) offered the interesting titbit that 'there is talk that the famous Mrs Langtry intends to play Hedda Gabler at the earliest opportunity'. Had this happened, Ibsen would doubtless have had the gratifying experience of having one of his plays attended by royalty, with one wonders what effect on the anti-Ibsen movement in England; but sadly (or perhaps, from an artistic viewpoint, fortunately) Mrs Langtry found other fish to fry.

On 31 January *Hedda Gabler* received its world premiere at the Residenztheater in Munich; but it was not well done, and Ibsen, who was present, was much displeased at the declamatory manner of Marie Ramlo in the title role. The audience was as baffled as the critics had been when the play was published. Ibsen took a call, and bowed to those who clapped; but there was a good deal of hissing and whistling. When someone commiserated with him afterwards, Ibsen shrugged his shoulders and murmured: 'The public likes to laugh.'[2]

On 9 February an Ibsen play was acted in Italy for the first time; Eleonora Duse, then thirty-one, acted Nora at the Teatro di Filodrammatici in Milan. Her translator, the novelist and critic Luigi Capuana, Pirandello's mentor, had asked Moritz Prozor (from whose French version he had made his own) for permission to change the last act so as to provide a happy ending; but a copyright agreement had recently been signed between Norway and Italy, which put Ibsen, at last, in a position to say No, and he did so. 'I can almost say', he wrote to Prozor on 23 January, 'that the whole play was written just for the sake of that final scene. And I think Herr Capuana is wrong in fearing that the Italian public would not be able to appreciate or understand my work if staged in its original form.' In Germany, he reminded Prozor, 'the play did not remain long in the repertory with the altered ending. But in its original form, it is still performed.'

The day after the Italian premiere of *A Doll's House*, *Hedda Gabler* was

---

[1] Letter to Charles Charrington, 30 March 1891 (Shaw, *Collected Letters, 1874–1897*, p. 287).
[2] Koht, II, p. 234.

staged at the Lessingtheater in Berlin. Ibsen went up for the occasion, but although the performance was better than in Munich it was not really a success. Even the critics normally friendly towards him found the play illogical, and the liberal journalist Theodor Wolff wrote a parody in *Berliner Tageblatt*. A Swedish producer, Adolf Paul, who was present, noted how Ibsen 'took a curtain call after each act, his face copper-red, and returned without the slightest change of expression to his box'.[1] The Danish novelist Henrik Pontoppidan, who was there too, thought that 'Ibsen cut a wretched figure. He looked like a troll that had been hauled up by the hair from the prompter's box.'[2] Ibsen gave a party for his friends before leaving the city, in a private room at the fashionable Dressel restaurant; the guests included Otto Brahm, Paul Schlenther, Paul Marx (the editor of *Der Tag*), Leo Berg and Ejlert Løvborg himself in the person of poor Julius Hoffory, now released from his asylum but a broken man, in dark glasses and black gloves. Ibsen moved among them, a genial host, constantly refilling their glasses with champagne.[3]

On 23 February *Rosmersholm* was staged for the first time in England, for two matinées at the Vaudeville Theatre in the Strand. Frank Benson, then a rising Shakespearean actor of thirty-one, played Rosmer, with Florence Farr as Rebecca; but it was evidently a far from satisfactory production. 'Archer was so disheartened by the rehearsals', wrote Bernard Shaw to Charles Charrington in Australia on 30 March, 'that I had the greatest difficulty in inducing him to come . . . Rebecca . . . got through by dint of brains and a certain fascination and dimly visible originality . . . Benson . . . forced his playing; but he did not distinctly fail except in the last act, which did not get for a moment on to the plane on which alone the catastrophe is credible.' At the second performance 'a sort of dim photograph of the play as it was meant to be was arrived at.'[4] 'Being ill produced and on the whole poorly acted,' commented Charles Archer, '[it] gave the anti-Ibsenites a plausible excuse to say "Aha".'[5]

---

[1] Adolf Paul, *Profiler* (Helsingfors, 1937), p. 114.

[2] Letter from Pontoppidan to Henri Nathansen, quoted in Elias Bredsdorff, *Henrik Pontoppidan og Georg Brandes* (Copenhagen, 1964), II, p. 135.

[3] Elias, *Ibsenminne af hans tyske oversetter*, pp. 405–406.

[4] Shaw, *Collected Letters, 1874–1897*, pp. 287–288.

[5] Charles Archer, p. 173. The main reason why the Vaudeville was so often chosen for early Ibsen productions seems to have been that it was regarded as an 'unlucky' theatre, and so was cheap and easy to hire. 'Who does not know', asked the *Academy* on 23 March 1901, 'the forlorn and furtive enterprises undertaken at "unlucky" theatres, with afternoon sunlight coming in through the side windows, at which Ibsen's masterpieces have been exposed to the admiration of the few and the laughter of the many?' Sir Lewis Casson, who as a young man attended several of these occasions, told me when he was over ninety that both William Archer and Elizabeth Robins imparted to the proceedings an atmosphere of puritanism to which Archer's translations also contributed, and that he thought this one reason why the tradition of presenting Ibsen's plays as totally humourless had, until very recently, survived in England.

His brother William collected some specimens of press reaction:

'A handful of disagreeable and somewhat enigmatical personages . . .
Ibsen is a local or provincial dramatist.'

The Times

'Impossible people do wild things for no apparent reason . . . Those
portions of the play which are comprehensible are utterly preposterous . . .
Ibsen is neither dramatist, poet, philosopher, moralist, teacher, reformer—
nothing but a compiler of rather disagreeable eccentricities.'

Standard

'A singularly gloomy and ineffectual function was that undergone at the
Vaudeville on Monday afternoon.'

Observer

'The stuff that Ibsen strings together in the shape of plays must nauseate
any properly constituted person.'

Mirror

'Ibsen's gruesome play . . . His repulsive drama . . . Greeted with the
silence of contempt when the curtain finally fell.'

People

'The whole affair is provincial and quite contemptible.'

Saturday Review

'To judge it seriously either as literature or as drama is impossible.'

St James's Gazette

'These Ibsen creatures are "neither men nor women, they are ghouls",
vile, unlovable, unnatural, morbid monsters, and it were well indeed for
society if all such went and drowned themselves at once.'

The Gentlewoman

'*Rosmersholm* is not very dramatic. It is hardly at all literary . . . It is
without beauty, without poetry, without sense of vista. It is not even
dextrously doctrinaire . . . The farce is almost played out.'

Mr F. Wedmore in The Academy

'There are certain dishes composed of such things as frogs and snails,
stews in which oil and garlic reek, and dreadful compounds which we taste
out of sheer curiosity, and which, if we expressed our honest, candid
opinion, we should pronounce to be nasty and unpleasant . . . *Rosmersholm*
is beyond me.'

Topical Times

'To descant upon such morbid, impracticable rubbish would be an insult to the understanding of every reader, except an Ibsenite ... If Herr Ibsen were well smothered in mud with his two creations [*A Doll's House* and *Rosmersholm*] and with every copy of his plays, the world would be all the better for it.'

*Licensed Victuallers' Gazette*

'Alas, poor Ibsen!' commented Archer. 'It is well that he does not read English, else who knows but the disesteem of the *Licensed Victuallers' Gazette* might drive him into his mausoleum in good earnest!'[1]

That last week in February was a bad one for Ibsen, or anyway for the theatres presenting his works. Two days after the *Rosmersholm* premiere in London, *Hedda Gabler* opened at the Royal Theatre in Copenhagen, and had the worst reception of any of his plays in Denmark. 'The public received *Hedda Gabler* coolly this evening', wrote Edvard Brandes in *Politiken* (26 February). 'Some hissed, a few even whistled; though there was also warm and loud applause ... After the close of the play the rival noises continued until the gong sounded ... The opposition to the play was not aesthetic ... People feel compelled to forbid authors to treat of the ugly side of life.' He admired Betty Hennings as Hedda, Emil Poulsen as Løvborg and Karl Mantzius as Brack, but thought that 'the play will not prove a financial success', and was right, for it was withdrawn after only five performances. In Bergen it managed only three; and when it was given in Christiania on 26 February the reception was again tepid. 'There was no real enthusiasm', reported Henrik Jæger in *Dagbladet* the next morning. '... The applause weakened as the play progressed. The net result was a success, but not one of those decisive successes we have grown used to when a new work by Ibsen or Bjørnson is performed.' The reason, Jæger concluded, was that Ibsen 'has treated the psychological conflicts portrayed here as Pasteur and Koch treat bacteria. The whole thing takes place in an abstract realm in which the public is not accustomed to moving.' Nor, the previous week, had the play fared better in Stockholm. 'No dramatic talent can make a character as obscurely complex as Hedda Gabler really clear and dramatically consistent', wrote Georg Göthe in *Ny Svensk Tidskrift* (1891, p. 175), and even Ibsen's champion J. A. Runström complained in *Ny Il-lustrerad Tidning* (14 March), of the obscurity which 'surrounds the central character like a thick fog'.

While Ibsen's latest play was baffling the Scandinavians, the ones he had written a decade earlier continued to be belatedly discovered abroad; and on

---

[1] William Archer, *The Mausoleum of Ibsen*, in the *Fortnightly Review*, July, 1893, pp. 79–80.

Friday 13 March 1891 there occurred one of the most famous of all theatrical occasions, as controversial and epoch-making as the first nights of Victor Hugo's *Hernani* or Synge's *Playboy of the Western World*: the London premiere of *Ghosts*.

Inspired by the example of Antoine's Théâtre Libre in Paris and the Freie Bühne in Berlin, a twenty-nine-year-old Dutchman named Jacob T. Grein, working for a tea merchant in Mincing Lane at £180 a year, had resolved to found a similar venture in London to stage plays from which the larger theatres shrank and which the censor would forbid. The era of the little theatres had begun, and it was from these that the new dramatists were to emerge; without the Moscow Arts there would have been no Chekhov as we know him, without the Dublin Abbey no Synge or O'Casey; in the following decade Strindberg was to found his own Intimate Theatre to perform his chamber plays. The next fifty years belonged not to the state- or city-subsidised theatres, still less to the commercial theatre, but to the little theatres, often possessing no locale of their own but performing in whatever halls or rooms they could afford to hire. They all lost money consistently and, except where saved by private patronage, ended by going bankrupt, as good theatres do.

The previous year Grein had produced Pinero and Henry Arthur Jones in his native Holland, and their plays had proved so successful that the Amsterdam Theatre sent him £50, to be used 'in the interest of art in England'. Thus, by a stroke of irony of which Ibsen would surely have approved, Jones, who had been chiefly responsible for the travesty *Breaking a Butterfly*, and was to be one of Ibsen's most vehement opponents in England, was also largely responsible for getting *Ghosts* on to the English stage. For it was principally with *Ghosts* in mind, since that play would obviously stand no chance with the Lord Chamberlain, that Grein added to his £50 another £30 which he had received for translating a play and founded, with Thomas Hardy, George Meredith and Henry James among its first members, the Independent Theatre Society, 'a modest organisation [as Charles Archer described it][1] of most slender resources, intended to give the non-commercial drama, both native and foreign, a chance upon the stage, by means of occasional subscription performances in theatres hired for the purpose. Since no money was to be taken at the doors, the performances would be technically private.'

The Society, then, opened its first season, as the Freie Bühne had opened its, with a single performance of *Ghosts*[2] at the Royalty Theatre in Dean Street,

---

[1] Charles Archer, p. 173.

[2] Plus a public dress rehearsal to hold the overflow. For a full account of the circumstances surrounding this production, see *Ghosts*, translated by Michael Meyer (London, 1962), pp. 95 ff.

Soho. Of the reception by the British press, William Archer noted: 'The shriek of execration with which this performance was received by the newspapers of the day has scarcely its counterpart in the history of criticism.' Three weeks after the performance, on 8 April 1891, he published in the *Pall Mall Gazette* an anthology of the choicest comments, worth quoting in full; for they show how Ibsen got under people's skin, whether they approved or disapproved of him:

## 'GHOSTS' AND GIBBERINGS

### DESCRIPTIONS OF THE PLAY

'An open drain; a loathsome sore unbandaged; a dirty act done publicly; a lazar-house with all its doors and windows open . . . Candid foulness . . . Offensive cynicism . . . Ibsen's melancholy and malodorous world . . . Absolutely loathsome and fetid . . . Gross, almost putrid indecorum'— *Daily Telegraph* (leading article). 'This mass of vulgarity, egotism, coarseness and absurdity'—*Daily Telegraph* (criticism). 'Unutterably offensive . . . Prosecution under Lord Campbell's Act . . . Abominable piece . . . Scandalous'—*Standard*. 'Naked loathsomeness . . . Most dismal and repulsive production'—*Daily News*. 'Revoltingly suggestive and blasphemous . . . Characters either contradictory in themselves, uninteresting or abhorrent'—*Daily Chronicle*. 'A repulsive and degrading work'— *Queen*. 'Morbid, unhealthy, unwholesome and disgusting story . . . A piece to bring the stage into disrepute and dishonour with every right-thinking man and woman'—*Lloyd's*. 'Merely dull dirt long drawn out'—*Hawk*. 'Morbid horrors of the hideous tale . . . Ponderous dullness of the didactic talk . . . If any repetition of this outrage be attempted, the authorities will doubtless wake from their lethargy'—*Sporting and Dramatic News*. 'Just a wicked nightmare'—*The Gentlewoman*. 'Lugubrious diagnosis of sordid impropriety . . . Characters are prigs, pedants and profligates . . . Morbid caricatures . . . Maunderings of nook-shotten Norwegians . . . It is no more of a play than the average Gaiety burlesque'—*Black and White*. 'Most loathsome of all Ibsen's plays . . . Garbage and offal'—*Truth*. 'Ibsen's putrid play called *Ghosts* . . . So loathsome an enterprise'—*Academy*. 'As foul and filthy a concoction as has ever been allowed to disgrace the boards of an English theatre . . . Dull and disgusting . . . Nastiness and malodorousness laid on thickly as with a trowel'—*Era*. 'Noisome corruption'—*Stage*.

### DESCRIPTIONS OF IBSEN

'An egotist and a bungler'—*Daily Telegraph*. 'A crazy fanatic . . . A crazy, cranky being . . . Not only consistently dirty but deplorably dull'—

*Truth.* 'The Norwegian pessimist *in petto* [sic]'—*Black and White.* 'Ugly, nasty, discordant and downright dull . . . A gloomy sort of ghoul, bent on groping for horrors by night, and blinking like a stupid old owl when the warm sunlight of the best of life dances into his wrinkled eyes'—*The Gentlewoman.* 'A teacher of the aestheticism of the Lock Hospital'— *Saturday Review.*

## DESCRIPTIONS OF IBSEN'S ADMIRERS

'Lovers of prurience and dabblers in impropriety who are eager to gratify their illicit tastes under the pretence of art'—*Evening Standard.* 'Ninety- seven per cent of the people who go to see *Ghosts* are nasty-minded people who find the discussion of nasty subjects to their taste in exact proportion to their nastiness'—*Sporting and Dramatic News.* 'The sexless . . . The unwomanly woman, the unsexed females, the whole army of unpre- possessing cranks in petticoats . . . Educated and muck-ferreting dogs . . . Effeminate men and male women . . . They all of them—men and women alike—know that they are doing not only a nasty but an illegal thing . . . The Lord Chamberlain left them alone to wallow in *Ghosts* . . . Outside a silly clique, there is not the slightest interest in the Scandinavian humbug or all his works . . . A wave of human folly'—*Truth.*[1]

One of the few English critics courageous enough to defend the play was A. B. Walkley. Writing in the *Star* (over the pseudonym of 'Spectator'), he asked: 'Do these people really find nothing in *Ghosts* but a mere hospital ward play? Is it really for them nothing but a painful study of disease? Have they no eyes for what stares them in the face: the plain, simple fact that *Ghosts* is a great spiritual drama? Like nearly all other great masterpieces of the stage, it is a drama of revolt—the revolt of the "joy of life" against the gloom of hide- bound, conventional morality, the revolt of the natural man against the law- made, law-bound puppet, the revolt of the individual against the oppression of social prejudice . . . This is the spiritual drama which I see in *Ghosts*.'

Bernard Shaw did not review this production (he had not yet a regular dramatic column), but he described the audience's reaction in a letter to Charles Charrington (in Australia with *A Doll's House*) a fortnight later. 'The Play was a most terrible success. After the first act the applause was immense. After the second, a third of the applauders were startled into silence. After the third four-fifths of them were awe-struck. When Grein came out, very nervous, to make his speech, a lady in the stalls said naïvely: 'Oh, is that Ibsen?,' throwing her neighbours into confusion. Then a man in the gallery cried out to Grein:

---

[1] The *Truth* article was by Clement Scott, who also wrote the *Daily Telegraph* review and leader.

"It's *too* horrible", and was instantly met with a sarcastic shout of "Why don't you go to the Adelphi?" [1]

The 1889 production of *A Doll's House* had established Ibsen as a force in the English theatre. The 1891 performance of *Ghosts* made his name a household word even among those Englishmen who never went to the theatre or opened a book. It elicited over five hundred printed articles. 'Behind the times indeed', writes a historian of the period, 'was the journal that omitted its daily column or so on Ibsen's iniquities . . . By the end of 1891 Ibsen was a name known to every reader of a London newspaper.'[2] In the November issue of the *Fortnightly Review* William Archer wrote:

'I can call to mind no other case in literary history of a dramatist attaining such sudden and widespread notoriety in a foreign country. His name is in every newspaper and magazine, his rankling phrases—call them catchwords if you will—are in every mouth. An allusion to Nora Helmer will be as commonly understood as an allusion to Jane Eyre. Hedda Gabler . . . is now as well known as Becky Sharp . . . This is the first time for half a century (to keep well within the mark) that a serious literary interest has also been primarily a theatrical interest'.

The following January a London critic was to declare: 'To contest the influence of Ibsen upon this country would be needless . . . It may be said of Ibsen's influence, as Napoleon said of the French Republic, that it is as obvious as the Sun in Heaven, and asks for no recognition.'[3]

One wishes that the people who imagined Ibsen as a 'crazy fanatic' and a 'gloomy sort of ghoul' could have seen the target of their abuse on his walks in Munich, with his top-hat, umbrella and order ribbons. On the day of the *Ghosts* premiere in London Ibsen was, in fact, occupied in writing a long letter to his sister Hedvig, his first to her for many years. She had written from Skien to inform him that a new civic centre was to be opened in the town and to convey an invitation from the committee to attend the inauguration ceremony. The thought of returning in triumph as an honoured guest to the town which he had last visited as a beggar must have tempted him; but Skien was always to remain the forbidden place. His conflicting emotions appear clearly in his reply:

*Munich, 13 March 1891*

*My dear Sister,*

*I thank you most warmly for your letter, which I received last month and to which I must no longer postpone a reply.*

[1] Shaw, *Collected Letters, 1874–1897*, p. 289.
[2] Franc, pp. 88 and 120.
[3] Justin Huntly McCarthy in *The Gentlemen's Magazine*, January 1892.

*It was with much pleasure that I learned that Skien, too, is now to have a civic centre. This will, I am sure, be both large and handsome, and no doubt modernly equipped in every respect, as befits the town and its present size.*

*And you tell me that this centre is shortly to be inaugurated with a series of celebrations.*

*Would indeed that I could have been present on that day! I suppose I would have met very few of those people I knew as a child. I would have found myself in the midst of a new and, to me, foreign generation. Yet perhaps, after all, not completely foreign. In all my many years of absence I have always felt that I still belonged to the town of my birth.*

*Had these festivities occurred a few years earlier, and had I known of them, I would have written a song or a poem and sent it home. I hope and believe that people there would have received it in friendship.*

*But I no longer write poems and songs of that kind. So there can be no talk of that. And yet I would very gladly be with you all in some way or other.*

*So you must tell people of this letter so that they shall all know that I am with you in my thoughts at your celebrations, just as I have so often been with you in my thoughts both in your afflictions, and in your confidence of happier days to come.*

*It was in 1850 that I was last at home in Skien.[1] Not long afterwards a time of spiritual tempest began to sweep the city and spread thence into wider circles.*

*I have always liked storms. And I was with you in this storm—though absent. That I was with you, a deal of my writing testifies.*

*Then great tragedies struck the town and harried it repeatedly. The house where I was born and spent my first childhood years, the church, the old church with its baptismal angel under the roof, were burned. Everything that my earliest memories could cling to—it was all burned.*

*How could I but feel, with all of you, deeply and personally touched by the blows which smote our mutual home town?*

*But you can also imagine with what vivid joy I read accounts of how our town raised itself again in beauty and splendour—how it has grown and how it has progressed in various fields of endeavour.*

*I think you must all feel happy and hopeful when you reflect upon our town's future.*

*Would that I could have said this to you all personally—and more. But I am there among you all the same, in my way.*

*And should I, as I hope, some time come up to Norway—yes, then I should like to see home again—the old and yet the new home.*

*This, my dear Hedvig, is what I wish to tell you today—I will do my best to see*

---

[1] But see *Henrik Ibsen; The Making of a Dramatist*, pp. 186–187.

*that you hear more from me later. Best wishes! My greetings to your husband and children, and to the rest of the family.*

Your affectionate brother

Henrik Ibsen.

The inhibited and semi-formal style, even allowing for the fact that he probably intended it to be read out at the celebrations, is that of a deeply divided man. They celebrated his birthday in Skien a week later, and sent him a telegram, to which he replied in an exceedingly formal letter of one sentence containing fifty-eight words.

On 31 March August Lindberg staged *Hedda Gabler* in Gothenburg, with his bright new star Julia Håkonsson (fresh from attempting Hjørdis in *The Vikings at Helgeland* and Svanhild in *Love's Comedy*) as Hedda and himself as Brack. It seems (as one would expect) to have been the most successful production of the play to that date; Karl Warburg, writing in *Handelstidningen*, though he felt that the play itself 'could scarcely arouse any enthusiasm', found the ensemble playing 'a brilliant triumph'. Julia Håkonsson's performance he thought 'among the finest that our audiences have had the chance to see during the past decade', and Lindberg's interpretation of Brack he found 'magisterially executed'.[1]

That spring the Freie Bühne in Berlin planned a party, and a member who was a waxwork artist conceived the idea of making a model of Ibsen to serve as a kind of patron saint to the proceedings. The man wrote to Ibsen asking if he would lend one of his old suits to dress the model in; but clothes, like religion, were a sacrosanct subject as far as Ibsen was concerned. 'Be so good as to tell this gentleman', he informed Julius Elias, 'that I do not wear "old suits", nor do I wish a wax model of myself to be clothed in an "old suit". Obviously I cannot give him a new one, and I therefore suggest that he order one from my tailor, Herr Fries, of Maximilianstrasse, Munich.'[2] Whether they solved the problem with a costume from stock, or whether they dropped the idea, is not on record.

There was an Ibsen festival in Vienna that April, with productions at different theatres of *The Pretenders*, *An Enemy of the People* and *The Wild Duck*. Ibsen was invited to attend, and accepted; it was the first time he had been there since the Exhibition of 1873. The productions were, like those in London and Berlin earlier in the year, an odd mixture of success and failure. *The Pretenders* on 11 April went splendidly. Ibsen was called after each act, and at the banquet which followed at the Kaiserhof, where the guests were mostly young enthusiasts for the 'new naturalism' which Ibsen had long since left behind him,

---

[1] Lindberg, p. 308.
[2] Elias, *Ibsen-minne af hans tyske oversetter*, p. 404.

*Top:* IBSEN at the naming of the Ibsenplatz, Gossensass, 1889

*Bottom left:* KNUT HAMSUN. Portrait by Alfred Emil Andersen, 1894

*Bottom right:* HERMAN BANG

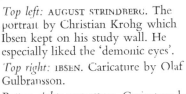

*Top left:* AUGUST STRINDBERG. The portrait by Christian Krohg which Ibsen kept on his study wall. He especially liked the 'demonic eyes'.

*Top right:* IBSEN. Caricature by Olaf Gulbransson.

*Bottom right:* BJØRNSON. Caricature by Olaf Gulbransson.

*Opposite*
*Top left:* EMILIE BARDACH
'*The May sun of a September life.*'

*Top right:* HELENE RAFF as an old woman
'*A voice within me cries for you.*'

*Bottom left:* HILDUR ANDERSEN
'*Here was my Empire and my Crown!*'

*Bottom right:* ROSA FITINGHOFF
'*People do not meet until they have to say goodbye.*'

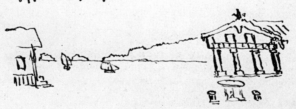

Extracts from Ibsen's manuscripts
*Top left:* Preliminary notes for *The Wild Duck*.   *Top right:* Last lines of *Hedda Gabler*.
*Bottom:* Preliminary notes for *When We Dead Awaken*

*Top:* 'Henrik Ibsen and the English tourists'. Caricature in *Vikingen*, 6 August 1898

*Bottom:* 'Ever higher'. Caricature in *Tyrihans*, 25 January 1895, showing Ibsen's upward progress from *The Vikings at Helgeland* (with a lapse for *Ghosts*) until, with *Little Eyolf*, he disappears from human view

*Top left:* SUZANNAH in 1884
*Top right:* SIGURD and BERGLIOT
in 1904
*Bottom:* IBSEN in 1901

*Top:* 'One of our leading dramatists'. Caricature in *Blæksprutten* of Ibsen's birthday banquet in Copenhagen, 1 April 1898
*Bottom:* IBSEN in 1905, paralysed

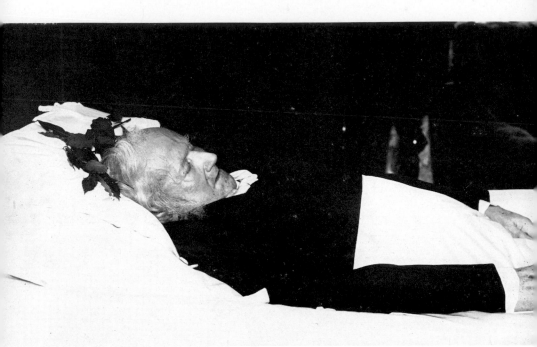

*Top:* IBSEN on his deathbed

*Bottom:* The mourners of a dramatist. Drawing by an unidentified artist in *Korsaren,* 1906. From left to right: Oswald Alving, Rebecca West, John Rosmer, Halvard Solness, King Skule (of *The Pretenders*), Hedvig Ekdal, Lady Inger of Østraat, Eyolf Allmers, Hedda Gabler, Brand, Catiline, Emperor Julian, Peer Gynt, and Hjørdis (of *The Vikings at Helgeland*)

he was acclaimed in both verse and prose. He replied in two lengthy Germanic sentences, saying that when anything made him happy and moved him it 'became a poem', and that he thought that this occasion too would 'become a poem'. (There is no evidence that it ever did; the 'joy of life' appears in his last works only as something never achieved or, if achieved, lost.) Later that evening a radical member of parliament expressed his amazement that a fellow-radical should sit covered in medals. Ibsen replied: 'I like to wear these orders which I have received from my King when I am with younger friends who I anticipate may continue celebrating into the small hours. It reminds me that I need to keep within certain limits'—evidence, as Halvdan Koht remarks, of the division between Ibsen and the Ibsenites.[1]

Radicals of every kind were claiming Ibsen as their champion. Some Viennese ladies, predictably, came to thank him for the pioneering he had done on behalf of their sex, and to name him an honorary member of the Society for Extended Female Education. It was in vain for him to protest that *A Doll's House* was not specifically about women's rights but about the rights of humanity in general, and he doubtless deemed it discourteous to point out that the play represented a phase in his work which he had now left behind him. A Freie Bühne was founded while he was in the city, on the model of the one in Berlin (another had been established in Munich), and they, too, elected him to honorary membership. *An Enemy of the People* went well on 15 April; but evidence that his more recent plays were less admired came the following evening when the newly-founded Deutsches Volkstheater opened its doors with a production of *The Wild Duck*, with Friedrich Mitterwurzer (who had toured *Ghosts* through the United States) as Hjalmar Ekdal. The play at first went well, and Ibsen was called after the second act; but thereafter it evoked increasing disapproval, expressed in whistles. At the final curtain his supporters countered with applause, and the hubbub of the rival factions did not cease until Ibsen, waving his hat at those who were applauding, left the theatre. Although the premiere had been sold out, so few people came afterwards that the production had to close after three performances. The director remarked that he had felt it a duty to open his theatre with an Ibsen play, but that it had cost him money.

On 18 April Ibsen's stay in Vienna was concluded with a final banquet at the Hotel Continental, given by the writers and journalists of the city. Many speeches were made, and the actor Max Devrient greeted him as the great liberator who had given mankind an 'inner freedom', banished ghosts and had the courage to admit daylight into corners that had previously been kept in

---

[1] Koht, II, p. 235.

darkness. Ibsen, as before, replied briefly ('I am no speaker', he declared), thanking the city both for the 'warm understanding' they had showed him, and also for the 'honourable opposition' which some had felt bound to express.

His return home, which he had hoped to make two days earlier, was further postponed, for he was persuaded to go on from Vienna to Budapest, where on 20 April the National Theatre gave a special performance of *A Doll's House* in his honour. Ibsen's reception here exceeded anything that he had yet experienced. When he took his call on the stage, and made a short speech of thanks in German, the cheering was such that, according to a newspaper report, he 'made huge eyes through his even huger spectacles'. The enthusiasm was not confined to the theatre, but followed him out into the street, where the students so mobbed him that he had to take refuge in a carriage. Two banquets were held for him. The first was official, with members of parliament, distinguished scientists and men of letters, and the press; the second, much more to his taste, was given by the students, two of whom made speeches of welcome in Norwegian. In his reply, Ibsen recalled that as a young man (at Grimstad) he had written a poem in honour of the Magyar freedom fighters.[1]

Ibsen's stay in Budapest was an unqualified triumph. The Hungarian press interviewed him on every possible subject, and German journalists who were present noted with amusement how passionately they questioned him and how little Ibsen answered. Strindberg, in the process of divorcing Siri von Essen, read of Ibsen's imperial progress with indignation. 'The "Lonely One",' he wrote to Ola Hansson on 12 May, 'has degenerated into a touring prima donna . . . a self-styled aristocrat who acclaims the new aristocracy in the shape of women and artisans . . . Farewell Ibsen, my youth's ideal!'[2]

Ibsen returned to Munich in the last days of April. While he had been away, two highly controversial premieres of his plays had taken place. On 20 April, the night that Ibsen was mobbed in Budapest, *Hedda Gabler* was performed at the Vaudeville Theatre in London, thanks to the enthusiasm of two American actresses resident there, both ardent feminists, Elizabeth Robins and Marion Lea. Such unkind comments as had been passed on the play by the Scandinavian and German critics paled before the abuse poured forth by the English press:

> 'It was like a visit to the Morgue . . . There they all lay on their copper couches, fronting us, and waiting to be owned . . . There they all were, false men, wicked women, deceitful friends, sensualists, egotists, piled up in a heap behind this screen of glass, which we were thankful for . . . What a horrible story! What a hideous play!'
>
> Clement Scott in the *Daily Telegraph*.

---

[1] *Ibid.*, pp. 236–237; *C.E.*, XIX, pp. 453–454.
[2] *August Strindbergs brev*, VIII, pp. 266–267.

'Hideous nightmare of pessimism . . . the play is simply a bad escape of moral sewage-gas . . . Hedda's soul is a-crawl with the foulest passions of humanity.'

*Pictorial World.*

'Tedious turmoil of knaves and fools'.

*The People.*

'Mean and sordid philosophy . . . Insidious nastiness of photographic studies of vice and morbidity'.

*Saturday Review.*

'Funereal clown [i.e., Ibsen] . . . For sheer unadulterated stupidity, for inherent meanness and vulgarity, for pretentious triviality . . . no Bostonian novel or London penny novelette has surpassed *Hedda Gabler.*'

Robert Buchanan in *Illustrated London News.*[1]

For the Ibsen enthusiasts, however, it was a great occasion, for this was plainly an unusually perceptive and powerful production. William Archer, who never allowed his passion for the cause to blind his eyes to bad acting, wrote in *The World*: 'In rapidity and subtlety of intellect, I find it hard to think of a woman in the whole range of the drama who can rival Hedda Gabler; and Miss Robins makes us feel throughout that her own mind could work as rapidly as Hedda's. She played upon her victims with the crisp certainty of touch of the consummate virtuoso. Behind every speech we felt the swift intellectual process that gave it birth . . . Miss Robins never forgot that Hedda is neither a hypocrite nor a fiend. I do not hesitate to call her performance in the last act the finest piece of modern tragedy within my recollection. Sarah Bernhardt could not have done it better; and it is long since Sarah attempted a scene so well worth doing.' Bernard Shaw, who saw the performance from the back of the pit 'in company with a large and intelligent contingent of Fabians'[2] wrote to Elizabeth Robins that same evening: 'You may safely accept all the compliments you get about the play and the part. I never had a more tremendous sensation in a theatre than that which began when everybody saw that the pistol shot was coming at the end . . . You were sympathetically unsym-pathetic, which was the exact solution of the central difficulty of playing Hedda.'[3] Thomas Hardy (who the previous Easter had noted in his diary that 'Ibsen's edifying is too obvious') went, and was sufficiently impressed to pay a second visit when it was revived in 1893. Oscar Wilde admired it too. 'I felt

[1] William Archer, *The Mausoleum of Ibsen*, pp. 81–82.
[2] Shaw, *Collected Letters, 1874–1897*, p. 291.
[3] *Ibid.*, p. 292.

pity and terror', he wrote to Lord Lytton, son of the novelist, 'as though the play had been Greek.'[1]

The production made at least one important convert. Henry James had been trying for two years to appreciate 'the northern Henry', as he called him, and had failed. 'How provincial all these Dear Norsefolk', he had written to Edmund Gosse in 1890. 'They all affect me like intensely domestic fowl plucking behind a hedge—the big bristling hedge of Germany.' He saw the bad Marie Fraser production of *A Doll's House*, which did not help; *Rosmersholm* he found dreary, and *Ghosts* shocked him. By April 1891 he was still unconvinced. 'Must I think these things works of skill?' he asked Gosse, dismissing them as 'moral tales in dialogue—without the objectivity, the visibility of the drama'.[2] But Elizabeth Robins's performance as Hedda won him over; six weeks later, after sitting through three performances, he wrote an essay on the play, which appeared that June in the *New Review*.

James's feelings towards Ibsen remained ambivalent. The plays still seemed to him (as to Yeats) grey and parochial, even ugly; yet what contemporary writer had probed so deeply into the depths of the human, and especially the feminine mind, and how could one forget those awkward questions which he was forever asking? How unlike James's own settings were 'the ugly interior on which his curtain inexorably rises, and which, to be honest, I like for the queer associations it has taught us to respect; the hideous carpet and wall-paper and curtains (one may answer for them), the conspicuous stove, the lonely centre table, the "lamps with green shades", as in the sumptuous first act of *The Wild Duck*, the pervasive air of small interests and standards, the sign of limited local life!' And yet, James reflected, 'the oddest thing happens in connection with this effect—the oddest extension of sympathy or relaxation of prejudice. What happens is that we feel that whereas, if Ibsen were weak or stupid or vulgar, this parochial or suburban stamp would only be a stick to beat him with, it acts, as the case stands, and in the light of his singular masculinity, as a sort of substitute—a little clumsy, if you like—for charm.' He went on to praise Ibsen's 'remarkable art, his admirable talent for producing an intensity of interest by means incorruptibly quiet, by that almost demure preservation of the appearance of the usual in which we see him juggle with difficulty and danger and which constitutes, as it were, his only coquetry. There are people who are indifferent to these mild prodigies; there are others for whom they will always remain the most charming privilege of art . . . His recurrent ugliness of surface, as it were, is a sort of proof of his fidelity to the real, in a spare,

[1] *The Letters of Oscar Wilde*, ed. Rupert Hart-Davis (London, 1962), p. 293.
[2] Leon Edel, *Henry James, The Treacherous Years* (London, 1969), pp. 23 ff.

strenuous, democratic community; just as the same peculiarity is one of the sources of his charmless fascination—a touching vision of strong forces struggling with a poverty, a bare provinciality, of life . . . He deals with a homely and unaesthetic society, he harps on the string of conduct, and he actually talks of stockings and legs, in addition to other improprieties. He is not pleasant enough nor casual enough; he is too far from Piccadilly and our glorious standards.' In a shrewd and memorable phrase, he summed up Ibsen's peculiar magic as 'the operation of talent without glamour'. The plays which James himself was about to write owe an obvious debt to Ibsen (*The Other House* carries clear echoes of both *Hedda Gabler* and *Little Eyolf*); but the most important lessons which Ibsen had to teach him as a dramatist James sadly failed to learn.

*Hedda Gabler* (originally presented only for five matinées) did well enough at the Vaudeville for the manager of the theatre to transfer it to the evening bill, where it ran for five weeks and was taken off at the height of its success. Archer seems to have sent Ibsen a somewhat coloured account of the whole business, for Ibsen, sending him two signed photographs for Elizabeth Robins and Marion Lea ('I have, as you will see, written the inscription in Norwegian and beg you to be so kind as to append an English translation underneath') expressed (29 April) his delight at Archer's information that *Hedda Gabler* 'has enjoyed a good and uncontested [!] reception on its performance in London'.

A week after the London premiere of *Hedda Gabler*, on 28 April, Paris had its first chance to see *The Wild Duck*, when André Antoine presented it at the Théâtre Libre, with himself as Hjalmar Ekdal—the first production of any Ibsen play in France apart from the same theatre's *Ghosts* eleven months earlier. It had a very mixed reception; some of the spectators showed their displeasure by quacking like the bird of the title, and it is indicative of how little the play was understood that Francisque Sarcey, writing in *Le Temps* (4 May), thought that Hedvig had shot herself out of grief because the wild duck was dead. 'La pièce est obscure', he concluded. 'Elle est incoherente; elle est insupportable.' Yet again, it excited a sizeable minority, especially among the young and the avant-garde. 'Ibsen's fame', wrote Georges Viollat in the *Revue Blanche* (1891, pp. 222 ff.), 'increases daily. It already equals that of Tolstoy'; and Edmond de Goncourt, whose efforts at play-writing had brought him nothing but failure, complained in his diary that to be noticed in the French theatre one needed to be a Scandinavian. The unconverted included Romain Rolland, who wrote to Lugné-Poe that November: 'I am sorry that all his works are getting into France; what have they to do with us? He is a man; but he is not of our race; let him stay in his fjords, the barbarian!'[1]

---

[1] *Correspondance: Romain Rolland, Lugné-Poe, 1894–1901*, ed. Jacques Robichez (Paris, 1957), p. 17.

The flood of Ibsen productions continued. On 10 May *The Pretenders* was staged by Max Grube at the Schauspielhaus in Berlin, and was a big success. The next evening Londoners had their first chance to see *The Lady from the Sea*, presented (for the usual five matinées) at Terry's Theatre in Eleanor Marx-Aveling's translation, and directed by her shady husband, Dr Edward Aveling, using the inappropriate pseudonym of Nelson. William Archer thought it 'an inadequate production', and Bernard Shaw, in a letter to Ellen Terry a year later, recalled how he 'went into an afternoon performance and found a poor ungifted, dowdy, charmless young woman [Rose Meller] struggling pathetically with Ibsen's *Lady from the Sea*. She was doing her best; and I thanked my stars that I was not a dramatic critic, and had not to go home and tell her that after all her study and toil she had done far more harm than good.'[1] *The Times* dismissed the play with contempt: 'It offers no opportunity for powerful acting, while its general analysis of character is shallow and its dialogue commonplace . . . Studies in morbid heredity are very well in a scientific treatise. On the stage, put forward as a public entertainment, they tend to perplex, irritate and repel, besides being useless for any practical purpose.'

Some time at the end of May *A Doll's House* had its first performance in France, privately at the salon of Madame Aubernon de Nerville, the part-original of Proust's Madame Verdurin.[2] 'Malheureusement', Ibsen wrote to her on 22 May (though the French wording was probably Sigurd's, since the letter is in his hand except for Ibsen's signature), 'il m'est impossible de quitter Munich, et je le regrette infiniment, car j'aurais été enchanté d'assister à la representation de *Maison de Poupée*.' A few days later the same play was revived for yet another single matinée in London, at the Criterion Theatre, with Rose Norreys as Nora.

As he was not writing a play this year, Ibsen decided to take a summer holiday. On 8 May he had written to Nils Lund that he was 'vaguely thinking of taking a trip north'. On 17 May, he told Julius Hoffory, who was threatening to descend on him in Munich, that he was 'considering going away for a longish time'. Suzannah was planning to revisit her relatives in Norway, but Ibsen seems to have been thinking only in terms of Denmark. 'It is still uncertain whether I myself shall come as far as Norway', he wrote to Didrik Grønvold on 6 June. 'I am for the moment tired and sated with travelling, of which I have had so much this year, first in Berlin and then in Austria and Hungary. I should like best to settle for a while by the beautiful Sound, which I so love and where I can see hundreds of ships sail in and out.'

---

[1] Shaw, *Collected Letters, 1874–1897*, p. 348.
[2] Unfortunately Proust was not at the performance. He did not join her circle until a few months later.

On 11 June he thanked Jacob Hegel for sending him 3,000 crowns and for the news that an eighth edition of *Peer Gynt* and a sixth edition of *Love's Comedy* were in the press (a third edition of *Catiline* had appeared earlier in the year). At the end of the month *The Vikings at Helgeland* was revived in Munich at the Residenztheater, and Ibsen attended it. Early in July he left for the north, leaving his furniture, paintings and other possessions in the apartment at Maximilianstrasse. He would have been surprised, possibly incredulous, if anyone had suggested to him that he would never return to Germany again, and that he was to spend the remaining fifteen years of his life in Norway, broken only by two brief visits to Denmark and Sweden. His twenty-seven years of self-imposed exile were over.

# PART THREE
# THE WINTER IN NORWAY

# EIGHT

# ❧ A Lion at Evening

# (1891)

IBSEN RETURNED TO Christiania on 16 July. Reporters from the two left-wing dailies, *Dagbladet* and *Verdens Gang*, greeted him at the quayside as he disembarked from the s.s. *Melchior*, and *Dagbladet* welcomed him on behalf of 'all liberal-minded Norwegian men and women'. Embarrassingly, the right-wing papers welcomed him too as a possible counterweight to Bjørnson. 'Our great and celebrated author', wrote *Aftenposten* on the day after his arrival, in language reminiscent of Dr Rørlund in the final act of *The Pillars of Society*, 'is now visiting his fatherland after several years' absence. His stay will, again, be brief; but we must express the hope that it may be long enough for him to assure himself that his compatriots, too, are able to appreciate the fame he has acquired by his distinguished works, and the honour he has thereby helped to bestow upon his country. As our readers will be aware, we do not share Ibsen's view of life or of social conditions; but we are well able to perceive and admire the mighty poetic power which his country has fostered in him—and we would wish that Herr Ibsen could emancipate himself from the bitter feelings which have for so long caused him to prefer other countries to his fatherland. For, after all, it is from the spiritual soil of his homeland that Henrik Ibsen has drawn his best strength, and should he decide to settle permanently among his fellow-countrymen, his sharp pen and acute critical mind would soon find worthy subjects here, where vulgarity still dominates the intellectual scene, and where superficiality and dilettantism hold sway under Bjørnson's leadership.' The words could scarcely have been more calculated to make Ibsen catch the next ship back to Germany.

He stayed in fact only a day or two in Christiania; the main purpose of his visit was to make the sea voyage up the west coast to the North Cape. He had never been further north than Trondhjem and, by the time he returned, his oft-expressed yearning for the open sea must have been amply satisfied. There are few more spectacular landscapes in the world than the west coast of Norway viewed from offshore, and one suspects that this voyage may considerably have influenced his subsequent decision to remain. Suzannah did not accom-

pany him. Some commentators have adduced this as evidence that they had
qua relled, but a more likely reason is that her by now crippling gout and
rheumatism would have made the journey, with its continual climbing and
descending of narrow stairways, agony for her; and she had seen it before.

He returned to Christiania on 7 August, and spent the next ten days at the
Grand Hotel. He had already decided to remain for some months; on 11 August,
thanking August Lindberg for inviting him to attend a performance at Gothenburg 'during my projected return to Germany', he explained: 'I am not planning to go south just yet, but intend to spend the winter here.'

Georg Brandes was also staying at the Grand. After the suspicions and
estrangements of recent years, they were now friends again, and on 15 August
Brandes gave a dinner for him. Ibsen was at first reluctant to attend, agreed
only on the understanding that it would be limited to a few friends, and was
much disturbed when he discovered that a number of left-wing writers, artists
and journalists had been invited. The resultant occasion was anything but
happy. 'Yesterday', wrote Brandes to Alexander Kielland the next day, 'we
had a small dinner of about twenty persons which I arranged for the Troll
King, H.I., and which failed most comically when he found all the praise that
was showered upon him insufficient, and behaved most coarsely and ill-
temperedly.'[1] The painter Erik Werenskiold, who was present, has left a fuller
account:

'Well, the evening arrived, and we were around 30–40 [sic] people. I was
fortunately placed so as to be able to see and hear everything. I had Fru
Augusta Sinding to table; Ibsen, who liked young ladies, had Fru Kitty
Kielland—not exactly beautiful nor young, but a well-known painter
and hard-boiled bluestocking. He was clearly not much pleased. After a
while Brandes rose and said: "He who comes at the eleventh hour is just as
good as he who comes at the seventh or ninth hour; but there is a difference,
none the less; we of the North have come at the seventh hour; we understood Ibsen earlier than others." Then Ibsen began to shake his heavy grey
head. Brandes was somewhat taken aback and began a long explanation to
show how we had understood him before the rest, but the more he
explained the more Ibsen shook his head; and when we finally stood to
drink Ibsen's health he merely half-rose from his chair and said: "One could
say much about that speech"—but did not enlarge further.

'The atmosphere was oppressive. Then O. Thommessen, [the editor of
Verdens Gang], who had Constance Bruun to table, thanked Ibsen on behalf
of the actors for all the great roles he had written for them. "I have not

---

[1] *Brandes Brevveksling*, IV, p. 368.

written roles for actors and actresses", snorted Ibsen. "I have written to portray human beings, not to create roles."

'Then Kitty Kielland began to talk earnestly to Ibsen. She said she thought everything worthwhile in Norway had been accomplished by people from the west coast. "You are from the west, are you not?" she asked. "I am Norwegian," replied Ibsen, "but I understand that you are from Stavanger [in the south-west]." A little later they were discussing *Hedda Gabler*. Kitty said she could not stand Mrs Elvsted—"those women who sacrifice themselves for men." "I write to portray people," said Ibsen, "and I am completely indifferent to what fanatical bluestockings like or do not like."

'Whew! At last dinner was finished. But then Ibsen got hold of my wife, whom he knew well from Munich, took her under one arm and her sister under the other, and strolled up and down the room with them in the most sparkling humour.

'Later that evening Thommessen mentioned to Ibsen that Brandes was going to apply for the Professorship after Skavlan. "Well," said Ibsen, "then he'd better not talk about Norwegian literature, because he doesn't know anything about it." It became rumoured that Thommessen repeated this to Brandes later, when they were having a drink in the café. This may just have been gossip. But the next day Brandes returned to Copenhagen. What a party!'[1]

Ibsen disliked big parties. Johannes Steen, who became Prime Minister that year, invited him and Bjørnson to an official reception. 'So the animals are to be put on show', commented Ibsen; but he accepted. There was a buffet supper, occupying several rooms. 'In one stood Bjørnson, the centre of a large circle of admiring guests; in another stood Ibsen, alone, holding his plate and facing a corner containing a tiled stove, presenting an unapproachable back to the gathering.'[2] On the other hand, he enjoyed small, select parties, especially if he was given an attractive young lady to take to the table, and then he could talk charmingly and rewardingly. He disliked the custom of paying thank-you visits after a party, and would send a visiting-card on which he had written beneath his name:' Active member of the Anti-Visit Society.'[3]

On 17 August Ibsen and Suzannah leased (though they did not move in until October) an apartment at 7B (later 13B) Viktoria Terrasse, yet another corner-house, situated in the centre of Christiania, only a few minutes from the palace

[1] Bergliot Ibsen, pp. 147–149.
[2] Bull, *Tradisjoner og minner*, p. 99.
[3] *Ibid.*, p. 101.

and the theatre. He saw two plays during the next couple of weeks. One was Strindberg's *The Father*, performed at the Tivoli Theatre by a Danish touring company under Hans Riber Hunderup, who had directed and played the lead in the original production of the play four years earlier at his Casino Theatre in Copenhagen. It was a tremendously hot evening, no less than 102° Fahrenheit (39° Centigrade), and the little theatre was almost empty (the night's takings were only 33 crowns, less than £2). Ibsen, records one of the actors, sat by himself in a box almost on the stage, 'staring at us in lonely majesty'. After the interval following the final curtain, when there was to have been a French farce to round off the proceedings, Ibsen and the other spectators had gone, and the theatre was completely empty; one old lady returned as the actors stood bewildered on the stage, but explained that she had only come to collect her programme; then she went home and so did the actors.[1] Ibsen's opinion of the performance is, sadly, not on record.

On 28 August he attended the Christiania Theatre, for the first time since 1874, when they had given *Love's Comedy* and *The League of Youth* for him on the occasion of his first return to Norway. Now, they offered *Hedda Gabler*, and Ibsen sat in the place of honour, in the stage box. He was greeted with applause as soon as he was seen, after each act and, thunderously, after the final curtain.

By this time, Ibsen had decided to make Norway his base. 'We do not of course intend to stay here all the year round,' he wrote to Hegel on 5 September, 'but to travel as hitherto. So it is just our starting-point which has altered. But we shall stay the winter and I have planned a big new dramatic work which I intend under all circumstances to complete up here. I have not for a long time felt in such good spirits as this summer. The voyage to the North Cape was quite glorious, and my wife has enjoyed the mountain air up at Valders. So my dream of spending a few months by my beloved Sound must be forgotten for this year; but henceforth it will be much easier for me to get down there.' He was not in fact to leave Norway for another six years.

On 14 September he was at the theatre again, for the hundredth performance of *The League of Youth*—a figure which none of his other plays had reached. He sat in the stalls, wearing his full panoply of medals, and again was greeted with tumultuous applause, which he acknowledged by rising from his seat and bowing; though, contrary to his custom in Germany, he refused to take a call from the stage. After the performance there was a banquet at the Tivoli restaurant, at which a speech in Ibsen's honour was made by Schrøder, the man who still obstinately refused to allow *Ghosts* to be staged at his theatre. Ibsen, to the delight of many present and the discomfiture of a few, devoted his reply

---

[1] Vilhelm Petersen, *Foran og bag Kulisserne* (Copenhagen, 1931), pp. 57–58.

to demanding that something should be done, and done quickly, about the building of the new National Theatre, which had so long been promised. He reminded his hearers that shares in the new theatre had been offered to the public as long as sixteen or seventeen years ago, yet no action had been taken. *Aftenposten* reported his speech:

'Were the speaker a member of the building committee, had he the power and authority of the building committee, he would commit himself to raise a million reichsmarks within a month. Had he total authority, he would undertake to start building within two years. (*Laughter*). Yes, you may laugh; but he, the speaker, would not sit and wait for contributions from rich men, for such contributions did not flow richly. He would go to the State Wine and Spirits Monopoly and . . . undertake to raise on such-and-such conditions a million at four or five per cent. He was a business man, as (he trusted) he had shown . . . He would ask Oskar Blumenthal how he had erected his beautiful Lessingtheater [in Berlin] in a single year. He would go to Ludwig Barnay and ask how he had built his fine Berliner Theater, then to Vienna to ask the director of the Volkstheater how he had raised two to three millions in eighteen months, then to Zurich, where eighteen months ago the theatre had been burned down but where they were not going to wait sixteen or seventeen years to lay a new foundation stone . . . He had a dream of a new occasion for celebration. This evening had been the hundredth performance of his play, a banquet of celebration for 18 October 1869, but if our city was to take its place among the capitals of Europe there must be a banquet to celebrate the laying of the foundation stone of the new theatre . . . The speaker concluded by thanking his listeners for the kindness they had shown him this evening and expressing the hope that he would see them again on the occasion of the laying of the new foundation stone this day two years hence.'

The speech, like so many of Ibsen's best, seems to have been spontaneous (he had opened by explaining that when accepting the invitation to attend he had made it a condition that he would not have to speak), and it reminds one how eloquently he could speak when he felt deeply about an issue, as opposed to conventional after-dinner speaking when people expected nothing but flattery and facile wit.

Most of his listeners that evening were establishment figures; but three days later he was equally fêted by his radical admirers. August Lindberg and his Swedish company were playing in Christiania that month, at the Tivoli Theatre, and Ibsen (possibly, one suspects, to needle Schrøder) expressed a desire to see their production of *Ghosts*. It was some time since the play had been in their repertory, but Lindberg managed to assemble the original cast; and so at last Ibsen saw it as it had first been staged in Europe. The audience, mainly young and left-wing, acclaimed him as their champion. Nor did he only attend their production of *Ghosts*. The company included a young singer named Sigrid Arnoldson; every time she sang, he came to the theatre, and when she left Christiania he was at the railway station with flowers and a portrait of himself.[1]

Yet while both political parties strove to make him their own, there were still many of the extreme right who regarded him as a pariah, and these included some of his old Holland friends. Christiania was by now full of people who regarded themselves as the originals of various characters in his plays; even the elderly Camilla Collett had improbably claimed to be the inspiration of Ellida in *The Lady from the Sea*. Professor L. L. Daae, who had been a friend of Ibsen's for years, was convinced that he was the original of Dr Kroll, the bigoted pedagogue of *Rosmersholm*, and cut Ibsen publicly in the street. More worrying was the number of people who claimed him as a brother-in-arms; he cannot have been pleased when the right-wing poet Kristofer Randers dedicated an aggressive volume to 'Henrik Ibsen, the poet of individualism, in deep gratitude for what he has taught me: to write verse and despise the masses.'

Suzannah's gout was proving so troublesome that she had gone south with Sigurd to take the cure at Salo on Lake Garda, leaving Ibsen to make the arrangements for moving into their new apartment. He was not, however, alone. He had found a new companion to replace Emilie and Helene. On his return from the North Cape in August he had renewed the acquaintance he had struck up in 1874 with Annette Andersen, the daughter of his old Bergen landlady Helene Sontum, and her daughter Hildur. Hildur, now twenty-seven, had fulfilled the musical promise of her youth, and was maturing into a distinguished concert pianist. A close and warm friendship quickly developed between her and Ibsen. When he first met her this year she had just returned from a holiday in the mountains, bronzed and fresh—exactly like Hilde Wangel at the latter's first entrance in the play which he was about to write. In Suzannah's absence Hildur became his constant companion on walks and visits to art galleries and theatres. She even got him along to an occasional concert, and helped him with the furnishing of his new apartment. The date 19 September held some particular significance for Ibsen in connection with their relationship, for he subsequently gave her a diamond ring with the date engraved on it, and referred to it in other letters and dedicatory inscriptions.

---

[1] Lindberg, p. 315.

Was it the date of their first meeting in 1874, or their first meeting this year, or did something particular once happen between them on that day? We do not know, just as we do not know whether anything happened on that same date two years earlier between him and Emilie Bardach.[1]

On 7 October they attended a lecture together at the Brothers Hals' Concert Hall, owned by his old friend the piano-maker. It was a notable occasion. The lecturer was a thirty-two year old working-class man named Knut Hamsun, who the previous year had caused a sensation with his first novel, the grim autobiographical *Hunger*. The advertised subjects of his three lectures, of which this was the first, were Norwegian Literature, Psychological Literature and The Literature of Fashion. It was known, for he had already delivered them in other Norwegian towns, that they contained an attack on both Ibsen and Bjørnson. Hamsun had boldly invited Ibsen to attend and, to the general amazement, up he turned, and sat in seat number one in the front row with Hildur beside him.

Hamsun pulled no punches. 'This evening', he began, 'I shall be as aggressive, as destructive as possible.' He attacked Ibsen, extraordinary as it now seems, for over-simplifying his characters and making them mere mouthpieces. For this, Hamsun largely blamed the literary form which Ibsen had chosen. 'A play', he declared, 'must always be easy for the gallery as well as the stalls to follow . . . Molière's Miser is only miserly, Shakespeare's Othello only jealous, Iago only a scoundrel and Rosmer in *Rosmersholm* only noble . . . I suggest that any psychology which is sufficiently clear, that is to say sufficiently shallow, to be understood and enjoyed in the theatre, is to an indefensible degree a coarse and false psychology.'

Hamsun went on to deliver a particular attack on the character of Rosmer. 'There is no more strength in his noble body than could be contained in my fist. He crumples aristocratically at the first hint of opposition . . . an exceedingly bourgeois conception of the meaning of aristocracy.' One reason for the inadequacy of Ibsen's psychology, he asserted, was 'the inherent stiffness and poverty of his emotional life'; and he attacked him for writing too much in 'fully-rounded, typical speeches instead of, at least occasionally, in fragments . . . There has never yet lived a dramatist on this earth who has been a sensitive psychologist. Not as a dramatist. We have grown so accustomed to believe everything the Germans say about Ibsen that we read him pre-conditioned to find wisdom there, determined to find everything good . . . If anything strikes us as odd, it is not the author's fault that we do not understand him.' Ibsen was too often wilfully obscure, as in *The Lady from the Sea*—'a book for Germans. I

---

[1] For a full account of the relationship between Ibsen and Hildur Andersen, see Francis Bull, *Hildur Andersen og Henrik Ibsen*, in Edda, 1957, pp. 47–54.

N

read and read and . . . cry in despair: "Damn you, man, talk clearly!" . . . But if I have in any way suggested that Ibsen is a small writer, that he has not earned his fame, that he is not worth much . . . then I have said something I did not intend, and I take it back, take it back most humbly. Ibsen's interest circles continuously around problems; that is his calling as a writer, and it is a sufficient calling . . . Let Ibsen write about problems and questions, it enriches our literature and occupies our minds; we must naturally be interested in what a man like Ibsen thinks about this and that . . . I say, too, that more than any other man Ibsen has raised our literature from being the literature of little Norway to the status of world literature, and that only a man of his mighty powers could have achieved this. But I say too, for it is a fact, that his writing is the literature of social questions, and that his personages are "characters" and types. I say this not in blame, but to state a fact.'[1]

Hamsun's contempt for the drama as a literary form, and even his disparagement of Shakespeare as a psychologist, were, one must remember, widely shared by nineteenth-century men of letters; and his condemnation of Ibsen as a man who wrote mainly about social problems has been echoed by many critics since. Bernard Shaw's *Quintessence of Ibsenism*, expanded from his Fabian lecture and published a couple of months before Hamsun's Christiania lectures, widely encouraged this view. To most people then, as (alas) now, he was the author of *The Pillars of Society*, *A Doll's House*, *Ghosts* and *An Enemy of the People*. If it seems incredible now that the author of *Brand*, *Peer Gynt*, *The Lady from the Sea* and *Hedda Gabler* should still have been regarded primarily as a social commentator, we must remember that in these plays, too, he viewed man as a creature at the mercy of social as well as of inner psychological forces —as a being, in other words, influenced by outward as well as by inward pressures. Today, the outward pressures have changed, the inward pressures remain the same; and *A Doll's House*, *Ghosts* and the rest survive because we are still conscious of those inward pressures. It is odd that Hamsun, who the previous year had published an essay entitled *From the Unconscious Life of the Mind*,[2] in which he demanded that writers should investigate the dark and inexplicable powers that haunt and motivate us, should have failed to perceive the true significance of *Rosmersholm*, *The Lady from the Sea* and *Hedda Gabler*. Yet his indictment expressed the irritation of many people with Ibsen then; and his condemnation of him for making his characters speak too roundedly, instead of in a broken and fragmentary style, would have been echoed by Strindberg, whose characters jump illogically (as Joyce's and Virginia Woolf's were to) from thought to thought, in a manner which many actors at first find dis-

---

[1] Knut Hamsun, *Paa Turné* (Oslo, 1960), pp. 31–38.
[2] *Samtiden*, 1890, pp. 325 ff.

turbing, but which gradually imposes its own remorseless logic on them and their listeners.

Ibsen, we are told, 'sat quiet and serious, with unmoved countenance ... His strong blue eyes did not leave the speaker for a minute.' Two days later he said to Hildur: 'Well, tonight we must go to Herr Hamsun's second lecture.' 'You don't mean,' said she, 'that you want to listen to that impudent fellow again?' to which Ibsen replied: 'Surely you realise we must go and learn how we are to write.'[1] And they attended both that lecture and the third three evenings later. Ibsen is not likely to have bothered overmuch about Hamsun's suggestion that he over-simplified his characters; but he must surely have found confirmation in the young man's words of the conviction he himself had already reached that a writer must explore the uncharted waters of the unconscious.

Hamsun's lectures held a further interest for Ibsen; they were revealing of something that increasingly intrigued him in his old age—the views of the young. Lugné-Poe, his youthful French champion, records (quoting an unnamed source) that Ibsen, during this first year after his return to Norway, showed an almost obsessive interest in the rising generation, and went out of his way to get to know the new artists and writers of Norway, as though afraid lest he might lose touch with the people who understood his plays most clearly.[2] His interest in Strindberg, a portrait of whom he was about to buy and hang in his study, is further evidence of this: and his next play was to present a confrontation between his own generation and theirs.

On 21 October Ibsen moved into Viktoria Terrasse, and the following month he wrote to Hegel asking for a further 2,000 crowns to cover furnishing expenses (he had requested 6,000 on 5 October). Suzannah was still in Italy; and he now initiated the ritual, which was to become so famous, of his daily walk across to the University, where he would check his watch (a 'frightful old Waterbury with no chain',[3] curiously out of keeping with his smart clothes) by the University clock, and down Carl Johan Gade to the Grand Hotel. This ritual has been described by many observers. Edvard Brandes noted that as he walked 'he kept his eyes to himself, so that one felt unwilling to greet him even if one knew him, and he was certainly not insulted if you avoided forcing him into a brief acknowledgment of your presence ... At the hotel ... he had a kind of reading-room to himself which in the nineties lay separate from both hotel and restaurant. [The Café which he was later to frequent had not yet been built.] But one could visit him there, more conveniently than at his home, if

---

[1] Bull, *Hildur Andersen og Henrik Ibsen*, pp. 49–50.
[2] Lugné-Poe, p. 74.
[3] P. Rosenkrantz Johnsen, *Om og omkring Henrik Ibsen og Suzannah Ibsen*, p. 17.

one had an errand to him or some topic for conversation that interested him. And it might happen that he became so interested that he would invite his visitor to take a glass with him. He always expressed his opinions in an individual and stylish form. The great master of dialogue chiselled and hammered out his words in short sentences, well considered, carefully shaped, and anyone who heard his slightly crackling voice and still retains the memory of it must regret not having noted at the time the sharp and forceful observations which emerged from those narrow lips.'[1]

Brandes adds the shrewd and probably correct surmise that the Grand Hotel somehow represented 'abroad' to him in the same way that the loft in *The Wild Duck* represented the forests of Højdal to Lieutenant Ekdal; and that had Ibsen been a poet instead of a dramatist no-one would have been surprised at his unapproachability.

That November a ghost appeared from the past to prick his conscience. Laura Kieler arrived in Christiania, and wrote Ibsen a letter. One might have expected him to avoid a further meeting with that sad and emotional lady. But her letter must have touched him, for he replied at once:

*Dear Laura Kieler!*

*I received your letter late yesterday evening. Today I am invited out and cannot meet you. But come tomorrow at 2.30, so that we can dine together and talk undisturbed about these things. Note the address: 7b. You will be most welcome.*

*Your affectionate*
*Henrik Ibsen.*

As an old woman, Laura remembered how they had talked for four hours. She told him her whole story. When she spoke of her hatred of illusion and her determination to look reality in the face, he replied: 'You and I are the same kind.' He was so moved that he wept. She said he must, even at this late stage, tell Georg Brandes the truth, to which he replied: 'No, I can't. That's impossible.' She said he must think it over and she would return the next day for his answer. He said: 'Oh, Laura, Laura, I can't let you go—but you mustn't come tomorrow. No, no, I can't do it. I can't. It's impossible.'[2] They never met or corresponded again. Did this really happen, or was it the confused and coloured fantasy of an old lady whose life had been a protracted tragedy? One suspects the latter; but Laura may not have been wrong in supposing that she

---

[1] Edvard Brandes, *Henrik Ibsens personlighed*, in *Politiken*, 20 March 1928, reprinted in Brandes's *Litterære Tendenser* (Copenhagen, 1968), pp. 231–238. Kristian Gloersen (*op. cit.*, pp. 348–349) tells that they kept a large armchair for him in this room, with his name on a plaque at the back.
[2] Kinck, pp. 528–531.

had given something at least to the character of another cruelly treated model, the deranged Irene in *When We Dead Awaken*.

The same month, Herman Bang, the young Danish writer whom Ibsen had known in Munich, sent him tickets for two lectures he was to give in Christiania, one on Guy de Maupassant and one on *Hedda Gabler*. Ibsen came to both, on 10 and 11 November. At the first, on de Maupassant, Bang thought he had never seen so indifferent a listener. Ibsen 'sat staring incessantly into the bottom of his silk hat, as though into the depths of a well'. But when Bang spoke of the story, *Une Vie*, in which the heroine is locked in a room with a fly which she cannot catch, and from which she cannot escape, symbolising the thought of death, Bang suddenly lifted his head and looked at Ibsen. Ibsen had raised his head and was staring at Bang. Such a look, Bang says, he had never seen except at the zoo, when a huge lion, before settling down to sleep at dusk, suddenly, with an indescribable emptiness of spirit, shot a glance from its half-closed eyes at the disappearing daylight. Such a glance Bang now saw in Ibsen's eyes, and the thought went through his mind: 'Yes, you should have guessed. He has lived and has achieved everything. Now he has only death awaiting him.'

The next evening Bang spoke on *Hedda Gabler*. The hall was full, largely (says Bang) because people wanted to see Ibsen listening to criticisms of himself. It was a perceptive lecture; Bang compared Hedda to the woman in Maupassant's *Notre Coeur* who owned a triptych mirror and shut herself up inside it every day for several hours. Ibsen again kept his eyes fixed on the bottom of his hat, so that it was impossible to know whether the lecture was interesting him. The following day Bang met Ibsen in the street. After a sly reference to Hamsun, Ibsen said: 'But you were kind to me.' Then, giving him a sidelong glance, he added: 'At least you read the stage directions.' He made no reference to Maupassant and the fly.[1]

On 17 December occurred the first attempt to stage Ibsen commercially in France. Albert Carré, the young director of the Vaudeville Theatre, impressed by Ibsen's growing reputation in artistic circles, decided to try out *Hedda Gabler* as a matinée play in the hope of transferring it to the evening bill should it prove a success. It did not. Marthe Brandes, a fashionable actress who was cast as Hedda, made no secret of the fact that she did not understand the play. 'People laughed,' records Lugné-Poe. 'There were smiles at this curious specimen of Scandinavian literature'; and he describes the production as

---

[1] Herman Bang, *Hedda Gabler*, in *Tilskueren*, October–November 1892, pp. 827–838; Lugné-Poe, pp. 91–93. Bang's lecture includes a reference to 'a London journalist, almost unknown', who claims that he has often taken Hedda Gabler into dinner. This obscure figure was Bernard Shaw.

'a crushing failure'. Francisque Sarcey wrote in *Le Temps*: 'In spite of everything, I am glad this play has been performed. Perhaps after this effort we shall be left in peace. Ibsen is now dead in France.'[1]

Despite the failure of *Hedda Gabler* on the stages of Scandinavia, 1891 had, thanks mainly to payments from German and Austrian theatres and various reprints, been a good year financially—Ibsen's best, indeed, since 1880:

| | crowns | £ |
|---|---|---|
| Royalties for *An Enemy of the People* at Wien Burgtheater | 2,259 | 126 |
| Fee for *The Pillars of Society* at Munich Hoftheater | 123 | 7 |
| Fee from Heinemann for English edition of *Hedda Gabler* | 2,720 | 151 |
| Fee for *Hedda Gabler* at Svenska Teatern,[2] Stockholm | 500 | 28 |
| Royalties for *A Doll's House* in Milan | 88 | 5 |
| Fee for *Hedda Gabler* at Christiania Theatre | 2,500 | 139 |
| Fee for *Hedda Gabler* at Finska Teatern, Helsinki | 250 | 14 |
| Fees from August Lindberg for *A Doll's House* and *The Vikings at Helgeland* | 250 | 14 |
| English monies from William Archer | 57 | 3 |
| Royalties for *An Enemy of the People* at Wien Burgtheater (extra performance) | 160 | 9 |
| Royalties for *An Enemy of the People* and *Hedda Gabler* at Munich Hoftheater | 420 | 23 |
| 3rd edition of *Catiline* | 540 | 30 |
| 8th edition of *Peer Gynt* | 1,815 | 101 |
| 6th edition of *Love's Comedy* | 800 | 44 |
| Unspecified royalties from Royal Theatre, Copenhagen | 772 | 43 |
| Further monies from William Archer | 90 | 5 |
| Unspecified royalties from Wien Burgtheater | 1,548 | 86 |
| Royalties for *The Vikings at Helgeland* at Munich Hoftheater (1 performance) | 96 | 5 |
| 3rd edition of *Lady Inger of Østraat* | 747 | 41 |
| 6th edition of *Poems* | 1,020 | 57 |
| Unspecified royalties from Munich Hoftheater | 296 | 16 |
| Fee for *Ghosts* at Bergen | 160 | 9 |
| Fee for Danish tour of *Hedda Gabler* | 40 | 2 |
| Royalties for *The Pillars of Society* at Mannheim Hoftheater (2 performances) | 53 | 3 |
| Royalties from Giacomo Brizzi, Milan | 39 | 2 |
| Unspecified royalties from Felix Bloch (German agent) | 2,120 | 118 |
| | 19,463 | 1,081 |

[1] Nyholm, pp. 51–55; Lugne-Poe, pp. 23–27.
[2] Formerly Nya Teatern; the name had been changed in 1888.

Thus, at the age of sixty-three, Ibsen, for the second time in his career, earned over a thousand pounds in one year. The fact that he received no payments for Norwegian productions of any of his earlier plays (apart from a few performances of *Ghosts* at Bergen) does not, of course, mean that none of them were staged. On the contrary, the 1890–1891 season at the Christiania Theatre included revivals of *The League of Youth*, *A Doll's House*, *The Lady from the Sea*, *The Vikings at Helgeland* and *Hedda Gabler*. But as the theatre had paid him in each case a lump sum for the rights, these extra performances brought him nothing. He was as dependent as ever on book sales and German theatre royalties.

# NINE

## ✵ The Master Builder

## (1892)

ON ONE OCCASION when visiting the Andersens Ibsen met Hildur's cousin, a young doctor named Christian Sontum. The two became good friends, and one of Dr Sontum's children, Bolette, who later settled in America, vividly recalled (in English) her first impression of Ibsen during that winter of 1891–1892:

'Ibsen came a great deal to our house, and I remember well the first time we children were allowed to see him. We were at my uncle's. My little brother and I were to play a duet sonata by Beethoven for the famous guest. We were both very frightened. I can still feel my fingers getting cold as they touched the keys. When we rose I sent a timid, beseeching glance at the old man standing in the doorway, in his long black frock coat with the broad lapels, which he always wore with the pride of a dandy. He came over to us at once and said: "How wonderful! How wonderful!" so kindly that our dread for the great silent old man disappeared at once. To him the simplest accomplishment of a child was always a wonder. No doubt it was our complete self-possession that awed him. Ibsen's real knowledge of the music was little better than our own.

'He had no idea of how to treat children and addressed one by the formal "De" (You) instead of the familiar "Du" (Thou), when I was only eight years old. That winter he came often to our house for dinner with a few other friends. He was always very prompt . . . I remember once we children went to speak to him while he was in the drawing-room. My mother was called out and my father was still busy with his patients; no other guests arrived, so we felt it our own duty to entertain our guest. My younger sister promptly asked: "Would you like to play dolls with us?" Ibsen wrinkled his heavy white eyebrows, but in a moment was ready, looking as though he were going to do a serious job, but meant to do it well. She trotted out of the room and soon came back loaded with dolls, dolls of all sizes and in all conditions, dolls with heads and without. She placed them all in his lap, and told him all their names, giving him a maternal account of their rag and bisque tragedies.

'One specimen, the doll Mette, who was perhaps worse-looking than any, had once been a great beauty in a wonderful red and white dress. Now she was headless and legless and of course my sister's pet. Mette had to have an honorary position on Ibsen's knee. My father opened the door just as the master of the Great Doll's House was taking all our dolls for a ride.'[1]

Another affectionate recollection of Ibsen that winter comes from a young actress, Elisabeth Dybwad. The actors of Christiania were holding a celebration at Tivoli to raise money for their building fund, and a bookseller had presented a complete bound set of Ibsen's works to be put up for auction. Elisabeth Dybwad was chosen to go up to Ibsen's apartment and ask him to write a few words in, or at any rate sign, one of the volumes, so that they would fetch a better price. On 21 February she went along with five volumes, and was duly admitted to the presence.

'He was very friendly and asked if all his works were contained in those five volumes.

' "No", I replied. "Each of the nineteen plays has a volume to itself."

' "What!" he said. "Have I written nineteen plays? That's many too many for one man, you must agree. What shall I write?" he asked.

' "I think it'd be enough if you wrote your name in one of the volumes —say, *Catiline*."

' "No, I must write a verse," he said. "But must you have it at once? I can't write poetry by artificial light."

' "No," I replied. "There's no hurry. Perhaps I might come back in a day or two?"

' "You can collect it tomorrow," said Ibsen.

'Next day, in the morning, I collected the book. In *Catiline* he had written a verse which, that same day, was telegraphed around the world— the postscript to *Burned Ships*:

> At long last he dismounted,
> Found open every door.
> Might not this homeless wanderer
> Have come somewhat before?'[2]

---

[1] Bolette Sontum, *Personal Recollections of Ibsen*, in the *Bookman* (New York, 1913), Vol. 37, pp. 247–256.

[2] Elisabeth Dybwad, *Et Ibsen-minde*, in *Urd*, *Ibsen-nummer* (Oslo, 1928), p. 158.

This verse, as Elisabeth Dybwad says, received wide publicity, not only in Norway, and was taken as a sign that Ibsen now felt totally at home in Christiania. And indeed, his letters of this year refer repeatedly to an unexpected sense of peace and euphoria. The set of signed volumes fetched over 400 crowns.

On 14 January *The Vikings at Helgeland* had been performed at the Moscow Little Theatre—the first Ibsen play to be staged in Russia since *A Doll's House* eight years earlier. Several of his later plays had apparently offended the Tsar's censor, but they seem to have enjoyed a kind of underground circulation.

That February, Hildur went to Vienna to pursue her music studies. Possibly her parents felt that, platonic as her relationship with Ibsen was, they were seeing a little too much of each other. The tongues of Christiania had begun to gossip. He corresponded frequently with her while she was away, by both letter and telegram. Hildur, who lived to be ninety-two, kept these letters almost—not, alas, quite—until her death.

On 7 March he attended the dress rehearsal of a new production of *Peer Gynt* at the Christiania Theatre—the first time he had seen the play staged—and two evenings later he was at the premiere. Bjørn Bjørnson played Peer, and a young actress named Johanne Dybwad was Solveig; she was later to be perhaps the greatest of all Aases. The production drew full houses for fifty performances.

Despite his abandonment of verse as a medium for public self-expression, Ibsen had developed the habit, when preparing a play, of composing a short poem to enshrine the theme, and on 16 March he wrote such a poem relating to the play that was taking shape in his head. It is the only one of these poems which has survived:

> They dwelt, those two, in so cosy a house
> In autumn and winter weather.
> Then came the fire—and the house was gone.
> They must search the ashes together.
>
> For down in the ashes a jewel lies hid
> Whose brightness the flames could not smother,
> And search they but faithfully, he and she,
> 'Twill be found by one or the other.
>
> But e'en though they find it, the gem they lost,
> The enduring jewel they cherished—

She ne'er will recover her vanished faith,
Nor he the joy that has perished.[1]

On 30 March, in the intervals of writing to Hildur, he sent a long and warm
letter (in Norwegian, which she had now learned) to Helene Raff in Munich:

*Dearest Frøken Raff,*

*Allow me to send you my warmest, my most heartfelt thanks for your dear letter,
which reached me on my birthday, and for your wonderfully beautiful picture, which I
had the inexpressible joy to receive some days ago. It now hangs in a good place in my
study, so that I can have it constantly before my eyes, and constantly feed my sight
with that prospect of the wide, open sea—and long even more to see again the dear,
dear, enchanting young girl who has created this exquisite little work of art. And who,
while creating it, has been thinking of me, far away. Ah, if only I could have the
chance to thank you personally, face to face—thank you as I would most wish to!
I love the sea. Your painting takes my thoughts and my mood to the thing I love.
Yes—you have indeed enriched me for life with your gift. Now little Solveig [the
painting she had done for his birthday two years earlier] shall hang beside the painting
of the sea. Thus I shall have you collected and complete before me—and within me—*

*My memories of Munich arose so powerfully in me when I received these greetings
from you in words and colours. How happy I would be to be there again! I feel so
deeply at home there. But there is so much in life which blocks and frustrates our
wishes and longings.*

*You have achieved an extraordinary fluency in Norwegian. Do you never think of
taking a summer holiday up here? Of dreaming a bright, fleeting summer night's
dream among the mountains or out at sea?*

*Answer me this, dearest Frøken Raff. Would you like to? It would give me in-
expressible pleasure—should you have the time and the opportunity—to receive some
further lines from you.*

*Your affectionate and grateful*
*Henrik Ibsen.*

But she does not seem to have written to him again; or if she did, he did not
reply.

Ibsen had seen little if anything of Bjørnson since his return to Norway.
Sigurd, however, had put himself very much in Bjørnson's good books by his
polemics against the union with Sweden, and Bjørnson invited him to stay at
Aulestad. He paid several visits there and, as Ibsen had forecast on his return

---

[1] A. G. Chater's translation. Ibsen incorporated this poem, with one alteration (*peace*
instead of *faith* in the penultimate line) in his first draft of *Little Eyolf* two years later. But
he deleted the poem in revision.

from Schwaz seven years earlier, fell in love with Bjørnson's young daughter, Bergliot. They became engaged; Bergliot has left a pretty account of how it happened:

'Much had been written and said of Sigurd, and we young ones were greatly excited at the prospect of his visit. One night I dreamed we were engaged, and was foolish enough to tell my brothers and sisters. They so teased me about it that I did not dare to show myself when he arrived, but hid behind a curtain. I didn't see much of him the first few days; he spent most of the time talking with Father. They had long conversations up in his study. Sigurd was very serious, and I didn't altogether like him. But one day he was standing with Father on the upstairs verandah and I was standing on the one below. Then suddenly Sigurd smiled and looked down at me with his beautiful eyes, and from that day I loved him, as I have loved him ever since ...

'We were very different. He was a true Ibsen, I a true Bjørnson, and a bigger contrast could not be imagined. Sigurd was by nature very melancholic; but how many times did I not succeed in making him laugh! When we got engaged he wanted to give me a ring, but I asked him instead to give me a concertina, as I did not much like ornaments. Sigurd could never forget this; it made him laugh even when he was old. But I got my concertina, and no girl ever received a more beautiful engagement gift. It was silver-plated, and sounded like a full orchestra. I still love to play it [she wrote in 1947] and then I remember the days at Aulestad when I used to play for him. The sun shone, the sky was blue, and I sat out in the fields with my concertina and sang, while Sigurd lay in the grass beside me and laughed till there were tears in his eyes.'[1]

The Bjørnsons were delighted, the Ibsens (according to Bergliot) less so. Certain 'so-called friends who were opposed to the engagement did their best to sustain Ibsen's distrust ... When Father and Mother came to Christiania they were not received with open arms as they had expected, and Father's enthusiasm and happiness changed. He became furious with Ibsen.'[2] Bergliot adds that her father's extremes of mood must always have had an unsettling effect on Ibsen, and that Ibsen consequently avoided him on his return to Norway because 'he knew what emotional explosions Father could arouse in him'. On his return to Aulestad Bjørnson wrote characteristically to his daughter:

---

1 Bergliot Ibsen, pp. 126–128.
2 *Ibid.*, p. 129.

Aulestad, 21 March 1892

Dear Bergliot,

You are much too young to understand all the *evil* Ibsen has done to me.
It could all have been forgotten. But he came back to Norway without
sending me a greeting . . . He even disavowed the engagement. He did
this repeatedly and to all kinds of people . . . He wants nothing more to
do with us. Very well! But then I shall be as free and shall say what I think
about him and his writings and personality . . . Your father and friend,
B.B.[1]

Whom is one to believe? Bergliot says that Ibsen received her 'amiably but
formally', and that the gossips of Christiania soon set to work, especially when
Sigurd went off again to Italy with Suzannah, which they took to be the first
sign that the engagement was short-lived. But they were wrong; and on 2 May
Ibsen wrote affectionately in Bergliot's album: 'Always be yourself, as you are
now. I know no better destiny I could wish you.'[2]

By now Ibsen was working busily on his new play, although since his
preliminary notes and first draft have disappeared we cannot, as with his other
plays (except *An Enemy of the People*), trace its first beginnings. On 4 May he
wrote to Jacob Hegel that it 'now occupies me completely and, as usual, takes
all my time and all my thoughts. I should gladly like to spend the summer
somewhere in Jutland. But alas, I dare not think of it; for I work best here in
my own apartment and at my own desk. I have made my study up here
very (to my mind) pleasant, comfortable and good for work, and can sit here
undisturbed. I couldn't do that in Munich, and often felt creatively inhibited
down there. So this summer I shan't leave Christiania.'

Suzannah had by now returned from Italy. They saw a few friends; the
Dietrichsons, with whom Ibsen had now patched things up, were invited to
dine 'very plainly, at 3', on 11 May; and he renewed one of his oldest friendships, with Christopher Due, his companion from Grimstad days, now a
retired customs officer. The meeting was evidently a success, for we find a
note from Ibsen on 9 May telling Due: 'I should be delighted if you could look
in again; I am usually to be found here between 11 and 12 of a morning.' Yet
even with so old a friend he retained an extreme formality. It was an ancient
custom, but one scarcely observed among old friends, that the senior of any
two walked on the right. Due records that one day 'Ibsen was walking at his
measured pace along Drammensveien when I happened to see him, caught up
with him on his left side and greeted him. After a friendly response a, to me,

---

[1] *Ibid.*, pp. 129–130.
[2] *Ibid.*, p. 133.

incomprehensible restlessness seemed to overcome him, and he shifted around me in a manner which I sought in vain to interpret, until I realised that he wanted to walk on my left. "No," I said, "you cannot expect me to walk on the right of one who holds the Grand Cross of St Olaf." "Certainly," replied Ibsen. "You are the elder." [1]

When Due remarked that Ibsen took his time over each play, since two years always elapsed before the next one appeared, Ibsen said: "And yet I work hard each day." "But not just at your plays?" "Yes, mostly on them. I spend at least five hours each day on creative work".' Due comments: 'Seeing Ibsen live this lonely life, I could not but think of him as a young man, when he was always so keen to have friends around him. Had life and humanity brought him so much disappointment that he had felt compelled to isolate himself and speak merely through his works?'[2]

On 5 June, a hundred miles to the south, occurred an event of which Ibsen probably never heard, since it was not of sufficient interest to appear in any newspaper. An old blind pauper woman died, aged seventy-four: Else Sofie Jensdatter, who had borne him a son nearly half a century before. It may have been around now (the year is not recorded, and indeed the whole story is based upon hearsay, though Professor Francis Bull, who is usually right in such matters, believes it to be true) that, for the first and last time, Ibsen met that son, Hans Jacob Henriksen, now a ne'er-do-well of forty-six. The story goes that Hans Jacob, penniless as always, knocked one day on the door of his father's apartment, revealed his identity and asked for financial help; to which Ibsen is said to have responded by handing him five crowns with the comment: 'This is what I gave your mother. It should be enough for you', and shut the door in his face. But there was so much malicious gossip about Ibsen in Christiania that there may be no truth in the story.

What is sure is that some of Ibsen's acquaintances, led by Christen Collin (later a professor at London University), hit on the idea of a fearful prank—to dress Hans Jacob, who, in build and general appearance, much resembled his father, in clothes such as Ibsen wore, and, having paid him a small sum to secure his willingness, to sit him in Ibsen's chair at the Grand to see what would happen when Ibsen himself walked through the door. But either they or Hans Jacob lost courage, and this macabre jest remained a thing of the imagination.[3]

Ibsen kept in touch with his sister Hedvig, and grew fond of her daughter Anna. A touching little note to his niece has survived from this summer, begging her to look him up before leaving town and not to be afraid of dis-

---

[1] Due, p. 53.
[2] Ibid., pp. 51–52.
[3] Information from Professor Francis Bull.

turbing him. Once he even attended a largish family party given in Christiania by one of his Paus half-uncles, and agreed, if only momentarily, to revisit Telemark. Among the guests at the party, relates Francis Bull (who had it from one of the Pauses present), was a gentleman named Løvenskiold who owned a large estate at Fossum, no distance from Venstøp, where Ibsen had spent so much of his childhood. Løvenskiold invited Ibsen to come and stay with him there, suggesting that it might amuse him to look over his old haunts. 'Ibsen,' continues Bull, 'was clearly pleased at the invitation and said that he would gladly come. It is easy to imagine how as a child he must have gazed longingly at the great house which a bankrupt's son could never hope to enter, and that the invitation must at first have seemed like the fulfilment of a childhood dream. But later in the evening Ibsen came back to Løvenskiold, very depressed and in a totally different mood. He had thought over the matter, he said, and regretted that he felt bound to refuse the invitation to Fossum, for he realised that once he came there he would inevitably be forced to revisit the town of his birth and revive old memories and acquaintances which he preferred to keep at a distance.'[1]

Bull also tells that at another party around this time Ibsen, on being presented to an attractive young lady, turned away in embarrassment on hearing her name. It transpired that her father, a lawyer, had been approached by Ibsen in 1862 for a loan. Ibsen had with him his manuscript of *Love's Comedy* as evidence that he would soon be in better financial conditions and be able to repay the money. The lawyer asked to read the play before deciding and, having done so, said that one passage offended him and that he would only lend the money on condition that Ibsen deleted it. Ibsen accepted the condition and took the money, but never forgot the humiliation and never repaid the loan, although the lawyer lived for several years after Ibsen's return to Christiania in 1891. They lived near each other, and when Ibsen saw him he would cross to the far pavement.[2]

Christian Sontum had by now become Ibsen's doctor. He was working that summer at a sanatorium at Grefsen, a short way outside Christiania, and Ibsen several times allowed himself the luxury of driving out to visit him. Little Bolette Sontum was there and remembered his visits:

'Nothing could be a better advertisement of the tonic air of Grefsen than this fact, that Ibsen actually drove out to inhale it. His fear of driving was a by-word in Christiania. However, only one particular horse and driver were trusted. Certainly he had little to fear from their energies. As

---

[1] Bull, *Tradisjoner og minner*, pp. 100–101.
[2] *Ibid.*, p. 100.

the funny little rig came creeping up the valley slowly and laboriously, like a very tired snail, it creaked and swayed with the roughness of the roads. Then the whole grotesque little outfit took up the motion—the old horse nodding from his ears to his tail, the fat lazy little coachman droning in his half-sleep, the reins lax in his podgy hands, his cap with its silver band tick-tocking like a pendulum. And behind on the soft, worn cushions sat Ibsen, conjuring up every accident possible to unrestrained speed . . .

'I used to run down to meet our old friend. "Welcome to Grefsen!" I would call out, very cautious with my best muslin dress and my most ceremonial curtsey. *"Goddag, goddag"* [Good day, Good day] he would call back, his whole face lighted up with smiles. Promptly, he would open the low door. "You will drive the rest of the way, my little friend?" Then I would spring up to the back seat more respectfully than timidly. "No, no, right here beside me," Ibsen would urge, and I, trembling with happiness, quickly obeyed, murmuring: "No, no, perhaps I had better not." "Grunt-grunt", he would reply. Each time he came we had our little comedy.'[1]

The political strife between the conservatives and liberals reached a pitch of particular bitterness that summer in Norway.

*The party newspapers outbid each other in abuse and accusations* [Ibsen wrote to Jacob Hegel on 5 July]. *Speeches, processions and torchlight displays are held, and other demonstrations are being prepared. Today a big procession of the conservatives is to go to the palace to greet the King. The conservatives are in a decisive majority here in Christiania . . . It interests me to observe all this at close quarters. But I don't involve myself in these conflicts personally; that would be against my nature. And this attitude of mine is respected up here. Since my return last year I am in the happy position of knowing, and daily experiencing, that I have both the right and the left behind me. I can therefore work with undisturbed peace of mind at my new play, and I do so daily. So I shall probably not leave town this summer. But the air here I find healthy and invigorating. I have not for a long time felt as well in myself as I do up here.*

All that summer of 1892 he was writing regularly to Hildur Andersen in Vienna, and she to him. Professor Francis Bull, who knew Hildur well, gathered from conversations with her that he discussed the progress of his play in detail in these letters. She promised to let Bull have them after her death; but most unfortunately for posterity, around the age of ninety, in the late nineteen-fifties, she underwent a change of heart and burned them. He is usually assumed to have destroyed his notes and first draft during the spring or early summer; but since, according to the date on the manuscript, he did not begin his final

---

[1] Sontum, p. 250.

draft until 9 August, it seems likely that he spent the summer writing a second draft and destroyed that too. *The Master Builder* was to be the most personal and revealing of all his plays, or at any rate the most consciously revealing, though *Hedda Gabler* possibly tells us more about him.

The final draft of the play went swiftly. Act One took him from 9 to 20 August, Act Two from 23 August to 6 September and Act Three from 7 to 19 September—six weeks in all. On 4 October he wrote Hegel that he was busy on the fair copy and hoped to let him have it soon after the middle of the month. In fact, due to a brief illness, he did not post it off until the end of the month.

On 11 October Sigurd Ibsen and Bergliot Bjørnson got married at Aulestad. Bjørnson, still offended at Ibsen's supposed coolness towards him, issued a frostily-worded invitation:

Aulestad, 3 September 1892

Dear Friend,

The wedding is now arranged for 11 October, and it is an honour and pleasure for Karoline and me to invite you to attend.

You will reach Lillehammer in the evening and can stay the night there or carry on and arrive here between 9 and 9.30. In that case you would need to have a carriage waiting at the quayside (telegraph the Victoria Hotel to book one). If you are very busy you could return to Lillehammer the same day as the wedding (scarcely twelve miles) and be in Christiania the following day.

Questions will be asked if you don't come and for the sake of the young couple only good questions should be asked. Moreover, since I (and probably Karoline) shan't attend the church ceremony, since we know it to be as much humbug for them as it is for us, you, who expressed the wish that it should take place, ought to be there, so that they won't be altogether parentless for the occasion, by which you set such store. For company on the journey I presume you will have Thoresen and my brother to keep you company.

No one except close relatives will be there. We shall do our best to make things pleasant for you. I could of course meet you on the quayside at Lillehammer, but it would only be a bother for both of us. Apart from that we shall try to arrange everything for you as comfortably as possible. Karoline sends her best wishes to your wife, and I too beg you to convey my most respectful greetings and warmest thanks for our last visit to you.

Everyone here is well and happy.

Your friend,
Bjørnst. Bjørnson.

A church ceremony would in fact have been far from humbug as far as Bergliot was concerned. 'I have always been a believer,' she comments, referring to the above letter. '. . . But it was useless to try to explain this to Father; he was so fanatical on this point that one dared not for the sake of one's life mention the subject of religion.'[1] As things turned out, when the day for the wedding came Ibsen was ill and could not come, so to please Bjørnson, Sigurd and Bergliot got married in his study. Suzannah, despite her gout, made the long journey with her brother, Judge Herman Thoresen. The predictions of the gossips who declared that for an Ibsen to marry a Bjørnson was asking for trouble were confounded. It was a profoundly happy and successful marriage, though relations between the two fathers remained distant for some time. When the important occasion of Bjørnson's sixtieth birthday occurred on 6 December that year, Ibsen sent him the coldest of congratulatory telegrams. It comprised, in Norwegian, seven words: 'Henrik Ibsen sends good wishes for your birthday.'[2]

In Berlin, meanwhile, the unfortunate Julius Hoffory had gone rapidly downhill. 'I am afraid he must be regarded as incurable', Ibsen had written to Rudolf Schmidt on 31 August; and on 1 November he told Julius Elias: 'He continually sends me old, paid hotel bills, private letters and the like, with no indication of what he expects me to do with them.' Next year, he added, he might take a trip south to meet all his German friends. Hegel sent word that a twelfth edition of *Brand* was in the press; and this news reminded Ibsen of an old promise. 'Twenty years ago', he wrote Hegel on 10 November, 'when the sixth edition of *Brand* was about to appear, we and the Falsens [Suzannah's younger sister and her husband] were living in Dresden. I did not then dream that I should ever live to see a *twelfth* edition of the poem, and I promised Dorothea that if such a thing ever happened she should have half my fee for it. Now it has happened; and she has turned up here and, like Hilde in my new play, demands that I keep my promise. May I therefore beg you to be so kind as to send her the sum in question?'

On 6 December, six days before *The Master Builder* was published in Scandinavia, William Heinemann issued an edition of twelve copies in Norwegian to safeguard his copyright; and the following morning, at 10 a.m., as a further safeguard, the play was read in Norwegian at the Theatre Royal, Haymarket. Edmund Gosse, who read Dr Herdal, described this strange occasion: 'Yesterday we had a curious little excitement. The new Ibsen play had to be nominally performed here to save copyright, it not having yet been played or published even in its own country. So Heinemann rented the Hay-

---

[1] Bergliot Ibsen, pp. 134–135.
[2] *Ibid.*, p. 135.

market Theatre, put a bill outside, and inside, with an audience of 4 persons, we read the play in Norwegian. I send you the bill (of which 12 copies only were printed); it marks my solitary appearance as an actor! It was odd to think that all this could go on in the very heart of London, where everybody thirsts for something new, and yet totally escape the newspapers. One journalist did discover the bill and wanted to make "copy" of the affair, but was promptly nobbled.'[1]

Consul H.L. (misprinted on the Bill as R.L.) Brækstad, appropriately for the man who had introduced Gosse to Ibsen's works, read Solness, and his wife Kaja. Elizabeth Robins and William Heinemann, who seem to have learned some Norwegian between them, read Hilde and Knut Brovik, and Amy Haldane read Mrs Solness.

Gyldendal published *The Master Builder* on 12 December in Christiania and two days later in Copenhagen, in a printing of 10,000 copies. Although many of the critics were bewildered, it got, overall, a better press in Scandinavia than any other play Ibsen had written since *A Doll's House*. Professor Bredo Morgenstierne predictably disliked it. 'It represents a step backwards', he lamented in *Aftenposten* (5 January 1893). 'The people we meet in it have little reality, or at best make a curiously airy and unreal impression . . . Solness and Hilde seem to belong to another world than the one we inhabit . . . We have difficulty in believing and understanding them. And the whole plot consists of a long string of improbabilities.' But Henrik Jæger in *Dagbladet* (27 and 30 December), after remarking that what was inhibited in Rebecca and Ellida was uninhibited and free in Hilde, concluded: 'The play is really a dialogue between Solness and Hilde, but a dialogue so powerful and brilliant that it is more gripping than the most exciting "scene". A poet who can write a play like *The Master Builder* has no reason to fear youth . . . His play is one long paean of praise to youth and the future.' Christian Brinckmann, in *Nyt Tidskrift* (1892–1893, pp. 272–281) also wrote admiringly of the play, in which 'despair resounds like jubilation and madness sounds like wisdom'.

In Sweden, opinions were similarly divided. Georg Göthe, in *Nordisk Tidskrift* (1893, pp. 153–157) found it 'essentially negative . . . It can be amusing to guess riddles; but when the riddles are so complex that one suspects that even the riddler himself does not really know the answer, the game ceases to be amusing . . . What are all these precious and pretentious abstract grandiloquencies which he has used so continuously since *The Lady from the Sea*? . . . Is it strange if some foreign observers find us Scandinavians abnormal?' The poet Gustav Fröding, however, praised the play in *Karlstads-Tidning* (4 February 1893), deploring 'the hateful attacks which the young have made on him'

---

[1] Bredsdorff, p. 48.

(presumably a reference to Hamsun); and Edvin Alkman reviewed it perceptively in *Svensk Tidskrift* (1893, pp. 138–152). Ibsen, he wrote, 'does not shrink from treating of phenomena which science has as yet barely and feebly started to illuminate, and which a few years ago were regarded by educated men as credulous and superstitious nonsense—such phenomena as hypnosis and telepathy'; and he shrewdly observed that the true subject of the play was 'self-love . . . and that curious power which men call God and which the egotist cannot endure because it sets bounds to his ego.'

Both the Brandes brothers praised it hugely. 'It is a masterpiece', wrote Edvard in *Politiken* (22 December). 'Only this man, already advanced in years and belonging to a small nation, could write such a play, in which supreme craftsmanship is allied to characteristic profundity . . . A work of genius.' And Georg, in *Verdens Gang* (28 December)—the first review he had written of an Ibsen play on publication since *Ghosts* eleven years previously—thought it his best yet. 'The play', he wrote, 'echoes in the mind long after one has read it. And when one has read it, one reads it again with increasing admiration. Technically faultless, profound and precise in its symbolism . . . Ibsen's new play is at the same time enthralling and liberating. Never has there existed a more perfect dramatic technique; never has dialogue been written like this.' Brandes's only regret, and it is a fair one, was that Ibsen had not made Solness more of an artist and established him more clearly as genuinely creative, a genius and not a mere tycoon. He concluded: 'Since Ibsen abandoned the matter and manner of his early plays, we have seen him acclaimed and attacked as a so-called "naturalist". Recently the so-called "symbolists" started a feud against "naturalism". That kind of catchword seldom means much, and all such are least applicable to Ibsen. For twenty years or more naturalism and symbolism have been harmonious partners in his work . . . Although both as a man and as a writer he loves reality, he is poet and thinker enough constantly to underlay the reality he portrays with a deeper interpretation.'

Great arguments developed as to the meaning of the play, and some extraordinary theories were advanced. Solness was variously taken to represent Ibsen himself, Bjørnson, the conservative party, the liberal party, Man rebelling against God, and (seriously) Bismarck, with Ragnar Brovik as the young Kaiser.[1]

---

[1] An anonymous critic in the London *Saturday Review* (4 March 1893, pp. 241–242) commented on these theories: 'We would undertake ourselves to get out of it a criticism of Mr Gladstone's Home Rule Bill, a system of phallic worship, a refutation of evolution and a diatribe against the Institution of British Architects . . . The fact of course is that it is of the essence of a fantasy piece to admit of almost any number of interpretations. And it is of the essence of the intelligent reader of a fantasy-piece not to insist upon any.' But the reviewer summed up *The Master Builder* as 'an impossible play . . . It will not stand examining.'

Ibsen never ceased to be amazed at the meanings people tried to read into his plays. Ernst Motzfeldt records a conversation he had with him shortly after the publication of *The Master Builder*:

'Ibsen said: "It's extraordinary what profundities and symbols they ascribe to me. I have received letters which ask if the nine dolls [of Mrs Solness] signify the Nine Muses, and the dead twins Scandinavianism and my own happiness. They have even asked if the dolls are connected with something in some Epistle of St Paul which I don't even know, or something in the Book of Revelation. Can't people just read what I write? I only write about people. I don't write symbolically. Just about people's inner life as I know it—psychology, if you like . . . I draw real, living people. Any considerable person will naturally be to some degree representative of the generality, of the thoughts and ideas of the age, so that the portrayal of such a person's inner life may seem symbolic. And I create such people. And with good reason. I have often walked with Hedda Gabler in the Munich arcades. And have undergone somewhat of the same experience myself.

'Solness and his wife are worthy people who don't suit each other and so aren't happy in their life together. They don't become what, being the people they are, they could and should have become—despite the fact that they aren't actually miserable, and despite their consideration for each other and a kind of tenderness and love. They keep each other down, cramp each other . . . Their worst characteristics are brought out, and they brood perpetually, because each goes his own way mentally and doesn't share with the other. Contrast Hilde and Solness. They are not portrayed as extraordinary persons, it is just that they feel spiritually akin, strongly attracted to each other, feel that they belong together and that life together would be immeasurably richer than it would otherwise be, and also that they themselves would be better people (Hilde immediately makes him do for Brovik what he wasn't willing to do before—did his wife ever try to make him do that?)—and that their relationship would elevate instead of debasing them, and give their lives greater meaning. Then the collision comes— when one still has a zest for life, a need for happiness, and feels unable to live without joy in subdued resignation. And so they decide to build a castle in the air and to live together in spirit. This lifts him up higher than before, to do things he had not been able to do for a long time (symbolically). But he stakes his life on it—and is killed. But was it so mad if it cost him his life, if he did it for his own happiness and only then, for the first time, achieved it?

'During our conversation he said it was wrong to think of unhappy love as when two people who love each other don't get each other. "No, unhappy love is when two people who love each other get married and feel they don't suit each other and cannot live happily together." '[1]

Despite the generally favourable reviews it received on publication, *The Master Builder* at first failed almost everywhere when staged. In Christiania it achieved only fifteen performances that season, and thirteen the next. In Copenhagen, it managed no more than eleven. In retrospect, this is not surprising. More than any play Ibsen had yet written, it demanded the kind of acting between the lines of which very few actors then were capable; and, like *The Lady from the Sea*, *The Father* and *Othello*, it needs a very particular kind of player in the leading role—an actor, as Yngvar Brun remarked when reviewing the Christiania production in *Morgenbladet* on 19 March 1893, 'as dazzlingly beautiful as love, as hideous as disease or egotism, as doubting and tormented as an evil conscience'. Another reason for its early failures on the stage was that in Scandinavia (then as now), and in Germany also, leading female roles tended to be awarded according to seniority rather than suitability. Edvard Brandes complained of the Copenhagen production (*Politiken*, 9 March 1893) that Betty Hennings was twenty years too old for Hilde.

Although today Hilde is usually played by actresses younger than Betty Hennings (then in her mid-forties), the age difference between her and Solness is still often under-emphasised. The Hilde too frequently looks thirty, the Solness a bare fifty or even less. For such a pair to become lovers strikes nobody as incongruous. Ibsen does not specify Solness's age—he merely calls him 'aging', probably to avoid too close an identification with himself—but he should surely be at least approaching sixty. Hilde is twenty-three; in other words, there should be not twenty, but nearly forty years between them; he should be old enough to be not merely her father but her grandfather. The theme of the play is an old man's fear of, and yearning for youth:

HILDE:  What do you want from me?
SOLNESS: Your youth, Hilde.
HILDE:  Youth, which you are so frightened of?
SOLNESS (*nods slowly*): And which, in my heart, I long for.

'Oh, high and painful joy—to struggle for the unattainable!' Ibsen had written in Emilie's album three years earlier in Gossensass. But if we see a handsome man of fifty wooing a girl of thirty, the point is lost. Even when

---

[1] Ernst Motzfeldt, *Af samtaler med Henrik Ibsen*, in *Aftenposten*, 23 April 1911 (also published as an offprint, Christiania, 1911).

Solness is played by an actor who is in fact sixty, one has too often seen him age himself down to forty-five.

Another fault too often committed by actors playing Solness is a tendency to push him up the social scale. Solness has fought his way up; his way of speaking is rough, not the language of one socially sure of himself. He is socially inferior not merely to his wife, but also to Hilde (whose language, by contrast, is immensely self-assured). Of course it is possible to argue that the son of 'pious, country people' (as Solness describes himself) need not be, or feel, socially inferior to the daughter of a country doctor; what is certain is that the play gains immeasurably if the social difference is there, between Solness and Hilde as well as between Solness and Aline. And he must be played sensually; one has seen Solnesses who behaved as though they would have not known what to do if Hilde had started to take her clothes off.

The character of Solness was the nearest thing to a deliberate self-portrait that Ibsen had yet attempted (though he was to follow it with two equally merciless likenesses in *John Gabriel Borkman* and *When We Dead Awaken*). He admitted in an address to the students of Christiania six years later that Solness was 'a man somewhat akin to me'; they shared an arrogancy and ruthlessness, a readiness to sacrifice the happiness of those close to them in order to further their ambition, and that longing for and fear of youth. The sensuality was Ibsen's, too, inhibited though he was about giving rein to it. Edvard Brandes noted that 'in his later years there lurked a strong sensuality in his bearing and speech'.[1]

Ibsen had, too, long regarded himself as a builder and his plays as works of architecture. In his youthful poem *Building Plans*[2] he had compared the artist to a master builder; and when the painter Erik Werenskiold, seeing him looking at some new building in Christiania, asked: 'You are interested in architecture?' Ibsen replied: 'Yes; it is, as you know, my own trade.'[3] And Ibsen, like Solness, had always had a fear of looking down from a great height or into a chasm, and this had become worse as he had grown older.

It has been argued by several commentators that Solness's development as

---

[1] Edvard Brandes, *Henrik Ibsens personlighed*, in *Litterære Tendenser* (Copenhagen, 1968), p. 231. And Gunnar Heiberg tells how Ibsen looked at a girl he introduced to him. 'I presented her and Ibsen looked emotionally at her face and cast a quick, admiring glance at her figure. He said nothing but his lips trembled. "She's very pretty, isn't she?" I said. Suddenly a smile flickered across his mouth. "She is", he said quietly and unwillingly, and his smile grew so that it illuminated his whole face. "Yes, she is", he repeated in a clear voice, this time directly to the young lady, as though in thanks.' (*Salt og sukker*, pp. 60–61). This took place in Christiania in the nineties.

[2] See *Henrik Ibsen: The Making of a Dramatist*, pp. 178–179.

[3] Koht, II, p. 257.

a builder corresponds precisely, if one reads between the lines, with Ibsen's career as a dramatist. 'The churches which Solness sets out by building', suggested William Archer, 'doubtless represent Ibsen's early romantic plays, the "homes for human beings" his social dramas, while the houses with high towers, merging into "castles in the air", stand for those spiritual dramas, with a wide outlook over the metaphysical environment of humanity, on which he was henceforth to be engaged.'[1] The theory may at first seem fanciful, of the kind that Ibsen himself derided; but the more one ponders it, the more truthfully it rings, whether the analogy was conscious or not. And one interesting variant between his extant draft and the final version of the play reveals how closely he identified himself with Solness. In the second act, when Solness is telling Hilde how success came to him, Ibsen originally made him conclude with the words: 'And now, at last, they have begun to talk of me abroad', which was exactly Ibsen's situation when he began work on the play. But he deleted the sentence in revision, doubtless because he felt that it made the identification too obvious.

Ibsen's interest in hypnosis, and the power that one human being could gain over the mind of another, has already been noted; and he carried it further in *The Master Builder* even than in his three preceding plays, concentrating here especially on how unexpressed wishes could sometimes translate themselves into actions. But if Solness is to be identified with Ibsen, Hilde is not to be identified with Emilie, Helene or Hildur. Was it from the needs of the play that Ibsen made her a harpy, or was it, remembering Elias's account of his maliciously untruthful description of Emilie, from a sense of guilt towards her and frustration with himself? Whatever the reason, from the time that Ibsen's letters to Emilie and Elias's story were published, both within a few months of Ibsen's death, everyone identified Emilie with Hilde, and for the remaining forty-eight years of her long life she was regarded as a predatory little monster. The play brought her as little joy as *A Doll's House* had brought to Laura Kieler.[2]

Nor was Emilie the only person to whom *The Master Builder* caused distress. The grim relationship between Solness and his wife was generally assumed, at any rate in Norway, to be a picture of the Ibsens' own marriage. Things seem

---

[1] Introduction to *The Master Builder* (London, 1907), p. xxviii.
[2] 'I didn't see myself', Emilie said, on seeing the play for the first time in 1908, 'but I saw him. There is something of me in Hilde; but in Solness, there is little that is not Ibsen.' Some commentators have suggested that Hildur Andersen was the original of Hilde. But he would hardly have modelled so unsympathetic a character on someone of whom he was so deeply fond, and he had originally created Hilde three years before he became interested in Hildur.

to have been getting difficult between Ibsen and Suzannah around this time (as we shall shortly see); and Magdalene Thoresen described their situation a couple of years later in words which precisely reflect the Solness marriage: 'They live in grand style, all most elegant, but in a suburban silence; for they are two lonely people—each for himself—each wholly for himself.'[1] The gossips of Christiania must have had a field day. And Francis Bull tells how a lady of his acquaintance who had known Ibsen in Munich was surprised, when Ibsen returned to Norway, to receive several invitations from him to dine out at restaurants. He seemed eager for her company and conversation until, suddenly, he stopped seeing her. She could not understand why until *The Master Builder* appeared. Then she recognised herself unmistakably in the character of Kaja Fosli, and realised that it was only as a model, not as a human being, that Ibsen was interested in her.[2]

Shortly before he had left Munich two years earlier (on 22 April 1890, according to her diary), Helene Raff had mentioned to him the legend of the master builder who had built St Michael's Church there and had thrown himself down from the tower because he was afraid the roof would not hold. Ibsen remarked that he thought the legend must have originated in Scandinavia, since he had heard it there, and when Helene observed that every famous cathedral in Germany had the same legend he replied that this must be because people felt instinctively that a man could not build so high without paying the penalty for his hubris. Did he perhaps feel that his plays, taken as a whole, were now approaching the size and seeming permanence of a cathedral, or that in some way he was challenging God? Of the repeated imagery of spires, which make an old man feel dizzy and a young girl hear harps in the air, the significance scarcely needs underlining; and I do not think it is reading too much into the play to assume that when Hilde, at the age of thirteen, saw Solness standing dangerously at the top of the tower in Lysanger, she had her first sexual orgasm, and that she drives him to the top of another tower in order to repeat it. Of their first meeting alone, when she says he kissed her and he denies it, we never know whether he wanted it so much that she thought it had happened, or *she* wanted it so much that she thought it had happened, or whether it did in fact happen and either a sense of guilt or mere forgetfulness caused him to forget. There is a close analogy with the film, *Last Year in Marienbad*, in which a similar situation occurs; and in both instances, part of the fascination lies in the fact that neither the people involved, nor we, ever know the truth.

[1] Magdalene Thoresen, *Breve, 1855–1901*, ed. J. Clausen and P. F. Rist (Copenhagen, 1919), p. 240.
[2] Bull, *Tradisjoner og minner*, pp. 101–102.

A few days after the publication of *The Master Builder*, on 16 December, there occurred a seemingly unimportant and almost unnoticed performance of an Ibsen play in Paris. The young Lugné-Poe presented *The Lady from the Sea* under the humble auspices of a theatre club which he had founded while still at school, Les Escholiers. He had lectured on the new dramatist of the North to his fellow-pupils, who included an awkward youth named Marcel Proust. The actors were all very young—Lugné-Poe himself played Dr Wangel—and it seems to have been a very bad production. Herman Bang, who saw it, declared that had Ibsen been present he would have 'wept blood or stared into his hat'. The symbolist movement in poetry and art was then at its peak in Paris—Paul Fort had founded his Théâtre de l'Art, the first symbolist theatre, in 1890, with Maeterlinck as his idol—and it was as a symbolist, not as a realist, that the French welcomed Ibsen. They drew delighted parallels between his plays and those of Maeterlinck, whose work Ibsen detested (Lugné-Poe records that he even refused to read *Pelléas et Mélisande* to the end, and that when Bang told him how in Paris they played Maeterlinck behind a transparent veil, Ibsen exclaimed violently: 'Why? What does it mean? I don't understand that kind of thing!').[1] Moreover, they had borrowed the worst methods that the Germans had been applying to Ibsen. 'In the German theatre', wrote Francisque Sarcey, 'it has become a tradition ... when they play Ibsen, that they strive to make the audience forget that these are real people of flesh and blood whom they see treading the boards. They move but little, use almost no hand-gestures and, when they do, make them broad, almost sacerdotal. Their whole delivery is characterised by a slow recitation, which seems to emanate from supernatural and symbolic lips.' Lugné-Poe confirms that 'faced with the difficulty of doing [Ibsen's plays] they hit on this monotonous, religious intonation, which we in our turn yielded to and plagued others with', and adds that Ibsen, 'when he heard of my friendly relations with his German interpreters and directors, took pains to urge me above all to avoid them.' But this contact between Lugné-Poe and Ibsen did not happen until later, so that *The Lady from the Sea* was practically a model of how Ibsen ought not to be acted—and yet it was a success among everybody enamoured of symbolism. Avant-garde magazines such as *Mercure de France*,

---

[1] Maeterlinck, ironically, appreciated better than most of his contemporaries what Ibsen was trying to do, especially his use of sub-text (*"dialogue du second degré"*). *Le Trésor des Humbles* (Paris, 1897, pp. 176–180) contains a penetrating section on *The Master Builder*: *"Hilde et Solness sont, je pense, les premiers héros qui se sentent vivre un instant dans l'atmosphère de l'âme, et cette vie essentielle qu'ils ont découverte en eux, par delà leur vie ordinaire, les épouvante ... Leurs propos ne ressemblent à rien de ce que nous avons entendu jusqu'ici, parce que le poète a tenté de mêler dans une même expression le dialogue intérieur et extérieur. Il règne dans ce drame somnambulique je ne sais quelles puissances nouvelles."*

*L'Ermitage* and *L'Académie Française* praised it glowingly, and its imagined obscurities were for months a talking-point in the cafés.[1]

And the occasion marked the beginning of an important partnership. Lugné-Poe was to do more for Ibsen than any other Frenchman, before or since; and within eighteen months, at the age of twenty-four, he was to be the first actor to succeed in the role of Master Builder Solness.

'A voice within me cries for you!' Ibsen wrote in the copy of *The Master Builder* which he sent to Helene Raff in Munich that New Year's Eve. He had not found any companion to replace Hildur Andersen. But he gave Hildur the manuscript of *The Master Builder*; also a copy of *Ghosts* inscribed with the lines from *Peer Gynt*:

> And the game can never be played again.
> Oh, here was my empire and my crown![2]

His earnings for 1892 had been as follows:

|  | crowns | £ |
|---|---|---|
| 6th edition of *Poems* (supplementary fee) | 20 | 1 |
| Unspecified royalties from Felix Bloch | 47 | 3 |
| Unspecified royalties from Wien Burgtheater | 540 | 30 |
| Unspecified royalties from Munich Hoftheater | 176 | 10 |
| Fee for provincial tour of *Hedda Gabler* by the Royal Opera, Stockholm | 150 | 8 |
| 4th edition of *Emperor and Galilean* | 1,600 | 89 |
| Unspecified royalties from Wien Burgtheater | 265 | 15 |
| „           „           „   Felix Bloch | 121 | 7 |
| „           „           „   Munich Hoftheater | 83 | 5 |
| Royalties for *The Wild Duck* from Royal Theatre, Copenhagen (14th–20th performances) | 1,848 | 103 |
| Unspecified royalties from Felix Bloch | 1,058 | 59 |
| „           „           „   Munich Hoftheater | 52 | 3 |
| 12th edition of *Brand* | 1,360 | 76 |
| Fee for illustrated edition of *Terje Vigen* | 250 | 14 |
| Royalties from Felix Bloch | 313 | 17 |
| Fee from French publisher, Savine, for Vols. 2 and 3 of Prozor's translations of the plays (250 francs) | 180 | 10 |
| Royalties from Munich Hoftheater | 138 | 8 |
| Fee for 1st edition of *The Master Builder* | 8,550 | 475 |

[1] Cf. Nyholm, pp. 38–39; Lugné-Poe, pp. 91–93.
[2] Bull, *Hildur Andersen og Henrik Ibsen*, p. 49.

|  | crowns | £ |
|---|---|---|
| Fee for German edition of *The Master Builder* (S. Fischer) | 533 | 29 |
| Fee from L. Dorsch and E. Zachrison for *The Vikings at Helgeland* in Sweden. | 50 | 3 |
| Fee from Dorsch and Zachrison for Swedish rights of *The Master Builder* for one year | 1,000 | 56 |
| Fee from Wm. Petersen for Norwegian provincial rights of *The Master Builder* for one year | 1,000 | 56 |
| Royalties from Royal Theatre, Copenhagen, for 21st performance of *The Wild Duck* | 123 | 7 |
|  | 19,457 | 1,086 |

# TEN

# ❧ 'Dull, Mysterious, Unchaste'

## (1893)

THE MASTER BUILDER had two world premieres simultaneously on 19 January 1893—at the Lessingtheater in Berlin (with Emmanuel Reicher as Solness), and in the little north Norwegian town of Trondhjem, under the humble auspices of William Petersen's travelling company, which had acquired the provincial rights. One might have expected the play to appeal to German taste, but it failed disastrously; the Berlin production had to be removed from the repertory after three performances. A touring Swedish company staged it in both Åbo (in Finland) and Helsinki that month; but, as with *Hedda Gabler*, the first successful production of the play took place in London, again thanks to the American actress Elizabeth Robins.

England was beginning to atone for its long neglect of Ibsen. Due very largely to him, the theatre was again beginning to attract men of letters; the previous year had seen the dramatic debuts of Oscar Wilde, Bernard Shaw and J. M. Barrie (to say nothing of *Charley's Aunt*), and the literary world of London awaited Ibsen's new play with immense expectation. Elizabeth Robins recalled the pre-publication fever; 'Months before *The Master Builder* reached these shores, the excitement that was set up by mere anticipation will never be credited in these times . . . Impatience for the play to come was exacerbated by the darkness that shrouded it . . . Neither the man who had committed himself to publishing it [William Heinemann] nor anybody else had even now the faintest idea what the play would be about. People lived on supposition, and were as hot over it as though they knew what they were contending for.'[1]

Among the enthusiasts who visited Miss Robins 'up those seventy-four steps' (as she described it) for news of the play were Henry James, Sidney Colvin, Sir Frederick Pollock, Mrs Humphry Ward, Rhoda Broughton, Bernard Shaw, the explorer Gertrude Bell, Beerbohm Tree, R. B. Haldane, Hubert Crackanthorpe, W. T. Stead, Arthur Symons and Oscar Wilde. The play arrived in instalments during November 1892, as each batch of proofs

---

[1] Elizabeth Robins, *Theatre and Friendship* (London, 1932), pp. 75 ff.

emerged from Gyldendal's presses—"in small, in very small, violently agitating spurts—or, as one might say, in volts, projected across the North Sea in a series of electric shocks.'[1]

But as the pattern of the plot emerged even the most ardent Ibsenites began to have qualms. 'More in the dark than ever', wrote Miss Robins to Florence Bell on 12 November. 'Think the old man's stark mad.' A few days later she reported that Archer himself 'is a good deal puzzled; but he says the 1st Act is powerful and fascinating though he can't "see it" on the English stage. I am desolate.' As the second act came in 'W.A. seems less hopeful . . . He writes: "The interest certainly hangs fire, etc. etc." I fear the thing is hopeless!' Henry James also found the first instalments unpromising. 'I have kindly been favoured with the communication of most of it', he wrote to Florence Bell on 16 November, 'and am utterly bewildered and mystified . . . It is all most strange, most curious, most vague, most horrid, most "middle-classy" in the peculiar ugly Ibsen sense—and alas most unpromising for Miss Elizabeth or for any woman. What is already clear is that a man is the central figure . . . and the man, alas, an elderly white-haired architect, or Baumeister, is, although a strange and interesting, a fearfully charmless creature.'[2]

Miss Elizabeth tried several of the established theatres; but her enthusiasm for Ibsen was not shared by the managements. 'I was told The Master Builder was simply unintelligible. Oh, it was wild! It was irritatingly obscure. It was dull, it was mad, it would lose money.'[3] She tried reading it to Herbert Beerbohm Tree, who 'was swept away by Solness, wants to play it'; but it transpired that before doing so he demanded 'amazing alterations' (including making all the characters English and Solness a sculptor), to which Heinemann and Archer refused to agree. Eventually Herbert Waring, who had played Helmer to Janet Achurch's Nora in 1889, agreed to act Solness on Ibsen's terms, and on 20 February The Master Builder was presented (for the usual five matinées) at the Trafalgar Square Theatre in St Martin's Lane (now the Duke of York's).

Henry James tried to encourage intelligent appreciation of the play by an article in the Pall Mall Gazette, three days before the premiere, in which he praised Ibsen's 'independence, his perversity, his intensity, his vividness, the hard compulsion of his strangely inscrutable art . . . [and] his peculiar blessedness to actors . . . No dramatist of our time has had more the secret, and has kept it better, of making their work interesting to them. The subtlety with which he puts them into relation to it eludes analysis, but operates none the less strongly as an incitement.' But this plug had little effect on the London

[1] Ibid., p. 78.
[2] Ibid., pp. 82–84.
[3] Elizabeth Robins, Ibsen and the Actress (London, 1928), p. 29.

dramatic critics, who greeted the play, like its predecessors, with a chorus of vituperation:

'Dense mist enshrouds characters, words, actions, and motives . . . One may compare it . . . to the sensations of a man who witnesses a play written, rehearsed and acted by lunatics.'

*Daily Telegraph*

'Platitudes and inanities . . . The play is hopeless and indefensible.'

*Globe*

'A feast of dull dialogue and acute dementia . . . The most dreary and purposeless drivel we have ever heard in an English theatre . . . A pointless, incoherent and absolutely silly piece.'

*Evening News*

'Assuredly no one may fathom the mysteries of the play, so far as it can be called a play . . . It is not for a moment to be understood that we personally recommend anyone to go and see it.'

*Standard*

'Rigmarole of an Oracle Delphic in obscurity and Gamp-like in garrulity . . . Pulseless and purposeless play, which has idiocy written on every lineament . . . Three acts of gibberish.'

*Stage*

'A distracting jumble of incoherent elements. There is no story; the characters are impossible, and the motives a nightmare of perverted finger-posts.'

*Saturday Review*

'Sensuality . . . irreverence . . . unwholesome . . . simply blasphemous.'

*Morning Post*

'Dull, mysterious, unchaste.'

*Daily Graphic*[1]

On the day after the opening performance Henry James wrote to Elizabeth Robins: 'I have looked at the papers, and there is little edification in them of

---

[1] William Archer, *The Mausoleum of Ibsen*, pp. 85–86.
Her Majesty's Censor (a Mr Pigott) shared these opinions. 'I have studied Ibsen's plays pretty carefully', he had declared in 1892, 'and all the characters appear to me to be morally deranged. All the heroines are dissatisfied spinsters who look on marriage as a monopoly, or dissatisfied married women in a chronic state of rebellion . . . and as for the men, they are all rascals or imbeciles.' (Quoted by Charles Archer, p. 189 n.)

course. They are stupid, angry and mean. The weaknesses of the play do indeed come out strongly in representation, but it would have been only honest in them to acknowledge also its *hold*, the odd baffling spell it works and the remarkable spell of the interpretation . . . I thought Waring *extremely good*—various and interesting, intelligent and coloured: BUT distinctly not loud enough. You were—keep it up, *up*, UP.'[1]

However, when he revisited the theatre for a subsequent performance James noted to his amazement that 'the house . . . was *full*'.[2] Intelligent opinion had decided to ignore the critics. George Moore wrote to Elizabeth Robins: 'I thank God I came a second time. It has grown upon me. I understand.'[3] Indeed, he came a third time. Oscar Wilde attended the final performance and was greatly impressed; and Bernard Shaw wrote to Elizabeth Robins after the first matinée: 'There is no saying what the papers will come out with tomorrow morning; so I had better send you my certificate of the perfect success of the play as far as I am concerned. It held me and moved me from beginning to end.'[4] Unfortunately, very few of Ibsen's supporters ran a dramatic column. 'The New Critics are to the Old Critics', William Archer had written in the *Fortnightly Review* the preceding August, 'in number as one to ten, in opportunities for disseminating their views as one to ten thousand.' And even two of the most prominent of these New Critics, sad to relate, disliked *The Master Builder*. A. B. Walkley, who had praised *Hedda Gabler* as 'a masterpiece of piquant subtlety, delicate observation and tragic intensity',[5] felt compelled to write coolly of *The Master Builder* in the *Fortnightly Review* that April, saying that he disliked symbolism on the stage; and Justin Huntly McCarthy, who had regarded both *A Doll's House* and *Hedda Gabler* as major plays, declared of *The Master Builder* in the *Gentlemen's Magazine*: 'A great man can blunder, and this great man has blundered.' Yet the play did well enough to be transferred on 6 March to the evening bill at the Vaudeville Theatre, where it continued until the end of the month.

A fortnight after the London premiere, on 8 March, *The Master Builder* was staged simultaneously in Christiania and Copenhagen; and in both cities it failed. On 23 March August Lindberg presented it in Gothenburg, with himself as Solness and another new discovery of his, Hilda Borgström, as Hilde; but although the production received splendid notices, it achieved only five performances, and the takings were so poor that Lindberg could not pay

[1] Robins, *Theatre and Friendship*, pp. 101–102.
[2] *Ibid.*, p. 103.
[3] *Ibid.*, p. 107.
[4] Shaw, *Collected Letters, 1874–1897*, p. 382.
[5] A. B. Walkley, *Playhouse Impressions* (London, 1892), p. 62.

Ibsen the thousand crowns (£55) he owed him. Ibsen had demanded two thousand crowns for the Gothenburg and Stockholm rights, half in advance and half after the fifth performance, and refused to allow Lindberg any grace, informing him (13 February) that 'last week I sent a large sum of money to Copenhagen to buy shares and have practically no money left,' and even wiring him on 3 April forbidding him to present his production in Stockholm until the money had been paid—churlish treatment, one might think, towards the man who had done more than any other actor-manager for his plays in the theatre. Fortunately, Lindberg managed to find a Norwegian friend (a chief of police, of all things) to lend him the money, and so was able to open in Stockholm (where again the production was acclaimed) and to tour it for a month; though when he asked to take it to Copenhagen, where Dagmars Theatre wished to present it, Ibsen and the Royal Theatre of Copenhagen prevented him from doing so.[1]

All this while, Sigurd was going through a very difficult time. Since leaving the diplomatic service in 1889 he had been without a permanent job, and was to remain so until 1899. Despite his outstanding ability and unquestioned patriotism, he was finding everywhere a resistance similar to that which his father had so often encountered in his field. Ibsen was so furious with the authorities for their ostracism of his son that he again seriously considered giving up his Norwegian citizenship, as witness the following extract from a letter to Sigurd (now living with Bergliot in the country near her parents) on 8 February 1893:

*On Sunday we had a visit from O. Arvesen [a Member of Parliament] and his wife, and I took the opportunity to have a talk with him, the gist of which was this. He began by saying that he had recently seen you and had suggested that you should come down here for a talk about your position vis-à-vis the foreign service. I then took occasion quietly but forcibly to express my personal opinion of the government's conduct towards you. I said that for a long time now you had placed yourself at their disposal, but that all their promises to you had remained unfulfilled. I told him that Steen [the Prime Minister] had, without my raising the subject, told me that it had been decided to create a political department within the Home Office in the near future. But I said that as far as I knew no steps had yet been taken and that I had therefore lost all confidence and trust in the government's promises. I ended by telling him slowly, coldly and forcibly that I was now considering giving up Norwegian citizenship and leaving the country next autumn to become naturalised in Bavaria, and that I would counsel you to do likewise.*

*This announcement appeared greatly to disconcert Arvesen, and his wife no less.*

---

[1] Lindberg, pp. 339–344. Bergliot Ibsen (pp. 175–176) defends Ibsen's conduct towards Lindberg, but not very convincingly.

P

*Both begged me most earnestly to pause before taking any final step. He said he would*
*use this statement of mine in a way that would, he hoped, quickly precipitate a decision*
*that would be satisfactory to both you and me. I assured him repeatedly that you knew*
*nothing of what I had in mind; so my remarks cannot harm your case. Whether it will*
*assist it and your prospects I cannot yet say.*

Ibsen's efforts on behalf of his son were unavailing. Sigurd's campaign to
rally opinion against the Union with Sweden had antagonised the Conservative
government which had been in office since 1889, and he continued to be
regarded as a political pariah, dependent on his pen to earn a living. He pam-
phleteered energetically for the cause that lay so near his heart; he insisted that
his book, *The Union*, should be priced as cheaply as eight øre (a penny) so
that it should be within the reach of every pocket, and continued the fight in
a further series of articles which formed the basis of another book, *Men and*
*Powers*. Yet he found surprisingly little support among his countrymen. The
apathy which his father had denounced in *Brand* remained. But Ibsen did not
carry out his threat to leave Norway. Sigurd was determined to stay there to
continue the fight, and Ibsen was more than ever, as he grew older, reluctant
to be far from him. And he had, after all, withdrawn from the political battle;
politics and current affairs were to play no further part in his writing.

In London, the Ibsen fever continued. From 29 May to 10 June *Rosmersholm*,
*Hedda Gabler* and *The Master Builder* (together with Act 4 of *Brand*) were
presented in repertory at the Opera Comique in the Strand. Elizabeth Robins
played Hedda and Hilde as before, and also Rebecca West, with Lewis Waller
as Løvborg, Solness and Rosmer; William Archer wrote in the *World* that he
thought her Rebecca West 'the largest, finest, most poetic thing [she] has yet
done'. Thomas Hardy visited all three productions within a week, and was
impressed; the doubts he had felt on reading Ibsen were, like Henry James's,
dispelled when he saw the plays staged. His companion to *The Master Builder*,
Florence Henniker, was 'so excited by the play as not to be able to sleep all
night',[1] and the final scene must curiously have reminded Hardy of his own
first published novel, *Desperate Remedies* (1871), which begins with a master
builder falling from one of his own towers. On 9 June Eleonora Duse opened
a season of *A Doll's House* in Italian at the Lyric Theatre, and on 14 June Herbert
Beerbohm Tree presented *An Enemy of the People* at the Theatre Royal,
Haymarket, with himself as Dr Stockmann. Archer found the text 'mon-
trously mutilated' and noted that 'the first actor-manager performance of
Ibsen, despite the excellent talents employed, was distinctly below the level of
the so-called "scratch" performances to which we have become accustomed';

[1] Florence Emily Hardy, *The Life of Thomas Hardy* (2nd edn., London, 1965), p. 256.

and Bernard Shaw thought that Tree's performance 'though humorous and entertaining in its way, was, as a character creation, the polar opposite of Ibsen's Stockmann'. But the play was a success, and Tree, who had originally presented it for seven performances only, made it a regular item in his repertory. Ibsen's reward from this expensive production came to approximately five guineas a performance; one wonders how many guineas Tree was getting.

In July William Archer published in the *Fortnightly Review* an article already cited, *The Mausoleum of Ibsen*, in which he surveyed Ibsen's progress in England since the break-through of 1889. Admitting that there had been a good deal of sane and competent criticism, and even some that had been extravagantly enthusiastic, Archer observed sadly that 'both in bulk and influence the favourable, or even the temperate criticism has been as nothing beside the angrily or scornfully hostile. All the great morning papers, the leading illustrated weeklies, the critical weeklies with one exception, and the theatrical trade papers, have been bitterly denunciatory.' And yet (he continued) the volume incorporating *The Pillars of Society*, *Ghosts* and *An Enemy of the People* which Walter Scott had published in the Camelot Classics at a shilling had, in less than four years (to the end of 1892), sold 14,367 copies, plus 16,834 copies of the five-volume edition published by Scott in 1891–1892 at 3s. 6d. Additionally, other publishers had issued single-volume editions of *A Doll's House*, *Rosmersholm*, *Ghosts*, *The Lady from the Sea*, *Hedda Gabler* and *The Master Builder*.

'Thus, I think, we are well within the mark in estimating that 100,000 prose dramas by Ibsen have been bought by the English-speaking public in the course of the past four years. Is there a parallel in the history of publishing for such a result in the case of translated plays? . . . The publishers to whom I proposed a collected edition of the Prose Dramas before Mr Walter Scott undertook it, dismissed the idea as visionary, roundly declaring that no modern plays could ever "sell" in England . . . For fifty years or more, the English public had lost the habit of reading plays . . . yet the fact remains that 100,000 of his plays are at this moment in the hands of the reading public . . .

'Except in omnivorous Germany, have translated plays ever been known to take very deep root on a foreign stage? In adaptation there has for centuries been a brisk international trade . . . but translations have been few and far between. In England least of all have we shown any appetite for them. Even of Molière we have made, for the stage, only crude and now almost forgotten adaptations. Since, then, Ibsen—translated, not adapted— has met with some acceptance in the English theatre, that fact is in itself practically unique. If he had indeed been "impossible" on the English stage, he would have had as companions in impossibility Corneille, Racine, Molière, Marivaux, Lessing, Goethe, Schiller, Lope and Calderon; no such despicable fraternity. As a matter of fact, and in the face of the unexampled tempest of obloquy in the Press, seven of his plays—not adapted, but faithfully translated—have been placed on the English stage. If our theatrical history presents any parallel to this, I shall be glad to hear of it; I certainly can think of none.'

Archer goes on to point out that of the seven Ibsen plays so far produced in London (excluding *The Lady from the Sea*, of which he knew no details, and *Ghosts*, which did not charge for its two performances), the receipts for *The Pillars of Society* (one matinée) and *Rosmersholm* (in 1891, two matinées) totalled £276. The three remaining plays—*A Doll's House*, *Hedda Gabler* and *The Master Builder*—took £4,600. *Hedda Gabler* made a profit, after paying all expenses, of £281 on its ten matinées. Yet he concluded with the surprisingly pessimistic forecast that 'It is scarcely to be expected . . . that they [Ibsen's plays] should take deep and permanent hold on the English stage', and expressed the hope that English successors to Ibsen would emerge and be played instead. He would have been happy to know that, over three-quarters of a century later, around twenty professional productions a year of those plays would regularly be mounted in the English theatre, television and radio.

The enemies of Ibsen, naturally, continued to fulminate. In the prologue to his play *The Tempter*, written this year, Henry Arthur Jones exhorted his audience to:

Shun the crude present with vain problems rife,
Nor join the bleak Norwegian's barren quest
For deathless beauty's self and holy zest
Of rapturous martyrdom, in some base strife
Of petty dullards, soused in native filth.[1]

On 11 July Sigurd and Bergliot had their first child, a boy. Mercifully rejecting the suggestion of their landlord that he should be called Bjørnstjerne (how could any child or man have lived up to the name of Bjørnstjerne Ibsen?),

[1] Two years later, in an essay entitled *The Renascence of English Drama*, Jones declared: 'A strong, dirty man has written plays, and now every feeble dirty person thinks himself a dramatist.' But in 1913, in *Foundations of a National Drama*, Jones recanted, and spoke of himself as one of 'those whom his shattering genius has at length conquered', referring to him in the same volume as 'a great destroyer; a great creator; a great poet; a great liberator . . . There is no serious modern dramatist who has not been directly or indirectly influenced by him.'

they christened him Tancred, a Norman name (writes Bergliot) so as to symbolise the union between the north and the south, between Scandinavia and the Mediterranean. Soon after he was born they moved to Christiania, and came to Ibsen to show him his first grandchild.

'I can still see Ibsen,' recalled Bergliot, 'drifting with his short steps around his wife as she sat in the centre of the room with Tancred on her lap. Each time he passed he bent down and looked at him, childishly gentle and happy because it was a boy.' They had him baptised by Christopher Bruun, the part-original of Brand; he wore the robe in which his grandfather had been baptised, and Suzannah carried him to the font. Ibsen was very nervous lest any accident should befall the child, and as Suzannah approached the font he rose, crossed over to Bergliot, took her arm and whispered: 'Do you think she'll drop him?' At the dinner afterwards in Viktoria Terrasse Ibsen made a speech thanking Bruun for everything he had meant to him, and Bruun replied with the eloquence which Ibsen had so admired in him in Rome.

For the first time, Bergliot was now seeing her parents-in-law regularly.

'It was a new and strange world. The Ibsens' home was as quiet as Aulestad had been full of fun and life. Few people visited them... There was one thing I could not understand at all. I came from the company of my own family, from Father, who believed in everything and everyone, the good that people told him and the bad; believed in people; both those who told the truth and those who lied; and then I came to the Ibsens, to Henrik Ibsen, who believed no one and nothing that anyone told him. I remember I would come up from town full of news which I enthusiastically recounted to them. Ibsen would sit and listen attentively, and when I had finished he would say: "Don't believe a word of it, it's all untrue." I had to hide my disappointment; but what surprised me most was that he was nearly always right.

'The strange thing about Ibsen was that he seemed so slow at grasping things. One always had to tell him a story twice. First he listened, the second time he always asked very searchingly for details, which lay very far from my Bjørnson nature. But he would insist. He took note of every detail; one could literally see him absorbing them. When anything particularly interested him, he would raise one eyebrow like Sigurd, and one of his eyes seemed much bigger than the other. But soon after he would go into his room; he was always occupied with his work.'[1]

That summer Ibsen renewed a friendship which had been allowed to lapse, with the only other Norwegian whose name was as internationally famous as

[1] Bergliot Ibsen, pp. 143–144.

230 HENRIK IBSEN

his own. Edvard Grieg had recently returned from Germany in a state of
poor health and extreme nervous exhaustion, and had gone to the sanatorium
at Grefsen to recuperate. One Sunday in July Ibsen was visiting Christian
Sontum and his family there, and Grieg walked over to join them. Bolette
Sontum was present and, in her awkward English, recalled the occasion:

'Ibsen sat brooding, solemn and relentless. But suddenly his face lighted
up radiantly as Grieg, light-hearted and buoyant as a sunbeam, tripped up
the steps. The two masters clasped hands. They had not met for years, and
there was a shot of questions and answers as between two boys, Ibsen's
deep basso vibrating thunders to Grieg's piping Bergen soprano. Half-
serious, half-jesting, they discussed the plan of Grieg's setting *The Vikings
at Helgeland* to music . . . After dinner at the sanatorium we induced Ibsen,
in behalf of the balmy summer afternoon, to walk with us to the "Little
Outlook", a particularly choice viewpoint on the Grefsen plateau, which
commands an excellent perspective of Christiania miles below in the valley.
Ibsen walked very slowly, his shoulders stooped, one hand against his back,
the other clasping the gold head of his walnut stick. This stick was as
personally associated with him as his big gold-rimmed spectacles. These he
had twisted so that the left eye always seemed larger and more drooping
than the right, and really exaggerated the severity of his piercing gaze.
The stick itself was a necessary complement to the glasses, as his near-
sightedness made him helpless one step beyond his immediate vision.
'We walked very slowly on his account, especially when climbing
the last steep round of the mountain. Finally, we came up breathless but
rewarded with the inspiring view of the fjord. Ibsen sat down heavily on a
rustic bench under one distinctly black fir, whose branches cut appealing
grotesques against the blue sky.'[1]

Ibsen was to remember this place, and the view of the distant city with its
factories, three years later when writing the final scene of *John Gabriel Borkman*.
But he was to write another play before that, and on 18 September he informed Jacob Hegel that he had begun to plan it, and 'intend to complete it
next summer'.

He seems to have kept largely to himself for the rest of that year; with
Hildur still abroad, he paid fewer visits to theatres and none to lectures or
concerts. Among his infrequent visitors was Jonas Lie's youngest daughter
Johanne, then at the start of her career as an actress. Ibsen, with her father,
attended her debut at the Christiania Theatre, and asked her to come and read
to him at Viktoria Terrasse. When she arrived, Suzannah admitted her with the

[1] Sontum, pp. 250–251.

daunting welcome: 'Dr Ibsen is expecting you', and showed her into his 'very small study'.

'Ibsen wanted to chat. And I got the feeling that this great writer was no cold satirist but a man of strong and lasting passions. He was not taciturn nor coldly curt; indeed, there was something confidential about his manner of talking. Suddenly there would be a flash of lightning under those bushy eyebrows, and one felt that this man could see right through one. I rose to leave, certain that he had forgotten about the reading. "No, now you must read for me" . . . I read him scenes [from *Love's Comedy*]. Dr Ibsen rose. "You shall play that part." And the amazing thing was that he actually wrote to Schrøder, the head of the theatre, and I did play Svanhild.'[1]

But she remembered how cold he could be to people he did not like, or who were over-familiar.

'I see Dr Ibsen standing in a doorway at a big party at Dr Bœck's at Munkedammen, looking straight ahead as though in a dream. A gentleman claps him on the shoulder. "Come on, Henrik, let's have a drink. Don't stand there brooding." Ibsen did not reply, but a motion of the hand dismissed the speaker mercilessly, like a feather that one blows away . . . He worked all the time, at home, on the street, in cafés . . . He was not especially afraid of death—only, when he was working on a play he would fear he might be taken away before he had said what he had to say to the world. And he did not want to die abroad.'

Once Johanne introduced another young girl to him as he was checking his watch by the University clock. 'Later that young girl often visited him at his home. She interested him.' Who this girl was we do not know, nor whether he used her in any of the three plays he had still to write. Like so many men who cannot fulfil themselves sexually for one reason or another (and I think there is little doubt that he could not, at any rate in old age), he needed a variety of attractive companions.

A Danish schoolboy, too, met Ibsen for the first time this year, and carried away an unusual impression. Jacob Hegel's son, named Frederik after his grandfather, was in the capital and had been told by his father to pay his respects. Aged thirteen, he arrived without warning: 'I rang; and Fru Ibsen warily opened the front door. When I told her who I was, she let me in, and Ibsen, who had been lying on the sofa with a rug over him, unwrapped himself slowly and came to greet me . . . He began to talk and talk of Denmark.

---

[1] Johanne Lie's reminiscences of Ibsen were published in *Urd, Ibsen-nummer* (Oslo, 1928), pp. 150–151.

What Denmark had meant to him. He spoke warmly, not grandly but humbly, softly and with deep emotion. He took me out on to the balcony and looked over Oslo [sic] as he spoke, and became more and more moved. Remarkable to relate, this lonely man opened his heart completely to the youth from Denmark whom he scarcely knew, and wept. He laid his head on my shoulder and wept . . . Fru Ibsen gave me an angry glance as I left. She sensed that something had happened.'[1] No wonder she gave young Hegel a resentful look. Although he does not say so, and may not have realised it, Ibsen only behaved this way when he was drunk, and Suzannah must have wondered what story the boy would take back to his father in Copenhagen.

1893 was, as we have seen, an important year for Ibsen in England, and it was to prove equally so in France. That autumn Lugné-Poe founded, together with Edouard Vuillard and Camille Mauclair, a 'little theatre' on the lines of Antoine's Théâtre Libre and Paul Fort's short-lived Théâtre de l'Art (in which Lugné-Poe himself had played the Old Blind Man in Maeterlinck's L'Intruse). They called their new enterprise Le Théâtre de L'Œuvre, and opened it on 6 October with Rosmersholm. Vuillard did the decor and designed the programme and posters; Lugné-Poe played Rosmer and Berthe Bady Rebecca. The production was much better than that of The Lady from the Sea the previous year, for Ibsen, on hearing about the latter effort from Herman Bang, had asked Bang to advise Lugné-Poe on the way his plays ought to be done; realistically, as opposed to ritualistically, and above all quickly. Antoine had the right natural-istic approach, but lacked any background of Scandinavian knowledge, and especially of Norwegian manners. Bang was able to provide this. The case was similar to that of Chekhov in England; he was never fully understood here until Theodor Komisarjevsky, in the nineteen-twenties, was able to explain that what had been assumed to be eccentric and symbolic was far more effective if played with the simplest realism.

On 10 November the Théâtre de l'Œuvre followed Rosmersholm with An Enemy of the People, as though to underline Ibsen's expressed hostility to overt symbolism in drama. Yet here again Ibsen showed his gift for reflecting topical issues anywhere and at any time, for the premiere occurred on a day when there were fierce anarchical demonstrations in the streets of Paris, and Dr Stockmann's hard words about the mob won an enthusiastic response from the young poets and artists who formed a large part of the audience and, odd as it may seem today, regarded themselves as an élite and dissociated themselves from the rioters outside. The dress rehearsal itself turned into a riot. It was preceded by a lecture, ostensibly about the play, by Laurent Tailhade 'which

[1] Frederik Hegel, Erindringer, I (Copenhagen, 1946), p. 115.

[writes Archer] consisted not so much of an exposition of the play as of a violent attack upon all the "leading men" in French literature and politics. Beside it, Dr Stockmann's harangue in the fourth act seems moderate and almost mealy-mouthed.' The writers attacked included several who were present, including Sarcey; and Tailhade compared Dr Stockmann to the prophet Elijah. Archer continues: 'The audience listened, not without protest, to M. Tailhade's diatribe, until he thought fit to describe the recent Franco-Russian fêtes as an act of collective insanity. At this point a storm of indignation burst forth, which lasted without pause for a quarter of an hour, and was not allayed by an attempt at intervention on the part of M. Lugné-Poe. The lecture closed amid wild confusion, and altogether the preliminary scene in the auditorium was like a spirited rehearsal of the meeting at Captain Horster's.'[1]

Thus Ibsen found himself acclaimed simultaneously as the opponent and the champion of anarchy. Clemenceau felt that the occasion recalled the brave days of 1830; the Théâtre de l'Œuvre came to be regarded as a centre of anarchy, and was the subject of a debate in the French Parliament; and a young anarchist named Auguste Vaillant who had been arrested for an attempt to cause a dynamite explosion named among the writers who had inspired him Darwin, Herbert Spencer and Ibsen, three singularly law-abiding men. But the play received tepid reviews. Apart from Henri Bauer in *Echo de Paris*, the French critics found it ill-constructed (which it certainly is not).[2]

One would like to be able to record the German productions of Ibsen that took place this year; but most of his royalties from that country were now coming through his agent, Felix Bloch, and are not separately itemised in his accounts, and the history of Ibsen on the German stage is lamentably ill-documented. W. H. Eller, in his book *Ibsen in Germany* (Boston, 1918), lists no new productions in 1892 and none in 1893 save the Berlin *Master Builder*; but although Ibsen's royalties from Bloch were down to 1,353 crowns in 1893, compared with 1,539 in 1892 and 2,120 in 1891 (an outstanding year), one doubts whether those sums can refer only to repeats of old performances. Even if they do, the figures show that, contrary to some supposition, he was still being frequently performed there. A windfall of £200 from Heinemann for the English edition of *The Master Builder* made 1893 a fair year for one in which Ibsen had written no new play:

| | crowns | £ |
|---|---|---|
| Royalties from Bloch | 204 | 11 |
| Fee from Heinemann for English edition of *The Master Builder* | 3,628 | 202 |

---

[1] William Archer, Introduction to *An Enemy of the People* (London, 1901), pp. xv–xvi.
[2] Nyholm, pp. 42–44.

| | crowns | £ |
|---|---|---|
| Fee for English edition of *Peer Gynt* | 242 | 13 |
| Fee from Christiania Theatre for *The Master Builder* | 3,000 | 167 |
| Fee from August Lindberg for Stockholm and Gothenburg rights of *The Master Builder* | 1,000 | 56 |
| Royalties from Bloch | 750 | 42 |
| 3rd edition of *The Pillars of Society* | 700 | 39 |
| Royalties for *The Master Builder* at Royal Theatre, Copenhagen (1st-5th performances) | 1,775 | 99 |
| Royalties from Societé des Auteurs Dramatiques (810 fr.) | 577 | 32 |
| Royalties from H. Beerbohm Tree for 1st and 2nd perfs. of *An Enemy of the People* in London (£11 7s. 0d.) | 205 | 11 |
| Royalties from Bloch | 204 | 11 |
| Royalties from Wien Burgtheater for *An Enemy of the People* | 120 | 7 |
| Royalties from Tree for 3rd–7th perfs. of *An Enemy of the People* in London (£25 5s. 0d.) | 458 | 25 |
| Royalties for *The Pillars of Society* at Munich Hoftheater | 135 | 7 |
| Royalties from Opera Comique, London, for *Rosmersholm*, etc. (£12 10s. 0d.) | 227 | 13 |
| Royalties for *The Master Builder* at Royal Theatre, Copenhagen (6th–11th performances) | 1,095 | 61 |
| Royalties from Bloch | 195 | 11 |
| 7th edition of *The Vikings at Helgeland* | 406 | 22 |
| 9th edition of *Peer Gynt* | 1,815 | 101 |
| Royalties for *The Pillars of Society* and *A Doll's House* at Munich Hoftheater | 456 | 25 |
| | 17,192 | 955 |

ELEVEN

## ❧ Little Eyolf

## (1894)

LUGNÉ-POE'S ENTHUSIASM for Ibsen continued unabated into 1894. On
3 April he directed and acted *The Master Builder* for his Théâtre de l'Œuvre at
the Bouffes du Nord. The production was received with derision. Gunnar
Heiberg records that the audience shouted their own answers to Hilde's
questions to Solness; the business about the crack in the chimney-pipe was
greeted with roars of laughter; and whenever (as happens several times in the
play) any character said: 'I don't understand this', the audience echoed:
'Neither do we'. Yet again, the mockery of the first-night audience represented
only one view. Heiberg, reporting on a revival of this production five years
later, comments; 'The general public liked neither the play nor the performance, but the young, the supporters of Ibsen and L'Œuvre, loved both.
"God, what a play!" exclaimed one young man with long hair.' But despite
Herman Bang's coaching, Heiberg still noted with regret the tendency of the
French to intone Ibsen like a mass and surround his plays with a kind of
mystique even (indeed, especially) when having to express everyday sentiments;
and he felt that Lugné-Poe acted Solness 'tastefully and intelligently, but
without suggesting a living person.'[1]

Yet two more distinguished judges than Heiberg found both the production
and Lugné-Poe's performance powerful and moving. When the company
visited London the following year, Bernard Shaw wrote: 'Comparing the
performance with what we have achieved in England, it must be admitted
that neither Mr Waring nor Mr Waller were in a position to play Solness as
M. Lugné-Poe played him. They would never have got another engagement
in genteel comedy if they had worn those vulgar trousers, painted that red
eruption on their faces, and given life to that portrait which, in every stroke,
from its domineering energy, talent and covetousness, to its half-witted

---

[1] Gunnar Heiberg, *Ibsen og Bjørnson paa scenen* (Christiania, 1918), pp. 81–86. During
the 1898 dress rehearsal a disaster occurred in the final act when the dummy figure that was
to drop from the flies (showing Solness's fall from his tower) burst and showered its contents
over the front stalls.

egoism and crazy philandering sentiment, is so amazingly true to life. Mr Waring and Mr Waller failed because they were under the spell of Ibsen's fame as a dramatic magician, and grasped at his poetic treatment of the man instead of at the man himself. M. Lugné-Poe succeeded because he recognised Solness as a person he had met a dozen times in ordinary life, and just reddened his nose and played him without preoccupation.'[1] How much better Shaw wrote about Ibsen when reviewing productions of his plays than in the *Quintessence*! The other authority who set the seal of his approval on the production and performance was, as we shall hear, Ibsen himself.

A fortnight after the *Master Builder* opening, on 20 April, Paris enjoyed another and more fashionable Ibsen premiere when Gabrielle Réjane played Nora at the Théâtre Vaudeville. Ibsen sent her a telegram thanking her for fulfilling his 'dearest dream, in creating Nora in Paris'. She enjoyed a great triumph in the role, thanks largely to Herman Bang, who advised on this production as he had on Lugné-Poe's. 'If I succeeded in overcoming the many difficulties in the part of Nora', Réjane wrote to Lugné-Poe, 'I owe it to Herman Bang'; and she added that she had never met a director who exuded so strong a personality in the theatre.

The production provided Ibsen with his first popular success in France, and even the critics who were usually hostile to him found something to praise. Sarcey himself declared *A Doll's House* to be the best constructed and most interesting foreign play yet performed in France, though he felt that it showed an obvious debt to Scribe and Sardou, and could not believe in Nora's abandonment of her husband and children. He summed it up as 'an enjoyable comedy, apart from its dénouement'. Nora's final action struck many observers as typifying the difference between Scandinavian and French manners. Edmund de Goncourt wrote in his diary that 'this naïvety, sophism and emotional perversion is characteristic of Scandinavian women', and Ernst Tissot thought it showed that Norwegian women read too much, with the result that 'a kind of intellectual hysteria forces itself into minds ill-equipped to think'.[2]

Numerous tributes reached Réjane from Norway; the artist Fritz Thaulow sent her a painting, Jonas Lie a poem and Edvard Grieg a piece of music. The success of *A Doll's House* and the interest created by the L'Œuvre productions opened the way for Strindberg in Paris. His *Creditors* was produced by

---

[1] *Saturday Review*, 30 March 1895, p. 413.
[2] Nyholm, pp. 55–59. Goncourt's diary (6 May 1894) shows how wildly Ibsen's contemporaries speculated about his literary ancestry: 'Zola declares Ibsen to have sprung from French Romanticism, especially Georges Sand, while Léon Daudet says he sprang from the German Romantics.'

the L'Œuvre that June and *The Father* in December, the latter play being especially acclaimed. The consciousness of his debt to Ibsen annoyed Strindberg. 'Pourquoi servirai-je comme chien de chasse à Ibsen?' he wrote to Lugné-Poe on 16 December 1894. 'J'ai été sa victime depuis dix ans,'[1] and he repeated his complaint that *Hedda Gabler* was a crib of *The Father*.

On 4 May London, for the first time, saw *The Wild Duck*—produced by J. T. Grein for his Independent Theatre Society at the Royalty in Soho, with Laurence Irving, the son of Henry Irving, as Relling. William Archer, who had been disappointed with the play on reading it, confessed himself 'utterly mistaken. The play now proved itself scenic in the highest degree . . . Hardly ever before, as it seemed to me, had I seen so much of the very quintessence of life concentrated in the brief traffic of the stage.' Not all the critics were enthusiastic; Clement Scott wrote that 'to call such an eccentricity as this a masterpiece, to classify it at all as dramatic literature, or to make a fuss about so feeble a production, is to insult dramatic literature and outrage common sense.'

The previous winter steps had been taken in Christiania to found an Authors' Society, for the protection of literary rights. Ibsen readily agreed to join, signed the invitations to the inaugural meeting on 7 May, and attended himself; but it was the last time he did so. Three days before the meeting an article by a young writer named Gabriel Finne appeared in *Dagbladet* attacking the project on the grounds that such a society would inevitably be controlled by old men, and that the old hated everything that was young, fresh and alive. He specifically excluded Ibsen from this generalisation, but at the supper following the meeting another young writer, Nils Kjær, jumped to his feet and delivered a violent denunciation of 'the old writers who have never been able to portray women but have always obstructed the ambitions of youth'. He did not name Ibsen but (despite the peculiar inapplicability of the words to him) aimed his speech at the table where the latter was sitting, and ended: 'We hate you! But your time is past! If you want to see the poet of Norway's future, here he sits!' So saying, he placed his hand on the shoulder of Gabriel Finne, who had fallen asleep with his head on the table. As Ibsen left, he said to Dietrichson: 'That was the most unpleasant occasion I have ever been present at. I shall never set foot in this society again.' Next day, Nils Kjær came to apologise to him, and received the immortal snub: 'Young man, the secret of drinking is never to drink less the day after.'[2]

Meanwhile, his new play had been maturing in his mind, and on 15 June he

[1] *August Strindbergs brev*, X, p. 332.
[2] Koht, II, pp. 251–252; Dietrichson, IV, pp. 416–417; Georg Brochmann, *Den norske forfatterforening gjennem 50 år* (Oslo, 1952), pp. 27–33.

wrote to Bergliot: 'Tomorrow I shall start writing the dialogue in earnest.' A week later he told Gerda Brandes that he was well under way, and by 10 July he had completed Act One. The next day he began Act Two, and a fortnight later, on 25 July, was able to inform Jacob Hegel: 'Yesterday I completed the second act of my new play, and have already today begun work on the third and last act. So I hope to have the final version finished in good time. This of course means that I cannot think of taking any summer holiday this year. But I don't need one. I am very content here, and happiest when I am working at my desk.' The third act he completed on 7 August, also in a fortnight. But he then revised the play so thoroughly that over two months elapsed before he was ready, on 13 October, to send *Little Eyolf* to the printers. As William Archer commented: 'Revision amounted almost to re-invention; and it was the re-invention that determined the poetic value of the play. The poet's original idea . . . was simply to study a rather commonplace wife's jealousy of a rather commonplace child. The lameness of Eyolf proves to have been an afterthought; and as Eyolf is not lame, it follows that the terrible cry of "The crutch is floating!" was also an afterthought, as well as the almost intolerable scene of recrimination between Allmers and Rita as to the accident which caused his lameness. We find, in fact, that nearly everything that gives the play its depth, its horror and its elevation came as an afterthought . . . In no case, perhaps, did revision work such a transfiguration as in *Little Eyolf*.'[1]

Georg Brandes was in Christiania again that August with his family, and Ibsen took especial delight in the company of Brandes's young daughter Edith. 'This evening', he wrote in her album on 15 August, 'two little girls sang so beautifully for me. Thank you for the song, Edith! I often think I hear it still.'[2] She lived, like so many of the other girls whom Ibsen liked, to a great age, and must have been one of the very few people who personally knew both Ibsen and Brecht.

On 3 October, while Ibsen was fair-copying *Little Eyolf*, Aurélien Lugné-Poe and his company from the Théâtre de L'Œuvre arrived in Christiania to give guest performances of *Rosmersholm* and *The Master Builder*. They were a very young group—'ten players', recalled Lugné-Poe, 'whose total ages came to less than two hundred years'. He himself, one may repeat, was only twenty-four. Their first morning they went to the Grand Hotel to catch a glimpse of their author. At the stroke of twelve, Ibsen made his ritual entry.

'We stood waiting for him, and recognised him immediately. As he walked through the hotel to the dining-room he reminded me of a doctor

---

[1] William Archer, *From Ibsen's Workshop* (London, 1912), p. 18.
[2] *Prinsessans Album*, (Edith Brandes's memories) in *Svenska Dagbladet*, 9 May 1965.

on the way to visit his patients. Saluted by the hotel porter, Ibsen paced
with careful steps to seclude himself in a corner of the large restaurant . . .
Berthe Bady . . . begged Hammer to introduce her to him. I observed the
scene from a distance. Ibsen was exactly as I had often heard described.
He rose and adjusted his gold spectacles, then kindly and smilingly
murmured a few words and sat down again. Then he took out a small
comb and smoothed his hair where it had been crimped by his hat. At
first glance his appearance struck me as correct and somewhat diffident,
his face luminous in a high white cravat . . . I would like to have had the
extraordinary gaze of this man. Indeed, I have never been able to forget his
eyes, which only the painter Edvard Munch once succeeded in repro-
ducing. One eye, as though half-asleep, reflected and pondered, while the
other observed Bady sharply and with intense and surprising animation
and warmth. The indeterminate colour of those eyes behind the spectacles
seemed to shine with an unusual brilliance. His brow was unique, proclaiming intelligence, order and distinction, its breadth and proportions
perfectly matched. Bady wept. At last she let Ibsen bury himself in his
newspaper and disappear behind it. We had imagined Ibsen to be gruff
and boorish, but after their conversation Bady told everyone: "He is
charming, and his face is quite pink—and his eyes are so gentle and good—
and how young his voice is!" '[1]

They were to play in the Carl Johan Theatre, 'a kind of large barn in the
old Tivoli Gardens . . . neither pleasant nor elegant'. Ibsen came to the first
night of *Rosmersholm*. 'During the whole performance Ibsen remained motionless. He seemed to wish to restrain the audience from demonstrating in any
way. Only at the end of every act did he applaud, without manifesting pleasure.
After the final act he rose, bowed to us actors, then to the audience who were
applauding him. That was all.'
At eleven the next morning Herman Bang took Lugné Poe to visit Ibsen
at Viktoria Terrasse.

'He received us, as before, with that exceptional amiability which I have
often remarked in him, like a doctor receiving a patient . . . Dare I say
without lack of respect that that morning Ibsen was *dans le décor*? . . . Very
*soigné*, his hair and beard shaggy yet combed in a curiously fastidious
style, his glasses on his nose, just as I had seen him in the Grand Hotel.
From time to time Bang came to my assistance. I felt so tall that the

---

[1] For these and subsequent details of Lugné-Poe's visit to Christiania, cf. his *Ibsen*
(Paris, 1936), pp. 75 ff.

furniture, the knick-knacks, the paintings on the wall, even my host himself, all made me feel gauche and clumsy. I waited for Ibsen to indicate that I might sit. He, somewhat small compared with me, seemed visibly ill at ease. His eyes bored deeply into mine as though exploring me.'

Bang explained that Lugné-Poe understood German, and Ibsen said he was grateful for the performance of *Rosmersholm* but was particularly looking forward to their interpretation of *The Master Builder*.

'He was not surly as we had been led to expect, nor seemed distrustful, but almost immediately made that remark in German which I subsequently repeated in Paris and which helped me greatly the following evening [when acting *The Master Builder*]: "French actors are more suited than many others to act my plays. People have not fully appreciated that a passionate writer needs to be acted with passion, and not otherwise" . . . As he saw us to the door he added something which I could not understand, but I heard two or three times the name Ulrik Brendel. When we left the Master after a reception that had been friendly and courteous, but nothing more, I expressed my amazement to Herman Bang that he had said nothing about the previous evening's performance of *Rosmersholm*. "Well", said Bang, "he was a little upset because in the last scene Brendel's entrance was lit by electricity. He doesn't want to have any stupid mysticism in his plays." '

Ibsen came to their opening performance of *The Master Builder* on 5 October and Herman Bang remembered his reaction:

'By general agreement, this strange play had not succeeded in the Scandinavian theatres . . . Ibsen took his place in his box. As usual he sat motionless throughout the first act . . . Towards the end of the act it was as though something had been awakened in him. In the second act Ibsen rose to his feet and leaned against the wall of his box. His eyes followed every movement of the actors, and the Master's eyes dwelling on them seemed to increase their power and magic . . . In the third act Ibsen leaned out over the balustrade of the box . . . When I went to the Grand that night Ibsen came to greet me. Only once have I seen him moved, and that was on this occasion. He stretched out both his hands to me; they were ice-cold, as though his excitement had drawn all the warmth from them. "This," he said, "was the resurrection of my play." '[1]

---

[1] *Ibid.*, p. 82. Bang originally recorded his memories of Ibsen in *Die Neue Rundtschau*, 1906, pp. 1498–1499.

Ibsen used his influence to recommend that Lugné-Poe should be awarded a medal, which the latter received soon after his return to France and which proved useful in a way that neither Ibsen nor King Oscar can have foreseen. 'Shall I confess', Lugné-Poe writes, 'that that medal rescued many a performance? Every time we found ourselves short of money for a new production, off it went to the pawnbroker, and Ibsen never learned what a service he had done us.'

The Swedish actor-manager Albert Ranft was in Christiania at this time, anxious if possible to obtain Ibsen's forthcoming play before the bigger Stockholm theatres. He put up at the Grand Hotel and, having unpacked his bags, went down to the reading-room, and was about to enter when he was stopped by a waiter with the words: 'You can't go in there. The Doctor's there and mustn't be disturbed.' 'What doctor?' asked Ranft. 'Is someone ill?' 'No, it's Dr Ibsen. He's reading the newspapers.' Ranft bribed the waiter with a tip and went in. Ibsen gave him a look as though to say: 'Who's this who dares to enter while I am here?' But when he learned who Ranft was and why he had come, he treated him with kindness and courtesy. Ranft asked if he might read *Little Eyolf* before publication 'to see if we can play it, and if so, buy it'. 'Ibsen said: "So you want to read it first and buy it later?" He stared at me in such astonishment that I feared I had said the wrong thing. "Well—". "I see, you want to read it first. Everyone else has wanted to buy it first and read it later. You shall have the play." And he shook my hand and said: "Won't you have a drink?" '

But when, later, Ranft began to question him about the play, he found Ibsen accommodating but totally unhelpful. 'Can't this line be interpreted thus, and spoken thus?' asked Ranft. 'Oh, yes.' 'But how do you think it should be said?' 'Oh, my dear fellow', replied Ibsen. 'You say it how you please, it's all the same to me.'[1] Similar evidence of Ibsen's indifference to how actors spoke his lines is given by Helena Nyblom, quoting the great Danish actor, Emil Poulsen. Poulsen told her that after Ibsen had attended a performance of *The Wild Duck* in Copenhagen the cast waited expectantly for his comments. 'But it seemed as though he no longer knew what he had meant by the play. He went around asking us actors, as though we should know better.'[2]

At the beginning of December Suzannah, accompanied by Sigurd, went south again to escape the worst of the winter, and on 11 December Ibsen wrote to her one of those touchingly Darby-and-Joan letters which they exchanged when parted:

[1] Albert Ranft, *Memoarer*, I (Stockholm, 1928), pp. 151–152.
[2] Helena Nyblom, *Mina levnadsminne*, I (Stockholm, 1922), p. 236.

*Dear Suzannah!*

*I have received your telegram, and now your letter. How happy and relieved I am to learn that everything has so far gone so well! I hope it will continue so! Here all is well. Frøken Blehr's[1] cooking suits me excellently. And there is plenty of it, so that we have ample left for supper should I want any. But I usually just have herring then, with the most beautiful potatoes which Lina [their maid] prepares in the new machine. She does everything for me most attentively. Bergliot had dinner with me on Sunday. Otherwise, no one has been here. The evenings are lonely, of course; but then I sit and read at the dinner table. In the morning I drink coffee, which I have brought to my bedroom at eight o'clock sharp. Indeed, everything goes like clockwork, just as if you were here. Every morning Augusta brings me a little tray with crumbs for the birds. Lina is good to her and gives her some of all the food that gets left over. My new play is being published today, both here and in Berlin and London. I got the fee from Heinemann yesterday, and am having Hegel invest 10,000 crowns for us. And later I hope a further 4,000, without having to leave ourselves short. I am overwhelmed with correspondence, as you can imagine. But I answer it all in as few words as I can—and so manage. Give Sigurd my warmest regards. I shall soon see his new book [Men and Powers] to which I greatly look forward. Greet also the Grønvolds, Frøken Klingenfeld and Frøken Raff—not to forget Clemence if she is still in Munich, and thank both the last-named deeply for the beautiful pictures! I wish you and Sigurd the happiest of times in our old haunts! Write soon again.*

*Your affectionate H.I.*

William Heinemann having safeguarded his copyright by a public reading at the Haymarket Theatre on 3 December, *Little Eyolf* was, as Ibsen stated, published simultaneously in Copenhagen, Christiania, London and Berlin on 11 December 1894—though it almost missed being on sale in Christiania that day, for a fog prevented the steamer from Copenhagen containing the copies arriving until the late afternoon, to the vexation of prospective purchasers who had been waiting in the bookshops since early morning. Surprisingly, for it is one of Ibsen's subtlest and most elusive plays, it received an almost unanimously favourable (if somewhat bemused) reception from the Scandinavian press. 'A new triumph', wrote the penitent Nils Kjær (who had so insulted Ibsen at the Authors' Society, but who was embarking on what was to be a distinguished career as a dramatic critic) in *Dagbladet* on 12 December. 'He has conjured forth another of those monumental dramas the architectonic perfection and severely symmetrical beauty of which will be enough to ensure the continuing admiration of the world'—though he suspected that 'for the latest vintage of Ibsen's admirers the play may disappoint because it is less symbolic

---

[1] A lady who ran a domestic science school in the same street.

and more realistic'. Kristofer Randers, who had severely criticised several of Ibsen's recent plays, praised this one highly in *Aftenposten* (13 December): 'Has our old poet become young again? Does he wish to put our younger writers to shame, so youthful he is here, so fresh, immediate and powerful?' An anonymous reviewer in *Verdens Gang* (12 December), after remarking on 'the feverish interest with which the famous poet's new play is awaited', thought it 'fully worthy of this attention; the view of life it expresses will arouse bitter opposition, but the play will live.' Georg Brandes, in an open letter to the same paper three days later, observed: 'There has always existed a duality in Ibsen; he advocates the cause of Nature, and he rebukes it . . . Now Nature has the voice over Morality, now the reverse. In *The Master Builder*, as in *Ghosts*, the advocate of Nature was dominant; here, as in *Brand* and *The Wild Duck*, he is the chastener.' By now, Brandes concluded, it was impertinent to criticise such a giant as Ibsen; one could merely thank him. Edvard Brandes (who that year had been appointed director of the Royal Theatre in Copenhagen) also praised the play, remarking (*Politiken*, 14 December) that it would not give rise to the violent debates and differing interpretations which had greeted most of Ibsen's works. 'Here no riddles are posed without solutions, no mighty questions which are not answered. Neither those who defend the social system nor those who have declared war on it will be able to use this play as ammunition.' Nils Vogt in *Morgenbladet* (15 December) found the third act weak but praised the play as a whole; and on 20 December Just Bing wrote a perceptive article pointing out that the play has a concealed meaning as well as its obvious one, and that, like Solness and Hilde, the Allmers are people through whom other powers speak. 'Ibsen's characters are at home in only one place—in Ibsen's plays. But there, they are totally at home. At the peak of crisis . . . they can breathe and move in their rightful atmosphere.'

Among the few dissident voices the leading one was, as usual, C.D. af Wirsén. 'As in *The Master Builder*', he protested in *Post- och Inrikes-Tidning*, 'the symbolism over-reaches itself, the action is thin, we do not believe in the characters' change of heart . . . A real decadence is revealed in these three plays, *Hedda Gabler*, *The Master Builder* and *Little Eyolf*. Where is the author of *The Pretenders* and *The Vikings at Helgeland*?'

Commercially, *Little Eyolf* was an immense success. The first edition of 10,000 copies sold out almost at once; a second edition of 2,000 appeared on 21 December, and a third of 1,250 on 20 January. A surprising proportion of these were sold outside Scandinavia. *Morgenbladet*'s Copenhagen correspondent reported on 15 December that, apart from the Scandinavian bookshops in America taking large quantities, 'there is scarcely anywhere in the world where people do not want to read Ibsen in the original and as quickly as possible. As soon as a new work by him is announced, orders begin to pour in to the publishers, not merely—indeed, perhaps least—from foreign booksellers, but from private individuals—in Germany, France, England, Russia, Rumania, Turkey, Greece, Italy . . . And these orders, as their language proves, do not come merely from Scandinavians. It is no exaggeration to say that myriads of people in foreign countries all over the world have learned Norwegian in order to read Ibsen's works in the original tongue.' The reporter added that on the day of publication P. A. Rosenberg, the director of Dagmars Theatre in Copenhagen, had given a public reading of the play in the Concert Palace, and that another theatre director named Neergaard had given another public reading a couple of days later—news which cannot have pleased Ibsen, remembering his strictures on Andreas Isachsen for doing the same thing with *Emperor and Galilean* twenty years earlier. But Rosenberg's reading, at least, was poorly attended, with only a few hundred people scattered around an auditorium holding three thousand. Most people evidently preferred to read it for themselves or wait until it was performed.

These were not the only irritations suffered by Ibsen in Denmark in connection with *Little Eyolf*; the plot had been leaked to the press before publication, something he so dreaded that he always requested Gyldendal to print the title page and list of characters last, lest any of the compositors or employees should feel tempted to turn a dishonest penny. The Norwegian novelist Thomas Krag had accidentally been sent proofs of *Little Eyolf* instead of some proofs of his own (or, according to another account, had purloined them). He told a journalist what they contained, as a result of which an inaccurate résumé of the first two acts appeared in *Politiken* on 14 November and was copied by many other newspapers. Ibsen was furious; but it is an old adage among publishers that any publicity is good publicity, and the brouhaha probably helped the sales.

Ibsen's fame in England was by now such that *Little Eyolf* was widely reviewed in the London press, though the reception was predictably mixed. The *Daily Chronicle* welcomed it, describing Ibsen as 'incomparably the most powerful influence in contemporary literature'; but the *Daily Graphic* thought the play exemplified his weaknesses as well as his strengths, and the *Daily News* found it wholly undramatic, the characters mere abstractions and the dialogue obscure and pointless.

Ibsen lost no time in informing Suzannah and Sigurd of the book's success. 'This has been a busy time for me, as you may imagine', he wrote them on 20 December. '. . . It has aroused a storm of enthusiasm, unanimous as never before. The first edition is sold out and a second is already appearing tomorrow. Director Ranft has bought the Swedish theatre rights and paid

3,000 crowns for them. The Christiania Theatre ditto. My English fee has been paid. I am straightway investing *seventeen thousand* crowns, which yet leaves a good deal over for us. The play has been accepted by the Royal Theatre in Copenhagen. And the Burgtheater [in Vienna] and the Deutsches Theater [in Berlin]. And doubtless by many other German theatres I don't yet know about.'

Bergliot came to spend Christmas Eve with him. Christmas had always meant a lot to Ibsen; Fru Werenskiold, the wife of the artist Erik Werenskiold, once visited him in Munich shortly before Christmas and was surprised to find him occupied in cutting out paper decorations for the tree, which 'he did very skilfully', as in his childhood when old Mother Maren had sold his products at her stall in the market place in Skien.

> 'Now [writes Bergliot] he no longer cut out paper decorations. Lina, the maid, had decorated the tree as Fru Ibsen liked it, just with candles and white cotton wool on the branches. We went in to the Christmas tree. Ibsen had a terror of fire, and was very worried about all the candles on the tree. Still, I had to light them, and a few moments later had to go out into the passage to fetch something. When I came back I saw to my astonishment Ibsen kneeling on the floor blowing the candles out, one after the other. The tree was on the floor and was not big. I can still see Ibsen's profile, and how his nose disappeared each time he blew.
>
> 'As we sat chatting afterwards, Ibsen told me he had discovered there were a lot of mice in the apartment. But he had his own way of keeping them at a distance. He said: "In the evening I take a glass of milk and some biscuits into my room. I put a little in a saucer for the mice and leave it in the next room, and then they don't come into mine." '[1]

On 28 December Ibsen wrote to Suzannah:

*Bergliot . . . has been up to me several times and has been very helpful with the Christmas things, which you prepared before you left; or rather, she did it all for me . . . I have bought you two pretty gifts, which are at present in the drawing-room. And a couple of landscapes from Lofoten . . . I have been invited out once or twice . . . Otherwise I sit at home in the evenings and read. Hegel has sent me several new books, and when I know where you are staying for the winter I will forward some to you. 29.12. I was interrupted at this point yesterday, first by the designer and then by the producer. They are painting new decor for the play and rehearsals are in progress . . . I have received many flowers and cards . . . even from America. If only I were through with answering them all! The most welcome and useful present was*

---

[1] Bergliot Ibsen, p. 153.

*from Bergliot. She gave me an enormous bath sponge, with which I wash and rub myself morning and evening; it suits me splendidly. Don't write your letters criss-cross. I have such difficulty with my eyes in deciphering it . . .*

With the two editions of *Little Eyolf*, various sales of the performing rights, reprints of (at last) *Ghosts* and *The Pretenders* and a miscellany of small royalties and honoraria, 1894 had been a bumper year for Ibsen, though it would have seemed nearly disastrous to an author of comparable stature in England, France, Germany or America. He had earned over £1,300, more even than in his previous best year, 1880:

| | crowns | £ |
|---|---|---|
| German royalties from Felix Bloch | 155 | 9 |
| Unspecified fee from Wien Burgtheater | 108 | 6 |
| Unspecified royalties from Munich Hoftheater | 182 | 10 |
| Fee for *The Master Builder* from P. Reclam (Leipzig publisher) (300 marks) | 266 | 15 |
| Royalties from Agence Roger, Paris (422 francs) | 300 | 16 |
| Royalties from Bloch | 201 | 11 |
| Royalties from Walter Scott and William Archer | 49 | 3 |
| Unspecified theatre royalties from Wm. Heinemann (£15) | 272 | 15 |
| Royalties from Munich Hoftheater | 58 | 3 |
| 8th edition *The Pretenders* | 1,200 | 67 |
| Fees owed by Bergen Theater | 760 | 42 |
| Royalties from Bloch | 324 | 18 |
| Royalties from H. Beerbohm Tree (8 gns.) | 152 | 8 |
| Royalties from Munich Hoftheater | 203 | 11 |
| Royalties from Bloch | 245 | 14 |
| 2nd edition of *Ghosts* | 666 | 37 |
| Royalties from Munich Hoftheater | 124 | 7 |
| Royalties from H. Beerbohm Tree and Walter Scott (£21 2s. 4d.) | 416 | 21 |
| Royalties for *Ghosts* at Lessingtheater, Berlin (3 perfs.) | 101 | 6 |
| 1st edition of *Little Eyolf* | 7,200 | 400 |
| English edition of *Little Eyolf* (Heinemann, £150) | 2,700 | 150 |
| Fees owed by M. Savine, Paris publisher | 215 | 12 |
| German edition of *Little Eyolf* (S. Fischer) | 885 | 49 |
| Fee for *Little Eyolf* at Christiania Theatre | 3,000 | 167 |
| Fee for *Little Eyolf* at Bergen Theatre | 400 | 22 |

| | crowns | £ |
|---|---|---|
| Fee for Swedish performing rights of *Little Eyolf* (2 years) from Albert Ranft | 3,000 | 167 |
| 2nd edition of *Little Eyolf* | 1,440 | 80 |
| | 24,622 | 1,366 |

As with *The Master Builder*, proofs of *Little Eyolf* had been sent to London as they came off the Gyldendal presses, in order that the translation might proceed without delay. Henry James persuaded William Heinemann to let him have an advance look at the English version, and on 22 November he wrote to Elizabeth Robins:

'Heinemann has lent me the proofs of the 2 first acts of the Play—the ineffable Play—and I can't stay my hand from waving wildly to you! It is indeed immense—indeed and indeed. It is of a rare perfection—and if 3 keeps up the tremendous pitch of 1 and 2 it will distinctly stand at the tiptop of his achievement. It's a masterpiece and a marvel; and it *must* leap upon the stage . . . The inherent difficulties are there, but they are not insurmountable. They are on the contrary manageable—they are a matter of tact and emphasis—of art and discretion. The thing will be a big *profane* (i.e., Ibsen and non-Ibsen *both*) success. The part—*the* part—is Asta—unless it be the Rat-hound in the Bag! What an old woman—and what a Young!'

But three days later, in a letter of apology for having talked indiscreetly about the play 'in the despair of a dull dinner—or after-dinner', he wrote to Miss Robins:

'I fear, in truth, no harm can be done equal to the harm done to the play by its own most disappointing third act. It came to me last night—and has been, to me, a subject of depressed reflection. It seems to me a singular and almost inexplicable drop—dramatically, *representably* speaking . . . The worst of it is that it goes back, as it were, on what precedes, and gives a meagreness to that too—makes it less interesting and less significant . . . I don't see the meaning or effect of Borghejm—I don't see the value or final *function* of Asta . . . I find the solution too simple, too immediate, too much a harking back, and too productive of the sense that there might have been a stronger one . . . My idea that Asta was to become an active, *the* active agent, is of course blighted.'

However, he admitted: 'Really uttered, *done*, in the gathered northern twilight, with the flag flown and the lights coming out across the fjord, the scene might have a real solemnity of beauty—and perhaps that's all that's required!' But, he concluded: 'I fear Allmers will never be thought an actor-manager's part.'

James's objections to the third act of *Little Eyolf* have been shared by many readers; yet, if properly understood and intelligently interpreted, this act is by no means meagre, nor the solution, as James supposed, simple. The great mistake is to imagine that Ibsen envisaged the ending as happy.[1] Surely it is obvious that devoting themselves to charity, sharing their 'gold and their green forests' with the poor, will not ultimately provide the answer and the peace which Alfred and Rita are seeking. They have reached rock-bottom; but unless they can prove that they have undergone a genuine change of heart, and are prepared to grapple with the realities of life, this will be no solution but merely another, more plausible but equally insidious 'life-lie'. They are only at the beginning of their long climb to salvation.

My own belief is that the third act of *Little Eyolf*, like the two that precede it, is among the greatest that Ibsen ever wrote, and that in it he achieved exactly what he set out to achieve, namely, to reveal the interior of what, in *Brand*, thirty years before, he had called 'the Ice Church'—the interior of a human soul in which love has died—so that, in Rita's words, all that is left to her and Alfred is to 'try to fill that emptiness with something. Something resembling love'. In Michael Elliott's delicate production of the play at the 1963 Edinburgh Festival, the two characters spoke the final lines of the play (after Alfred has hoisted the flag to the top of the mast), not facing, but half-turned away from each other, so that the effect was not of facile optimism, but of fear and uncertainty.

Yet James was right in one thing, at least—the reluctance of actors of the 'actor-manager' type to play Alfred. Like John Rosmer, and Torvald Helmer in *A Doll's House*, Alfred Allmers is weaker than the woman with whom he is in love, and leading actors tend to be conscious of what is nowadays called their image (which means the kind of man their fans mistakenly imagine them to be). 'How', asked Bernard Shaw in his review of the first English production of the play in 1896, 'could he recommend himself to spectators who saw in him everything they are ashamed of in themselves?' Allmers is usually, in practice, either romanticised or (like Rosmer) played as sexless; and a sexless or romanticised Allmers and a happy ending are burdens that no production of *Little Eyolf* can hope to survive. *A Doll's House*, *Ghosts* and *Hedda Gabler* are robust plays; they can be ill-cast, ill-directed and ill-acted, and yet make a goodish evening. *Little Eyolf*, like *The Lady from the Sea* and *When*

---

[1] Witness his own remark to Caroline Sontum, p. 251 below.

*We Dead Awaken*, is fragile; if it is not done well, one would rather it had not been done at all; performed as it was written to be performed, it is a haunting and memorable experience. Nowhere else does Ibsen probe so mercilessly into the complexities of human minds and relationships; it is like a long, sustained and terrifying operation. On the occasion of the first English production William Archer wrote: 'I rank the play beside, if not above, the very greatest of Ibsen's works, and am only doubtful whether its soul-searching be not too terrible for human endurance in the theatre.'

# TWELVE

# ❧ John Gabriel Borkman

## (1895–1896)

SUZANNAH STAYED ABROAD for nearly a year. It was the longest time they had been separated during their marriage. She spent the winter at Meran in the southern Tyrol, and he wrote to her regularly and at length, enquiring solicitously after her health, warning her against this or that possible excess and giving her dull little pieces of news and local or family gossip; his letters are more than ever those of a man to whom correspondence is an agony. He was 'overwhelmed' with preparations for the Christiania production of *Little Eyolf*, which in fact can have made little demand on him, and 'bombarded' with requests that he visit Berlin for the German premiere, 'which is of course an impossibility'. Susannah's niece, Magdalena Falsen, meeting him on the street and suggesting that she visit him, was told that 'he was so occupied with business matters that he could not receive anyone.' Bergliot came to dine with him on Sundays; no one had filled the gap left by Hildur's absence.

The world premiere of *Little Eyolf* took place on 12 January at the Deutsches Theater in Berlin, with Emmanuel Reicher as Allmers and Agnes Sorma as Rita; it was a measure of the international fame which Ibsen now enjoyed that critics (or at least reporters) from all over the world attended. It was not a success, any more than *The Master Builder* had been in Germany, and like the latter play it does not seem to have been performed for several years in any other German town. Ibsen's 'social' dramas were continually revived (his royalties from Bloch were considerably up this year), but his recent plays struck the Germans as less realistic and topical and therefore less interesting.

In Christiania, by contrast, *Little Eyolf* proved such a success that it was performed thirty-six times that year, compared with eighteen performances for *Hedda Gabler* and fifteen for *The Master Builder* during their first seasons. Ibsen attended the premiere on 15 January, together with Christian and Caroline Sontum and young Bolette:

> 'Ibsen was very anxious about the reception. He kept saying to my mother, who sat next to him: "Do let's get out before the curtain comes down." It was always a torture to him to see his own plays . . . *Little*

*Eyolf* was received with great enthusiasm, and there were many curtain calls, but, persistently as they clapped, the audience could not persuade the author to take a bow. Finally, the stage manager promised to convey their congratulations personally to him.

'Ibsen, meanwhile, was driving to the Grand Hotel in a shabby little sleigh as fast as the plodding horse could carry him through the streets. It was snowing heavily . . . When Ibsen reached the Grand, he was much overcome by the performance and exceedingly nervous. He begged my mother to order the supper for him, and seemed like a child asking for protection. The heavy food and some good wine soon raised his spirits. When my mother, still full of the play, said "Poor Rita, now she has to go to work with all those mischievous boys", Ibsen replied: "Do you really believe so? Don't you rather think it was more of a Sunday mood with her?" . . . The only other remark I can recall him ever making on his own plays was in discussing *Love's Comedy* with my mother. "But Svanhild should not have engaged herself to Guldstad," she said. "Console yourself, dear friend," he replied. "The next day she will have a rendezvous with Falk." '[1]

Before the end of January, *Little Eyolf* was also staged in Bergen, Helsinki and Gothenburg; Milan and Vienna saw it in February. On 3 February he had another Russian premiere, when (of all plays) *The Feast at Solhaug* was performed in prose—only the third of his plays to be seen in that country.

At the beginning of February Sigurd returned to Norway, leaving his mother at Meran. He had published a caustic article on Swedish liberalism in the December number of the Stockholm magazine *Nyt Tidskrift*, extracts from which had been quoted in the Christiania press. Ibsen proudly wrote to Suzannah on 6 February that the piece 'has excited much attention, and not only in Norway; as have his articles on the consular question'. With equal pride he added: 'Can you guess how much I have already invested of the royalties that have come in? No less than 20,000 crowns [£1,111]! And I hope in the near future to be able to put by another 4,000 crowns, without our having to pinch in any way.' The winter in Norway, he told her, was the coldest for years; not merely shipping, but even railways, were at a standstill; but 'the air is brilliantly clear and clean'. Sigurd looked in only occasionally; otherwise 'I sit by myself and read the newspapers, and am quite content.' He was economising as much as ever as regards food. His lunch was being sent in; and for the evening 'I have hot soup and fish or meat left over from lunch, so that we hardly ever have to send out for anything.'

[1] Sontum, pp. 251–252.

Georg Brandes sent him an essay he had written about the young Marianne von Willemer's infatuation with Goethe when the latter was sixty-six, and its stimulating effect on the poetry of Goethe's old age. He could scarcely have chosen a subject closer to Ibsen's heart (and he must have heard about Emilie and Hildur). 'I cannot forbear', wrote Ibsen to him on 11 February, 'to send you especial thanks for your *Goethe and Marianne von Willemer*. I didn't know anything about the episode you describe in it. I may have read about it years ago in Lewes's book, but if so I had forgotten it, because at that time the affair held no particular interest for me. But now things are somewhat different. When I think of the quality which characterises Goethe's work during that period, I mean the sense of renewed youth, I ought to have guessed that he must have been graced with some such revelation, some such reassurance of beauty, as his meeting with Marianne von Willemer. Fate, Providence, Chance, can be genial and benevolent powers now and then.' Ibsen must have been comforted to know that other great writers had become emotionally involved with girls forty years their junior; and certainly his own last five plays, after his meeting with Emilie, have, like the aged writings of a young poet just then emerging into fame, W. B. Yeats, all the vigour and sharpness of youth.

Camilla Collett died in March at the age of eighty-two. 'I met her son Robert almost daily in the street', Ibsen wrote to Suzannah on 12 March, 'and he said she lay there talking ceaselessly of Welhaven and us, and of her time with us abroad.' Ibsen went to her funeral service. 'Upon the coffin, beside the Queen's wreath, lay a large and handsome wreath from you, with long white ribbons and gold letters saying "To Camilla Collett, greetings from Suzannah Ibsen". I sent a big bay wreath with ribbons in the national colours.'

His sixty-seventh birthday was looming, but any hope he might have had that it could be allowed to slip by peacefully in Suzannah's absence had been knocked on the head.

*For the dreadful day, 20 March* [he continued in this same letter of 12 March], *Bergliot must manage as best she can, since you will have it so. And I shall receive everyone, even the spies, as politely as I can. I hope Falsen* [his brother-in-law, a *generalkonsul* married to Suzannah's sister Dorothea] *won't be able to come. Dorothea and Magdalena* [her daughter] *have influenza; so they won't be able to. Incidentally, I hear they have moved to Parkveien. Herman has twisted his foot and can't go out. Then I must tell you that a* third *edition of* Little Eyolf *is printing and will probably be out next week. The day after tomorrow the play will open in Copenhagen. Hegel has commissioned a big portrait of me from Eilif Petersson, and I am now sitting for him. There is a very widespread epidemic of influenza in the city. But so far I haven't noticed any signs. On Sunday evening there was a fire upstairs in Fru Bjørn's boarding-house. They had overfilled a lamp, which of course exploded. The fire brigade arrived, and there was a great scene, with screaming on the stairs; but the fire was soon put out. At the Exhibition I bought a fine painting by Chr. Krohg. It is actually a portrait of Strindberg; but Sigurd calls it 'The Revolution', and I call it 'Insanity Emergent'. Sigurd urged me to buy it, for the ridiculously cheap price of 500 crowns [£28]. Sigurd and his family are well. Bergliot has been so good as to give me some gammelost and pickled herring and a splendid joint of roast pork, which I enjoy in the evenings. I hope you are having a good time down there.*

Ibsen hung the painting of Strindberg (a very large one) on the wall of his study; it helped him, he explained to astonished enquirers, to work with 'that madman staring down at me'. He especially liked the 'demonic eyes', and once remarked: 'He is my mortal enemy, and shall hang there and watch while I write.'[1] August Lindberg, who knew Strindberg, tells that Ibsen once asked him if it was a good likeness and, 'in a whisper that he perhaps did not intend to be heard, muttered: "A remarkable man!" '[2] As with the visits to the Hamsun lectures, it seemed as though he wished to remind himself of the younger generation challenging and threatening him. Some writers are enervated by competition and hostility; Ibsen thrived on it. Bergliot recalls that once when Bjørnson was so ill that he was not expected to live, but recovered, Ibsen, on being gently taunted by Sigurd, declared with deep feeling: 'It would not have been easy to lose one's only rival.'[3]

He was (he told Suzannah on 3 April) sitting each day for Eilif Peterssen; otherwise 'everything is as usual except that we have begun to cook meals here. Frøken Blehr's food got worse from day to day until it was practically uneatable. Lina, on the other hand, cooks quite excellently, just the kind of food she knows I like; a lot of fish, and excellent potatoes.' Ten days later he informed her proudly that he had invested 24,000 crowns-worth of royalties and hoped soon to be able to invest a further 6,000 (£1,667 altogether), and that his total investments now totalled 166,000 crowns (£9,222) 'which I venture to say is not bad'. So far from indulging in any luxuries, apart from the Strindberg painting, he boasted a few weeks later (2 July) that his household expenses over the past quarter had averaged 116 crowns (less than £6 10s. 0d.) a *month*—'including laundry and everything'.

He did a lot of modelling that spring, for as soon as Peterssen had finished

[1] Koht, II, p. 250.
[2] Lindberg, p. 308.
[3] Bergliot Ibsen, p. 191.

his portrait Erik Werenskiold moved in to paint another. 'This puts me somewhat behind in my work, I mean my correspondence,' he confessed to Suzannah on 27 April. 'But I find it an agreeable distraction, and a change, and it doesn't greatly inconvenience me since it all takes place in my study. After Werenskiold, Sinding is coming to model the statue for the new theatre.'

Both Erik Werenskiold and Stephan Sinding recorded their impressions of Ibsen. Werenskiold remembered him as an excellent model, who 'stood still as a pillar . . . stood happily for a couple of hours on end, he was so immensely strong. Even the last time I saw him, he was as round and firm as a rolling-pin.' He found Ibsen 'extraordinarily winning, delightfully agreeable and full of jokes'. Before he started to paint Ibsen liked to sit and chat, and 'was exceptionally curious, asking question after question; he was especially interested about women. Whenever I was able to tell him about some unusual woman he would sit there like a bird of prey and would not let me stop until I had told him everything I knew'. He remembered that Ibsen once used the phrase 'the terrain of the face', and rightly comments that 'it wasn't a phrase *anyone* would use'. Impressed by the size of Ibsen's forehead, he asked if anyone had ever measured his brain-pan; Ibsen replied that a German professor had, and had told him it was the largest he had ever come across. Werenskiold also recalled that every Saturday some little boys from a school in the street would come to Ibsen's apartment, and that he would give them each 25 øre (3d.). When his charlady complained that they dirtied his floors and would only spend the money on cakes, Ibsen replied: 'Why shouldn't they buy cakes?'[1]

Stephan Sinding found Ibsen equally courteous and patient but (through no fault of his) a most awkward subject to model. 'I worked and worked and couldn't get it right. I discarded one effort after another. While I was working on the sixth it occurred to me to ask Ibsen to take his spectacles off. He laid them aside and looked at me. I have never seen two eyes like those. One was large, I might almost say horrible—so it seemed to me—and deeply mystical; the other much smaller, rather pinched up, cold and clear and calmly probing. I stood speechless for a few seconds and stared at those eyes, and spoke the thought that flashed into my mind: "I wouldn't like to have you as an enemy!" Then his eyes and his whole body seemed to blaze, and I thought instinctively of the troll in the fairy tale who pops out of his hole and roars: "Who's chopping trees in *my* forest?" '[2]

Werenskiold made no less than six portraits of Ibsen during the first six

---

[1] *Dagbladet*, 20 March 1928.

[2] Kristofer Visted, *Henrik Ibsen i karikaturen*, in *Boken om Bøker*, II (Oslo, 1927), pp. 145–147.

months of that year,[1] including one delightful one painted from memory entitled 'The Laughing Ibsen'. It is the only laughing painting or photograph of him in existence; Werenskiold notes at the foot of the portrait that it was a remark of Ibsen's own that put him into this good humour. Recalling a bad portrait that a Norwegian artist named Ole H. B. Olrik had painted of him in Rome in 1879, Ibsen said to Werenskiold: 'For a long time he had been painting nothing but saints, so I wasn't a very suitable subject for him.'[2] Peterssen, Werenskiold and Sinding were not the only artists to portray Ibsen that winter and spring. Edvard Munch had done the first of his lithographs of Ibsen just before the turn of the year, and Hans Heyerdahl and Christian Krohg painted him too. A contemporary Danish caricature by Alfred Schmidt shows Ibsen surrounded by Norwegian artists trying to capture his likeness.

Hildur Andersen had by now returned to Christiania, and Ibsen had been seeing a good deal of her. Their frequent appearances in public together had, naturally, Christiania being what it was, led to a good deal of gossip; the rumour had spread that Ibsen was considering divorcing Suzannah, and her stepmother, Magdalene Thoresen, thought fit to write to Suzannah and tell her of this. Suzannah, still in Meran, wrote to Ibsen asking him if there was any truth in the gossip, an action which is, perhaps, less surprising when one remembers that they had, for the first time in nearly forty years, been separated for six months. Ibsen replied on 7 May in a letter which one is surprised, though grateful, that she kept:

*Dear Suzannah,*

*It hurt me deeply to read your last letter, dated 1 May. And I hope that, on closer reflection, you will regret having sent it. So your stepmother, that damned old sinner, has been at work again trying to cause trouble by setting us against each other. But it's easy to guess who is behind that poor twisted woman. It is of course her good daughter, who is still wandering around the streets here and is doubtless angry with me because whenever I see her I slip into a side-street, which I have done once or twice. And now she is trying to take her revenge. And you can let yourself be fooled by that!*

*I don't understand your stepmother's hysterical utterances and sham profundities. I never have understood them. But when she writes this rubbish about my 'wanting freedom at any price'—then I can most solemnly and sacredly assure you that I have never seriously thought or intended any such thing and that I never shall think or intend it. What I may have blurted out in a temper when your moods and humours drove me to a temporary despair is something quite different and to which no weight should be*

---

[1] Reproduced in *C.E.*, XX, pp. 237–47.
[2] *Ibid.*, p. 215.

*attached. But my earnest advice is that if you wish to retain the peace of mind necessary if you are to be cured you should break off all correspondence with your mentally confused stepmother. It is possible that she means well. But that woman's intervention in any matter or situation has always proved disastrous. If you don't want to tell her this yourself, I will. But I must have your consent first. Enough of this for today.*

*And now I come to the next main point in your letter. You beg me to lease a new apartment. And of course, since you so positively demand it, I shall do this. But in your letter you reproach me for taking our present apartment without consulting you. (At that time you were in Valdres and in no frame of mind for me to consider asking your advice.) Now when you come home and find this new apartment leased and furnished, you must remember that I have acted in accordance with your expressed wishes and that on this occasion, too, I have been unable to consult your opinion. And the task of finding something that will suit you in every respect is one that I shall indeed not find easy. Remember how Sigurd and Bergliot had to search and search before they at last and at great expense found something suitable. Our difficulties will be even greater. You don't want to live on the ground floor because the floors will be cold, and you won't or can't live higher up because of the stairs. But, as I say, your demand will be met. A new apartment will be leased.*

*I neither can nor wish to write about other matters today. Nor have I anything to say as regards myself. Werenskiold is here every morning and paints for an hour, otherwise the household routine remains unchanged. I presume Sigurd and the newspapers keep you in touch with political events.*

*And let me soon receive a calm, and calming, letter from you. And above all, keep these damned witches out of your life! That is the best advice and the best wishes that I can send you. Warmest regards,*

*Your affectionate*

*H.I.*

On 21 June he wrote again to Suzannah, by now in Monsummano, a spa near Pisa with a natural steam-bath in a grotto:

'*Well, I have now terminated our lease of Viktoria Terrasse and taken the first-floor apartment in a new house which the brothers Hoff are building on the corner of Arbins gade and Drammensveien. It was Sigurd and Bergliot who suggested this, and I think you will be happy with it. I have a big study with a door direct to the hall, so that people visiting me will not have to enter any other room in the apartment. You will have for your exclusive use a large corner room with a balcony and, next to it, an almost equally large drawing-room leading into the dining-room, which will hold 20–22 people and has an alcove for a sideboard, which I shall get. The dining-room leads straight into a large library and thence into your bedroom, which is much bigger than your one here. My bedroom is next to it and has a balcony.*

*You won't need to use the corridor except when you want to go to the bathroom.*
*There is also of course a big, light kitchen, a pantry and a servery, and many built-in*
*wall-cupboards. As I say I think you will be pleased.*

It was to be the last of their many apartments, and both Ibsen and Suzannah
were to die there.

William Archer, enclosing a couple of money drafts from Beerbohm
Tree that summer, seems to have suggested to Ibsen that he should visit
England to meet his many and distinguished admirers there. What a gathering
that would have been! But Ibsen was as timid as ever of visiting a country
where he could not speak the language. 'More and more do I feel it a painful
deficiency', he replied on 27 June, 'that I did not in time learn to speak English.
Now it is too late! Had I mastered the language I would now come at once to
London. Or rather, I would have been there long ago. I have been thinking
over many things, recently, and now feel sure that my Scottish ancestry has
left deep marks in me. But this is just an idea—possibly the wish is father to the
thought.' And indeed it must have been, for his only Scottish ancestor had
been seven generations earlier, in the seventeenth century. There seems to
have been something of a conspiracy to get him to England this year, for
Georg Brandes also wrote (on 16 December), but got the same reply.

By now, Ibsen had become a kind of tourist attraction in Christiania. Foreigners gathered at the Grand to see him make his entry; among them was the
English poet Richard le Gallienne:

'The large café was crowded, but we found a good table on the aisle,
not far from the door. We had not long to wait, for punctually on the
stroke of one, there, entering the doorway, was the dour and bristling
presence known to all the world in caricature—caricatures which were no
exaggerations but as in the case of Swinburne, just the man himself. The
great ruff of white whisker, ferociously standing out all round his sallow,
bilious face as if dangerously charged with electricity, the immaculate
silk hat, the white tie, the frock-coated martinet's figure dressed from
top to toe in old-fashioned black broadcloth, at once funereal and professional, the trousers concertinaed, apparently with dandaical design, at
the ankles, over his highly polished boots, the carefully folded umbrella—
all was there, apparitionally before me; a forbidding, disgruntled, tight-
lipped presence, starchily dignified, straight as a ramrod; there he was, as I
hinted, with a touch of grim dandyism about him, but with no touch of
human kindness about his parchment skin or fierce badger eyes. He might
have been a Scotch elder entering the kirk.

'As he entered and proceeded with precision tread to the table reserved

R

in perpetuity for him, which no one else would have dreamed of occupying, a thing new and delightful—to me a mere Anglo-Saxon—suddenly
happened. As one man, the whole café was on its feet in an attitude of
salute, and a stranger standing near me who evidently spoke English and
who recognised my nationality, said to me in a loud but reverent aside:
'That is our great poet, Henrik Ibsen'. All remained standing till he had
taken his seat, as in the presence of a king, and I marvelled greatly at a
people that thus did homage to their great men.'[1]

A grand-daughter of Queen Victoria, the lively young Princess Marie Louise,
was intrigued to note that he carried a small mirror in the crown of his hat
and used it like a woman when combing his hair.[2] Foreigners did their best to
obtain introductions; that summer he was visited by a Russian Count Galitzin,
who (he wrote to Suzannah on 2 July), 'has been General in the Caucasus and
has seen all the Russian borderlands touching India, Tibet and China, and
the whole of the north coast of Siberia'. The Hungarian novelist Giula Pekar
visited him too, as did his French translator Count Prozor and a Serbian Prince,
Bojidar Karageorgevitch, 'whose father ruled until the present régime came
into power'. On one occasion 'a group of forty to fifty tourists cheered me
loudly outside the Grand Hotel, led by an Austrian Lieutenant-Field-Marshal';
indeed, he was (he complained) 'properly plagued' by tourists, one of whom,
an American, gained entry to his apartment and, as Ibsen glared at him, slid
round him into his study, seized a pencil from the desk and disappeared with
it through the door. All this, except the last incident,[3] he reported to Suzannah
and Sigurd in his letters of that summer, urging Sigurd not to let Suzannah
hurry home since 'I manage excellently alone'. Apart from two dinners, he
told Suzannah (22 September), he had not been outside the city all summer.

Lugné-Poe was in Christiania again, after his theatrical triumph of the
previous autumn (which he had repeated in London that spring). He had
staged Little Eyolf and Brand in Paris that summer, evoking the usual violently
mixed reactions. On 10 August a dinner was given for him, which Ibsen
attended—'I cannot avoid going, little as I feel inclined to', he grumbled to
Suzannah the previous day. However, he seems to have enjoyed himself, for
Lugné-Poe tells that he stayed until one in the morning, joined in a game of
cards, and kept saying to him: 'I am so happy for your sake.'[4]

---

[1] Richard le Gallienne, The Romantic Nineties (London, 1926), pp. 59–60. Le Gallienne's
daughter, Eva, became a distinguished interpreter of Ibsen on the American stage.
[2] H.R.H. Princess Marie Louise, My Memories of Six Reigns (London, 1956), pp. 213–
214.
[3] Bergliot Ibsen, p. 150.
[4] Lugné-Poe, pp. 85–86.

On 15 October he moved with Bergliot's help into the new apartment at Arbins gade. Despite the pride with which he had written of it to Suzannah, it was to be as cheerless and unindividual as Viktoria Terrasse, or any of the furnished apartments they had inhabited abroad. 'Here he lodged for the eleven years that remained to him', writes Gerhard Gran. 'I say "lodged" deliberately, for these rooms never acquired the character of a home. They seemed cold and unlived-in, as regards not merely ordinary comfort and intimacy, but every personal stamp or individuality of taste. The only room which possessed a little of this was his study.'[1] A young child who lived in the flat below and occasionally visited Ibsen's kitchen for titbits from their maid Lina remembered it as drab and icy-cold; she also recalled the incessant sound above her head, when she was in her own room, of footsteps pacing back and forth, back and forth.[2] King Oscar gave him a key to a private section of the palace grounds known as the Queen's Park, so that he could walk there undisturbed.

August Lindberg, who had taken his productions of *Peer Gynt* and *Little Eyolf* to St Petersburg that March, was in Christiania in October preparing a production of *Brand*, and asked Ibsen if he could meet him to discuss it.

'He agreed to see me one evening at the Grand Hotel. The room where we were to meet was out of the way and quiet, lit only by a couple of candelabra. I was a few minutes late, and he was already seated when I arrived. He sat with his back to the door and the powerful head seemed even bigger in the large, dark room with its curious lighting. Quietly I closed the door behind me and went forward to greet him. He was in a brilliant humour, so I cried: "I'm sure you must have some mischief cooking, to judge from your smile." "Yes," he replied. "Some of those little imps are flocking around me, and I only have to put them in order." I thought he looked like an old wizard, and felt that the men who long ago had created the old sculptures in the great cathedral up at Nidaros [Trondhjem] must have looked like him.'

Ibsen asked whom Lindberg had in mind to provide the music.

'I'd thought of Grieg, naturally.'
'Why Grieg?'
'Well, he wrote the music for *Peer Gynt*.'
'Oh', said Ibsen. 'You think that's good, do you?'

---

[1] Gran, II, p. 330.
[2] Told by Fru Signe Meyer, née Hansen, to Herr Gordon Hølmebakk, who told me.

They wrangled about the price. Ibsen asked 3,000 crowns (£167), but Lindberg managed to beat him down to a thousand, and on 21 October his production opened at the Eldorado Theatre in Christiania, the first time *Brand* had ever been seen in Norway. The actors were all Swedish and, the question of the Union being a subject of more than usual controversy just then (thanks not least to Sigurd's pamphleteering) Swedes were less than popular in Norway; but Lindberg's performance overcame chauvinistic feelings, and the production proved a great success. He toured it, in repertory with *Peer Gynt*, to Bergen and Trondhjem, where he played to full houses for nearly a month; his company, containing as it did several young players who were to be the great names of the future, was better than the resident companies at the big theatres in any of the Scandinavian capitals.[1]

1895 had been an important year for Ibsen in America. Although there is no record of any native performances, apart from a *Little Eyolf* in Chicago in the spring, New Yorkers had had the opportunity to see three European productions: Janet Achurch in *A Doll's House*, Gabrielle Réjane in the same play, and Tree's *An Enemy of the People*. Of this last production, Lucy Monroe wrote in the magazine *Critic*: 'With a singular lack of faith in the discretion of the public, it was reserved for the close of the engagement and put on then, apparently more as an experiment than with any expectation of success. But the enthusiasm was of a kind not easily provoked in an American audience. The house was keenly appreciative throughout, and after the third act it fairly rose to the play, shouting and cheering.'[2] By the following year, an American was to write: 'Ibsen has become so familiar to the American public that one need scarcely touch upon the incidents of his career.'[3]

It had been another fair year financially. New editions of *Brand*, *Little Eyolf*, *Love's Comedy* and *The League of Youth* had brought him 4,610 crowns (£256), but this represented only about one-fifth of his income; the rest came from performing rights. His German and Austrian royalties aggregated 9,067 crowns (£503), his French royalties 2,947 crowns (£164), his Danish royalties 3,420 crowns (£190). His English royalties (from Tree's *Enemy of the People*) were, one is ashamed to record, only £17 10s. 0d.; and for Norwegian performing rights he received 580 crowns (£32), made up of 80 crowns owed him from Bergen for the previous year and 500 crowns for the touring rights of *Little Eyolf*.

[1] Lindberg, pp. 372–378.
[2] *Critic*, 1895, nr. 26, pp. 208–209.
[3] Edgar O. Achorn, *Ibsen at Home*, in *New England Magazine*, 1896, nr. 13, pp. 737–748.

| | crowns | £ |
|---|---|---|
| German royalties from Felix Bloch | 333 | 18 |
| Royalties from Lessingtheater, Berlin | 82 | 4 |
| Fees from Bergen for previous season | 80 | 4 |
| Fees for *Little Eyolf* at Svenska Teatern, Helsinki and Finska Teatern, Helsinki | 359 | 20 |
| Royalties for *The Pillars of Society* at Wien Burgtheater | 2,413 | 134 |
| 13th edition of *Brand* | 1,870 | 104 |
| Royalties for *The Pillars of Society*, *A Doll's House* and *An Enemy of the People* at Munich Hoftheater | 546 | 30 |
| Fee for provincial rights in Norway of *Little Eyolf*, excluding Christiania and Bergen (Olaus Olsen) | 500 | 28 |
| 3rd edition of *Little Eyolf* | 780 | 43 |
| French royalties from Societé des Auteurs Dramatiques | 2,947 | 164 |
| German royalties from Bloch | 1,726 | 96 |
| Royalties for *The Pretenders*, *The Pillars of Society* and *Little Eyolf* from Wien Burgtheater | 1,790 | 99 |
| Unspecified royalties from Munich Hoftheater | 84 | 5 |
| Royalties from H. Beerbohm Tree for *An Enemy of the People* (£17 10s. 0d.) | 317 | 17 |
| Fee from Oda Nielsen for *Little Eyolf* | 600 | 34 |
| German royalties from Bloch | 930 | 52 |
| Unspecified royalties from Wien Burgtheater | 805 | 45 |
| 7th edition of *Love's Comedy* | 800 | 45 |
| 6th edition of *The League of Youth* | 1,160 | 65 |
| Royalties from Royal Theatre, Copenhagen, for *The Wild Duck* (21st–26th performances) | 595 | 33 |
| Ditto for *Little Eyolf* (1st–7th performances) | 1,625 | 90 |
| Fee for *Lady Inger of Østraat* at Dagmars Theater, Copenhagen | 600 | 33 |
| German royalties from Bloch | 85 | 5 |
| Royalties from Wien Burgtheater | 123 | 7 |
| Fee for *Brand* from August Lindberg | 1,000 | 56 |
| Royalties from Munich Hoftheater | 150 | 8 |
| | 22,300 | 1,239 |

Suzannah had returned home during the autumn, to settle for the first time in their new apartment; so he wrote no more letters to her, and few to anyone that have survived from 1896. Edvard Brandes visited him that winter and was amused to see how he enjoyed studying the harrowed and embittered face of his adversary hanging on the study wall. The Strindberg portrait seemed to Brandes to provide the sole example of individuality in the furnishing of Arbins gade. When he remarked on it, Ibsen half-closed his eyes and said: 'I like to look at that face.'[1]

He spent the first months of the year brooding on his new play, getting his 'little imps' into order. 'I am busy with preparations for a big new work', he wrote to Georg Brandes on 24 April, 'and don't want to put it off for longer than I need. I could so easily have a tile fall on my head before I had "managed to write the last verse". And what then?' On 11 July he began his draft, and on 27 July was able to inform Jacob Hegel that it was 'progressing quickly and easily, despite the more than southerly warmth we are having up here this summer'. It went smoothly indeed, for by 26 August he had finished his draft.

As he was revising it, in September, the great explorer Fridtjof Nansen returned from his Greenland voyage, and practically the whole population of Christiania flocked to the quayside to greet him. Edvard Brandes, who was in the city, tells how he was walking through the deserted streets when, near the Post Office, he encountered Ibsen. The two stood facing each other, seemingly alone in Christiania. 'You here, Herr Doctor, and not at the reception?' asked Brandes. 'Ibsen's face stiffened. "No," he replied, almost angrily. "This is an Indian deed to be celebrated with an Indian dance, at which I don't belong." And he walked on.'[2] Brandes surmises that to Ibsen Nansen's voyage was an athletic feat which hardly deserved "the acclamation of a nation", but that seems a cynical and unjustified comment. Returning heroes, like Coronations, are not to everyone's taste.

On 3 October he thanked Georg Brandes for sending him his 'great monumental book on Shakespeare', which 'I have not merely read but have buried myself in, as I have done with scarcely any other book.' One wonders if he recalled the youthful lecture he had given on Shakespeare in Bergen forty-one years before to the week. A week later he wrote again to Brandes, this time to deny (as so often before) various supposed influences upon his own writing. The French dramatist and critic Jules Lemaître, in an article on the influence of Scandinavian literature in France,[3] had suggested that Ibsen had said and done nothing that George Sand and Dumas fils had not said and done before him. Brandes put this to Ibsen, who replied (11 October): 'I hereby swear on my honour and conscience that I have never in my whole life, neither in my youth nor later, read a single book by George Sand. I once began Consuelo in translation, but put it aside as soon as I realised it was the

---

[1] Edvard Brandes, Henrik Ibsens Personlighed, in Politiken, 20 March 1928, reprinted in Litterære Tendenser (Copenhagen, 1968), p. 235.

[2] Ibid., pp. 237–238.

[3] Reprinted in Lemaître's Les Contemporains, VI (Paris, 1896), pp. 225–270. Brandes's reply, Henrik Ibsen en France, appeared in Cosmopolis, January 1897, pp. 112–124. Cf. Sprinchorn, p. 322.

work of a dilettante philosopher and not of a writer. But I read only a few pages, so I may be mistaken in this . . . I owe Alexandre Dumas nothing whatever in respect to dramatic form—expect that I have learned from his plays to avoid certain gross faults and misconceptions of which he is not infrequently guilty.'[1]

On 18 October he finished fair-copying his new play—he had spent eight full weeks polishing it—and two days later he posted it off to Hegel with the prophecy: 'I think we shall both have joy from it.'

Happy with his English publisher, William Heinemann, Ibsen was less content with S. Fischer in Germany. 'I am afraid', he wrote on 1 November to Julius Elias, who was handling his book rights there, 'I am not rich enough to go on using Herr Fischer as a publisher, which more or less amounts to giving him my books gratis. I have had to pay most of the translation fees myself, since I have had to grant the translators half my theatre royalties while Herr Fischer himself has paid the merest trifle for their labours. My fee last time was 1,000 marks [887 crowns, £49]; and in a letter I received at the same time as your telegram he very generously offers to pay me a full 200 marks more! Now, when the work is protected by the Berne Convention! . . . By comparison, let me tell you how Herr Albert Langen of Munich feels able to pay for my new book without any compulsion to talk of sacrifices. Herr Langen is paying me 5,000 marks as author's fee, and all theatre royalties will come to me, since Herr Langen is paying for the translation. Bearing this in mind I hope you will appreciate that I cannot continue to carry the financial burden of having Herr Fischer as my publisher. As a further example for comparison with Herr Fischer's offer I may tell you that my English publisher, Mr W. Heinemann, London, has paid me the same fee as Herr Langen for each of my last two plays and, now that I am protected by the Convention, will pay me even more.'[2]

Ibsen's threat worked. Fischer, unwilling to lose so profitable an author, matched Langen's terms—and was well rewarded, for by his own statement he published 40,000 copies of the German collected edition (according to the widow of Julius Elias, who co-edited it, he in fact published twice that number).[3]

In France, Lugné-Poe had presented *The Pillars of Society* that June; and on 12 November, greatly daring, he followed it with the French premiere of *Peer Gynt*. Bernard Shaw, went over to Paris for the performance, and found it disappointing. 'The characteristic Northern hard-headed, hard-fisted humour,

[1] Dumas, however, apparently admired Ibsen (cf. Jules Claretie's account of a conversation with Ibsen in *Figaro*, 20 July 1897, reprinted in *Morgenbladet*, 24 July 1897, and in *C.E.*, XIX, pp. 208–211).

[2] Heinemann's fee for *John Gabriel Borkman* was in fact £200, compared with Langen's £245.

[3] Bergliot Ibsen, p. 177.

the Northern power of presenting the deepest truths in the most homely grotesques, was missed', he wrote in the *Saturday Review* (21 November). 'M. Lugné-Poe, with all his realism, could no more help presenting the play sentimentally and sublimely than M. Lamoureux can help conducting the overture to Tannhäuser as if it were the Marseillaise; but the universality of Ibsen makes his plays come home to all nations; and Peer Gynt is as good a Frenchman as he is a Norwegian, just as Dr Stockmann is as intelligible in Bermondsey or Bournemouth as he is in his native town . . . Peer Gynt will finally smash anti-Ibsenism in Europe, because Peer is everybody's hero. He has the same effect on the imagination that Hamlet, Faust and Mozart's Don Juan have had.' Yet the press (according to Bjørn Bjørnson, who was also there) was surprisingly good, and Shaw records that the play aroused such interest in Paris that Prozor's translation 'was sold out immediately after the performance'. The Old Man of the Mountains was played by a twenty-three year old actor who was the secretary of the Théâtre de L'Œuvre—Alfred Jarry (appearing under the pseudonym of Hemgé), whose play *Ubu roi*, written for marionettes when Jarry was a schoolboy of fifteen, had been performed by the L'Œuvre that year, with Bonnard, Vuillard and Toulouse-Lautrec among the designers of scenery and masks.

On 23 November *Little Eyolf* was staged in England for the first time, at the Avenue Theatre (later the Playhouse) behind Charing Cross station. The cast was the strongest that had yet been assembled in England for an Ibsen play. Not only were Janet Achurch and Elizabeth Robins paired together for the first time, as Rita and Asta; Allmers was played by Courtenay Thorpe, who had been a remarkable Oswald in New York in 1894, and a West End star, Stella Patrick Campbell, who had burst into fame as Pinero's Mrs Tanqueray in 1893, was secured for the part of the Rat-Wife. Bernard Shaw, in the *Saturday Review* (28 November) commented: 'The performance was, of course, a very remarkable one. When, in a cast of five, you have the three best yet discovered actresses of their generation, you naturally look for something extraordinary . . . Miss Achurch was more than equal to the occasion. Her power seemed to grow with its own expenditure . . . As Rita she produced almost every sound that a big human voice can, from a creak like the opening of a rusty canal lock to a melodious tenor note that the most robust Siegfried might have envied. She looked at one moment like a young, well-dressed, very pretty woman; at another she was like a desperate creature just fished dripping out of the river by the Thames Police. Yet another moment, and she was the incarnation of impetuous, ungovernable strength . . . It is encouraging to see that the performances are to be continued next week, the five matinées—all crowded, by the way—having by no means exhausted the demand for places.'

The production was such a success that it was transferred to the evening bill; but in the hope of ensuring a commercial success the new backers removed Janet Achurch from the part of Rita and replaced her with Mrs Patrick Campbell who (according to Shaw in the *Saturday Review*, 12 December) 'succeeded wonderfully in removing all unpleasantness from the play', and thereby ruined it. It was not to be the last time that an Ibsen production was to be spoiled by the replacement of the right player by a supposedly more magnetic star[1] (though in the next century Mrs Campbell was to be a memorable Hedda Gabler and Mrs Alving, with the young John Gielgud as Oswald).

Not all the critics, naturally, admired the play. *The Theatre* called it 'dull, wordy, unpleasant and prodigiously tiresome', and the *Times* wrote: 'Gloom, depression and a sense of the remoteness of the action from all living human interests overcome the spectator, whose abiding impression of the play is that of having seen in a dream the patients of a madhouse exercising in their yard.'

On 5 December *Emperor and Galilean* was staged for the first time, in a shortened form at the Leipzig Stadttheater, and the same month *Love's Comedy* also received its German premiere, at the Belle-Alliance Theatre in Berlin— the first performance of that play outside Scandinavia. But neither was a great success.

On 15 December *John Gabriel Borkman* was published, in, thanks to the success of *Little Eyolf*, the unprecedently large edition of 12,000 copies. Even this proved insufficient; the demand was such that Hegel had to reprint another 3,000 before publication. It was even better received than *Little Eyolf*—not surprisingly, the critics found it less obscure. 'Ibsen has never climbed so high as a dramatic master builder', wrote Nils Vogt in *Morgenbladet* (24 December), and he thought the play 'fascinating and exciting.' Georg Brandes, in *Verdens Gang* (19 December), found it magnificently constructed 'as though built of iron on a foundation of granite. The play moves with the speed of youth, but the voice is that of age and wisdom, a stern wisdom'—and yet, too, of 'a deep sympathy for human suffering which yet has not retracted a single one of its demands'. Carl Nærup, reviewing the play again in the same newspaper on 21 December, also spoke of 'the breath of youth', and found the characters 'bigger, stronger—not the centre-less, crumbling characters of his earlier plays, at the mercy of every emotional wind and weather. They choose for themselves.' In Sweden J. A. Runström, in *Ny Illustrerad Tidning* (27 February

---

[1] Lugné-Poe (*op. cit.*, p. 22) tells that Ibsen hated to hear of any actor doing a play 'for his own sake', and that when a Parisian theatre director told him that the great Le Bargy was thinking of acting Oswald, Ibsen exploded: 'Of course, like that Italian actor who acts the whole play.' He was referring to Ermete Zacconi.

1897) wrote that it was 'in the opinion of many people the author's finest play since the days of *An Enemy of the People* and *The Wild Duck*. The much debated obscurity which has enveloped Ibsen's latest creations is here dispelled . . . *John Gabriel Borkman* is a mighty play.' The Danish magazine *The Corsair* printed a cartoon, humorously entitled *A Disappointment*, showing Ibsen offering a bowl marked 'No Problems' to a forlorn gathering of critics.

Naturally, there were dissidents, most of whom reacted against the play's apparent pessimism. Kristofer Randers, in *Aftenposten* (20 December), found it 'a curious play, dark and obscure, full of bitter contempt for humanity . . . This is the blackest and most comfortless play Ibsen has yet written . . . *Vanitas vanitatum*, the poet seems to cry, all is emptiness. Empty the ambitious dreams of power, empty the belief in the happiness of marriage . . . Only one thing is true—the love of a steadfast woman—but that is seldom found, and when found it is shamed or betrayed. Shall this philosophy be the aged master's last words as the twilight shadows gather? We must hope not.' C. D. af Wirsén similarly complained: 'These are lofty heights onto which Ibsen leads us through the whirling snow. But they are cold and empty. However brilliant this play may be, it is unlikely to warm or rejoice a single human heart.'[1] And an anonymous reviewer in *Nordisk Tidskrift* (1897, pp. 160–162) wrote, perhaps rather wishfully; 'Undoubtedly the tight phalanx of Ibsen's admirers has been thinned by this work . . . The whole play makes an empty and hollow impression, and we turn disappointed to the author and ask: "Why?" . . . His technique is failing him.' But the Ayes had it. *John Gabriel Borkman* was acclaimed as none of his plays had been since *A Doll's House*.

*John Gabriel Borkman* tells the story of a miner's son who becomes a financier and, for idealistic reasons, embezzles and is sent to prison. Released after eight years, he lives alone in an upstairs room of his house refusing to see his wife, visited only by an old clerk and waiting in the conviction that the people will demand that he emerge to save them. As a young man he had married not for love but to get his foot on the ladder; now his wife's twin sister, whom he had loved and rejected, comes to reproach him and to beg that she be given charge of his son, and that this son, Erhart, should take her name. Borkman agrees, but his wife, who overhears their conversation, refuses; as the two women argue, Erhart arrives to announce that he is leaving with a woman nearly twice his age. Borkman wanders out and dies on the mountainside.

The plot is based on a story which Ibsen had heard long ago in his student days. In 1851 a high-ranking army officer had been charged with embezzlement. At first he denied the charge but then, like Old Ekdal in *The Wild Duck*,

---

[1] Wirsén, p. 120.

he unsuccessfully tried to shoot himself. He was sentenced to four years penal servitude and, when released, shortly before Ibsen returned to Christiania to run the Møllergaden Theatre, shut himself up in his house and spent the rest of his life brooding in solitude, unable even to speak to his wife. Later, in the eighteen-eighties, a great scandal had occurred at Arendal; a bank director speculated and embezzled his clients' money, and was sent to prison.

After the obsessive references to bankruptcy in his earlier plays Ibsen had not touched on the subject since *The Wild Duck* twelve years before; and in several other ways, *John Gabriel Borkman* marks a curious return to the past. His youthful poem *The Miner*, written when he was twenty-three in the year the officer was charged, perfectly crystallises the theme of the play:

> ... Here in the darkness there is peace.
> Peace and rest for eternity.
> Heavy hammer, break me the way
> To the heart-chamber of what lies hidden there ...
>
> When I first entered here
> I thought in my innocence:
> 'The spirits of the dark will solve for me
> Life's obscure riddles.'
>
> No spirit has yet taught me that strange answer.
> No ray has shone from the depths.
>
> Was I wrong? Does this path
> Not lead to the light?
> But the light blinds my eyes
> If I seek it in the mountains.
>
> No, I must go down into the dark.
> Eternal peace lies there.
> Heavy hammer, break me the way
> To the heart-chamber of what lies hidden there.
>
> So blow follows blow
> Till he sinks weak and tired.
> No ray of morning shines.
> No sun of hope rises.

And as a young man, Ibsen had had a friend named Vilhelm Foss, an old copying clerk who had once published a collection of verses and still lived in the hope that he might some day achieve poetic fame. He had remembered Foss when planning *The Lady from the Sea*, in the notes of which Foss makes a phantom appearance. Ibsen discarded him from that play, but he kept him in mind, and at last Foss achieved immortality as Vilhelm Foldal, the clerk who spends his life polishing a youthful play which he dreams he may one day see acted.

The gossips of Christiania, naturally, took the loveless marriage of the Borkmans to be a picture of Ibsen's relationship with Suzannah, especially now that Hildur Andersen was back in town.[1] It is hardly that; yet, despite Ibsen's demand that we should treat his plays as pure fiction, one may be forgiven for suggesting that *John Gabriel Borkman* does in fact represent a sad survey of the dramatist's bleak emotional life. The Ibsens were not precisely the Borkmans; the immense tie that bound Henrik and Suzannah together is absent from the marriage in the play; a kind of love, perhaps the most profound and lasting kind, existed between the Ibsens, but it was not, and never had been, romantic love, the kind that Ella Rentheim represents. Ibsen, like Borkman, had turned his back on romantic love for a woman who could enable him to achieve his ambitions, and Emilie Bardach, Helene Raff and Hildur Andersen were living symbols of what he had rejected. By choosing, and remorselessly pursuing, the career of an author he had sacrificed his chance of that other kind of happiness; and he may have felt that to some extent he had sacrificed Suzannah's chances too. The recent quarrel with Suzannah about his supposed intention to divorce her must have helped to make *John Gabriel Borkman* the guilt-ridden play it is. In a sense the play is about what Ibsen's marriage might have been like had he failed as a writer; in another sense, it is about emotional bank-ruptcy, the buried treasures of the heart that lie unmined; how a man may gain the whole world and lose his soul. Edvard Munch called *John Gabriel Borkman* 'the most powerful winter landscape in Scandinavian art'.

Formally, the last act of *Borkman* marks a return to the epic and poetic symbolism of *Brand* and *Peer Gynt*. As we have seen, Ibsen had deliberately suppressed the poet in him while writing the "social" plays, from *The Pillars of Society* to *The Wild Duck*; there are no moments of poetry in them, save perhaps Mrs Alving's speech about the ghosts that 'lie as thick as grains of sand'. But in every play he had written since *The Wild Duck*, with the solitary

---

[1] As an example of the malicious rumours that circulated in Christiania about Ibsen and Suzannah, William Archer tells that 'my brother was one day going to call upon him in Christiania and remarked to a friend resident in the town that if Ibsen was not at home he hoped he might see Fru Ibsen. "Oh, no," said his friend. "You won't see her. She hasn't been able to live with him for years." My brother paid his call and the first person he saw on crossing the threshold was Fru Ibsen. The incident was typical.' (*Ibsen as I Knew Him*, p. 10.)

exception of *Hedda Gabler* (and was the laconic shorthand of that play the result
of a desire not to let his hidden feelings break the surface?), there are times when
we are aware of the buried river. A poet who delves into the dark unconscious,
as Ibsen had done in these last plays, cannot wholly suppress the poet within
him, far less the symbolist. But it is not, I think, until the final act of *John
Gabriel Borkman* that we find the writer of realistic dialogue being edged aside
by the symbolist and the poet:

BORKMAN (*stops by the precipice*): Come, Ella, and I shall show you.

ELLA:    What will you show me, John?

BORKMAN (*points*): See how the country stretches out before us, open and
    free—far, far away.

ELLA:    We used to sit on that seat, and stare into the distance.

BORKMAN: It was a country of dreams we gazed into.

ELLA:    The country of our dreams, yes. Now it is covered with snow.
    And the old tree is dead.

BORKMAN (*not listening to her*): Can you see the smoke from the great steamers
    out on the fjord?

ELLA:    No.

BORKMAN: I can. They come and go. They create a sense of fellowship
    throughout the world. They bring light and warmth to the hearts
    of men in many thousands of homes. That is what I dreamed of
    creating.

ELLA:    But it remained a dream.

BORKMAN: Yes. It remained a dream. (*Listens*) Listen. Down there by the
    river the factories hum. My factories. Listen how they hum. The
    night shifts are working. They work both night and day. Listen,
    listen! The wheels whirl and the pistons thud, round and round,
    in and out. Can't you hear them, Ella?

ELLA:    No.

BORKMAN: I hear them.

ELLA (*frightened*): No, John, you can't.

BORKMAN: Ah, but these are only the outworks surrounding my kingdom.

ELLA:    What kingdom?

BORKMAN: My kingdom. The kingdom I was about to take possession of
    when I died.

ELLA:    Oh, John, John.

BORKMAN: And there it lies, defenceless, masterless, abandoned to thieves
    and robbers. Ella! Do you see those mountains far away? Range
    beyond range, rising and rising? That is my infinite and in-
    exhaustible kingdom.

ELLA:     Ah, but it's a cold wind that blows from that kingdom, John.
BORKMAN: To me it is the breath of life. It is a greeting from the spirits that
          serve me. I feel them, those buried millions. I see those veins of
          iron ore, stretching their twisting, branching, enticing arms
          towards me. I've seen you all before, like shadows brought to
          life—that night when I stood in the vaults of the bank with the
          lantern in my hand. You wanted to be freed. And I tried to free
          you. But I failed. Your treasure sank back into the darkness. But
          let me whisper this to you now, in the stillness of the night. I
          love you where you lie like the dead, deep down in the dark. I
          love you, treasures that crave for life, with your bright retinue
          of power and glory. I love you, love you, love you.

That is the voice of the young Ibsen, the author of *Brand*. In his next play, the
movement away from realism, or rather from the realism of prose towards the
realism of poetry, was to be carried a stage further. In *When We Dead Awaken*,
as in *Brand* and *Peer Gynt*, Ibsen seems to be writing for a theatre of the mind—
though, like them, *When We Dead Awaken* works powerfully on the stage,
given the right quality of imagination in the staging.

As though to underline the message of *John Gabriel Borkman*, that the quest
for material success may lead to emotional bankruptcy, 1896 had proved, in
terms of money, Ibsen's richest year yet:

|  | crowns | £ |
|---|---|---|
| German royalties from Felix Bloch | 50 | 3 |
| Royalties from Wien Burgtheater | 225 | 12 |
| Fee from Bergen Theatre for previous year (360) | 360 | 20 |
| Fee for *Love's Comedy* at Folketeater, Copenhagen | 1,200 | 67 |
| Royalties from Munich Hoftheater | 98 | 5 |
| Fee for *Little Eyolf* at Royal Theatre, Copenhagen (8th–13th performances) | 1,276 | 71 |
| 4th edition of *A Doll's House* | 675 | 38 |
| 9th edition of *The Pretenders* | 1,020 | 56 |
| French royalties from Societé des Auteurs Dramatiques | 144 | 8 |
| Royalties from Bloch | 145 | 8 |
| Royalties from English book sales (Archer: £2 7s. 1d.) | 43 | 2 |
| Royalties from Wien Burgtheater | 448 | 25 |
| 10th edition of *Peer Gynt* | 1,815 | 101 |
| 1st German edition of *Catiline* (A. Langen of Munich) | 400 | 22 |
| Fee from August Lindberg for 3 performances of *Brand* at Folketeater in Copenhagen | 300 | 17 |

| | crowns | £ |
|---|---|---|
| Royalties from Bloch | 75 | 4 |
| Royalties from Wien Burgtheater | 120 | 7 |
| Royalties from Munich Hoftheater | 83 | 5 |
| Royalties from Bloch | 26 | 1 |
| Royalties from Munich Hoftheater | 52 | 3 |
| 1st edition of *John Gabriel Borkman* | 11,160 | 620 |
| 1st German edition of *John Gabriel Borkman* | 4,444 | 247 |
| Balance on German edition of *Little Eyolf* | 444 | 25 |
| 2nd edition of *John Gabriel Borkman* | 2,790 | 155 |
| English edition of *John Gabriel Borkman* (£200) | 3,600 | 200 |
| Swedish performance rights for two years of *John Gabriel Borkman* (Albert Ranft) | 3,000 | 167 |
| Fee from August Lindberg for Norwegian provincial rights of *John Gabriel Borkman* (2 years) | 1,000 | 55 |
| | 34,993 | 1,944 |

# THIRTEEN

## ❧ Irritations

## (1897)

1897 OPENED WITH a row with an Englishman. Robert Harborough Sherard, the friend (and later biographer) of Oscar Wilde and a great-grandson of William Wordsworth, had visited Norway the previous summer and autumn, and on 3 January he published in the New York magazine *The Humanitarian* a purported interview with Ibsen at the latter's home. In this article Sherard attributed to Ibsen several outspoken remarks about Norwegian manners—*inter alia*, that Christiania was 'the most immoral city in Europe', and that one of the reasons for his living there was that 'there is nowhere else where a student of social life can find better subjects. One can, for example, say that marriage in a practical sense no longer exists here.' One cause, he allegedly added, was that the suppression by the police of licensed prostitution 'throws young people into their neighbours' arms ... *Ménages à trois* flourish and, thanks to the present equality of the sexes, the third party is often a woman.'

The publication of these remarks naturally caused a sensation in Norway, and Ibsen immediately issued a refutation in *Aftenposten*, declaring that 'partly because of the Grüttefien affair [a German journalist of that name had printed supposed interviews with Bjørnson and King Oscar the previous summer, which turned out to have been faked], partly because the gentleman in question [Sherard] gave the impression of being untrustworthy', he had refused to receive him and had merely conversed with him for a couple of minutes in public without discussing Christiania or Norway at all; 'there is not a true word in what the Englishman writes'. Sherard sent a telegram to *Aftenposten* which appeared on 8 January standing by his article, to which Ibsen replied (in the same issue) that a journalist who tells a lie always pretends it is true.

If Frank Harris had written the article, one would have no doubts as to what had happened; but Sherard was a rather guileless man, not given to falsification. Ibsen is hardly likely to have uttered the above remarks to a journalist, or directly to a stranger; yet they are precisely the kind of things he might have said over a glass to friends, and a sneaking suspicion remains: would an intelligent and quite reputable writer like Sherard, the friend and biographer

272

not merely of Wilde but of Zola, Daudet and Maupassant, have invented such a tissue of lies? Sherard, in his telegram to *Aftenposten* on 8 January, referred to friends in Christiania as witnesses; did he perhaps sit in on a conversation in which Ibsen was indiscreet, perhaps not realising that Sherard was a journalist as well as an author of books? We shall never know (if there were such friends present they would scarcely have risked their friendship with Ibsen by support-ing Sherard's story); but I do not think Ibsen's denial should be accepted without a certain reserve. Grüttefien had published fake interviews, but Sherard was not a fake.

*John Gabriel Borkman* received two simultaneous premieres on 10 January in Helsinki, when both the Finnish and Swedish theatres staged it. On 16 January it was performed at Frankfurt-on-Main. The German censor had ordered the excision of two passages which he found offensive, Ella's line in Act Two about 'the sin for which there is no forgiveness' (to murder love in a human being), and Mrs Wilton's remark in Act Four about the advisability of Erhart having another girl to fall back on if he should tire of her, or she of him. Here, as in Helsinki, the play was a success. Three days later it received its Norwegian premiere, under bizarre circumstances. August Lindberg had secured from Ibsen the rights to present it in the Norwegian provinces, and managed to stage it at the little town of Drammen, a bare thirty miles from Christiania, six days before the Christiania Theatre were ready with their production. He enterprisingly ran special trains from the capital to Drammen and so drew off a proportion of the Christiania Theatre's public, which probably caused Ibsen no displeasure (as he had received a fixed fee for both productions, it did not matter to him which one people attended). The provincial production got much the better reviews.

Lindberg had one or two meetings with Ibsen while preparing the production, to ask him about various points, 'but he always answered briefly and evasively.' Lindberg thought his attitude towards his plays was like what, as an apothecary, he must have felt towards his medicines; once he had mixed them, there was an end to it. 'I had to console myself with the thought that we actors were as air to him.'

One day Ibsen invited him to lunch at the Grand Hotel at noon.

'I met him in the foyer and saw how he took out a small girl's comb and combed his hair meticulously, surveying himself in a small mirror in the crown of his hat. When we arrived at the table reserved for him there stood on it nothing but a carafe of schnapps and a bottle of light brown ale. The head waiter came, and was commanded to lay another place. Immediately there arrived another carafe of schnapps and bottle of beer. Ibsen helped

s

himself and bade me do likewise. Then he raised his schnapps glass and said:
"Skaal!" I repeated the word but did not drink. He continued: "What I
like about this schnapps is that it's a healthy drink and a native one. I don't
order Hungarian wine in Bavaria or Bavarian lager in Hungary. One
should do as the natives do, and since schnapps is the only wine this country
produces one must enjoy it as such. Skaal!"

"But what about something to eat?" I asked squarely and without
thinking.

"You want something to eat?"

"Well, I'm sorry," I said. "But didn't you invite me to lunch?"

"Are you hungry at this hour?"

"I must at least have a sandwich."

He rang for the head waiter and ordered him to bring "a sandwich for
the director".'[1]

Before the end of January, *John Gabriel Borkman* had also been staged in
Stockholm, Berlin (where Hermann Nissen played the title role with a make-
up suggesting both Ibsen and Bjørnson) and Copenhagen (where Emil Poulsen
clearly identified the character with the author). The play proved a greater
success in the theatres than any Ibsen had written since *A Doll's House*. No one
could find this obscure, or politically or morally offensive—though Edvard
Brandes, seated beside Ibsen at the Christiania dress rehearsal, noted his misery
at the actors' failure to give the play life.[2] In London Ellen Terry tried to
interest Henry Irving in the role. He was ill, and she took advantage of his
enforced immobility by reading him the first two acts; he read the third to her.
'What a play!' he commented, with an inflection that left no doubt of his
opinion. To his notebook Irving confided: 'Threadworms and leeches are an
interesting study; but they have no interest to me.'[3]

If Irving found *Borkman* uninteresting, Henry James did not. In a London
Letter to *Harper's Weekly* of New York, dated 15 January and published on
6 February, James declared:

'The author who, at the age of seventy, a provincial of provincials, turns
out *John Gabriel* is frankly for me so much one of the peculiar pleasures of
the day, one of the current strong sensations that, erect as he seems still to
stand, I deplore his extreme maturity and, thinking of what shall happen,
look round in vain for any other possible source of the same kind of
emotion. For Ibsen strikes me as an extraordinary curiosity, and every time

[1] Lindberg, pp. 384–386.
[2] Edvard Brandes, *Henrik Ibsens Personlighed*, pp. 236–237.
[3] Laurence Irving, *Henry Irving* (London, 1951), p. 601.

he sounds his note the miracle, to my perception, is renewed. I call it a
miracle because it is the result of so dry a view of life . . . There is a positive
odour of spiritual paraffin. The author nevertheless arrives at the dramatist's great goal—he arrives for all his meagreness at intensity. The meagreness, which is after all but an unconscious, an admirable economy, never
interferes with that; it plays straight into the hands of his rare mastery of
form. The contrast between this form—so difficult to have reached, so
civilized, so 'evolved'—and the bareness and bleakness of his little northern
democracy is the source of half the hard frugal charm that he puts forth. In
the cold fixed light of it the notes that we speak of as deficiencies take a
sharp value in the picture. There is no small-talk, there are scarcely any
manners. On the other hand there is so little vulgarity that this of itself has
almost the effect of a deeper, a more lonely provincialism. The background
at any rate is the sunset over the ice. Well in the very front of the scene
lunges with extraordinary length of arm the Ego against the Ego, and rocks
in a rigour of passion the soul against the soul—a spectacle, a movement,
as definite as the relief of silhouettes in black paper or a train of Eskimo
dogs on the snow. Down from that desolation the sturdy symbolist comes
this time with a supreme example of his method. It is a high wonder and
pleasure to welcome such splendid fruit from sap that might by now have
shown something of the chill of age. Never has he juggled more gallantly
with difficulty and danger than in this really prodigious *John Gabriel*, in
which a great span of tragedy is taken between three or four persons—a
trio of the grim and grizzled—in the two or three hours of a winter's
evening; in which the whole thing throbs with an actability that fairly
shakes us as we read; and in which, as the very flower of his artistic triumph,
he has given us for the most beautiful and touching of his heroines a sad old
maid of sixty.'[1]

But, when it was staged in London, at the Strand Theatre on 3 May, it was
very inadequately done. 'Mr Vernon's Borkman was not ill acted', commented
Bernard Shaw. 'Only, as it was not Ibsen's Borkman, but the very reverse
and negation of him, the better Mr Vernon acted, the worse it was for the
play'—a statement which could be applied to many subsequent Ibsen performances by this actor and that. Shaw also denounced the poverty of the
sets, which seem to have been dire even for an experimental production.
'I beg the New Century Theatre',[2] he wrote, 'when the next Ibsen play is

[1] Cf. *The Scenic Art*, pp. 291–294.
[2] A private subscription society founded by Elizabeth Robins, William Archer, H. W.
Massingham and Alfred Sutro, and patterned on Grein's Independent Theatre Society,
which was about to close after six brave years.

ready for mounting, to apply to me for assistance. If I have a ten pound note, they shall have it; if not, I can at least lend them a couple of decent chairs.'[1]

After the quiet of the previous year, when only *Little Eyolf* of Ibsen's plays had been staged in London, the summer of 1897 saw a renewed flurry of activity. A week after the *Borkman* opening, *A Doll's House* was revived for a series of matinées at the Globe Theatre, with Janet Achurch in her old part and Courtenay Thorpe (who was playing Hamlet in the evenings) as Helmer. 'He plays Helmer with passion,' wrote Bernard Shaw. 'It is the first time we have seen this done; and the effect is overwhelming. We no longer study an object-lesson in lord-of-creationism, appealing to our sociological interest only. We see a fellow-creature blindly wrecking his happiness and losing his "love-life", and are touched dramatically.'[2] On 17 May *The Wild Duck* followed at the same theatre (likewise for five matinées), and on 24 June *Ghosts* was revived at the Queen's Gate Hall for three performances, with Mrs Theodore Wright (who had played Mrs Alving in the first London production) and Courtenay Thorpe as Oswald, the role in which he had startled New York. The production coincided with Queen Victoria's Diamond Jubilee, which led Bernard Shaw to draw an irreverent comparison:

> 'On the one hand, the Queen and the Archbishop of Canterbury; on the other, Mrs Alving and Pastor Manders. Stupendous contrast! . . . Suppose the Queen were to turn upon us in the midst of our jubilation and say: "My Lords and Gentlemen! You have been good enough to describe at great length the changes made during the last sixty years in science, art, politics, dress, sport, locomotion, newspapers and everything else that men chatter about. But you have not a word to say about the change that comes home most closely to me? I mean the change in the number, the character and the intensity of the lies a woman must either believe or pretend to believe before she can graduate in polite society as a well-brought-up lady.' If Her Majesty could be persuaded to give a list of these lies, what a document it would be! . . . Depend upon it, seventy-eight years cannot be lived through without finding out things that queens do not mention in Adelphi melodramas. Granted that the Queen's consort was not a Chamberlain Alving . . . it is possible to have better luck than Mrs Alving without missing all her conclusions.'[3]

In Norway, meanwhile, the spring of 1897 had brought a bitter personal

---

[1] *Our Theatres in the Nineties*, III, p. 123.

[2] *Ibid.*, pp. 131–132.

[3] *Ibid.*, pp. 177–178. This passage has given rise to a curious myth among Ibsen commentators that Queen Victoria saw *Ghosts* performed (e.g., Koht, II, p. 224; Ollén, p. 104).

disappointment to Ibsen. Three years previously Sigurd had proposed, in a series of articles, that a new chair of sociology be established at Christiania University. There was opposition to the scheme in the Storthing, which compromised by granting sufficient money for a series of lectures to be held during the autumn of 1896, leaving the question of the professorship open. (According to Sigurd's wife Bergliot, several of his colleagues in the Liberal Party disliked the idea of his becoming too important.) At all events, Sigurd delivered his lectures that autumn, with a panel of five professors present; the attendances were very large, and there was an atmosphere of great excitement. But on 29 April 1897 the panel published its verdict that: 'Dr Ibsen has not in his lectures succeeded in demonstrating such qualities that one could confidently at the present juncture entrust him with a university teaching post in sociology.'

Sigurd immediately left for Italy. 'Never since I left the diplomatic service', he wrote to Bergliot, 'have I been as angry as I am this week ... It looks as though they have all conspired to make it impossible for me to live in Norway.' His father was, if possible, even more outraged. He had attended all Sigurd's lectures with immense pride; and when the University invited him to a banquet he replied curtly: 'I shall never enter those doors again.' Suzannah wrote to Bergliot from Monsummano: 'The truth is that Sigurd's talent, with his European viewpoint, does not suit their academic outlook. It is foreign and unpleasing to them, as his father's was, which they only accepted when the world acclaimed him. We owe nothing to Norway, and all the humbug and mean-mindedness we have experienced there makes me weep. They are trying to bar every road to Sigurd.'

Indignation was widespread in Christiania. 'It was clear to everyone', writes Bergliot, 'that Sigurd did not lack the qualifications. But they were afraid of his liberal views and of his consequent influence on the young.' The University tried to compromise by offering him a new series of lectures with a different panel of judges, but Sigurd refused. 'I dread the prospect of returning to Christiania', he wrote to Bergliot from Monsummano on 17 July.[1]

The affair caused Ibsen to think seriously again of finally abandoning Norway. 'Can you guess', he wrote to Georg Brandes on 3 June, 'what I am dreaming and planning, and picturing to myself as so delightful? It is to settle by the Sound, between Copenhagen and Elsinore, in a free, open place, where I shall be able to see all the deep-sea ships coming from afar and going afar. Here I can't do that. Here every sound is locked (in both senses); every channel of understanding is stopped. Oh, my dear Brandes, one does not live for twenty-seven years out in the great, free, liberating world of culture for nothing. Here

---

[1] Bergliot Ibsen, pp. 156 ff.

among the fjords is my native land. But—but—but—where shall I find my
home? The sea is what draws me most. I live here alone and plan some new
dramatic work. But I can't yet see clearly what shape it will take.' Twelve days
later, thanking Bjørnson for a note of condolence about Sigurd's treatment,
he wrote: 'If all roads are barred to Sigurd in Norway, I do not see that I have
anything more to do here. And I have other places I could go to. I have lived
long enough in Munich to acquire Bavarian nationality, and I can be sure I
would be welcomed there. In Italy too. I must say, Norway is a difficult
country to have as a fatherland.'

Yet he stayed. Suzannah, no doubt, would have found Munich or Italy more
convenient for her gout cures. But Ibsen, at sixty-nine, was reluctant to up-
root himself. His letters to Suzannah that summer are full of touching little
domestic details.

*The hydrangea has begun to show its buds again as abundantly as last year. I have
had to order a dozen new dress-shirts, for the ones I had from Munich are now quite
worn out. As regards food, I have been eating very much to my taste: smoked mutton,
scrambled eggs, a lot of salmon done different ways, spiced-beer soup, and other good,
wholesome summer dishes. So I am very content—and in my solitude I have begun to
hatch and germinate plans for a new play. I already sense the general theme; but as
yet I see only one of the characters clearly. Well, the others will come too.*

Thus on 13 June; and on 2 July:

*Last week there was a great to-do here; my study was spring-cleaned from ceiling
to floor. The paintings have been taken down for cleaning, and now glitter and shine
so that it is a joy to see them. The curtains have been washed and the walls also. The
floor was scoured and then lacquered, so that you would not recognise it. It took six days
to dry, during which time the furniture had to stand in the yard and got a thorough going-
over. I used the red room while this was happening. Now it is the turn of the blue room,
the floor of which is likewise to be lacquered, as is that of the dining-room. I can eat in
the library; it is lucky we have enough rooms, and Mina* [the new maid] *is very good;
she has had the charlady to help her for a couple of days. I am now busy with correspondence about the German collected edition, which is to fill nine thick volumes. There are
already masses of tourists here, and yesterday a flock of journalists arrived from the
congress in Stockholm; most of them have left their cards on me or spoken with me here
and at the hotel. I am really very content, and don't think I could be more so anywhere
now that it is summer. And I have begun to think about a new play! To that purpose I
have extended my walks, and start each day by strolling to Skillebæk and back, and
then down into town; and find this very contenting. But the most important thing is how
the steam cure is suiting you this year. The iodine tincture which you found painful in*

*Labers you must of course throw away and get a new bottle down there. Let me know
how everything is with Sigurd . . . I sent Bergliot a telegram on 16 June. That is her
birthday, isn't it? . . . Well, I have rambled on; but I felt I had to write to you today.
We have the most wonderful summer weather; it is lovely to breathe.*

Lugné-Poe revisited Christiania later that summer. He had courageously
followed his production of *Peer Gynt* with one of *Love's Comedy* on 23 June.
Gunnar Heiberg attended the public dress rehearsal in Paris and, imperfect
though the performance was, found the electricity and driving power of the
young company stimulating; and 'a better, or anyway a more responsive
public, no theatre, actor or dramatist could wish for. They are artists, writers,
joyful malcontents of every profession . . . They are young, these Frenchmen,
as I have never seen young people in Norway or anywhere else . . . They shout
with joy. They rejoice and cry bravo and think life is full of meaning and
beauty when such men as Ibsen are around.'[1] At the premiere next evening,
however, the play was less successful—not surprisingly, the general public
found it small beer after the works of Ibsen's maturity.

Lugné-Poe brought to Christiania his young actress-wife Suzanne Desprès,
who had replaced Berthe Bady as Hilde in his *Master Builder*, and had played
Solveig in *Peer Gynt*. They met Ibsen at the Grand Hotel; Ibsen expressed the
desire to hear some of her Solveig, so they got hold of Henrik Klausen, who had
played Peer in the original production of 1876, and together they read all the
great scenes between the two characters, Klausen in Norwegian, Suzanne in
French. Ibsen also persuaded her to read some scenes from *The Master Builder*,
and praised her warmly.[2]

Ibsen's letters that autumn show him in a prickly mood; perhaps it was the
change of the year, perhaps his loneliness was beginning to weigh on him.
On 19 September he wrote a discourteously irritable note to the faithful Julius
Elias forbidding him to include *St. John's Night* in the German collected
edition which Elias was preparing with Georg Brandes and Paul Schlenther
(though for some reason he allowed them to use the much inferior *Warrior's
Barrow*).[3] He wrote so rudely, indeed, that a fortnight later he sent Elias an
apology for 'my unseemly way of expressing myself'. Then the Christiania
Theatre annoyed him by arranging a revival of *The Feast at Solhaug* without
informing him, so that he first heard through a third party. When Schrøder
penitently invited him to attend rehearsals and the premiere, he replied curtly
(3 December): 'Dr Ibsen is grateful for the information but will not attend

---

[1] Heiberg, *Ibsen og Bjørnson paa scenen*, pp. 71–79.
[2] Lugné-Poe, p. 88.
[3] Cf. *Henrik Ibsen, The Making of a Dramatist*, pp. 117–118.

rehearsals and does not wish to have tickets for the performance.' And when
Paul Clemenceau, brother of the statesman, raised his hat to him on Drammensveien and began: 'Cher maître! Permettez-moi de vous exprimer ma profonde
admiration—' Ibsen replied: 'Je ne parle pas français' and walked on.[1] In a
kindlier mood, he wrote (18 October) a charming little note of congratulation
to his doctor's wife, Caroline Sontum, on the birth of a new child; and when
young the poet Sigbjørn Obstfelder, lately released from an asylum and shortly
to die of consumption, sent him a volume of his poems, Ibsen thanked him
(10 December) with the assurance that he had 'already begun to read the book,
which fascinates and interests me.'

Despite the absence of any reprints, save only a small fourth edition of *An
Enemy of the People*, Ibsen's income again exceeded £1,000 in 1897. Over two-
thirds of this came from Germany and Austria, where his performing rights
totalled as much as 7,902 crowns (£439), and where Fischer gave him a not
very generous flat fee of 8,000 crowns (£444) for the Collected Edition, from
which that firm was to make immense sums over the next fifty years. From
England he got only £18 6s. od. for the Independent Theatre Society productions of *The Wild Duck* and *A Doll's House*, and £2 15s. 11d. from the book
sales of *Peer Gynt* in the translation by the Archer brothers. France did him a
little better with £40 for the publication of *John Gabriel Borkman* in the *Revue de
Paris* and £11 in performing rights. The Russians had done *The Pillars of
Society* on 24 September, but of course he got nothing for that; and from
Norway he received nothing but £167 for the Christiania production of
*Borkman* and £32 from Bergen:

|  | crowns | £ |
| --- | --- | --- |
| German fees and royalties from Felix Bloch | 5,119 | 284 |
| Royalties from Wien Burgtheater | 2,295 | 128 |
| Royalties from Munich Hoftheater | 403 | 22 |
| Royalties from Leipzig Stadtheater | 85 | 5 |
| Fee from S. Fischer for German collected edition | 8,000 | 444 |
| Fee for *John Gabriel Borkman* at Christiania Theatre | 3,000 | 167 |
| Fee from Bergen for 1 perf. of *John Gabriel Borkman* | 400 | 22 |
| Fees from Bergen for performances in 1896 | 180 | 10 |
| Fee for *John Gabriel Borkman* in Helsinki | 300 | 17 |
| Fee for *Ghosts* at Dagmars Theatre, Copenhagen | 600 | 34 |
| Fee for *Little Eyolf* at Royal Theatre, Copenhagen (13th–16th performances) | 434 | 24 |
| 4th edition of *An Enemy of the People* | 899 | 50 |

[1] Bull, *Tradisjoner og minner*, p. 99.

|                                                                              | crowns | £     |
|------------------------------------------------------------------------------|--------|-------|
| French royalties from Societé des Auteurs Dramatiques                        | 202    | 11    |
| Fee from *Revue de Paris* for publication of *Borkman* (1,000 fr.)           | 725    | 40    |
| Fee for London productions of *The Wild Duck* and *A Doll's House* (£18 6s. od.) | 332    | 18    |
| Share of English book sales of *Peer Gynt* (£2 15s. 11d.)                    | 50     | 3     |
|                                                                              | 23,024 | 1,279 |

During 1897 he had invested as much as 34,000 crowns (nearly £1,900) in securities, representing his entire earnings of the preceding year.

FOURTEEN

 The Other Side of the Medal

(1898)

IN NORMAL CIRCUMSTANCES, Ibsen would have spent the first months of 1898 hatching his new play, so as to be ready to write it in the summer and autumn. But this was the year of his seventieth birthday, always an occasion of special celebration in Scandinavia, and in Ibsen's case this involved a series of distractions not merely in Norway, but in Denmark and Sweden too. Moreover, the proofs of the German collected edition had now begun to arrive, several thousand pages of them. For the first time since *The Pillars of Society* in 1877, there was to be a three-year gap between one play and the next.

Jacob Hegel sent him the good news in January that he was proposing to issue a cheap popular edition of the plays. Ibsen was delighted; as he said in his reply of 16 January, it would bring them 'into strata of society where the more expensive editions have difficulty in gaining entry'. He went on: 'Where do I intend to spend my birthday this year? Well, I don't yet know. If the choice were mine alone I would escape up to the mountains somewhere or other, where I could be beautifully alone. But that time of year is unsuited to such a recreation, so I suppose I shall stay where I am. But I hope this won't exclude the possibility that I may later be able to fulfil my favourite dream, which is to see again the Sound and my Danish friends.'

As his birthday approached, the messages began to arrive. Among the earliest was a telegram of congratulations from Emilie Bardach, the first contact between the two for seven years. His reply of 13 March has already been quoted.[1] On the day itself, telegrams, flowers and gifts of every kind poured in from all over the world. One of the first gifts to come was a handsome set of silver from his British admirers, comprising a loving-cup (a facsimile of one executed for King George II in 1730) and an original ladle and small cup of the same period, the three pieces being fitted into a case of polished oak. The contributors included Thomas Hardy, Henry James, Bernard Shaw,

---

[1] See p. 138 above.

J. M. Barrie, William Archer, Edmund Gosse, Richard Garnett, A. C. Bradley, Gilbert Murray, A. W. Pinero, Elizabeth Robins, Herbert Beerbohm Tree and the future Prime Minister, H. H. Asquith.

Since none of these were able to make the journey, Karl Keilhau, the editor of *Norske Intelligenssedler*, presented the gift, together with a vellum address and a list of the subscribers' names. Keilhau reported to Gosse and Archer: 'He was obviously very much moved. While we were standing in front of the oak case and admiring, visitors began to arrive—a deputation from the Storthing, headed by the leader of the House, deputations representing the University, the Christiania theatres, etc., etc. Ibsen then asked me to translate the address, and I took out of my pocket a translation of it, which I read to him and to the others. He then himself read out all the names of the subscribers from the flyleaf. Ibsen repeated again and again that it was a splendid present, and all the afternoon he was occupied in taking his hundreds of visitors, in parties, up to the case, showing them the objects and explaining their origin.'[1]

Performances to celebrate Ibsen's birthday were given that evening in many countries; at two theatres in Christiania, two in Copenhagen, three in Stockholm, four in Vienna and six in Berlin. In London, surprisingly, there were none—indeed, there were no Ibsen productions there in 1898, 1899 or 1900. The Christiania Theatre gave *The Feast at Solhaug*, with selected scenes from *Peer Gynt*, and Centraltheater did *Ghosts*. For the following evening a gala performance of *The Master Builder* was planned, and Bergliot records that when a deputation came from the theatre to ask Ibsen and Suzannah to honour them with their presence, Suzannah thanked them but asked that he and she should each sit in a separate box. 'Ibsen must sit alone,' she said. 'This is your evening, and I have nothing to do there.' And, despite his protests, so it was. Similarly, when the students came to honour him with a torchlight procession: 'I can still see Ibsen walk over to her with his short steps, and hear him say: "Won't you come with me to the window?" But she replied: "No, you must stand there alone." . . . She never bothered to borrow the reflected glory of his fame. She cared only about him, and that his work should succeed.'[2]

A *festskrift* had, naturally, been arranged, headed by a tribute from King Oscar, and containing contributions from, amongst others, Snoilsky (whose poem is one of the best things in the book) and two future Nobel Prize winners in Verner von Heidenstam and Selma Lagerlöf. Two unexpected names in the

---

[1] Bredsdorff, pp. 48 ff. and 180 ff. The appeal was not launched publicly, but by private approach. Forty subscribers contributed £50 8s. od. between them. Several of those not approached, including J. T. Grein, voiced their discontent, and Shaw, though among the subscribers, criticised in the *Saturday Review* of 26 March the way the thing had been done.

[2] Bergliot Ibsen, p. 171.

list are those of John Paulsen and Nils Kjær, who had both so insulted him;
Kjær, since that unfortunate drunken outburst, seems to have undergone a
remarkable change of heart. Old friends such as Georg Brandes and Jonas Lie
reminisced affectionately, and August Lindberg and Emil Poulsen spoke for the
acting profession. But what an opportunity was wasted by not inviting foreign
admirers to contribute! Hardy, Henry James, Shaw, Hauptmann—other
admirers such as Freud, Rilke, Pirandello and Joyce were scarcely if at all
known, and Tolstoy[1] would not have contributed, but Chekhov and Zola
might have. Strindberg nearly did. In a letter to Gustaf af Geijerstam later that
year asking him to send Ibsen a copy of *To Damascus*, Strindberg told him to
tell Ibsen that: 'Strindberg is ashamed that as a prominent Swedish author he
did not join in the homage to the Master, from whom he learned much. But he
was in a state of depression and did not think his homage could honour or
gladden anyone.' Fearful lest this might be taken to imply a modification of his
antagonism to Ibsen's general view of life, he assured Geijerstam that his
homage would have been 'to the master of dramatic art, not the philosopher',[2]
at whom he continued to snipe until, and even after, Ibsen's death.

On 23 March the city of Christiania gave an official banquet for Ibsen. In his
reply Ibsen, after a conventional paragraph of thanks, asked:

'Were you perhaps expecting that I should speak about my books? That
I could not do, for then I should have to bring in my whole life. And that
alone would make a very thick book. And talking of that, I am indeed just
now thinking of writing such a book—a book which will knit my life and
my work together into an integral and explanatory whole. For I think I
have now reached a sufficiently mature age to permit myself a short
breathing-space—take a year's holiday; for such a book would be a holiday
task compared with the nagging and exhausting work of dramatic com-
position. And I have not had a real holiday since I left Norway thirty-four
years ago. I think I could do with one now. But, ladies and gentlemen, you
must not therefore suppose that I intend to lay down my pen as a dramatist
for good. No, I intend to take it up again and to cling tightly to it until the
end. For I still have a few lunacies in my locker which I have not yet found
the opportunity to express. Only when I have got them off my chest will
it be time for me to stop. And how easy would it not be to stop then, in
contrast to the time when I was still a beginner! What a silence and empti-

---

[1] The day before his birthday *Ørebladet* printed an interview in which Ibsen, after prais-
ing *Anna Karenina*, described Tolstoy as 'a great man when he isn't being crazy . . .
Tolstoy . . . spends his life abusing me . . . But that is natural in view of his beliefs.'
(*C.E.*, XIX, p. 214.)

[2] Sten Linder, *Ibsen, Strindberg och andra* (Stockholm, 1936), p. 95.

ness surrounded one then! One's fellow-combatants were scattered, isolated and apart. It often seemed to me, after I had gone away, as though I had never been here. Nor my work, neither.

'But now! Now the place where I stood is crowded. Young forces have arisen, confident of victory. They need no longer write for a tiny circle. *They* have a public to speak to, an entire people to whom to address their thoughts and feelings. Whether they meet with opposition or acceptance does not really matter. What destroys a writer is indifference and rejection. That is what I encountered.

'I regret deeply that I have come into so little contact with many of those who are to continue my work in this country. Not because I would have wished to influence them, but so that I myself might achieve a deeper understanding. And I would especially have used this closer contact to dispel a misconception which has in many ways been a hindrance to me— I mean, the idea that unqualified happiness is a necessary consequence of the rare and saga-like fate which has befallen me, of winning fame in many foreign lands. I have, too, won friendship and understanding in those countries. That is the most important thing of all.

'But true, inward happiness does not fall from heaven. It must be earned at a price which may often seem heavy. For the point is this: that he who has won a home in many foreign lands feels in his heart of hearts nowhere truly at home—scarcely even in the country of his birth.

'But perhaps this may happen yet. And I should like to think of this evening as a starting-point.

'For here I see something that resembles an entity. Here every view-point, every divergent opinion, has been assembled with a single purpose. I have no longer the painful sense of being regarded as the spokesman of a party. This party or that party. A writer must have all his people around him, whether they agree with him or whether they oppose him. And then the idea of unity can march forward, to higher goals and grander ambitions. That is my hope and my belief.

'And so, ladies and gentlemen, I ask you to accept my warmest thanks for all your goodness and kindness towards me.'[1]

The book he was considering writing—'A Dramatist's Apology', he might have entitled it—had, as we have seen, been in his thoughts for years; only the opposition of his old publisher and counsellor Frederik Hegel had discouraged him from attempting it earlier. Yet he was fated never to write it; though in some ways, the theme was to be that of his next and final play.

[1] *C.E.*, XV, pp. 412–414.

Meanwhile, there were other capitals besides Christiania waiting to acclaim him, and on 29 March he left for Copenhagen to attend the celebrations which had been prepared there. It was the first time he had left Norway since his return seven years earlier. The editor of *Morgenbladet*, Nils Vogt, accompanied him on the journey, by train through south-west Sweden and across the Sound. Vogt later recalled that Ibsen was a little feeble on his feet, the first evidence we have that age was beginning to tell on him; the Swedish railways courteously arranged that food should be brought to his carriage at the various stops, to save him the trouble of getting out. When they reached Gothenburg Ibsen found a telegram awaiting him from Peter Hansen, who had been his companion on the trip to Egypt and was now head of the Royal Theatre in Copenhagen, telling him that he had been awarded his most impressive medal yet, the Grand Cross of the Danish Order of Dannebrog. Ibsen was hugely gratified. 'I can recall many Norwegians', he said proudly to Vogt, 'who are Knights or Commanders of Dannebrog, but none who has the Grand Cross' (a statement which was not quite accurate but which Vogt prudently refrained from correcting). As they approached Denmark on 31 March Ibsen sat long at the window staring silently out across the water. Suddenly he said: 'Do you know, when I come from Norway to the Sound I feel as though I was emerging from a tunnel into the sunshine.' Then, after a pause, he added: 'But please don't tell them that in Norway, at any rate until I am dead.'[1]

Jacob Hegel and Peter Hansen met him on his arrival in Copenhagen, and took him to the Hotel Angleterre, where the royal suite had been placed at his disposal and the Norwegian flag was flying in his honour. As they entered the suite the first thing that met their eyes was a small box on the table. Ibsen opened it and there, resplendent, lay the Grand Cross. He gazed at it. 'How beautiful!' he exclaimed. 'This is indeed a great honour. No Scandinavian writer since Oehlenschläger has received so high a Danish decoration.' Suddenly his expression changed. 'But what is this?' he cried. 'This is no medal! It is papier-mâché!' Hegel and Hansen were as amazed as he; on enquiry, however, they learned that it was the custom for the recipient of this great honour to buy the medal himself from the court jeweller, only a papier-mâché copy being provided by the state.

Hegel gave a small lunch for Ibsen that day, the only other guests being Vogt and the Norwegian poet and novelist Alexander Kielland, who happened to be in town. In the evening, the Royal Theatre gave a gala performance of *The Wild Duck*. It was not the most inspired of choices, for Ibsen had already seen this

---

[1] For the details of Ibsen's visit to Copenhagen, cf. Nils Vogt, *Paa reise med Henrik Ibsen*, in *Samtiden*, 1906, pp. 329 ff., and Peter Nansen in *Aftenposten*, 4, 7 and 11 March 1917.

production twice with the same cast, and Betty Hennings, the country's leading actress, was now, at forty-eight, more than ever too old for the role of Hedvig. But the theatre had omitted to do anything about arranging a new production of any of Ibsen's plays until it was too late. Still, the performance was royally attended, for not only were the King and Queen of Denmark there, but also their daughters, Princess Alexandra of Wales and the Tsarina of Russia, all in the royal box with Ibsen seated majestically alone in the box opposite.

The unfortunate Peter Hansen, already under fire for not having remembered to arrange a new production, was to have a bad evening. His troubles began immediately after the performance when, in his tactless way, he issued a military-sounding directive that the actors were to be ready to be presented to Ibsen immediately after the performance. They were so offended at being thus commanded that they refused in a body. Hansen was desperate. Amongst other things, this refusal meant that Ibsen got no refreshment during the long interval, for Peter Nansen of Gyldendal (not to be confused with Hansen) records that when he mentioned the matter to Hansen the latter replied: 'I really have no time to think about refreshments', and Ibsen had to go thirsty.

When the performance ended, at first all went well. The entire audience, including the crowned heads, rose and bowed to Ibsen in his box, applauding, while he bowed aristocratically back. He then waited for the company to be presented; but the company held to their refusal, and all Hansen could rustle up was a few of the younger actors who were sufficiently frightened of him to obey. With some presence of mind he presented them as 'my most promising actor', and 'my most promising dancer', and so partially saved the situation.

But Hansen's troubles were by no means over. The students of Copenhagen had decided to greet Ibsen with a torchlight procession before he left the theatre. He stood on the theatre balcony acknowledging their applause; meanwhile, Hansen went on to the hotel, where he found Kielland waiting. As they chatted, there was a fearful noise outside, and Ibsen shot in 'like a cannonball from a gun, dazed, his coat torn, his top hat at the back of his head and his medal dangling outside his overcoat', with a mob of students pushing and cheering him, so that 'it was a miracle that the helpless little old man survived unharmed'. Peter Hansen, however, seemed by now to have forgotten his famous guest. Not only had his company mutinied against him; that same evening one of his star actors, Karl Mantzius, had given notice because his wife had not been re-engaged. So Ibsen stood dishevelled and forgotten in a corner.

His fellow-Norwegian, Alexander Kielland, was furious. 'God Almighty, how typically Danish!' he cried. 'Typical bloody Danish! The Royal Theatre has the most famous author in Scandinavia as its guest and doesn't even hire a carriage to take him home! He ought to have been driven across the square in a bridal carriage with white horses and the director of the theatre as postilion, and a proper dinner awaiting him. Instead of which the old man has to fight his way through a mob on foot and no one even bothers to ask whether he's hungry or thirsty!'

Nansen said to Hansen: 'Ibsen would like to have something to eat.'

The distraught Hansen turned to Ibsen. 'You want something to eat?'

'Yes, please.'

'Waiter! Bring a sandwich menu. Thank you. Now [to Ibsen] just tick off what you'd like. Steak, sausage, salmon, anything you like. Perhaps you'd like a drink too?'

'Yes, please.'

'A beer for Dr Ibsen. Do you want a schnapps too?'

Ibsen said yes. So he got three sandwiches, a schnapps and a glass of beer, and thus his first day in Copenhagen ended.

The next day, which was 1 April, began no more promisingly and ended even more disastrously. Nils Vogt and Peter Hansen, the latter no doubt anxious to redeem himself after his showing of the previous evening, had the pleasant idea of going out first thing to the court jeweller to buy Ibsen his expensive Grand Cross of Dannebrog. They bore this to Ibsen in his suite at the Angleterre but, as they entered, were much embarrassed to see one already lying in its box on the table. Ibsen, an inveterate early riser, had been to the jeweller before them. As the three stood there in confusion, the Minister of Culture was announced, and entered carrying a third Grand Cross as a personal gift from the King. The other two were silently removed and returned with apologies to the jeweller.

That evening a gala banquet was held for Ibsen at the Angleterre. Unusual difficulty had been experienced by the organisers in securing appropriate people to make the speeches of welcome. Georg Brandes was away. His brother Edvard was suggested but (says Nansen) he was 'as hated then as he was beloved later', and anyway was editor of the radical newspaper *Politiken*, so that for him to have made the principal speech would have offended the conservatives present. Eventually they chose the Professor of Philosophy, Kroman, with Peter Hansen following as the second speaker and Professor Sophus Schandorph as number three. So that was settled; but now the organisers learned that several of the invited guests considered the price of a ticket for the dinner (25 crowns, around 27s.) as excessive. (Nansen admits that it was 'a then unheard-of price'). Among the objectors was Betty Hennings, whose husband had just become deeply religious. She declared it to be immoral to spend so much on a dinner, and could not be persuaded to attend.

The banquet was an almost total disaster. At two o'clock Professor Kroman, the principal speaker, sent word that he was too ill to come (Nansen suspected it was an attack of nerves). Five hours was not enough to find a substitute, and as Kroman had been going to make the formal speech, to be followed by Hansen in lighter vein, they had to compromise by persuading Hansen to introduce serious matter into a set comic speech of his which had been successful on previous occasions and which Ibsen had not heard. But Hansen found the time at his disposal insufficient to make the adaptation, so that his speech turned out an unhappy mixture of jokes and formality. Amongst other gaffes, he referred to Ibsen as 'one of our leading dramatists' and thanked him for the 'many full houses' he had brought the Royal Theatre.

A profound embarrassment settled on the company, and Ibsen, who had clearly prepared a speech on the assumption that it would be in response to the usual courteously formal welcome, made the briefest reply. 'Professor Hansen's speech has confounded me, and rendered inappropriate the reply I had intended to make . . . I must therefore improvise, and ask your indulgence. Today is 1 April. This same day in 1864 I visited Copenhagen for the first time. That is now thirty-four years ago. Mark well the date and the year! I travelled south, through Germany and Austria, and crossed the Alps on 9 May.' He went on to describe his first sight of Italy, in words already quoted,[1] and concluded: 'This feeling of being released from darkness into light, of emerging from mists through a tunnel into the sunshine—this feeling I had again now, as I gazed along the Sound . . . I felt that these two journeys had some hidden connections, and I therefore give you my most grateful thanks.'

As usual when Ibsen improvised, the result was almost certainly more interesting than what he had prepared. That crisis, then, seemed to have been bridged; but the troubles of the evening were by no means over. Professor Sophus Schandorph, who rose to speak next, proved to be so drunk that he had to support himself on the shoulders of his two neighbours, a Count and a Bishop. The guests, already embarrassed, began to titter and interrupt, at which Schandorph, clutching the Bishop closer to him, thundered what can most faithfully be translated as: 'Shut your fucking mouths while I speak!'

He was allowed to finish, and a cantata, specially composed by Holger Drachmann, partially restored order, as did two tactful and appropriate speeches by younger guests, Professor Vilhelm Andersen and Dr Poul Levin. But now a new unrest developed as several of the guests began to complain about the food. The German proprietor of the hotel, one Heene, anxious to celebrate the occasion in style, had composed a gastronome's menu of real turtle soup, duckling and out-of-season asparagus. The Danes, who had come

---

[1] Henrik Ibsen, The Making of a Dramatist, p. 238.

T

expecting the enormous steak that was customarily served on such occasions, were now feeling hungry. 'If we'd charged twelve crowns and given them a piece of fish, a steak, cheese and an ice', said Heene to Nansen, 'they'd have been happy. That's what they're used to.' Heene was so disillusioned by the whole business that he left the Angleterre shortly afterwards.

When the meal ended Ibsen rose and made his way to the door, escorted by the Count and the Bishop who had supported Schandorph. Suddenly an old painter named Thorvald Niss, in a flush of, amongst other things, enthusiasm, rushed from his place, embraced Ibsen, shook him backwards and forwards and cried: '*Du er kraft steile mig en gut! Tak for alt, gamle dreng!*' (something like: 'You're a right lad! Thanks for everything, old cock'). Ibsen stared in horror and murmured: 'Take this man away.'

As he sat drinking his coffee, Peter Nansen presented some young writers to him. He was courteous and affable to them until Nansen introduced a popular playwright of intellectual pretensions. 'I don't know, Dr Ibsen', said Nansen, 'if you have heard of Sven Lange', to which Ibsen in his silkiest tones replied: 'Of course I know of Sven Lange, the Scribe of Denmark.' Nansen tells that he did not dare to look at the unfortunate man (who had contributed a vapid article on 'Henrik Ibsen and the young Europe' to the *Festskrift*).

So, as they say in the sagas, that day ended.

The next morning, Saturday 2 April, Ibsen was received by King Christian to be formally handed his medal, and was presented to the Tsarina of Russia and the Princess of Wales. Ibsen's impression of the meeting is not on record but King Christian's, surprisingly, is. Not long afterwards the Speaker of the Storthing, Hegsbro, was received by the King and, on the latter's enquiring after his health, replied 'Well, Your Majesty, one notices that one's getting old'. 'You should talk about growing old,' said the King. 'I'm several years older than you, and I don't notice any weakness. I felt rather proud some while ago. I had to receive the Norwegian writer, Henrik Ibsen. He was seventy, and I was ten years older. I thought: "It won't be easy to make conversation with such a genius. What is one to say to him?" But I must honestly confess I thought he seemed much older than me. He was really most timid and unhelpful. I had to keep nudging him along.'

By contrast, when, later that day, a young girl came to Ibsen's suite to offer him flowers and found herself speechless, Ibsen sat her down and put her at her ease with the greatest charm. After she had left, he said to Nansen: 'How pretty the young ladies of Copenhagen are!' Nansen adds that Ibsen would sometimes fantasise to young girls of what he would do if he were very rich—how he would buy the finest ship in the world, engage a gipsy orchestra and sail to some tropical island with a few good friends and 'the most beautiful young women in the world'—very much as Solness must have spoken to Hilde Wangel during their first encounter at Lysanger.

They kept him busy in Copenhagen, for he attended two receptions that same afternoon and evening, one given by the Women's Literary Guild and one by the Students' Union. At the latter, Valdemar Vedel (another contributor to the *Festskrift*, on 'Ibsen and Denmark'), began his speech of welcome with the familiar second person singular ('*Mester, Du—*') which Ibsen so detested. Accounts vary as to what happened next. According to some, Ibsen immediately rose and left the room.[1] Peter Nansen simply tells that he left without replying to the speech; and Nils Vogt, who accompanied him to the dinner as to everything else on this trip, says that he merely left early, and remarked to Vogt on the way downstairs: 'Vedel's a good fellow, but I can't remember having drunk "Du's" with him.' And Georg Brandes's daughter Edith, who accompanied Ibsen to the dinner in a carriage (and recalled that he was much annoyed on arrival to find that he was not sitting next to her, as he had assumed, but to the much less youthful and attractive suffragette Amalie Skram, to whom he did not address a word all evening) writes that he said simply 'Thank you' after the speeches of Vedel and Harald Høffding, made no speech himself, but, although he had ordered a carriage for 10.30, did not leave till 11.[2] What is sure is that as he left (whenever it was) some wit recited Ibsen's own poem *Gone*, substituting 'he' for 'she':

He was but a guest
And now he is gone.

which was greeted with laughter and cheers.

The next day, Sunday 3 April, the privately owned Dagmars Theatre, now under solvent management, gave a gala performance of *Brand*. It was a new production, the company was young, and Nansen wondered with some trepidation how Ibsen would survive a performance lasting five hours or more. But against all expectations, the evening turned out to be the peak event of Ibsen's visit. Martinius Nielsen, the head of the theatre, who was acting the title role, had, with more foresight than Peter Hansen at the Royal Theatre, supplied the royal box in which Ibsen sat with an excellent cold collation, accompanied by 'champagne, beer, whisky, coffee, liqueurs and flowers'. Nansen records: 'It was a *young* people's performance, and he liked it far better than *The Wild Duck*. He clapped loudly at the fall of each curtain and showed

---

[1] Cf. letters from Bengt Zinglersen, Otto Zahle and Valdemar Petersen in *Politiken*, 14, 16 and 18 January 1966. My attention was drawn to these letters by Dr Elias Bredsdorff.
[2] *Prinsessans Album*, in *Svenska Dagbladet*, 9 May 1965.

no signs of tiredness.' It was the first time he had seen *Brand* played, and another observer, P. A. Rosenberg, tells that 'he seemed moved and several times dried the tears from his cheek during the fourth act. "Don't blubber!" ("*Ikke tude!*") he muttered to himself.'[1] He said to Nielsen's wife Oda, who sat next to him: 'This moves me. This is—my youth. I haven't thought about *Brand* for thirty years.' At the end he led the applause, which the audience then directed towards him. Although the performance lasted until midnight he did not return home, but stayed at a party which the actors improvised for him, and did not leave until 3 a.m. He was very lively and talked continuously. Of Nielsen's performance, he said: 'That is my Brand. That's how I saw him.' 'You haven't cut much,' he said to Rosenberg, and when told that they had in fact cut a third of the play he asked to see the prompt book and, as he leafed through it, seeing page after page deleted, murmured: 'I'll be damned. Yes, I suppose I've forgotten most of it.'

As they at last broke up, at three o'clock, Ibsen said: 'I must go home now. I must be at my desk at 7.' 'Not *this* morning?' exclaimed Rosenberg. 'Yes,' he replied. 'Come and see. I'll be there at 7.' 'But you won't have had enough sleep,' said Nielsen. 'Yes, I will,' said Ibsen. 'Under such circumstances I sleep more energetically. Thank you for tonight. It has been a good night.' As a favour he asked that his two companions at table, Fru Nielsen and Fru Rosenberg (who had played Agnes), should accompany him home in the carriage, declaring: 'Their husbands can manage without them for a few minutes.'

Yet (we are told) he did not sleep, but lay awake most of that night.[2] As he lay there he may have remembered that thirty years before, just after *Brand* had brought him the recognition he had longed for, he had remarked to Georg Brandes (26 June 1869) that Brand 'could as well have been a sculptor or a politician as a priest'. The chief character in his new play was to be a sculptor, of the same uncompromising ruthlessness as Brand; and, like Brand, he was to die in an avalanche near the top of a mountain, his pride crushed, with a Latin blessing cried out to him as though from a forgiving deity at the moment of death.

The next day, luckily, was a rest day; and on 5 April, his last day in Copenhagen—the last that he was ever to spend there—Jacob Hegel gave a farewell dinner for him at his villa, Skovgaard. According to Vogt, Ibsen enjoyed himself, but the evening was spoilt by Sophus Schandorph, who had delivered the drunken speech at the Angleterre and now, in a fit of remorse and en-

---

[1] For the details of this evening, cf. Nansen in *Aftenposten*, 11 March 1917; Rosenberg in *Nationaltidende*, 28 July 1926 (reprinted in *C.E.*, XIX, pp. 215–220); Kinck, p. 537.
[2] A. Fibiger, *Henrik Ibsen* (Copenhagen, 1928), p. 14.

thusiasm, attempted to kiss Ibsen on the cheek, causing him to leave early. However, on the way home with Vogt, in a carriage drawn by two white horses (like the ones in *Rosmersholm*, reflected Vogt, though he was tactful enough not to mention it), Ibsen thawed again. Speaking of a classical scholar of rigid conservative views, he said: 'He has no idea of what real classicism and humanism are. He has read some books in Latin and Greek which I, for good reason, have not. But I have lived myself into its spirit by studying its buildings and art, as you may possibly have gathered from *Emperor and Galilean*. X's aesthetic and intellectual horizon stops at Lübeck and Greiswald.'

Ibsen particularly disliked the narrower type of academic mind, especially after the treatment Sigurd had received from the professors of Christiania. Once during this visit to Copenhagen he asked Vogt: 'Can't you help to get Georg Brandes a professorship in Norway? Never mind that he's unreliable on odd details, and to many people personally antipathetic—he makes people think, and forces us to be aware of the intellectual currents of our time, and how many of our professors do that?'

On 6 April Ibsen left Copenhagen by train for a further round of celebrations in Stockholm. They installed him in the best suite at the Hotel Rydberg in Gustav Adolfs Torg and gave him a couple of days to recover his breath; then, on 9 April, he was received at the Palace by King Oscar and given another medal to add to his collection, the Grand Cross of the Northern Star. The King, during the conversation, graciously employed the phrase 'we two Kings', and spoke with some apprehension about Sigurd. The Norwegian government was considering setting up its own Foreign Office, something that Sigurd had urged ever since he had been a young attaché, and they had in mind to appoint him head. King Oscar expressed gloomy doubts. 'He doesn't want me as King of Norway,' he said to Ibsen. 'But let that pass. As long as that wife of his doesn't make him too much of a radical and an agitator!' The combination of the leading pamphleteer against the Union and Bjørnson's daughter in joint charge of Norwegian affairs must have been an alarming prospect to that conservative monarch. Ibsen assured him that Bergliot's views were not as extreme as her father's. That evening, the King gave a banquet for Ibsen at the Palace; among the guests was the explorer Sven Hedin, whom he had met on the Göta Canal eleven years previously, and whom he afterwards took back to his hotel and proudly showed his medals, carefully arranged on a table in little red and black boxes.[1]

During the meal the King said to his guest of honour: 'But you shouldn't have written *Ghosts*, Ibsen. That's not a good play. Now, *Lady Inger of Østraat*—

---

[1] Bergliot Ibsen, pp. 183–184; Hedin, p. 79.

there's a good play.' Ibsen was embarrassed and remained silent. Queen Sophie tried to rescue him by speaking of other things; but after a long pause, Ibsen exclaimed: 'Your Majesty, I *had* to write *Ghosts*!'[1]

Two days later, the Swedish Society of Authors gave a dinner for Ibsen at Hasselbacken Restaurant on Skansen. 'I'm not very curious about him,' wrote the poet Oscar Levertin to a friend that morning. 'Great men are best appreciated at a distance, and every utterance that the Sphinx has delivered during these past weeks of divine revelation seems to me about as empty as the usual wisdom of Sphinxes.' And the evening indeed was not a great success. Carl Snoilsky, who took the chair, had promised that there would be no speeches, but unfortunately Gustaf af Geijerstam improvised one, full of Ibsen quotations, and at the end of the evening Levertin, despite his lack of enthusiasm for Ibsen, made another. Ibsen replied (untruthfully) that he did not think he had ever belonged to any Society and that this was the first time he had attended one. 'I am pretty sure there is a Society in Christiania of the same name as this, but I am a member of that only for appearance's sake and for various reasons never partake in its meetings.' (He had still not forgotten how he had been insulted at the inaugural meeting.) He went on: 'A Society is not a thing for me. And in a way it might seem that a Society is least of all appropriate for authors, for they must go their own wild ways—yes, as wild as they wish, if they are to fulfil their life's calling.' (Loud applause). However, he granted that such a Society might serve to protect writers 'which can often be very necessary', and concluded by expressing the hope that it might also encourage Scandinavians to read each other in the original language and not in translation—a hope which has hardly been fulfilled. To a foreigner, it is amazing how reluctant Scandinavians are to read each other in the original, despite the close similarity of Norwegian, Danish and Swedish.

After dinner, the Swedish writer and artist Albert Engström sang some Swedish country songs, which Ibsen, despite the view he had just expressed, was unable to understand; and (records a lady who was there) 'despite being primed with punch and other stimulants, he remained stiff and unapproachable. No amount of effort could provoke any Ibsenian profundities, far less any witty conversation. At last he turned to a lady seated near him and began: "Can you tell me—?" The lady in question adopted an expression of deep concentration. "Can you tell me if I can go direct to Christiania by the night train, or if I have to change at Laxå?" '[2]

Engström himself tells that Ibsen spent the second half of the evening

---

[1] Bull, Introduction to *Ghosts*, *C.E.*, IX, p. 13.
[2] Gurli Linder, pp. 129–133.

surrounded by elderly authoresses, from whom he tried repeatedly to rescue
him by saying: 'May I drink with you, Doctor?' for which Ibsen was grateful.
'At last it grew late and the ladies departed, accompanied by some of the
gentlemen. I had rescued Ibsen at least ten times during the evening. And
now, when there were only a few young people left, he became a new man.
He joked and toasted us continuously. It was just midnight when he declared
that his age no longer allowed him to exceed a certain limit. So we gathered
around him and he said a few words, very simply, rather shyly; but I think
that we who heard them will remember them and the mood of that moment.
He clasped our hands in farewell. To me he said: "Do you know how many
brandies you've made me drink tonight, my dear Engström? I've lost count." '[1]

Next evening, 12 April, he attended a performance at Vasa Teater of
The Pretenders, with a distinguished cast: Emil Hillberg (the original Brand)
as Bishop Nicholas, Tore Svennberg as Skule and a new young star, Anders de
Wahl, as Haakon. Harald Molander directed. Ibsen sat in a box with Gustaf af
Geijerstam, and towards the end of his long life de Wahl recalled: 'I had
received a flower arrangement in the form of a long, tall Viking ship, and the
thought occurred to me that I ought to present these flowers to the author . . .
I noted that the gentlemen had put this ship on the edge of their box so that
they were invisible to us and the audience. During one of the intervals I was
summoned to pay my respects . . . I was determined to have every sense alert
so as to memorise every word the great man might utter, note every glance,
engrave every nuance of the occasion on my memory and, at some future
date, tell the world of this great meeting. Thus prepared, I entered the box on
trembling legs. There he sat, the great man, beside my Viking ship, at a small
table covered with glasses and bottles. "What, what, what . . . what d'you
want?" In a word, he was drunk. As I came closer he pointed at me and said:
"You're dolled up. Do you think Haakon was a dandy?" '[2]

On 13 April the city gave an official banquet for Ibsen at the Grand Hotel,
and in reply to Snoilsky's speech of welcome Ibsen said that his life had been
'a long, long Passion Week' which, however, had now been 'transformed into
a poem, a fairy tale . . . a midsummer night's dream.'[3] Next day a deputation

---

[1] Albert Engström, Åt Häcklefjäll (Stockholm, 1914), pp. 13 ff. Strindberg was unfortunately in Paris, though one doubts whether he could have been persuaded to attend. On
being asked during this visit by a Swedish journalist what he thought of Strindberg, Ibsen
described him as 'a very great talent. I don't know him personally—our paths have never
crossed—but I have read his work with great interest. Not least, his last book Inferno
[written the previous year] has made a powerful impression on me.' (Interview in Aftonbladet, 13 April 1898, reprinted in C.E., XV, pp. 429–432.)
[2] Per Lindberg and Sten af Geijerstam, Anders de Wahl (Stockholm, 1944), pp. 40–41.
[3] C.E., XV, pp. 432–433.

of students from Upsala brought him greetings; and in the evening the Royal
Theatre gave *Lady Inger of Østraat*, that play of which King Oscar approved
and which he now graced with his presence. 15 April seems to have been a rest
day, but on the 16th Ibsen, who so disliked the company of elderly bluestockings, found himself the guest at Skansen of the two Women's Societies of
Stockholm, Nya Idun and the Fredrika Bremer Society. The officials of these
two formidable bodies, indignant that the dinners arranged for Ibsen had
been mainly male affairs, had managed to persuade him to stay an extra day in
Stockholm to meet their members. When they put the idea to him 'Ibsen
became nervous, waved his arms and exclaimed: "No, no, I shall be like Carl
XII, I shall be carried across the frontier a corpse!" '[1] But a historian present
reminded him that when Carl XII had crossed the frontier from Sweden to
Norway, he had been very much alive (he had been killed on the other side of
the border at Frederikshall in 1718); so Ibsen had accepted.

Perhaps he hoped that he might have at least one reasonably youthful and
attractive lady to table. But as usual on these occasions, he found himself
flanked by dragons, in this instance the presidents of the two societies, Ellen
Key and a Fru Anckärsvard; nor did Ellen Key help matters by beginning her
speech: "*Du . . .*", as Valdemar Vedel had done in Copenhagen. She thanked
him for his 'new religion, under which every human being will obey his or
her own laws without being daunted by a sense of guilt, and self-fulfilment
shall be deemed as justifiable and meaningful as self-sacrifice'.

To entertain their guest the ladies had arranged an exhibition of folk dancing,
and here at least there were some young faces. One, twenty-six years old,
especially attracted his attention. Her name was Rosa Fitinghoff, the daughter
of a well-known popular authoress, Laura Fitinghoff (whose *The Children from
Frostmoor Mountain* is still a favourite children's book in Sweden). Ibsen
spoke to Rosa several times during the evening, expressing particular admiration of her long and beautiful hair, and asked her to see him off at the station
next day. She was to be the last of his dream girls, following in the footsteps of
Emilie, Helene and Hildur.

Ibsen's rather pathetic longing for young girls was demonstrated several
times during these days in Stockholm. Gurli Linder tells that he received several
in his hotel room, gave them signed photographs of himself, said: 'You are
just like my Hilde', and kissed them; and that when a lady at one of the receptions told him that she had once been in the same town as him in Norway and
had only with difficulty restrained herself from running up to him, seizing his
hand and saying: 'Thank you!' he replied: 'Do you know what I would have

---

[1] For the account of this dinner, cf. Gurli Linder, pp. 130–132.

done if you had? I would have hugged you to my breast and kissed you many times'—precisely as Hilde Wangel claimed Solness had done to her.[1]

On 17 April he returned to Christiania. He had been away for over a fortnight of almost unbroken celebration, but his constitution seemed unimpaired. 'I am always well,' he had told an interviewer on 19 March. 'I have never been ill, not for a single day in my life. I have never consulted a doctor. I have never used a prescription. Despite the fact that I have often lived in feverish atmospheres and exposed myself to illnesses.'[2] It was not quite true; he had been ill in 1861, 1889 and 1892; but even then he had probably not consulted a doctor, though the period of his immunity was almost past.

Eight days after his return he sent a photograph of himself to Rosa Fitinghoff, with an accompanying letter:

*Dearest Miss Fitinghoff!*

*When I received your beautiful postcard yesterday it was as though you had entered my house yourself with a spring greeting to warm my heart. There was music and dance in what you wrote; and it was through dance and music that we met. That is the happy part of the story. The sad part is that we did not meet until my last evening. Parties are often like life; people do not meet until they have to say goodbye. But go on writing to me. Write of everything you wish to, and can—and make happy*

*Your affectionate*
*Henrik Ibsen.*

On 26 May he had another formidable body of ladies to face. The Norwegian Society for Women's Rights gave a banquet for him in Christiania. Suzannah, appropriately for one who had for so long been a champion of that cause, for once attended with him. In his reply to the toast Ibsen said something that must have disconcerted his hearers, and that every dramatic critic ought to learn by heart before reviewing any production of *A Doll's House*: 'I have been more of a poet and less of a social philosopher than people generally tend to suppose. I thank you for your toast, but must disclaim the honour of having consciously worked for women's rights. I am not even quite sure what women's rights really are. To me it has been a question of human rights. And if you read my books carefully you will realise that. Of course it is incidentally desirable to solve the problem of women; but that has not been my whole object. My task has been the portrayal of human beings.'

On 29 May he informed Julius Elias that, owing to the distractions occasioned by his birthday celebrations, it was doubtful if he would be able to finish his

---

[1] *Ibid.*, pp. 130–131.
[2] Interview with Hans Tostrup in *Ørebladet*, 19 March 1898 (reprinted in *C.E.*, XIX, pp. 211–215).

projected new play that year, adding: 'I have never planned to complete my
so-called "Memoirs" in the immediate future.' (He presumably regarded the
childhood memories which Jæger had incorporated in his biography as the
foundation). On 26 June he wrote again to Rosa Fitinghoff thanking her for a
profile photograph of herself 'so that now I can sit each day and look at you
from the side without your knowing. And when I want to look into your
eyes I take out the big group photograph. There you sit so still and thoughtful,
as though you were dreaming and had no idea that anyone was looking at
you . . . Your letters can never be too long for me. But I must, alas, limit
myself to telegraphic brevity. But do not think ill of me for this. What I do
not write I say to your photograph.' On 8 July he wrote suggesting that she
should visit him in Christiania on her way back to Stockholm from her holiday
with her mother on the Swedish west coast. This visit did not materialise, but
she wrote to him twice from Lysekil and continued the correspondence on her
return to Stockholm.

Gustaf af Geijerstam visited him in Christiania that August; so did William
Archer, who was somewhat surprised to see 'holding a very prominent position in his study, a bright corner-room looking out upon the palace park, a
huge gilt-edged and brass-clasped family Bible. "You keep this close at hand?"
I said, pointing at it. "Oh, yes," he replied. "I often read in it—for the sake of
the language." ' (Bolette Sontum likewise records that she heard him assure
people, 'gazing fiercely at them', that he read it only for the language. 'But we
knew him to be a faithful reader of the Bible, as the worn pages of his own
huge copy testify.') On Archer's expressing further surprise at seeing the
portrait of Strindberg, Ibsen replied: 'I think he looks so delightfully mad.'[1] The
same month Ibsen received news from Hegel that they had decided to increase
the first printing of the popular edition of his collected works to 15,000—the
more gratifying since Bjørnson's works in the same series were being printed
in an edition of only 4,000.

In September he received his first letter for over a year from Georg Brandes.
Brandes had been gravely ill and, quarrelsome as ever, had apparently rebuked
Ibsen for not writing, 'You know how much I owe you,' Ibsen replied on
30 September, 'recently as well as of old, and that I gratefully acknowledge
this. And if you doubt it, would a written assurance help? Good God, you
know how easy it is to put together a French-general-staff kind of letter. I can
therefore not feel that the crime of silence is sufficient to justify your addressing
a friend of many years' standing as "Respected Sir". I don't think it worthy of
you to take this attitude because of a couple of unwritten letters—especially

[1] *Ibsen as I Knew Him*, p. 16; Sontum, p. 263.

from someone whose main passion is certainly not correspondence, even with his best and dearest friends.' Of Ibsen, Bjørnson and Brandes, which was the most difficult to remain friends with? Yet somehow, against the odds, the friendships survived.

On 3 October Ibsen sent a photograph of himself to his sister Hedvig with a tender little note: 'I think we two have been close to each other. And so it will continue.' In a similar mood he inscribed a copy of Peer Gynt that Christmas for a two-year-old boy, Odd Arstal:

To little Odd!
*You shall have this book for Christmas. But you won't read it till you've grown into a big boy. And then, please remember the man who wrote this book.*

H. Ibsen.

On 29 December he wrote to Bjørnson that he was asking the National Theatre (it was now nearing completion, and the old contracts with the Christiania Theatre would not apply to it) to pay him ten per cent of the gross intake instead of the flat fees he had opted for since the failure of Rosmersholm. It is a sad comment on the position of dramatists then that he felt compelled to add in his letter to Bjørnson that 'according to the law ... copyright continues until fifty years after the author's death'. The copyright position of dramatists was (despite the Berne Convention) by no means watertight. Bernard Shaw had written to the publisher T. Fisher Unwin on 11 February that it was by no means clear whether a play could be 'performed from the printed copies without illegal copying ... For instance, all Ibsen's stage rights are voided here except those which Heinemann so ingeniously secured by his performances of the last two or three plays in Norwegian at the Haymarket before they were translated.'[1] As Ibsen's account books show, some of the productions in London and other English cities (and all American productions) still brought him nothing.

Thanks to the 75,000 crowns (£4,167) for the popular edition of his works, Ibsen earned over three times as much in 1898 as in any previous year. Without this windfall, however, his earnings would have fallen well below £1,000:

|  | crowns | £ |
| --- | --- | --- |
| German royalties from Felix Bloch | 2,821 | 156 |
| Royalties from Munich Hoftheater | 538 | 30 |
| Royalties from Wien Burgtheater | 1,909 | 106 |
| Swedish rights from Albert Ranft for 5 years of The Pretenders, The Vikings at Helgeland and A Doll's House | 2,000 | 111 |

[1] Shaw, Collected Letters, 1874–1897, p. 595.

|                                                                                              | crowns | £ |
|----------------------------------------------------------------------------------------------|--------|-------|
| Fee from Royal Theatre, Stockholm, for 1 perf. of *Ghosts*                                   | 55     | 3     |
| Fees from Dagmars Theatre, Copenhagen, for *Brand*, *Love's Comedy* and *Rosmersholm*        | 3,000  | 167   |
| Fee for *The Wild Duck* from Helsengren                                                       | 300    | 17    |
| Old fees from Royal Theatre, Copenhagen                                                       | 950    | 53    |
| English book sales (£1 16s. 5d.)                                                             | 32     | 2     |
| French royalties via G. Roger                                                                | 925    | 51    |
| Extra fee from Philippe Reclam (Leipzig publisher)                                           | 880    | 49    |
| Fee from Gyldendal for popular edition of Collected Works                                    | 75,000 | 4,167 |
|                                                                                              | 88,410 | 4,912 |

It is ironical to note that for most of the birthday performances in Scandinavia he received nothing, thanks to the fixed fee system which gave a theatre rights to a play in perpetuity.

FIFTEEN

# ❧ The Top of a Cold Mountain

## (1899)

DURING THE FIRST weeks of 1899 Ibsen at last got down to work on his
new play. On 13 February he wrote Hegel that he had 'now begun to grapple
with it in earnest', and on 20 February he made his first notes. Two days later
he began to write the dialogue, giving the play the provisional title of *The
Day of Resurrection*. But spring came, and summer, and still he, who normally
wrote so rapidly, had not finished the first act. No doubt the theme was partly
to blame: this play was to be about an artist's final reckoning with himself.
Perhaps, too, he found it difficult to adapt himself to the unusual task of writing
in winter instead of, as had for so long been his habit, during the summer or
autumn.

On 19 February an important event (though Ibsen would not have realised
its significance, and received no money from it) occurred in Russia. The
Moscow Arts Theatre staged their first Ibsen production—*Hedda Gabler*,
with Konstantin Stanislavsky as Løvborg. They were to perform seven more
of his plays during the next nine years: *An Enemy of the People*, *When We Dead
Awaken*, *the Wild Duck*, *The Pillars of Society*, *Ghosts*, *Brand* and *Rosmersholm*.
Surprisingly, only *An Enemy of the People* and *Brand* were complete successes.
One would have expected plays such as *Ghosts* and *The Wild Duck* to have
been perfectly suited to the Stanislavsky method, but the company seem to
have found as much difficulty in comprehending their realism as other countries
at first did with Chekhov. 'More's the pity I was not a Scandinavian', mourned
Stanislavsky, 'and never saw how Ibsen was played in Scandinavia. Those who
have been there tell me that he is interpreted as simply, as true to life, as we
play Chekhov.'[1]

In March Ibsen wrote to Edvard Brandes, asking him to look after Hildur
Andersen who was visiting Copenhagen to play in a concert. He was still
seeing much of her, and corresponding with Rosa Fitinghoff. On 17 April he
wrote to Rosa thanking her for sending him a little blue flower—' "*die blaue*

---

[1] Stanislavky, p. 345.

*Blume"*, which signifies so much and is so seldom found. And thank you for thinking of me and of 11 April last year. I shall never forget that day. Be assured of that! Your letters live in a special little place in my desk and when I go to my work in the morning I always look into that little drawer and greet my Rosa.' His memory had slipped; it had been on 16 April that he had first met her; 11 April had been the date of the Society of Authors' banquet in Stockholm.

On 15 June he attended the last performance of the Christiania Theatre, which was to close its doors after seventy-two years to make way for the National Theatre. The play was *The Pillars of Society*, with Lucie Wolf, who had worked under Ibsen as a young actress at Bergen, in her old role of Lona Hessel, which she had played in the original production twenty-one years before. As Øyvind Anker has written,[1] it must have been a moving occasion for Ibsen; this was the theatre which had rejected his early work and had employed him at a starvation wage, and of which he had so long advocated the demolition. He had first written for it as a young rebel; now he sat himself among the pillars of society, loudly cheered from both the auditorium and the stage.

His play still eluded him; but July brought good news for the family. Sigurd was appointed head of the new Foreign Office; after eight years in the wilderness, he was to return to active politics. 'At last, at last!' he wrote to Bergliot, adding: 'My parents were transported with joy.'[2] He was a tremendous success in his new post, far-sighted, able and popular; importantly, too, he and Bergliot established an admirable relationship with the suspicious old King. Sigurd would have made a great Prime Minister; but his cosmopolitan and independent outlook, and lack of chauvinism, were always, as hitherto, to make him an object of distrust in political circles, a kind of Norwegian Churchill.

Rosa at last visited Christiania that month, with her mother (inevitably) in tow. They met Ibsen at the Grand Hotel, where the three drank champagne on the verandah. Thirty years later Rosa remembered how he had spoken of 'the emptiness of Christmas'. He invited them back to his home, and told her how he kept small pieces of paper, each bearing the name of a character in the play he was writing, on a string in front of his desk. When a character died, he pulled off that piece of paper and tore it up. 'One doesn't want too many bits of paper in front of one's nose,' he explained. She remembered his alternations of deep brooding and urchin merriment. 'Sometimes,' he said, 'all these characters I have imagined weary me with their squabbles and griefs and

---

[1] Anker, *Henrik Ibsens brevveksling med Christiania Theater, 1878–1899*, pp. 67–68.
[2] Bergliot Ibsen, p. 181.

lovings and hatings, and when I get really tired I pull out the drawer of my desk and look into this little box.' He showed it to her; it contained her letters. 'Then I sit and talk with you and after a little while I can carry on with the people I'm writing about.' He spoke of the play he was writing. 'If only my powers last! But they must, they must! This play will be the best and the biggest I have ever written.'[1] On her departure, on 26 July, he gave her a photograph of his study with the inscription: 'In memory of a summer meeting in Christiania, 1899'.

Rosa's visit may have helped to thaw his inspiration, for on 31 July he finished the first act. On 2 August he began the second act, and finished it on 23 August; and on 25 August he started the third and final act, completing it on 21 September. By this time he had altered the title from *The Day of Resurrection* to *When the* [sic] *Dead Awaken*.

On 1 September the National Theatre was formally opened. Bjørnson's son, Bjørn, had been appointed director, and faced the ticklish problem of which dramatist should be performed on the first night. Clearly, it had to be a Norwegian writer, and to have performed either Ibsen or Bjørnson would have mortally offended the other; and although Bjørnson had written half-length plays, Ibsen had not, so that there could be no question of sharing the evening between them. Ibsen reminded Bjørn that he was the senior of the two. Bjørn replied: 'There is a Norwegian dramatist who is senior to both of you', and diplomatically solved the question by presenting an evening of extracts from Holberg. When the day came statues of Ibsen and Bjørnson were unveiled in front of the theatre, Ibsen staring pensively at his feet, Bjørnson, as Ibsen uncharitably but accurately observed, looking as though he were competing in a spitting contest. At the performance, they sat in the centre of the dress circle in separate boxes, tactfully segregated by a vast garland of red and white roses. 'They were the objects of universal attention,' noted Edmund Gosse, who was there, 'and the King never seemed to have done smiling and bowing to the two most famous of his Norwegian subjects.'[2] Bolette Sontum, who was also present, tells that 'the whole house cheered as they entered. Bjørnson stood and bowed gracefully to each salute, while Ibsen sat rigid, looking straight at the curtain, nervously tapping his chair.'[3]

Earlier that day Gosse had met Ibsen for the first time, twenty-seven years after having first introduced his name to the English reading public. Being the man of letters that he was, Gosse was a little shocked at seeing in his apartment 'no books at all, except the large Bible which lay always at his side'—referring

---

[1] *Nya Dagligt Allehanda* (Stockholm), 4 March 1928.
[2] Edmund Gosse, *Ibsen* (London, 1907), p. 221.
[3] Sontum, p. 253.

presumably to Ibsen's own study; he cannot have seen the room they proudly
called the library, which was full of books. Gosse mentioned Tolstoy, and
Ibsen exclaimed: 'Tolstoy! He is mad!'—'with a screwing up of the features
such as a child makes at the thought of a black draught'. Gosse adds that Ibsen
had read of Tolstoy 'with contemptuous disapproval, only some of the polemical pamphlets'—another inaccurate observation, for we know that Ibsen
admired *Anna Karenina*.[1] He also remarked to Gosse that 'it was almost useless
for actors nowadays to try to perform the comedies of Holberg, because there
were no stage directions and the tradition was lost', an observation which
doubtless sprang from his own frequent productions of the plays in earlier
years.[2]

Gosse noted 'the smallness of his extremities' in contrast to his burly figure
and huge head of hair. 'His little hands were always folded away as he tripped
upon his tiny feet . . . His voice was uniform, slow and quiet. The bitter
things he said seemed the bitterer for his gentle way of saying them . . . His
movements were slow and distrait.' Some time that day or the next, presumably
at the theatre at one of the receptions afterwards, Gosse witnessed 'his *sang-
froid* under distressing circumstances. Ibsen was descending a polished stair-
case when his feet slipped and he fell swiftly, precipitately, downward. He
must have injured himself severely, he might have been killed, if two young
gentlemen had not darted forward below and caught him in their arms. Once
more set the right way up, Ibsen softly thanked his saviours with much frugality
of phrase—"*Tak, mine Herrer*"—tenderly touched an abraded surface of his
top-hat and marched forth homeward, unperturbed.'[3]

The following evening, 2 September, the National Theatre performed
*An Enemy of the People*. Gosse describes the scene:

'He occupied, alone, the manager's box. A poem in his honour, by
Nils Collett Vogt, was recited by the leading actor, who retired, and then
rushed down the empty stage, with his arms extended, shouting: "Long
live Henrik Ibsen!" The immense audience started to its feet and repeated
the words over and over again with deafening fervour. The poet appeared to
be almost overwhelmed with emotion and pleasure; at length, with a
gesture which was quite pathetic, smiling through his tears, he seemed
to beg his friends to spare him, and the plaudits slowly ceased. *An Enemy
of the People* was then admirably performed. At the close of every act
Ibsen was called to the front of his box, and when the performance was

---

[1] See *Henrik Ibsen: The Farewell to Poetry*, p. 122.
[2] Gosse, *Ibsen*, pp. 238, 243, 263.
[3] *Ibid.*, pp. 238–239.

over, and the actors had been thanked, the audience turned to him again with a sort of affectionate ferocity. Ibsen was found to have stolen from his box, but he was waylaid and forcibly carried back to it. On his re-appearance, the whole theatre rose in a roar of welcome, and it was with difficulty that the aged poet, now painfully exhausted from the strain of an evening of such prolonged excitement, could persuade the public to allow him to withdraw. At length he left the theatre, walking slowly, bowing and smiling, down a lane cleared for him, far into the street, through the dense crowd of his admirers. This astonishing night, 2 September 1899, was the climax of Ibsen's career.'[1]

No wonder that the next day, refusing an invitation from J. B. Halvorsen, he wrote: 'The interruptions during these past few days of my normal routine have much affected my strength, and now I must catch up on almost a whole week's neglected work.' But in less than three weeks, on 21 September, he had finished his draft. He took a full two months revising it; but on 20 November he was able to telegraph Gyldendal that *When We Dead Awaken* was ready. On 19 December Heinemann published the now customary London edition of twelve copies in Norwegian to cover general copyright,[2] and on 22 December the Gyldendal edition appeared. Hegel printed 12,000 copies, as for *John Gabriel Borkman*, and again he had to reprint a further 2,000 before publication.

The press reaction in Scandinavia was, predictably, respectful, despite the obvious problems that the play presented. 'The work the aged dramatist has now completed', wrote an anonymous reviewer in *Morgenbladet* (21 December), 'is superior rather than inferior to its predecessors.' Kristofer Randers, who had been critical of so many of the earlier plays, described it in *Aftenposten* (22 December) as 'less a truthful and objective picture of life than a personal expression of his own needs and feelings—a confession from the heart, a desperate cry of doubt, an apotheosis of love. It is as though the aging poet wishes to say: "Let everything in life fail, woman will not fail; let everything in life break, the power of love will hold." And never has he proclaimed this gospel more beautifully and powerfully than here.' Carl Nærup in *Verdens Gang* (21 December) wrote admiringly of 'an extraordinary lyricism stronger

---

[1] *Ibid.*, pp. 221–222.

[2] There was a row with Heinemann about the English edition. Heinemann demanded that the Gyldendal edition be postponed on some obscure copyright ground. Ibsen refused. Heinemann wired Gyldendal: 'In that case inform Ibsen I only pay half fee.' Ibsen wrote to Archer on 16 December: 'Let him keep the whole fee on condition I am freed from all future commitment to him.' Eventually they compromised on a fee of £120, only two-thirds of what Heinemann had paid for *John Gabriel Borkman*. (Tysdahl, pp. 255–257).

V

than in any of his earlier plays' in this 'apocalyptic tragedy of an artist'. Georg
Brandes, in the same paper on 28 December, wrote: 'This work is born of no
happy view of art, any more than Zola's *oeuvre* . . . With sad bitterness he
dwells, as in *The Master Builder*, on what Art and Genius cost the artist and,
especially, what they cost others . . . It speaks as every artist, even the greatest,
speaks in the moments of despair and bitterness . . . Whatever [Ibsen's plays]
say, they always keep something in reserve . . . One is never finished with any
Ibsen play, but always feels the need to take it up again and study it afresh. So,
in general, one does not fully understand or assess a new play by Ibsen until
several years after it has appeared. One's first immediate verdict on it is totally
inadequate . . . Ibsen's plays are like certain human beings; they improve with
the years.' And Edvard Brandes, in *Politiken* (20 December) declared: 'The
deeper one digs into the play, the better one is able to appreciate its greatness.'

*When We Dead Awaken* tells of an aged sculptor, Arnold Rubek, who has
achieved fame at the expense of personal happiness. His marriage with a much
younger wife, Maja, is on the rocks. Returning to Norway after a long absence,
he meets a former model, Irene, who had loved him but in whom he had been
interested only as an artist. She is now deranged. She accuses him of destroying
her life (as Ella had accused John Gabriel Borkman); together, painfully, they
dredge up the past; then she asks him to climb with her to the top of the
mountain on different levels of which the action of the play takes place. They
climb together, and near the top meet Maja and a huntsman, Ulfhejm, with
whom she has become enamoured. As a storm rises, Maja and Ulfhejm go down
the mountain to safety, while Rubek and Irene continue towards the top,
where, like Brand, they are killed by an avalanche. In other words, Maja and
Ulfhejm return to what they think is life but what Rubek and Irene regard as
death, while Rubek and Irene climb upwards to what the others regard as
death but they regard as life. As long as people remain imprisoned in flesh,
Ibsen seems to say, they are dead; it is only when the body dies that the dead
awaken.

It is a very short play, much the shortest Ibsen ever wrote; in performance,
it lasts under two hours (unless one is foolish enough to have two intervals, of
which more anon). The third and final act occupies only a quarter of an hour.
This brevity is curious; and so is the language in which the play is written.
In the last act of *John Gabriel Borkman*, Ibsen had moved into a heightened prose
very near to poetry; in *When We Dead Awaken*, he uses this heightened prose a
great deal more—for most, indeed, of the dialogues between Rubek and
Irene. I well remember that when I translated this play I found myself continually feeling how much easier my task would have been if he had written it in

poetry. There is a certain kind of abstract high-flown writing which in any prose sounds grandiose, even windy (when I translated *Brand* I tried at first to put it into prose, and found exactly this result). I cannot but feel that *When We Dead Awaken* would have been a much greater play if he had written it in poetry—as he nearly did. He told C. H. Herford, a Welshman who translated *Brand* into English, that he would probably write his last play in verse 'if only one knew which play would be the last'.[1] To have done this with *When We Dead Awaken* would have been tantamount to an acceptance that he would never write any more. Yet the straining is clearly there.

The shortness of the last act is a mystery; not merely its shortness but its (to my mind) inadequacy. It is the only less-than-great final act that Ibsen wrote after *The Pillars of Society* (whatever objections may be raised against the endings of *The Lady from the Sea* and *Little Eyolf*, they both work wonderfully well if—to borrow Henry James's phrase—really *done*). There are, I think, two possible explanations. One is physical exhaustion; he was within a few weeks of his first stroke, and there are hints of weakness that summer and autumn—his remark to Rosa: 'If only my powers last! But they must, they must!', his remaining seated at the theatre as the audience applauded, while Bjørnson stood, his fall down the steps, his words to Halvorsen about his strength being 'much affected', Gosse's observation that his movements were 'slow and distrait'.[2] He may have sensed that he had not an indefinite time left, and perhaps felt unequal to the immense strain of executing an appropriate final act, especially to so self-searching a play.

But it is also possible that he felt some strange compulsion to leave it as a fragment. Another sculptor, Henry Moore, once remarked: 'There is a fact, and for me a strange fact, about the really great artists of the past; in some way their late works became simplified and fragmentary, become imperfect and unfinished. The artists stop caring about beauty and such things, and yet their works get greater.'[3]

This is one way to assess *When We Dead Awaken*, as a marvellous and flawed fragment, like those unfinished statues of Michelangelo's old age which Ibsen may have seen, and drawn inspiration from, on his way to Rome thirty-five years before. Many admirers of Ibsen dislike and even dismiss it; but on some it has always exercised a peculiar fascination. 'His magic is nowhere more potent,' wrote Bernard Shaw. 'It is shorter than usual. That is all.'[4] And the young James Joyce proclaimed: 'On the whole, *When We Dead Awaken* may

---

[1] William Archer, *Ibsen as I knew him*, p. 7.
[2] See also p. 312 below.
[3] *Sunday Times* (London) colour magazine, 16 February 1964.
[4] Shaw, *The Quintessence of Ibsenism*, 3rd edition (1922), p. 147.

rank with the greatest of the author's work—if indeed it be not the greatest.'
It is not the greatest; but he is at his greatest in it, and in some ways it is a more
moving memorial to him than if it had been a perfected whole. As Michael
Elliott, who staged the play memorably at the 1968 Edinburgh Festival, has
written: 'Like the last quartets of Beethoven, *When We Dead Awaken* has all
the intensity of the master at the height of his powers . . . It too is a quartet.
At times it may seem impossible to rise to the music, but the score itself can
only be regarded with wonder.'[1]

It needs gigantic yet delicate acting: a Rubek who can suggest genius, an
Irene who can suggest madness without alienating our sympathy. Rubek is
sometimes played soft on the excuse that Irene accuses him of being 'soft and
self-indulgent, and so ready to forgive all your own sins'. But it should come as
a shock to us when she says that: he should seem a figure of granite, a Sibelius,
a Hemingway. Like *Brand* and *The Master Builder* and *John Gabriel Borkman*,
*When We Dead Awaken* has to be played big or it had better not be played at
all. It is no place for gentlemanly or ladylike understatement; Rubek and Irene
are the shadows of mighty archetypal creatures moving near the sun. And the
way to solve the briefness of that last act is to have no interval between Acts
Two and Three. The scene-change, from one level of the mountain to another,
can easily be made during a brief black-out.

It is significant that *When We Dead Awaken* should have so appealed to
Joyce, for although Ibsen sub-titled it 'A Dramatic Epilogue', he took pains to
make it clear that he intended it, not as his final word, but as a declaration that
he had now finished with the realistic type of drama through which he had
won international recognition, and was intending to break out into new and
experimental fields. When, a few days before the publication of the play, the
Danish newspaper *Politiken* assumed from the sub-title that 'with this play the
author will have said his last word, and will thereby have written *finis* to his
dramatic work', the correspondent of *Verdens Gang* asked Ibsen if this were
true. Ibsen replied: 'No, that conclusion has been too hastily reached. The word
"epilogue" was not meant by me to have any such implications. Whether I
write any more is another question, but all I meant by "Epilogue" in this
context was that the play forms an epilogue to the series of plays which began
with *A Doll's House* and which now ends with *When We Dead Awaken* . . . It
completes the cycle, and makes of it an entity, and now I am finished with it.
If I write anything more, it will be in quite another context; perhaps, too,
in another form.'[2]

On 5 March 1900 he wrote to Moritz Prozor: 'If it be granted to me to

---

[1] In the programme note to that production.
[2] *Verdens Gang*, 12 December 1899.

retain the strength of body and spirit which I still enjoy, I shall not be able to absent myself long from the old battlefields. But if I return, I shall come forward with new weapons, and with new equipment.'

I do not think there is much doubt that, by these remarks, Ibsen meant that he was finished with orthodox realism and was intending to move, as Strindberg had recently done, back towards poetry and symbolism. In 1898 Strindberg had sent Ibsen the first two parts of his highly symbolic drama, *To Damascus*, and it is known that he read both volumes. One can only speculate on what Ibsen would have written if illness had not struck him down and rendered him helpless; but *When We Dead Awaken* gives us a hint, and one may speculate on its possible influence on Joyce, who was to make the same decision to abandon realism in favour of symbolism barely a dozen years later.

Ibsen had been planning to write an autobiographical book which would relate his life to his work. Did he perhaps, before starting *When We Dead Awaken*, decide to write that book in dramatic form? For the play certainly covers that ground; it is Ibsen's final account with himself. He had portrayed different facets of himself in most of his plays: the unsatisfactory husband preoccupied with his work (Tesman in *Hedda Gabler*, Allmers in *Little Eyolf*), the uncompromising idealist who brings unhappiness to those he loves most (Brand, Gregers Werle, Dr Stockmann), the egotistic artist (Ejnar in *Brand*, Hjalmar Ekdal, Lyngstrand in *The Lady from the Sea*), the ruthless old man who despises the world and neglects his wife (Solness, Borkman). But nowhere do we find so complete and merciless a self-portrait as the character of Arnold Rubek. The aging artist, restless in his married life, restless in the homeland to which he has returned after a long sojourn abroad, restless in his art, shocked, like Brand, near the top of a mountain, into the realisation that to reject love is to reject life; such is Ibsen's Portrait of the Dramatist as an Old Man, painted at the age of seventy-one.

*When We Dead Awaken* received its premiere at Stuttgart on 26 January 1900, and within the next few weeks was performed in Copenhagen, Helsinki, Christiania, Stockholm and Berlin. Despite the acclaim with which it had been received on publication, it failed everywhere (in Christiania it achieved only eleven performances that season), for the same reason that *The Master Builder* had failed; it was beyond the range of any of the actors who tackled it. 'The play is good enough, big enough,' wrote Edvard Brandes on the occasion of the Copenhagen premiere (*Politiken*, 29 January 1900). 'The actors were too small.'

Ibsen's earnings for 1899 had been as follows:

|  | crowns | £ |
|---|---|---|
| German royalties from Felix Bloch | 1,664 | 92 |
| Royalties from Wien Burgtheater | 699 | 39 |

|                                                                                                                          | crowns | £ |
|--------------------------------------------------------------------------------------------------------------------------|--------|------|
| Royalties from Munich Hoftheater                                                                                         | 570    | 32   |
| Fee from S. Fischer for German edition of *When We Dead Awaken*                                                          | 4,444  | 247  |
| Fee from Gyldendal for 1st edition of *When We Dead Awaken*                                                              | 9,360  | 520  |
| Fee from Gyldendal for 2nd edition                                                                                       | 1,560  | 87   |
| 14th edition of *Brand*                                                                                                  | 1,870  | 104  |
| 8th edition of *The Vikings at Helgeland*                                                                                | 520    | 29   |
| 10th edition of *The Pretenders*                                                                                         | 1,200  | 67   |
| Swedish performing rights of *When We Dead Awaken* (Albert Ranft)                                                        | 3,000  | 167  |
| Royalties from Royal Theatre, Copenhagen, for *The Lady from the Sea* (12th–14th performances) and *The Pillars of Society* (26th performance) | 1,460  | 81   |
| Fee for *Rosmersholm* from Dagmars Theatre, Copenhagen                                                                   | 600    | 33   |
| Unspecified fees from Bergen Theatre                                                                                      | 260    | 14   |
| Extra fee from Christiania Theatre following 50th performance of *A Doll's House*                                        | 220    | 12   |
| Fee from Olaus Olsen for 1 perf. of *Lady Inger of Østraat*                                                              | 100    | 5    |
| Fee for Danish provincial rights of *The Pretenders*                                                                     | 500    | 28   |
| Fee for Danish provincial rights of *The League of Youth*                                                                | 400    | 22   |
| French royalties from Societé des Auteurs                                                                                | 1,024  | 57   |
| Unspecified fees from Mr Perrin and M. Prozor                                                                            | 279    | 15   |
|                                                                                                                          | 29,730 | 1,651 |

He invested more than this amount during the year in gilt-edged securities—34,000 crowns (£1,890).

SIXTEEN

## ❧ The Running Demon

## (1900—1906)

> O friend, if you should venture to that country,
> Pass guardedly, be unseduced
> By its too subtle promises of peace.
> Its quiet is of a kind you should not seek . . .
> This is a very ancient land indeed;
> Aiaia formerly or Cythera
> Or Celidon the hollow forest called;
> This is the country Ulysses and Hermod
> Entered afraid; by aging poets sought,
> Where lives no love nor any kind of flower—
> Only the running demon, thought.
> > Sidney Keyes, *Sour Land*.

The new century dawned, and Ibsen, though approaching seventy-two and at last showing signs of physical fallibility, seemed as intellectually vigorous as ever. Ernst Motzfeldt visited him on New Year's Day: 'He was then already weakened by illness, but said that when he had taken a short rest and settled a few business matters, he would start on a new play. "Then your last play, which you have described as an Epilogue, is not your final work?" I asked. "No, it is only a phase which is now completed. Now I want to start on a new one." When I asked him if he would not publish some guide to the meaning of this "recently completed phase", about which there was so much speculation, Ibsen said: "No. Just as I myself claim complete freedom as far as the public is concerned in my choice and treatment of material, so the public too must have complete freedom in interpreting my writings as they choose. I have no right to deny the public that freedom." And I did not question him further.'[1]

That he had at last had cause to break his proud record of never having

---

[1] Ernst Motzfeldt, *Af samtaler med Henrik Ibsen*, in *Aftenposten*, 23 April 1911.

consulted a doctor is evidenced by a letter he addressed to Christian Sontum three days later:

*Dear Dr Sontum,*

*I can no longer permit myself to parade in your files as an unreliable debtor from the last century. And since you take no steps to secure what is due, I must take the matter into my own hands, and presume to send you the enclosed trifle as compensation for your trouble and time. The rejuvenation you have caused I could not repay with its weight in gold. A Happy New Year to you and yours.*

*Your most grateful friend*
*Henrik Ibsen.*

On 15 January he wrote to Jonas Lie, who had likewise returned to live in Norway, that he was thinking of giving himself a holiday that summer, the first since his trip to the North Cape nine years previously, and that 'it would be delightful if we could chat about all things as we did in Berchtesgaden twenty years ago'. He was well able to afford it; on 6 February he asked August Larsen of Gyldendal to invest a further 32,000 crowns (£1,778) in gilts, a sum which a decade earlier would have represented three years' normal earnings. Yet that same evening he did not attend the premiere of *When We Dead Awaken* at the National Theatre, and it is not easy to imagine what other cause but illness could have prevented him.

On 5 March he wrote to Moritz Prozor that he still enjoyed intellectual and physical strength; but within a few days his health had deteriorated badly. 'I have been very poorly since the day after the palace ball', he confessed to Nils Vogt on 2 April, and on 30 April he had to tell August Larsen: 'I have been sick (though not bedridden) since the beginning of March, and my doctor has forbidden me the use of pen and ink. But now that is over, and I have leave to write short letters to my closest friends.' It seems likely that he had suffered his first stroke,[1] resulting in a partial paralysis of his right side, and he was never to be a fully fit man again.

On 1 April the *Fortnightly Review* in London published a review of *When We Dead Awaken* by an eighteen-year-old Dublin student, the first example of the young man's work to appear in print outside school and university magazines. The student's name was James Augustus Joyce; his enthusiasm for Ibsen, which was to last throughout his life, had probably been fired by his fellow-Irishman Shaw's *Quintessence*, a book which Joyce is known to have read as a boy, though unlike Shaw Joyce admired Ibsen not for his sociological icono-

---

[1] Thus Francis Bull (*Norsk litteratur-historie*, IV, pp. 463–464). Koht (p. 294) dates Ibsen's first stroke as coming the following year, but a lesser illness would hardly have caused him to be forbidden to use a pen.

clasm so much as for what, in *A Portrait of the Artist as a Young Man*, he called 'a spirit of wayward boyish beauty' that blew through him 'like a keen wind'. At first he read him only in translation, drinking him, as Yeats unkindly put it, through William Archer's hygienic bottle (though his opinion of *When We Dead Awaken* was based on a reading of the French translation). On 20 January Joyce had read an essay in the Physics Theatre of University College on *Drama and Life*, in which he had praised Ibsen for the way he put real life on the stage— life 'as we see it before our eyes, men and women as we meet them in the real world, not as we apprehend them in the world of faery . . . *Ghosts*, the action of which passes in a common parlour, is of universal import—a deep-set branch on the tree, Igdrasil, whose roots are struck in earth but through whose higher leafage the stars of heaven are glowing and astir'. He had concluded this essay by quoting Lona Hessel's line from *The Pillars of Society*: 'I will let in fresh air, Pastor.'[1]

Joyce had written to the editor of the *Fortnightly*, a confirmed anti-Ibsenite Oxford don named W. L. Courtney, asking if he would consider a general article on Ibsen's work. Courtney had rejected this idea, but had suggested that Joyce review *When We Dead Awaken*. His letter reached Joyce on the morning he was to read the essay in the Physics Theatre. For this article, Joyce received the then handsome sum of twelve guineas.

It is an extraordinary eulogy. 'It must be questioned', declared Joyce, 'whether any man has held so firm an empire over the thinking world in modern times. Not Rousseau; not Emerson; not Carlyle; not any of those giants of whom almost all have passed out of human ken . . . His genius as an artist faces all, shirks nothing.' After a detailed appreciation of the play, Joyce expresses particular admiration of Ibsen's understanding of women, and perceptively observes: 'If one may say so of an eminently virile man, there is a curious admixture of the woman in his nature. His marvellous accuracy, his faint traces of femininity, his delicacy of swift touch, are perhaps attributable to this admixture. But that he knows women is an incontrovertible fact. He appears to have sounded them to almost unfathomable depths. Beside his portraits the psychological studies of Hardy and Turgenieff, or the exhaustive elaborations of Meredith, seem no more than sciolism. With a deft stroke, in a phrase, in a word, he does what costs them chapters, and does it better.' He also shrewdly notes (and one must remember that this is a boy of eighteen writing): 'One cannot but observe in Ibsen's later work a tendency to get out of closed rooms. Since *Hedda Gabler* this tendency is most marked. The last act of *The Master Builder* and the last act of *John Gabriel Borkman* take place

---

[1] Richard Ellmann, *James Joyce* (London, 1959), pp. 54–55, 72–75.

in the open air. But in this play the three acts are *al fresco* . . . And this feature, which is so prominent, does not seem to me altogether without its significance'.[1] The article concludes:

> 'Henrik Ibsen is one of the world's great men before whom criticism can make but feeble show. Appreciation, hearkening, is the only true criticism. Further, that species of criticism which calls itself dramatic criticism is a needless adjunct to his plays. When the art of a dramatist is perfect the critic is superfluous. Life is not to be criticised, but to be faced and lived. Again, if any plays demand a stage they are the plays of Ibsen . . . At some chance expression the mind is tortured with some question, and in a flash long reaches of life are opened up in vista . . . In this play, Ibsen has given us very nearly the best of himself . . . On the whole, *When We Dead Awaken* may rank with the greatest of the author's work—if, indeed, it be not the greatest. It is described as the last of the series which began with *A Doll's House*—a grand epilogue to its ten predecessors. Than these dramas, excellent alike in dramaturgic skill, characterisation and supreme interest, the long roll of drama, ancient or modern, has few things better to show.'

This article, over eight thousand words long, came to Ibsen's attention, and despite his faulty command of English, he took the trouble to send his new admirer a personal message of thanks via William Archer.

*Christiania, 16 April 1900*

*Dear Mr William Archer,*

*I should long ago have thanked you for* Wehn [sic] We Dead Awaken, *but I have been ill for five weeks and my doctor has forbidden me to write during all that time.*

*The English edition looks handsome and in every way distinguished, and I have found it quite easy to read and understand most of it; though I am sure the book has been difficult to translate.*

*I have also read—or rather, spelt out—a review by Mr James Joyce in* Fortnightly Review, *which is very benevolent and for which I should greatly like to thank the author, if only I had sufficient command of the language . . .*

*Your ever affectionate and grateful*
*Henrik Ibsen.*

---

[1] The six plays from *The Pillars of Society* to *Rosmersholm* are all set entirely indoors. By contrast, four out of five acts of the 'optimistic' *The Lady from the Sea* take place out of doors. Then followed the meeting with Emilie and the darkly pessimistic *Hedda Gabler*, again set totally indoors. But the last act of *The Master Builder*, the last two acts of *Little Eyolf*, the last act of *Borkman* and all of *When We Dead Awaken* are out of doors; surely, as Joyce, observed, not without significance.

Archer relayed Ibsen's message to Joyce on 23 April. Five days later Joyce replied:

> 13, Richmond Avenue,
> Fairview, Dublin.
> April 28, 1900.

Dear Sir,

I wish to thank you for your kindness in writing to me. I am a young Irishman, eighteen years old, and the words of Ibsen I shall keep in my heart all my life.

> Faithfully yours,
> Jas. A. Joyce.

William Archer, Esq.,
Southampton Row,
London.

Joyce's biographer, Richard Ellmann, comments: 'Before Ibsen's letter Joyce was an Irishman; after it he was a European.'[1] A few months later, in one of the prose poems which he called 'Epiphanies', Joyce, describing a dream which he interpreted as being about Ibsen, wrote: 'But here he is himself in a coat with tails and an old-fashioned high hat . . . He walks along with tiny steps, jutting out the tails of his coat . . . My goodness! how small he is! He must be very old and vain . . . But then he's the greatest man on earth.'[2]

Within a year, Joyce was to write a passionate letter of admiration to Ibsen himself, an admiration which he was never to lose. Both *Ulysses* and *Finnegans Wake* are full of references to and echoes of Ibsen.[3]

Dr Sontum was working at Sandefjord, a watering-place on the Christiania fjord, that summer, and Ibsen, anxious to be near him in case he should suffer another stroke, went there on 8 June. Suzannah, after several months back in Norway, was about to leave again for Italy, and on 13 June Ibsen wrote what was to be his last letter to her:

---

[1] Ellmann, p. 78.

[2] *Ibid.*, p. 89.

[3] For example, from *Finnegans Wake*: 'For peers and gints, quaysirs and galleyliers, fresk letties from the say and stale headygabblers, gaingangers and dudder wagoners, pullars off societies and pushers on rothmere's homes.' (Cf. J. S. Atherton, *The Books at the Wake: a Study of some Literary Allusions in James Joyce's* Finnegans Wake, London, 1959, pp. 152–157 and 257-258.) *Kejser og Galilaeer, Gengangere* and *Naar Vi Døde Vaagner* are the Norwegian titles of *Emperor and Galilean, Ghosts* and *When We Dead Awaken. Peer Gynt, The Lady from the Sea, Hedda Gabler, The Pillars of Society* and *Rosmersholm* are the other plays punned upon in this passage. Atherton lists over sixty such examples of puns on Ibsen's plays (or his name) in *Finnegans Wake*.

*Dear Suzannah!*

*Thank you for your letter, which I have just received. Everything goes excellently. Sleep well. Appetite ravenous at every mealtime. I have massage daily, and it does me remarkable good. No trace of pain. I can already walk as far as I wish without my foot feeling tired.*

*This is the last time I shall write to you before you leave. I received Sigurd's letter yesterday.*

*The room must not be locked without Helga* [their maid] *having access to the key. This is because of the insurance. Be sure to remember this! Otherwise I shall not have an hour's peace down here.*

*Well, I wish you with all my heart a good and successful trip. I shall at least celebrate the red-letter days 18 and 26 June[1] quietly here. May you receive as much benefit from the grotto as I from the massage. My best wishes to Sigurd.*

*Your affectionate*

*H.I.*

According to Bolette Sontum, he had had Sandefjord in mind when describing the setting for the first act of *When We Dead Awaken*. Ironically, he found himself attended, like Irene in that play, by a nun. Soon after his arrival, erysipelas developed in his right foot, and the attack was sufficiently critical for Suzannah to be summoned back from Italy. But he recovered rapidly. A beautiful old house, Hjertnes hovedgaard, was secured as a retreat for him where he could enjoy privacy, and he ate many of his meals with the Sontums. Bolette remembered:

'While he was ill, we were allowed to pay him short visits. My youngest sister was only three years old, and a very popular little pet among the patients. She had heard so much about the Great Man, and was anxious to see him. One day when my mother went to take tea with Mrs Ibsen she brought little Ellen with her. While Mrs Ibsen and my mother were chatting, Ibsen was busy in his study with some letters, and as the little girl thought the tea-time very long and tedious, she left them to hunt for the Great Man herself. Ibsen was just stepping out on the verandah with his nurse when little Ellen came peeping in the door. When she saw him she stopped, opened her baby lips round and said: "Oh, are you the Great Man?" Her little face showed how disappointed she was that any Great Man was not a Great Big One.

'Ibsen was much amused and winked at the nurse. To make up for her disappointment he took her around to his study, and as he never knew how

[1] Their wedding anniversary and Suzannah's birthday.

to treat children or what to give them, he offered her some claret. Shortly afterwards she came tripping in to her mother, her eyes shining from the wine. 'I have had such a good time with a little, kind man in there!" she said . . .

'Since his illness my father had ordered a special shoe for him, flat and broad. He did not like these, as they were not nearly as neat as his own patent leathers, but he was partially consoled when my father told him he could have them tan.'[1]

Bolette wanted to photograph him, and as she was about to click the shutter Ellen came running down the street. Ibsen tried to catch her and asked why she was in such a hurry. 'It's dinner-time,' she replied. 'Papa says I must get there early today because the old doctor is coming.' As he paused a moment, his hand on her shoulder, Bolette snapped them together—one of the very few occasions when Ibsen was photographed off his guard.

He was as regular in his routine on the promenade at Hjertnes as on his walks down Carl Johan in Christiania. Bolette recalled: 'When my sister said one day: "The old doctor is my clock", it so pleased Ibsen that he told my father that he thought his little daughter was extremely intelligent. The last day of our summer vacation he gave a special dinner for us, as my mother too was going to the city. He slyly gave us children champagne when our parents were not looking. In a little speech he thanked us for the pleasant summer and hoped we would study hard and please our teachers.'[2]

On 11 August he wrote to his niece, Anna Stousland:

*My dear little Anna,*

*Thank you for your kind and dear letter. It warmed my heart to read it, and I wished I had you here with me. You may certainly continue to call me your 'Sun God'. All the fire of my youth still burns in me.*

*I am almost completely well again and take long walks on the roads.*

*Your 'Sun God'.*

But during the autumn his health began to fail again. 'I went to see him a couple of times,' writes Bolette—'and he looked pale and thin, but was still interested in everything . . . One day when my father made his daily call at noon Ibsen handed him a parcel, saying that his brother-in-law had brought something for him, if my father would give it to me on my Confirmation Day. It was a beautiful brooch with a large amethyst in an exquisite setting.'[3]

[1] Sontum, p. 254.
[2] *Ibid.*, p. 255.
[3] *Ibid.*, p. 255.

It must have been this 19 September, nine years since their meeting, that he sent Hildur Andersen a bouquet of roses with a card:

*Nine red roses for you, nine rose-red years for me. Take the roses as thanks for the years.*

*H.I.*

He also sent her, probably this year or the next (it must have been after the appearance of *When We Dead Awaken* and before he became unable to write) a set of his collected works, twenty-four plays plus the *Poems*, bearing the dedication:

*Hildur!*
*These twenty-five twins are all ours. Before I found you I wrote seeking, groping. I knew you were somewhere in the world, and once I had found you I wrote only of princesses in varying forms.*

*H.I.*[1]

On 4 November he sent Dr Sontum a photograph of himself with an inscribed message of thanks, and the children were amused to see that he had ruled pencil lines so as to be able to write straight—a sad sign of how shaky that iron hand had become.[2] But three weeks later he felt well enough to allow himself to be interviewed, by Hans Tostrup for the newspaper *Ørebladet*. He declared that he was in excellent health save that 'perhaps my left leg is not quite as it should be; but that is a trifle . . . I do most of my walking now on my home ground—the handsome pavements out here on Drammensveien.' He was, he said, mooting a new play and doing a bit of groundwork for it; but this year, being the one following that in which he had produced a work, he would regard as a rest year, as was his custom. Tostrup asked Ibsen's opinion of

[1] Neither the card nor the dedication exist; shortly before her death Hildur destroyed not merely Ibsen's letters to her but also several pages bearing dedicatory inscriptions. Her servant remembered these two items, however, and told Francis Bull (cf. his *Hildur Andersen og Henrik Ibsen*, pp. 44, 48).

On 14 August 1962 the provincial newspaper *Halden Arbeiderblad* reported that two letters and two visiting cards in Ibsen's hand had been found in a house previously occupied by Hildur's housekeeper, Valborg Ottersen. These were: (1) a letter dated 7 January 1893 addressed to 'My wild forest bird' and signed: 'Your, your master builder' (2) a visiting card dated 5 October 1893 addressed: 'To the princess' (3) a letter dated 22 October 1893 addressed to: 'My own dearest, most beautiful princess' and (4) a visiting card inscribed: '19 September 1891–1895. Thank you for everything, everything in these four crowded years. A thousand greetings!' But no more has been heard of these items, and it has proved impossible to discover whether there is any substance in the report. A veil of silence has descended, and one can only presume, eight years later, that the report proved to be unfounded.

[2] Sontum, p. 255.

Nietzsche, who had died in Weimar that August. Ibsen replied that he 'did not know so much about him', but that he was 'a rare talent who, because of his philosophy, could not be popular in our democratic age'. When Tostrup remarked that some people regarded Nietzsche as 'a spirit of darkness, a Satan', Ibsen cut in: 'No, he wasn't that'. And when asked about the Boer War, which had been in progress for just over a year, he surprised his interviewer, and no doubt many who read the interview, by saying that his sympathy for the Boers was somewhat divided. 'Remember that the Boers themselves took possession of the country illegally by driving out the original inhabitants. And they came only as a half-civilised people, not with the purpose of spreading civilisation. And now a more civilised people, the British, come and force their way in. That is no worse than—indeed, it is not as bad as—what the Boers have done. The British are simply taking what the Boers themselves have stolen.'[1]

These remarks naturally offended the Dutch, and a young journalist, Cornelius Karel Elout, editor of the Amsterdam *Algemeen Handelsblad*, attacked Ibsen's attitude in the Copenhagen newspaper *Politiken* on 7 December. Ibsen defended his viewpoint with dignity in an open letter to *Algemeen Handelsblad* on 9 December, saying: 'I owe a deep personal debt of gratitude to your country. But you cannot ask me to repay part of this debt by denying my convictions.'[2] It was the last public appearance that he was to make in print.

Thanks mainly to performing rights, especially German and Danish, the first year of the new century had been a good one. German royalties and fees alone had amounted to nearly £800.

|  | crowns | £ |
|---|---|---|
| Royalties for *An Enemy of the People* at National Theatre, Christiania | 2,950 | 164 |
| Unspecified royalties from Wien Burgtheater | 535 | 30 |
| Fee for *The Pillars of Society* at Mannheim Hoftheater | 80 | 4 |
| German royalties from Felix Bloch | 13,479 | 749 |
| Additional royalties from National Theatre, Christiania | 3,106 | 172 |
| French fees from Societé des Auteurs | 1,869 | 104 |
| Fee from *Revue de Paris* | 725 | 40 |
| 11th edition of *Peer Gynt* | 1,815 | 101 |
| 8th edition of *Love's Comedy* | 625 | 35 |
| English edition of *When We Dead Awaken* (Heinemann) | 2,160 | 120 |
| Extra fee from Archer for book sales | 24 | 1 |

[1] *C.E.*, XV, pp. 435–436.
[2] *Ibid.*, p. 383.

|                                                                                 | crowns | £ |
|---------------------------------------------------------------------------------|--------|-----|
| Royalties from Royal Theatre, Copenhagen:                                       |        |     |
| *The League of Youth* (25th–31st performances)                                  | 1,299  | 72  |
| *The Lady from the Sea* (15th–18th performances)                                | 1,035  | 57  |
| *The Pretenders* (20th–28th performances)                                       | 2,224  | 124 |
| *The League of Youth* (32nd–35th performances)                                  | 451    | 25  |
| *The Lady from the Sea* (19th–23rd performances)                                | 489    | 27  |
| Swedish rights of *The League of Youth* and *The Pillars of Society* (A. Ranft) | 1,600  | 89  |
| Unspecified rights from Danish director (Stephensen)                            | 300    | 17  |
|                                                                                 | 34,766 | 1,931 |

On 1 January 1901 he received 1,836 crowns from the National Theatre and 2,460 crowns from Felix Bloch. These are the last entries in his account book, apart from a note on 21 January that he had bought 5,000 crowns' worth of shares in the Sundsvall Cellulose Company, bringing his total investments to 338,310 crowns, or £18,795. Over half of this amount, 171,000 crowns, he had purchased in the past four years—34,000 in 1897, 25,000 in 1898, 34,000 in 1899, 73,000 in 1900 and this last purchase of 5,000 in January 1901.

Ibsen's optimism about his health proved sadly false. He was very ill that winter, with repeated small apoplectic fits, and Bolette Sontum remembered how 'we were all very anxious every time the night telephone rang and my father was called out.'[1] These fits paralysed his right arm and leg and the right side of his face, left his speech slurred and occasionally caused hallucinations.[2] Henceforth his health showed little change. Occasionally there were small improvements. The newspapers prepared their obituaries; but his strength carried him through, and he even spoke confidently of writing a new play. It was, he told Christian Michelsen (later to become Prime Minister), to deal, like *John Gabriel Borkman*, with the conflict between love and the desire for power, a conflict finally to be resolved by a third driving passion, envy.[3] But this he was never to begin.

One hopes he was well enough to appreciate a remarkable letter of tribute which arrived for his seventy-third birthday that March from his young Irish admirer, James Joyce. Joyce wrote it in Norwegian, which he had begun to teach himself so as to be able to read his idol in the original;[4] this letter has not

[1] Sontum, p. 255.
[2] Gran, II, p. 339, quoting information given him by Dr Edvard Bull.
[3] Bull, *Henrik Ibsen*, in *Norsk litteratur-historie*, IV, p. 463.
[4] As did Thomas Mann and Stefan George.

survived, but luckily Joyce drafted it in English first, and the draft remains:

8, Royal Terrace,
Fairview, Dublin.
March 1901.

Honoured Sir,

I write to give you greeting on your seventy-third birthday and to join my voice with those of your well-wishers in all lands. You may remember shortly after the publication of your latest play, 'When We Dead Awaken', an appreciation of it appeared in one of the English reviews—The Fortnightly Review—over my name. I know that you have seen it because some short time afterwards Mr William Archer wrote to me and told me that in a letter he had from you some days before, you had written: 'I have read or rather spelt out a review in the "Fortnightly Review" by Mr James Joyce which is very benevolent and for which I should greatly like to thank the author if only I had sufficient knowledge of the language.' (My own knowledge of your language is not, as you see, great but I trust you will be able to decipher my meaning.) I can hardly tell you how moved I was by your message. I am a young, a very young man, and perhaps the telling of such tricks of the nerves will make you smile. But I am sure if you go back along your own life to the time when you were an undergraduate at the University as I am, and if you think what it would have meant to you to have earned a word from one who held as high a place in your esteem as you hold in mine, you will understand my feeling. One thing only I regret, namely, that an immature and hasty article should have met your eye, rather than something better and worthier of your praise. There may not have been any wilful stupidity in it, but truly I can say no more. It may annoy you to have your work at the mercy of striplings, but I am sure you prefer even hot-headedness to nerveless and 'cultured' paradoxes.

What shall I say more? I have sounded your name defiantly through a college where it was either unknown or known faintly and darkly. I have claimed for you your rightful place in the history of the drama. I have shown what, as it seemed to me, was your highest excellence—your lofty impersonal power. Your minor claims—your satire, your technique and orchestral harmony—these, too, I advanced. Do not think me a hero-worshipper. I am not so. And when I spoke of you, in debating-societies, and so forth, I enforced attention by no futile ranting.

But we always keep the dearest things to ourselves. I did not tell *them* what bound me closest to you. I did not say how what I could discern dimly of your life was my pride to see, how your battles inspired me—not the

W

obvious material battles but those that were fought and won behind your forehead—how your wilful resolution to wrest the secret from life gave me heart, and how in your absolute indifference to public canons of art, friends and shibboleths you walked in the light of your inward heroism. And this is what I write to you of now. Your work on earth draws to a close and you are near the silence. It is growing dark for you. Many write of such things, but they do not know. You have only opened the way—though you have gone as far as you could upon it—to the end of 'John Gabriel Borkman' and its spiritual truth—for your last play stands, I take it, apart. But I am sure that higher and holier enlightenment lies—onward.

As one of the young generation for whom you have spoken I give you greeting—not humbly, because I am obscure and you in the glare, not sadly because you are an old man and I a young man, not presumptuously, nor sentimentally—but joyfully, with hope and love, I give you greeting.

Faithfully yours,

James A. Joyce.

Mr. Henrik Ibsen,
Arbiens Gade 2,
Kristiania.

A second stroke in the summer of 1901 left Ibsen virtually unable to walk; though occasionally he would obstinately struggle out for a few painful paces. An observer recalled one such occasion as he crossed Drammensveien on his way from Arbins gade to the Queen's Park twenty yards from his door. 'A young man held him firmly under one arm while he struggled forward with short, dragging steps, his body heavily slouched, his head bowed, his eyes on the ground. His mouth, which had always looked like a line, had acquired an underlip.'[1]

That summer of 1901 Dr Christian Sontum himself became afflicted by an illness which in a few months was to prove fatal. He and his family had to return from Sandefjord to Christiania. Bolette records: '[Ibsen] called every day at our house to hear how the patient was. I usually went down to his carriage . . . He was so kind and sympathetic to us all in our sorrow . . . He was so touching when one day he asked me if he might go in and see my father for the last time. "I cannot walk, you know, but they can carry me." My father was too ill to see anybody so Ibsen asked me to take his card in to him. On it was written in pencil and with a trembling hand the word "*Tak*" [thanks] . . . After my father's death Ibsen called again and when I came down to his carriage he took my hand and his voice quivered as he said: "How are

---

[1] Peter Egge, *Minder fra nord og syd* (Oslo, 1962), pp. 26–27.

you all? I am thinking about you all the time. I, too, have lost my best friend." '1

Dr Sontum's successor as Ibsen's private physician was an eminent Professor of Medicine at the University, but his unpunctuality greatly annoyed Ibsen; and when, on one occasion, he arrived an hour late, Ibsen, sitting up in bed with a sweater up to his neck, ordered him from the house and swore he would never consult him again. He asked his friends if there was a good doctor in the capital who could be relied on to arrive in time, and was recommended Edvard Bull, a Bergenser aged fifty-six. An appointment was fixed for two o'clock and, as the hour of Dr Bull's appearance approached, Ibsen sat waiting with his watch in his hand. From five to two, Ibsen glanced cynically every minute at Dr Bull's recommender, who was sitting with him. As the clock struck two, Ibsen opened his mouth triumphantly, but before he could speak the doorbell rang.² Edvard Bull remained Ibsen's doctor until the writer's death.

Ibsen took the air daily in his carriage, accompanied either by Dr Bull or by the masseur who now attended him, Arnt Dehli. He would make the coachman stop before the University clock, so that he could set his watch by it as he had been wont to do on his walks down Carl Johan to the Grand Hotel, and he was now as familiar a sight on his rides he had been during those walks, a top hat on his head in summer, a round fur hat covering his ears in winter. The great muff of white hair that had surrounded his neck for the past few years was now shaven at the front of the chin. Once he decided that instead of riding he would take a walk. By now he had a nurse permanently in attendance; she helped him down the stairs and no sooner had they reached the street than Ibsen commanded her to disappear. When she hesitated (Suzannah told Bergliot) 'Ibsen swung his stick at her so that she fled back into the house. And all the way down the street Ibsen kept turning to see if she was still there.' Bergliot had never heard Suzannah laugh so as when she told this story. 'She was always amused when Ibsen got angry. He always jutted out his underlip, showing his lower teeth. He hated being ill. He never addressed a barber who visited him each day, except once, when he suddenly hissed at him: 'Ugly devil!'³

Exaggerated reports of his state of health were printed from time to time in most western countries, and in August the New York *Critic* published a long letter purporting to be from Georg Brandes which stated that Ibsen could not possibly live beyond the autumn. Brandes denied authorship, pointing out that so far from having been at Ibsen's side, as the latter claimed,

¹ Sontum, p. 255.
² Information from Dr Bull's son, Professor Francis Bull.
³ Bergliot Ibsen, pp. 212–213.

he had not been in Christiania since 1893. But similar rumours continued to appear over the next five years.

That autumn the first Nobel prize for literature was awarded. The world speculated which living writer would be the first to receive this honour: Tolstoy, Ibsen, Zola, Chekhov, Hardy? But the Swedish Academy chose the French poet Sully-Prudhomme, the first of many curious decisions which that body was to make over the years. Incredible as it seems, none of the five great writers named above ever received it, though Ibsen was to live another five years, Chekhov three, Tolstoy nine and Hardy twenty-seven. Nor did Strindberg, Gorki, Proust, Henry James, Joseph Conrad, H. G. Wells or James Joyce. Bjørnson was to be awarded it in 1903, in Ibsen's lifetime; but Ibsen enjoyed one small piece of revenge. When Bjørnson went to Stockholm to receive the prize, he tried to enter the palace through a side door but found his way barred by a sentry. 'My good man,' Bjørnson informed him. 'I am Norway's greatest writer.' 'Oh,' said the sentry, making way. 'I beg your pardon, Herr Ibsen.'[1]

On 10 September Ibsen's second grandchild was born. Sigurd and Bergliot named her Irene, after the heroine of *When We Dead Awaken*. Ibsen became very devoted to her, and called her 'my little princess', as he had called the young girls who had been the dream images of his old age, from Emilie Bardach to Rosa Fitinghoff. 'Little Irene is beautiful', he once said to Suzannah. 'But my Irene was also beautiful.' He greatly missed Sigurd, who was able to make only infrequent visits from Stockholm. On one such visit 'as soon as he caught sight of Sigurd, he raised both arms towards him and cried despairingly: 'Oh, I have been so sick—so sick.' He took Sigurd's hand between his and so they stood.'[2]

Yet on 24 November he felt well enough to give another interview to Hans Tostrup of *Ørebladet*. 'Dr Henrik Ibsen [wrote Tostrup] sits in his black morning coat with a pocket watch before him at the corner window of his apartment ... He looks well, and his complexion is healthy. His eyes shine with the same sharpness as before. Only his hair has grown somewhat whiter than when we saw him last. We asked how he was and Ibsen replied: "Thank you, better than I have been for a long while. But I cannot walk easily nowadays. To drag myself through the streets would cause me such difficulty that I have to drive. My head is all right. That is fine. But I get tired easily, and my doctor has forbidden me to work very much." He spoke of his hope of completing a new play once he had regained his full health, and even of travelling abroad, though not in the immediate future, since "I would then have to take a masseur

---

[1] Told by Bjørnson's son Bjørn, in *Hjemmet og vennerne* (Oslo, 1932), pp. 191–192.
[2] Bergliot Ibsen, p. 205.

and a servant with me, and it would be no fun to travel with such an army."
He managed to accompany his interviewer through three large rooms to the
front door.'¹

On 8 December 1902 Bjørnson celebrated his seventieth birthday, and surprised Ibsen with a visit. Both Ibsen and Suzannah were much moved that he
should have come on such a day, and Suzannah left them alone together in
Ibsen's study. On returning home, Bjørnson told his family that Ibsen had said
to him: 'When I think back—I can't think ahead, I'm too ill for that—when
I think back, my dear Bjørnson, in spite of everything it's you who have been
closest to my heart all these years. And in that play, you know—the one about
the doctor at the baths—' 'The doctor at the baths?' asked Bjørnson, puzzled.
'The one about those microbes. You know.' 'No.' They both pondered.
'*The* [sic] *Enemy of the People*', said Ibsen eventually. 'I was thinking of you
when I wrote it. Partly. Of course, you're not a bourgeois like him. But it's
you all the same.' When Bjørnson finally rose to leave Ibsen suddenly gripped
his hand tightly and would not let it go. They remained thus for a long time.
At last Ibsen said: 'You are the dearest of all men to me.' It was the last time
they met.²

About this time Georg Brandes saw him for the last time. 'His mind', he
recalled, 'was as brilliant as ever. An extraordinary mildness pervaded his
manner, supplanting his former sternness. His charm had grown, while his
distinction of manner was as great as ever. Yet the general impression was one
of weakness.' And Brandes remembered Oswald's terrible cry in *Ghosts*:
'Never to be able to work again! To be dead, yet alive! Can you imagine
anything more horrible?'³

On 19 February 1903 he granted Hans Tostrup a last interview:

'As we crossed Drammensveien yesterday morning we caught a glimpse
behind the corner window on Arbins gade of a handsome, white-bearded
and white-haired old head, staring with a friendly and gentle expression,
half-dreaming, half-observing, down the street towards the wintry trees of
the Palace park.

' "Well, Henrik Ibsen looks brisk and well!" we thought, so we go
up and visit him. It is long since any word was heard from him . . . We
announced ourselves and were received.

¹ Reprinted in *C.E.*, XV, pp. 439–441.
² Bjørn Bjørnson, *Hjemmet og vennerne*, pp. 257–258; *Fra barndommens dage*, p. 11.
³ Georg Brandes, in *Century Magazine* (New York), February, 1917, pp. 541 and 546.
Brandes adds that 'he no longer spoke with bitterness of Norway, but merely complained
about its slow development. Norwegian ideas and theories seemed old-fashioned and out of
date to him.'

' "I don't usually receive anyone now. I don't feel really strong in the daytime, and conversations, much as I'd like them—no, no, do sit down."

'So we sat beside him in the corner window, enquired after his health, and the old poet was friendliness and kindness itself.'[1]

Unfortunately, the interview dealt only with the question of closer co-operation between the Scandinavian kingdoms, and Ibsen's views on the subject, that small nations could achieve more by co-operation than by squabbling—a useful reminder at a time when squabbling was the order of the day, but one would have liked to have learned his views on something less parochial as he moved, in Joyce's phrase, near the silence.

On 28 March Magdalene Thoresen died, at the age of eighty-three; luckier than her stepson, she had retained her physical and mental vigour to the last. That spring Ibsen had another stroke. He tried to learn to write with his left hand, practising every day; he sadly remarked to Suzannah: 'Strange that I, who was once quite a dramatist, now have to learn to write the alphabet.'[2] Yet on 17 August he let the sculptor Gustav Vigeland, who had made busts of him in 1901 and 1902, make sketches for a new one. These sketches show a sad change, the mouth slack, the expression almost vacant.[3] Gunnar Heiberg, who was present on one of these occasions, tells that Ibsen 'complained that there was a limit to how long he could sit in that cold room; his health would not stand it, and anyway he had not promised to give so many sittings. Vigeland gave him a look but said nothing. Ibsen glanced at the clock and said he was expecting someone.' Heiberg said he had to go; Ibsen accompanied him to the next room, where he stumbled and had to grasp a chair. 'I asked if he would like to lean on my arm. No, he replied, there was nothing wrong. His face was stern and splendid; he looked like a Jupiter betrayed.' As they got to the door Heiberg asked who was the visitor he was expecting, and Ibsen gave a little smile and replied: 'The tailor'. Heiberg remembered that Ibsen was bitter because he felt that the National Theatre, under Bjørn Bjørnson's direction, was playing too much of Bjørnson's work and too little of his own.[4]

On 14 February 1904 Ibsen wrote the last word we have from his hand: 'Tak', shakily pencilled on a card to Dr Bull, who told his son that it took Ibsen three days to write it.[5] On 19 March he granted his last interview, to Verdens Gang:

---

[1] C.E., XV, pp. 442–443.
[2] Bergliot Ibsen, p. 214.
[3] They are reproduced in C.E., XIX, pp. 429–435.
[4] Aftenposten, 16 April 1911, reprinted in Heiberg's Salt og sukker, pp. 45–46.
[5] Bull, Tradisjoner og minner, p. 97.

'Tomorrow the poet celebrates his seventy-sixth birthday. One of our colleagues who visited him yesterday reports that Dr Ibsen is comparatively well and has in general been in quite satisfactory health all winter.

' "There is nothing much wrong with me just now," said the poet. "I just have to be careful, and Dr Bull says that March with its changeable weather could be dangerous for me. I find walking a little difficult, but as soon as the air becomes milder I shall try to take a stroll outside. I am allowed to enjoy myself in the Queen's Park, which gives me great pleasure." Our colleague extended his best wishes to the poet for his birthday and asked if he was receiving any visitors. "No," he replied. "It is so difficult to speak with so many people that I am not receiving anyone." '[1]

Halvdan Koht, who had recently edited Ibsen's letters, visited him during the autumn of 1904.

'He had difficulty with his speech and forgot his words, sometimes using the wrong ones, e.g. "lexicon" instead of "letters". [Arnt Dehli was present at the meeting to interpret his meaning when the right words would not come]. One could see how it pained him. His eyes were dull and had lost their colour. But they could still sparkle. It happened twice during our conversation, once when I greeted him from old German friends of his whom I had recently seen, and again when I mentioned that I knew his sister, Hedvig Stousland of Skien. Both times his eyes suddenly went steel-blue and shot like a flash at me.'[2]

That same autumn Bolette Sontum saw him for the last time, before going to America to study at the Carnegie Library School in Pittsburgh:

'He was very much changed, so thin and white and, oh, so little. His shoulders, always so proudly erect, had shrunken pathetically, and his lion head had grown so small that it was only the intense fire of his eyes that quickened it. It seemed to pain him that he did not have the strength to keep up a conversation. Yet he recognised me, and smiled when I came in, and in a few minutes he regained his interest and asked about all my America plans. Mrs Ibsen had told him that I was sailing for New York and had come to say goodbye. We talked about the happy days at Grefsen and my father. Then he said: "And now you are going to America. Are you going to write books?" "Oh, no," I laughingly answered. "I am going to learn how to put them correctly on the shelves." He said: "Yes, their libraries are famous," and then he sat thinking. "It must be a great country with many

---

[1] *C.E.*, XIX, p. 227.
[2] Koht, II, pp. 294–295.

chances", he repeated slowly, twice. "But it seems so far away. You must
be careful with yourself. My son says, beware of the iced water and the hot
bread." Mrs Ibsen also asked me not to have too many of those American
dishes. Chivalrous as always, despite his absolute frailty, Ibsen wanted to
see me to the door, but asked me to excuse him, adding he was so tired. He
kissed my hand and I left him. When I was out on the street I looked up to
his window where he was standing in his black frock coat, and I waved my
last goodbye to "the old Doctor".'[1]

Hildur Andersen does not seem to have visited him during these years of
sickness; presumably Suzannah, despite Ibsen's protestations of innocence,
still took their relationship seriously. Nor, being unable to go out alone, did he
visit her. One's winter's day, driving in his carriage, he saw her on the pavement. Raising his hand, he called weakly: 'Bless you! Bless you!' It was the
last time they saw each other.[2]

Yet the old man lived on. One January night in 1905 he was heard to cry
in his sleep: 'I'm writing! And it's going splendidly!'[3] Dreams, too, brought
him occasional comfort and joy. He, who had always been so taciturn and self-
contained, was now pathetically grateful for someone to talk to him, provided
it was someone he knew. Jens Wang, the artist, paid him several visits to
show him his designs for new decor and costumes, and he especially enjoyed
these occasions. He even allowed an American photographer to take two
portraits of him, rigid-faced and clutching the arm of his chair.[4] But his
helplessness increased; that spring another visitor noticed that he sat with a
piece of paper in his hand wishing to put it on the table but unable to do so.
His guest did it for him and received a grateful glance.[5] A frequent visitor at
this time was Christopher Bruun, who half a century earlier had helped to
inspire Ibsen with the character of Brand. One day he tentatively brought up
the question of Ibsen's relationship with God. Ibsen 'went red in the face with
anger and said: "Leave that to me!"'[6]

Sigurd, meanwhile, had run into trouble over the question of dissolving the
union with Sweden. His skilful diplomacy in Stockholm, where he had taken
up residence in 1903, and especially the trust and friendship he had inspired in
King Oscar, had achieved what a few years earlier had seemed impossible. The
King (who, on Sigurd's first mentioning the question of dissolution soon after

[1] Sontum, pp. 255–256.
[2] Bull, *Hildur Andersen og Henrik Ibsen*, p. 54.
[3] Bull, *Henrik Ibsen*, in *Norsk litteratur-historie*, IV, p. 464.
[4] See illustration no. 18.
[5] *Da Henrik Ibsen døde*, anonymous article in *Morgenbladet*, 23 May 1931.
[6] Bergliot Ibsen, p. 214.

taking office, had replied: "If anyone suggests that to me I shall shoot him with my own hand") now seemed not totally to reject the idea, and several Swedish newspapers began actively to support it. Unfortunately, this produced a reaction, and a new and chauvinistic Swedish Prime Minister, E. C. Boström, enraged Norwegian opinion by closing down on the proposals for a separate consular service. The Norwegian government resigned and the new Prime Minister, Christian Michelsen, wanted Sigurd to remain in charge of foreign affairs; but Sigurd believed that the Treaty of Union should be dissolved legally by changing the constitution and not violently by a *coup d'état*, and refused. As a result, he was suspected by jealous circles in Norway of having played a double game, and felt compelled to resign. 'I am one of those', he commented to Bergliot, 'who work for eleven hours of the day and at the twelfth hour have to look on while others gather the fruits of my labour.'[1]

At least this meant that for the last year of his life Ibsen had Sigurd constantly with him in Christiania. Bergliot tells that when Sigurd returned, Ibsen 'not only was no worse; he was up again, and followed Sigurd's account of the latest developments in Stockholm with great interest. Fru Ibsen listened silently while Ibsen asked question after question. The conversation continued through dinner. I can still see Ibsen as he sat there, his hands far apart gripping the table edge. He looked like some powerful judge. When Sigurd had finished Ibsen suddenly rose and said loudly and firmly: "Sigurd shall give up politics. He shall continue my life's work." '[2] Sigurd was beginning to write a philosophical work called *The Quintessence of Man*, which was to take him several years; and one day when he asked his father about one of his plays which had just been revived with great success, Ibsen waved his hands and said: 'Don't talk about my things, I'm only interested in everything you write.'[3]

That summer Sigurd arranged the outright sale of his father's Danish and Norwegian copyrights for a lump sum of 150,000 crowns (£8,333), of which 20,000 crowns was to be paid forthwith, 10,000 annually for the next eight years and 5,000 annually for the following ten. Sigurd signed the contract on his father's behalf on 3 June. It seems a terribly bad bargain from the point of view of Ibsen's grandchildren; but the news galvanised Bjørnson into demanding 200,000 crowns from Gyldendal for the outright purchase of his copyrights. 'Ibsen is a rich man and I a poor one', he told Peter Nansen, who negotiated on behalf of Gyldendal, 'and who knows whether my work won't last longer than Ibsen's?' He got the sum he asked, spread over twenty years.[4]

---

[1] *Ibid.*, p. 209.
[2] *Ibid.*, pp. 211–212.
[3] *Ibid.*, p. 212.
[4] Harald Grieg, pp. 156 ff.

On 7 June Michelsen's government, by a *coup d'état*, dissolved the union with Sweden. Dr Edvard Bull told Ibsen that people now referred to a famous restaurant called The Queen as 'Fru Michelsen', and was able to report to his family that the joke had made Ibsen smile, something Dr Bull had seldom seen.[1] His difficulty in speaking had, however, now worsened, though his other senses remained sharp. He liked to sit hour after hour at his corner window gazing out, and tourists would stand in the street below to catch a glimpse of him, just as (noted Peter Nansen) a few years earlier the old Kaiser Wilhelm had been exhibited like a mummy in a window of his palace in Berlin.[2] His only pleasure was when Sigurd came; he would sit with his watch before him, waiting for the visit.[3] In 1906 Sigurd and Bergliot had their third child, another girl.

'She was only a few weeks old when Sigurd and I took her up to the Ibsens. Ibsen was sitting in an armchair at the table in the library when we came in. I showed him the baby, and he looked at her for a long time. Then I asked him if we could call her Eleonora. He became very moved, so that he could only slowly reply: "Yes." Then he turned towards me and added: "God bless you, Bergliot." He was happy to see his family grow. When we had gone he said to Fru Ibsen: "My Nora was also called Eleonora."

'That was one of the last times Sigurd and I saw him up. Afterwards, Ibsen lay mostly in his bed. His wife was the only person whom he allowed to give him food; and when he was up he only wanted to eat in her bedroom, which lay next to his.

'He lived in a permanent fear lest she should die before him. He said: "If you die before me, I shall die five minutes later." Towards the end he had difficulty in speaking and always called her *"Fruen"* [Ma'am]; it was easier to say, and he always heard the nurse call her that.

'Once I was sitting with him—it was the last time. He lay holding my hand, and his eyes and face shone with kindness as he spoke many loving words to me. It is a beautiful memory. Sigurd was with his father every day. One evening his father said to him: "Soon I shall go into the great darkness." '[4]

---

[1] Bull, *Tradisjoner og minner*, p. 97.
[2] Interview in *Aftenposten*, 4 March 1917.
[3] Bergliot Ibsen, p. 214.
[4] *Ibid.*, pp. 216–217. Ibsen enjoyed stressing that 'Nora' in *A Doll's House* was the kind of affectionate abbreviation that one uses to a child, and that Helmer employed it as Nora's father had done, her real name being Eleonora.

That February another Eleonora came to Christiania. Duse was visiting Norway for the first time, largely in the hope of meeting the dramatist who had provided her with her greatest triumphs. On her arrival she sent a letter and flowers to Ibsen asking if she might call merely to say: 'Thank you'. Suzannah, however, telephoned that Ibsen was too ill to receive anyone. Lugné-Poe, who was with Duse at the time, tells what followed: 'I remember very well that morning when she had just received this sad message. I went in to her and found her swathed in the long white *palandrane* which she loved to wear. She sat fearful, annihilated, hollow-cheeked, her face tired and lined as though life was abandoning her. She asked me: "What shall I do? Please, what shall I do?" ... What could I do for her? I had hoped so much, for her sake ... Next morning around noon Duse and I found ourselves outside Henrik Ibsen's house. She had bought Norwegian boots, for she wished to go there on foot. We walked round the left of the palace, and at the stroke of twelve we stood beneath the corner window where, every day at this time, people could see Dr Ibsen in person, sometimes with a secretary or someone at his side. Duse stood there waiting in the cold and snow. Who, even thirty years later, would not be shaken by the memory of having been present at that sad and silent meeting? Eleonora Duse on the pavement, looking for the old poet's silhouette behind the big window?'[1]

His seventy-eighth birthday passed, and still death would not come to relieve him. Suzannah, herself in almost constant pain, sat by his side. 'I could not do without her greatness', he told Bergliot; and the nurse told her that she heard him say to Suzannah: 'You have been my guiding star. You were the eagle that showed me the way to the summit.'[2] Occasionally, little spurts of strength seemed partially to revive him. Once when Dr Bull asked the masseur how Ibsen was, Dehli replied: 'Not too bad. He's sworn a couple of times.'

From 16 May he was too weak to stand, and lay in a coma, occasionally muttering a word or two indistinctly and incoherently. At noon on 22 May he opened his eyes, pressed Dr Bull's hand and murmured: 'Thank God!' A little later, the nurse said to the others who were in the room that he seemed to be a little better. From the bed came the single word: "*Tvertimod!*" ("On the contrary!") It was the last word Ibsen ever spoke;[3] and it came appropriately from one who had devoted his life to the correction of lies.

---

[1] Lugné-Poe, pp. 95–97.
[2] Bergliot Ibsen, p. 238.
[3] Some deny this, but cf. Dr Edvard Bull's journal, quoted in Lis Jacobsen's *Ibsens sidste ord*, in *Ibsen-Årbok*, 1957–1959, p. 81. There is a legend that in his last moments Ibsen cried: 'No!' but this seems to be without reliable foundation.

He died at 2.30 p.m. on 23 May 1906. Bergliot was present:

'One morning our telephone rang and we were told we must come at once. We came in to Ibsen, who lay calm and beautiful with closed eyes. Fru Ibsen sat crying in the next room. We went in to her. It was so strange to see her cry. Most people distort their faces when they cry, but not she. Tear after tear simply streamed down her cheeks. I can still see her large, clear face as she sat and spoke of the one she loved and must now lose. The nurse came and asked us to go in to Ibsen, since she thought the end was near. We went quickly in, but Fru Ibsen, who had difficulty in walking, came slowly after. Death brings with it a sublime stillness, and in this stillness we heard her approach with very short steps. First the stick was heard, then her foot which she dragged after her. It seemed an eternity. I can still see her as she stood as though lost above his bed. Now it was finished.

'There was a majestic peace and greatness about Henrik Ibsen's departure from this world. We remained with him a long time and then went and sat down in the library. There she told us very emotionally that the previous night,[1] before falling into a doze, his last words to her had been: "My dear, dear wife, how good and kind you have been to me." This had made her happy. After a while she rose, and said: "Now I must go. Ibsen liked me to look after the house." In this sad atmosphere we again heard her small steps and the sound of the stick growing weaker and weaker until at last they were gone.

'Before he was taken away from Arbins gade we gathered for the last time around his open coffin. His face was transfigured in death; all the tightness and severity that had marked it in life were smoothed away. It was as though for the first time I saw how beautiful he was; the mighty brow lay smoothly serene, and the chiselled features stood classically forth.'[2]

The Norwegian government granted him a state funeral, and this took place on 1 June at Trinity Church. Bolette Sontum, now back from America, was among the mourners: 'For the last time he was dressed in his black frock coat with the broad lapels and laid out in state ... The day before the funeral people flocked to the church and thousands stood outside waiting for their turn to pay their last respects to him. In the choir the coffin stood loaded with flowers and around it the students of the University kept a guard of honour. The organ played softly and the crowd [estimated at 12,000] filed past the

---

[1] But Dr Bull's journal states that he was in a coma from the afternoon of 22 May. Bergliot recorded her memories over forty years later, and may have misremembered Suzannah's exact wording; or she may have been right and Dr Bull wrong. It hardly seems to matter.

[2] Bergliot Ibsen, pp. 217–218.

coffin. There was nothing in the white little Ibsen that awed them now. The task of the fiery judge was done.'[1]

Suzannah was forbidden by Dr Bull to attend the ceremony, and remained alone in the apartment at Arbins gade. Afterwards, Bergliot and Sigurd returned there. 'There seemed an enormous emptiness in all the rooms. I sat and watched Sigurd and his mother as they talked together. Now those three had become one.'[2] A column was erected over Ibsen's grave bearing the simple and appropriate symbol of a hammer.

---

[1] Sontum, p. 256.
[2] Bergliot Ibsen, p. 219.

# SEVENTEEN

## ❧ Epilogue

SUZANNAH LIVED ON for eight years at Arbins gade; she died there on 3 April 1914. Only once during that time did she leave the apartment, when she had herself carried down the stairs and driven to see her husband's grave. Despite her condition, she would never let anyone else dust the paintings which Ibsen had brought so proudly back from Italy. Twice a month she would have steps brought in, send her maid out of the room and painfully climb up to wipe the dust off each picture. Dr Bull once suggested to her that her discomfort would be eased if he designed a special chair for her to sit in; and she thanked him, moved that anyone should think of her, who had always lived in the shadow of her husband. But the next time he came, and showed her the drawing, she asked what it would cost, and when he replied: 'About a hundred crowns' [£5 10s. od.], she declared that having managed for so long without such a luxury, she could continue for the short time that was left to her. Dr Bull's son Francis once visited her with his mother, and remembered that before she rang the bell his mother told him to take a deep breath so as to have fresh air in his lungs, since the atmosphere in the closed apartment was so suffocating. 'I remember that I was shocked at how unbeautiful Fru Ibsen was, and how lacking in any kind of feminine charm; but when she spoke of the old days, she became alive.'[1]

A few days before she died she spoke to Bergliot about the early years of her marriage. 'With great difficulty she said: "When we were young, many so-called friends came to Ibsen, but I sent them away." After a long pause: "I had many unkind words for it, but I didn't care. He had to have peace for his work." After another long pause: "Ibsen had no steel in his character—but I gave it to him." Finally she said: "I have never spent a day in bed in my life, and I don't want to die there. I want to die standing or sitting."[2] She died in her armchair early one morning.

Sigurd never returned to politics. The year after his father's death he settled in Italy, but three years later, at Suzannah's request and with the greatest

---

[1] Bull, *Tradisjoner og minner*, pp. 102–104.
[2] Bergliot Ibsen, p. 237.

reluctance, came back to Norway. Despite his gifts, he remained unwanted there, and could obtain no permanent post, even in journalism or teaching. His philosophical work, *The Quintessence of Man*, was translated into many languages and was especially successful in America; Eugene O'Neill, in his autobiographical play *Ah, Wilderness!*, made his hero name it as one of the influential progressive books of his youth. In 1913 he published an interesting play, *Robert Frank*, about the conflict between the proletariat and the Old World; it was translated into English, French and German, but was as viciously attacked in Norway as his father's early works had been. After Suzannah's death he re-settled in Italy, and died in 1930. Bergliot lived on until 1953. Their son, Tancred, became a pioneer aviator and a distinguished film director; he and Ibsen's other grandchildren, Irene and Eleonora, are still alive at the time of writing, and there are many great- and great-great-grand-children.

Jonas Lie and Edvard Grieg died within a year of Ibsen, and Bjørnson in 1910, in a Paris hotel. Bergliot was at her father's deathbed, as she had been at Ibsen's, and noted that where Ibsen had said: 'Soon I shall enter the great darkness', Bjørnson spoke of ascending into 'the great whiteness'. Strindberg died of cancer in 1912, aged 63; Georg Brandes in 1927, aged 85.

The young girls whom Ibsen loved in his last years all lived to a ripe age. Helene Raff achieved some success as a painter and novelist, and died in Munich in 1942 at the age of 77. Emilie Bardach survived until 1 November 1955. By good fortune she left Vienna for Switzerland before Hitler's invasion and settled in Berne; during the Second World War she was called before Hitler's Austrian representatives there and (being a Jewess) stood in danger of being returned to her native country, but (writes Basil King's daughter, Mrs Reginald Orcutt, whose husband was instrumental in persuading the Swiss authorities to let her remain) 'she was too old and dotey to travel and obviously harmless ... She was sweet and kind up to the last.'[1] So she escaped the gas chambers. She died a spinster. Hildur Andersen lived even longer; she died in December 1956 at the age of 92. She, too, never married; nor did Rosa Fitinghoff, who died on 27 March 1949, aged 76. Rosa wrote several novels and children's books of moderate quality, and a trivial autobiography, *Minnenas kavalkad*, which contains no reference to her friendship with Ibsen. Her Swedish publisher, Dr Ragnar Svanström of Norstedts, remembers her as 'a rather eccentric little old lady always accompanied by about ten poodles'. During the Second World War she turned up in Oslo at the offices of Cappelin and asked if they would be interested in publishing a book about poodles. On being asked:

---

[1] Letter to the author, 14 February 1969.

'Would you not consider writing something about Ibsen?', she left without reply.

IBSEN'S CONTRIBUTION TO the theatre was threefold, and in each respect the drama owes more to him than to any other dramatist since Shakespeare. First, he broke down the social barriers which had previously bounded it. As explained, he was the first man to show that high tragedy could be written about ordinary people and in ordinary everyday prose, and the importance of that seemingly simple achievement can hardly be exaggerated. Soon after his work had been introduced to England, W. L. Courtney, the editor of the *Fortnightly Review*, who also wrote dramatic and literary criticism for the *Daily Telegraph*, complained that Ibsen's plays were 'singularly mean, commonplace, parochial . . . as if Apollo, who once entered the house of Admetus, were now told to take up his habitation in a back parlour in South Hampstead. There may be tragedies in South Hampstead, although experience does not consistently testify to the fact; but, at all events from the historical and traditional standpoint, tragedy is more likely to concern itself with Glamis Castle, Melrose Abbey, Carisbrooke or even Carlton House Terrace.'[1] In other words, as William Archer commented, Ibsen's characters were not what the Victorians called 'carriage people'. Before Ibsen, tragedy had (always excluding Büchner) concerned itself with Kings and Queens, Princes and Princesses or, at the lowest, Montagus and Capulets. Ibsen showed that high tragedy could and did take place at least as frequently in back parlours as in castles and palaces. He was, of course, not the first dramatist to attempt this, any more than the Wright brothers were the first people to build an aeroplane; they were the first to build one that got off the ground, and *Ghosts* is, after *Woyzeck*, the first tragedy about back parlours that gets off the ground.

His second great contribution was technical. He threw out the old artificialities of plot which are usually associated with the name of Scribe, but of which Shakespeare and Schiller were also guilty; mistaken identities, overheard conversations, intercepted letters and the like. It was a slow and painful process to rid himself of these; something of the old machinery is still there as late as *A Doll's House*; but his last ten plays are free of it. As A. B. Walkley noted as early as 1891: 'Whatever we learn we learn at first-hand, from the characters

---

[1] Quoted by William Archer, *The Real Ibsen*, in *The International*, February 1901, p. 196.

themselves, not from a Dumasian commentator or *raisonneur*.'[1] Equally importantly, he developed the art of prose dialogue to a degree of refinement which has never been surpassed; not merely the different way people talk, and the different language they use under differing circumstances, but that double-density dialogue which is his peculiar legacy, the sub-text, the meaning behind the meaning. Through this he was able to create characters as complex as the most complex characters of Flaubert or Henry James, without the aid of explanatory narration or monologues. And this demanded, and opened the way for, a new kind of acting, analytical, penetrating, self-effacing and sensitive. There was no place in his plays for the old operatics.

What nowadays seem technical limitations, such as the over-exposition in the opening scenes, the excessive and sometimes repetitive planting of information needful to the audience, were dictated by the limitations of those audiences; as we have seen, when he tried in *Hedda Gabler* to reduce his exposition to a modern minimum, the reaction was almost total bewilderment (even Henry James on reading it was left 'muddled and mystified'[2]). It is no coincidence that this, the least popular in his own time of his mature plays, is the one most frequently performed today and the one for which fewest allowances have to be made.

But none of these technical contributions explain the continued life of Ibsen's plays on the stage today; and one regrets the (very natural) tendency of the compilers of programme notes to stress his importance as an innovator. Few things put an audience off a play as much as reading beforehand that its author was the first man to do this or that; it is like being asked to sit for three hours in the first armchair, or in the first house to have been equipped with central heating. Ibsen's enduring greatness as a dramatist is due not to his technical innovations, but to the depth and subtlety of his understanding of human character (especially feminine character) and, which is rarer, of human relationships. None of the great novelists, Stendhal and Flaubert included, created more memorably observed women than Agnes, Nora, Helen Alving, Rebecca West, Ellida Wangel, Rita Allmers or Ella Rentheim. And he created a succession of male characters of a size and strength that represent a challenge to any actor equal to that of Hamlet or Lear—Brand, Peer Gynt, Oswald Alving, Thomas Stockmann, Halvard Solness, John Gabriel Borkman, Arnold Rubek—characters which defy shallow or 'clever' acting, but which, worthily interpreted, offer as rewarding experiences as it is possible to receive in a theatre. Yet so delicate was Ibsen's understanding of human relationships that a selfish actor can only partially succeed in these roles. Unless the relationships with the

---

[1] *Playhouse Impressions* (London, 1892), p. 56.
[2] *The Scenic Art*, p. 246.

other characters are right, the performance fails. And it can never be sufficiently
stressed that, as Ibsen himself insisted, his leading characters are almost without
exception passionate characters, even when these passions are inhibited. They
are never sexless (though how often has one not seen them played so!). It would
be an exaggeration, perhaps, to say that Ibsen's plays are about sex, for they are
about so much besides; but there is none of his plays, except *Brand* and *An Enemy
of the People*, in which sex is not a major and decisive element.

Ibsen's uniqueness among dramatists as a contributor to the social debate
has been noted, but one must underline an essential difference in this respect
between him and his great contemporaries. A major writer's biography is only
partly the story of his life; perhaps more importantly, it is the story of a series of
explosions which he causes in places he has never seen and among people he
has never met. With a poet, a novelist or a philosopher, these explosions occur
in myriads of individuals reading in their homes. But this was only partially
true of Ibsen. Unlike Tolstoy or Zola, Mill, Nietzsche, Freud or even Marx,
unlike, indeed, any writer before him, more like a preacher, a Savonarola or a
Wesley, he wrought his effect most powerfully on crowds, gathered together
not in a market-place or a church or chapel, but in a theatre. It is a commonplace that a man may more easily be converted in a crowd than alone, and it is
not the least of Ibsen's numerous contributions to the theatre that he turned it
from a place of entertainment and occasional catharsis into a place from which
men emerged compelled to re-think basic principles which they had never
before seriously questioned. Euripides had done this, but no dramatist since, or
anyway not on the same scale. Shakespeare never questioned the established
tenets and beliefs of his time as Ibsen did. There were more social abuses in
Shakespeare's England than in Ibsen's Norway, but Shakespeare never chal-
lenged one of them. Who ever walked out of a Shakespeare play, in his time
or since, feeling compelled to re-think his basic concepts of life? Yet that was
the effect of Ibsen's 'social' plays on his contemporaries, like reading Darwin
or Marx or Freud.

Nowadays we tend to regard his later plays, less appreciated in his time, as
his greater. But because Ibsen's supreme quality was his understanding of the
human mind and his ability to portray its depths and nuances (so that no actor
or actress can ever honestly say that he or she has totally explored or filled that
character), and because he did this as surely in the 'social' plays as in everything
else he wrote, *A Doll's House* and *Ghosts* and *An Enemy of the People* remain as
hypnotic today as when it was their messages rather than their psychology
that buzzed like a caged fly in the minds of their audiences. As Desmond
MacCarthy wrote: 'Ibsen's theatre is the theatre of the soul. Important as he
was, and is, as a social reformer, it is that which makes him even more important

as an artist. Society changes quickly, the mind hardly at all; it is that which makes his work permanent.'[1]

Ibsen's two great successors in the realm of tragedy explored fields that he did not. Strindberg, like no writer before him, mapped that no-man's-land where reality and fantasy, sanity and insanity, abut; and he wrote of sex with a frankness which Ibsen, being Ibsen, could not match, especially of sex divorced from love and riding hand in hand with contempt or hatred. The only other dramatist since Ibsen who is his peer in stature is Chekhov, and to argue whether he or Ibsen is the greater is like arguing whether Bach is superior to Beethoven. Chekhov's feelings about Ibsen were as mixed as Strindberg's. He read him, we must remember, in bad translation (by non-Russians), and Stanislavsky remembered only his frequent expressions of distaste for Ibsen's work. 'I recall A. Chekhov once being present at the rehearsals of The Wild Duck. He looked bored. He did not like Ibsen. He said: "Look here, Ibsen does not know life. In life it does not happen like that." ' 'Just as much as Chekhov disliked Ibsen's plays, he liked Hauptmann's.' 'At a rehearsal of Hedda Gabler at the Moscow Arts, Chekhov said: "Look here, Ibsen is not a playwright." ' And in his autobiography Stanislavsky summed up: 'Chekhov did not like Ibsen as a dramatist, although he placed Ibsen's talents very high. He thought him dry, cold, a man of reason.' But this may have been due to the bad translations and the unrealistic way in which Ibsen was played in Russia. And towards the end of his life, Chekhov's attitude seems to have changed. On 30 October 1903, when planning to visit Moscow, he wrote to Stanislavsky: 'I haven't yet seen The Lower Depths, The Pillars of Society or Emperor and Galilean. I very much want to see all three'; and a week later, on 7 November, he wrote to A. L. Vishensky: 'You know Ibsen is my favourite writer.'[2]

Pirandello and O'Neill had none of Chekhov's doubts. 'After Shakespeare', declared Pirandello, 'I unhesitatingly place Ibsen first';[3] and O'Neill found him 'much nearer to me than Shakespeare'. 'O'Neill said that people are too

---

[1] New Statesman, 26 May 1917.

[2] Cf. Stanislavsky, p. 345; Chekhov, Literary and Theatrical Reminiscences, trans. and ed. S. S. Koteliansky (London, 1927), pp. 156, 161; Life and Letters of Anton Chekhov, trans. and ed. S. S. Koteliansky and Philip Tomlinson (London, 1925), p. 293. Martin Nag, (op. cit. p. 111) argues persuasively that The Wild Duck, which had been translated into Russian in 1892, four years before Chekhov wrote The Seagull, may well have influenced the latter play, which likewise has a dead (or about to be killed) bird as its central symbol. But we must remember Ibsen's warning against confusing parallelisms with influence. It is interesting to note that the Theatre Literary Committee of St Petersburg approved The Seagull for performance only after much criticism, condemning, in the words of the report, 'its symbolism, or more correctly, its Ibsenism' as ineffective and unnecessary. (Ernest J. Simmons, Chekhov, London, 1963, p. 365).

[3] Quoted by Zucker (title page), and in several other books about Ibsen.

apt to think of Ibsen as merely dreadful and deep. "He's deep all right," O'Neill continued, "and sometimes dreadful, like life itself, but he's also intensely human and understandable. I needed no professor to tell me that Ibsen as a dramatist knew whereof he spoke. I found him for myself outside college grounds and hours. If I had met him inside, I might still be a stranger to Ibsen.'[1]

A reaction against Ibsen's work inevitably set in, even before his death. In 1902 Max Beerbohm, reviewing a production of *The Lady from the Sea*, noted with dismay that Ibsen already seemed old-fashioned. ' "Byron is dead!"—can that message have fallen with a more awful suddenness on our grandfathers than "Ibsen is old-fashioned" falls on us? . . . But Time is a cyclist. The things of the day before yesterday are nearer to us than the things of yesterday, and nearer still are the things of the day before. Ellida and the rest, creatures of yesterday, will grow gradually younger, and will doubtless be much admired at the close of the century.'[2]

Beerbohm was right as far as England is concerned. It has not been the same in all countries; in the Mediterranean lands (because they and their ways of acting are southern, or because they are Catholic?) he is not often played, and then usually in the wrong way for the wrong melodramatic reasons; to the French Ibsen is still, as Georg Brandes wrote in 1902, a Protestant who protests too much.[3] In Germany, where, not unpredictably, Bertolt Brecht dismissed him as 'very good—for his own time and his own class',[4] he is, as he was recently in England, in urgent need of reassessment. But in England his reputation stands higher than ever and he is performed with annually increasing frequency, and it is difficult to imagine that other western countries will not soon follow suit. As a Swedish critic has written, Ibsen is the Rome of modern drama. All roads ultimately lead from him and to him.[5]

Ibsen was a poet, who used prose as other poets have used the sonnet, as a medium which, by its strict confinement, intensifies and liberates. Let the last word on him be spoken by a poet. Four years after Ibsen's death Rainer Maria Rilke addressed to him, in *The Notebook of Malte Laurids Brigge*, one of the most eloquent and penetrative tributes ever paid by one great writer to another:[6]

---

[1] Croswell Bowen, *The Curse of the Misbegotten* (London, 1960), p. 125.

[2] Max Beerbohm, *Around Theatres* (London, 1953), pp. 207–208.

[3] Georg Brandes, *Henrik Ibsen i Frankrig*, in *Norden*, 1902, pp. 29–47.

[4] Willy Haas, *Die Literarische Welt* (Hamburg, 1955), p. 134.

[5] Martin Lamm, *Det moderna dramat* (Stockholm, paperback edition, 1964), p. 83.

[6] *The Notebook of Malte Laurids Brigge*, translated by John Linton (London, 2nd edition, 1950), pp. 76–79. It is one of the great English translations of this century.

'Loneliest of men, withdrawn from all, how rapidly have they overtaken you by means of your fame! But lately they were fundamentally
opposed to you, and now they treat you as their equal. And they carry your
words about with them in the cages of their presumption, and exhibit
them in the streets and excite them a little from their own safe distance:
all those wild beasts of yours.

'When I first read you, they broke loose on me and assailed me in my
wilderness—your desperate words—desperate, as you yourself became in
the end, you whose course is wrongly traced on every chart. Like a fissure
it crosses the heavens, this hopeless hyperbola of your path, that only once
curves towards us and draws off again in terror. What mattered it to you
whether a woman stays or goes, whether one is seized with vertigo and
another with madness, whether the dead live, and the living appear to be
dead: what mattered it? It was all so natural to you; you passed through it,
as one might cross a vestibule, and did not stop. But yonder, within, you
remained stooped, where our destiny seethes and settles and changes colour,
farther in than anyone has yet been. A door had sprung open before you,
and now you were among the alembics in the firelight. Yonder where,
mistrustful, you took no one with you, yonder you sat and discerned processes of change. And there, since your blood drove you to reveal and not
to fashion or to speak, there you conceived the vast project of magnifying
single-handed these minutiae, which you yourself first perceived only in
test-tubes, so that they should be seen of thousands, immense, before all
eyes. Then your theatre came into being. You could not wait until this
almost spaceless life, condensed into fine drops by the weight of centuries,
should be discovered by the other arts, and gradually made visible to the
few who, little by little, come together in their understanding and finally
demand to see the general confirmation of these extraordinary rumours in
the semblance of the scene opened before them. For this you could not
wait. You were there, and you had to determine and record the almost
immeasurable: the rise of half a degree in a feeling; the angle of refraction,
read off at close quarters, in a will depressed by an almost infinitesimal
weight; the slight cloudiness in a drop of desire, and the well-nigh im-
perceptible change of colour in an atom of confidence. All these: for of
just such processes life now consisted, our life, which had slipped into us
and had drawn so deeply in that it was scarcely possible even to conjecture
about it any more.

'Given as you were to revelation, a timeless tragic poet, you had to translate this fine-spun activity at one stroke into the most convincing gestures,
into the most present things. Then you set about that unexampled act of

violence in your work, which sought ever more impatiently, ever more desperately, equivalents among things that are seen to the inward vision. There was a rabbit, a garret, a room where someone paced to and fro; there was the clatter of glass in a neighbouring apartment, a fire outside the windows; there was the sun. There was a church and a rock-strewn valley that was like a church. But that did not suffice; towers had ultimately to be brought in; and whole mountain ranges; and the avalanches that bury landscapes destroyed the stage, overladen with things tangible used for the sake of expressing the intangible. And now you could do no more. The two extremities that you had bent together, sprang apart; your mad strength escaped from the flexible shaft, and your work was as nothing.

'Who should understand, otherwise, why in the end you would not leave the window, headstrong as you always were? You wanted to see the passers-by; for the thought had occurred to you that some day one might make something out of them, if one decided to begin.'

*January 1965–March 1970*
*London, Stockholm, Oslo.*

# Select Bibliography (Volumes I–III)

AGERHOLM, Edvard. *Henrik Ibsen og Det Kongelige Teater*, in *Gads Danske Magasin* (Copenhagen, 1910–11).

AMDAM, Per. *Ibsen og Molde in Edda* (Oslo, 1952).

ANKER, Øyvind. *Christiania Theaters repertoire, 1827–99* (Oslo, 1956).

ANKER, Øyvind. *Henrik Ibsens brevveksling med Christiania Theater, 1878–99* (Oslo, 1965).

ANKER, Øyvind. *Kristiania Norske Theaters repertoire, 1852–63* (Oslo, 1956).

ANDERSEN, Annette. *Ibsen in America*, in *Scandinavian Notes and Studies* (Menaska, Wis., 1935–7).

ANDERSEN, Hans Christian. *Brevveksling med Edvard og Henriette Collin*, ed. C. Behrend and H. Topsøe-Jensen, IV (Copenhagen, 1936).

ANDERSEN, Hans Christian. *Dagbøger og Breve, 1868–75*, ed. Jonas Collin (Copenhagen, 1906).

ANDERSON, Rasmus B. *My Life Story* (Madison, 1915).

ARCHER, Charles. *William Archer* (London, 1931).

ARCHER, William. *Ibsen as I Knew Him*, in *Monthly Review* (London, June, 1906).

ARCHER, William. Introductions to *The Collected Works of Henrik Ibsen*, revised and edited by William Archer, I–XII (London, 1906 ff.).

ARCHER, William. *The Mausoleum of Ibsen*, in *Fortnightly Review* (London, July, 1893).

ARCHER, William. *The Theatrical 'World' of 1893, 1894, 1895, 1896, 1897* (London, 1894 ff.).

ARVESEN, O. *Oplevelser og erindringer* (Christiania, 1921).

BANG, Herman. *Teatret* (Copenhagen, 1892).

BANG, Herman. *Ti Aar* (Copenhagen, 1891).

BERGGRAV, Eivind, and BULL, Francis. *Ibsens sjelelige kriser* (Oslo, 1937).

BERGMAN, Gösta M. *Den moderna teaterns genombrott, 1890–1925* (Stockholm, 1966).

BERGSØE, Vilhelm. *Henrik Ibsen paa Ischia og 'Fra Piazza del Popolo'* (Copenhagen and Christiania, 1907).

BEYER, Harald. *Søren Kierkegaard og Norge* (Christiania, 1924).

BJÖRKLUND-BEXELL, Ingeborg. *Ibsens Vildanden, en studie* (1962, unpublished).

BJØRNSON, Bjørn. *Bare ungdom* (Oslo, 1934).

BJØRNSON, Bjørn. *Fra barndommens dage* (Christiania, 1922).

BJØRNSON, Bjørn. *Hjemmet og vennerne* (Oslo, 1932).

BJØRNSON, Bjørnstjerne. *Gro-tid (brev fra aarene 1857–70)*, ed. Halvdan Koht, I, II (Christiania, 1912).

BJØRNSON, Bjørnstjerne. *Brytnings-aar (brev fra aarene 1871–8)*, ed. Halvdan Koht, I, II (Christiania, 1921).

BJØRNSON, Bjørnstjerne. *Kamp-tid (brev fra aarene 1879–84)*, ed. Halvdan Koht, I, II (Oslo, 1932).

BJØRNSON, Bjørnstjerne. *Breve til Karoline, 1858–1907*, ed. Dagny Bjørnson-Sautreau (Oslo, 1957).

BJØRNSON, Bjørnstjerne. *Brevveksling med danske, 1875–1910*, ed. Øyvind Anker, Francis Bull and Torben Nielsen, I–III (Oslo, 1953).

BJØRNSON, Bjørnstjerne. *Brevveksling med svenske, 1858–1909*, ed. Øyvind Anker, Francis Bull and Örjan Lindberger, I–III (Oslo, 1960–61).

BLANC, T. *Christiania Theaters historie, 1827–77* (Christiania, 1899).

BLANC, T. *Norges første nationale scene* (Christiania, 1884).

BLYTT, Peter. *Minder fra den første norske scene i Bergen* (Bergen, 1894).

BOTTEN HANSEN, Paul. *Henrik Ibsen* in *Illustreret Nyhedsblad* (Christiania, 19 July 1863).

BRANDES, Edvard. *Litterære Tendenser* (Copenhagen, 1968).

BRANDES, Edvard. *Om Teater* (Copenhagen, 1947).

BRANDES, Edvard, and BRANDES, Georg. *Brevveksling med nordiske Forfattere og Videnskabsmænd*, ed. Morten Borup, Francis Bull and John Landquist, I–VII (Copenhagen, 1939–42). **"Brandes Brevveksling."**

BRANDES, Georg. *Henrik Ibsen* (Copenhagen, 1898).

BRANDES, Georg. *Henrik Ibsen i Frankrig* in *Norden* (Stockholm, 1902).

BRANDES, Georg. *Henrik Ibsen og hans Skole i Tyskland* in *Tilskueren* (Copenhagen, June 1890).

BRANDES, Georg. *Henrik Ibsen: Personal Reminiscences and Remarks about his Plays* in *Century Magazine* (New York, February, 1917).

BRANDES, Georg. *Levned*, I–III (Copenhagen, 1905–8).

BREDSDORFF, Elias. *Sir Edmund Gosse's Correspondence with Scandinavian Writers* (Copenhagen, 1960).

BULL, Francis. *Essays i utvalg* (Oslo, 1964).

BULL, Francis. Introductions to *Catiline, The Warrior's Barrow, Norma, St. John's Night, The Feast at Solhaug, Olaf Liljekrans, The Vikings at Helgeland, Love's Comedy, Peer Gynt, Ghosts, The Wild Duck, Rosmersholm* and *The Lady from the Sea*, in **C.E.**

BULL, Francis. *Henrik Ibsen* in *Norsk litteratur-historie*, ed. Francis Bull, Fredrik Paasche, A. H. Winsnes and Philip Houm, IV (Oslo, 1960).

BULL, Francis. *Hildur Andersen og Henrik Ibsen* in *Edda*, 1957.

BULL, Francis. *Nordisk kunsterliv i Rom* (Oslo, 1960).

BULL, Francis. *Tradisjoner og minner* (Oslo, 1945).

BULL, Francis. *Vildanden og andre essays* (Oslo, 1966).

BULL, Marie. *Minder fra Bergens første nationale scene* (Bergen, 1905).

CHESNAIS, P. G. la, Introductions to *Oeuvres complètes d'Henrik Ibsen, traduites par P. G. la Chesnais*, I–XVI (Paris, 1914–45).

COLLIN, Christen. *Bjørnstjerne Bjørnson, hans barndom og ungdom*, I, II (Christiania, 1902, 1907).

DAAE, Ludvig. *Paul Botten Hansen* in *Vidar* (Copenhagen), 1888.

DARDEL, Fritz von. *Dagboksanteckningar, 1873–6* (Stockholm, 1916).

DARDEL, Fritz von. *Dagboksanteckningar, 1881–5* (Stockholm, 1920).

DERRY, T. K. *A Short History of Norway* (London, 1957).

DIETRICHSON, Lorentz. *Svundne Tider*, I–IV (Christiania, 1894–1917).

DOWNS, Brian W. *Ibsen: the Intellectual Background* (Cambridge, 1946).

DUE, Christopher. *Erindringer fra Henrik Ibsens ungdomsaar* (Copenhagen, 1909).

DUVE, Arne. *Symbolikken i Henrik Ibsens skuespill* (Oslo, 1945).

EITREM, Hans. *Ibsen og Grimstad* (Oslo, 1940).

ELIAS, Julius. *Ibsenminne af hans tyske oversetter* in *Samtiden* (Oslo, 1940).

ELLER, W. H. *Ibsen in Germany, 1870–1900* (Boston, 1918).

ELLMANN, Richard. *James Joyce* (London, 1959).

FENGER, Henning. *Georg Brandes Læreår* (Copenhagen, 1955).

FENGER, Henning. *Ibsen og Georg Brandes indtil 1872* in *Edda*, 1964.

FLEETWOOD, Carl Georgsson. *Från studieår och diplomattjanst*, I, II (Stockholm, 1968).

FORESTER, Thomas. *Norway in 1848 and 1849* (London, 1850).

FRANC, Miriam. *Ibsen in England* (Boston, 1919).

GEIJERSTAM, Gustaf af. *Två minnen om Henrik Ibsen*, in *Ord och Bild* (Stockholm, 1898).

GEORGE, David E. R. *Henrik Ibsen in Deutschland*: *Rezeption und Revision* (Göttingen, 1968).

GLOERSEN, Kristian. *Henrik Ibsen: minder fra mit samvær med ham i utlandet*, in *Kringsjaa* (Christiania, 1906).

GOSSE, Edmund. *Ibsen* (London, 1907).

GOSSE, Edmund. *Two Visits to Denmark, 1872, 1874* (London, 1911).

GRAN, Gerhard, ed. *Henrik Ibsen: festskrift i anledning af hans 70de fødselsdag* (Bergen, 1898).

GRAN, Gerhard. *Henrik Ibsen: liv og verker*, I, II (Christiania, 1918).

GRANVILLE BARKER, Harley. *The Coming of Ibsen* in *The Eighteen-Eighties*, ed. Walter de la Mare (Cambridge, 1930).

GREGERSEN, H. *Ibsen in Spain* (Cambridge, Mass., 1936).

GRIEG, Harald. *En dansk forlegger og fire norske diktere* (Oslo, 1955).

GRØNVOLD, Didrik. *Diktere og musikere* (Oslo, 1945).

GRØNVOLD, Marcus. *Fra Ulrikken til Alperne* (Oslo, 1925).

HALVORSEN, J. B. *Henrik Ibsen* in *Norsk forfatter-lexicon, 1814–80*, III (Christiania, 1892).

HAMMER, S. C. *Kristianias historie*, IV (Christiania, 1923).

HAMRE, Kari. *Clemens Petersen og hans forhold til norsk litteratur i aarene 1856–9* (Oslo, 1945).

HAMSUN, Knut. *Paa turné* (Oslo, 1960).

HEDIN, Sven. *Stormän och kungar* (Stockholm, 1950).

HEIBERG, Gunnar. *Ibsen og Bjørnson paa scenen* (Christiania, 1918).

HEIBERG, Gunnar. *Salt og sukker* (Christiania, 1924).

HEIBERG, Johan Ludvig. *Om Vaudeville og dens Betydning paa den danske Skueplads* (Copenhagen, 1826).

HEIBERG, Johanne Luise. *Et Liv gjenoplevet i Erindringer*, III (Copenhagen, 1892).

HØST, Else. *Hedda Gabler: en monografi* (Oslo, 1958).

HØST, Sigurd. *Ibsens diktning og Ibsen selv* (Oslo, 1927).

IBSEN, Bergliot. *De tre* (Oslo, 1949).

IBSEN, Henrik. *Samlede verker, hundreårsutgave*, I–XXI, ed. Halvdan Koht, Francis Bull and Didrik Arup Seip (Oslo, 1928–58). **C.E.**

IBSEN, Henrik. *Efterladte skrifter*, I–III, ed. Halvdan Koht and Julius Elias (Christiania and Copenhagen, 1909).

JÆGER, Henrik. *Henrik Ibsen: et livsbillede* (Christiania, 1888).

JAMES, Henry. *The Scenic Art* (London, 1949).

JANSON, Kristofer. *Hvad jeg har oplevet* (Christiania, 1913).

JOHNSEN, P. Rosenkrantz. *Om og omkring Henrik Ibsen og Suzannah Ibsen* (Oslo, 1928).

JOSEPHSON, Ludvig. *Ett och annat om Henrik Ibsen och Kristiania Teater* (Stockholm, 1898).

JUST, Carl. *Schrøder og Christiania Theater* (Oslo, 1948).

KINCK, B. M. *Henrik Ibsen og Laura Kieler* in *Edda*, 1935.

KING, Basil. *Ibsen and Emilie Bardach* in *Century Magazine* (October and November, 1923).

KNORRING, Oscar von. *Två månader i Egypten* (Stockholm, 1873).

KNUDTZON, Frederick G. *Ungdomsdage* (Copenhagen, 1927).

KOHT, Halvdan. *Henrik Ibsen: eit diktarliv*, I, II (revised edn., Oslo, 1954).

KOHT, Halvdan. Introductions to *The Pretenders, Brand, The League of Youth, Emperor and Galilean, The Pillars of Society, A Doll's House, An Enemy of the People* and *Hedda Gabler*, in **C.E.**

KOMMANDANTVOLD, K. M. *Ibsen og Sverige* (Oslo, 1956).

KONOW, Karl. *Bjørnson og Lie* (Oslo, 1919).

LAMM, Martin. *Det moderna dramat* (Stockholm, 1948).

LEFFLER, Anne-Charlotte. *En självbiografi* (Stockholm, 1922).

LIE, Erik. *Erindringer fra et dikterhjem* (Oslo, 1928).

LIE, Erik. *Jonas Lie, oplevelser, fortalt af Erik Lie* (Christinia, 1908).

LINDBERG, Per. *August Lindberg* (Stockholm, 1943).

LINDER, Gurli. *Sällskapsliv i Stockholm under 1880– och 1890–talen* (Stockholm, 1918).

LINDER, Sten. *Ibsen, Strindberg och andra* (Stockholm, 1936).

LINDSTRÖM, Göran. *Strindberg contra Ibsen*, in *Ibsen-Årbok, 1955–6* (Skien, 1956).

LUGNÉ-POE, Aurélien. *Ibsen* (Paris, 1936).

LUND, Audhild. *Henrik Ibsen og Det Norske Theater, 1857–63* (Oslo, 1925).

MCFARLANE, J. W., ed. *The Oxford Ibsen*, II, IV-VII (London, 1960–66).

MEYER, Michael. Introductions to and Stage Histories of *The Pretenders, Brand, Peer Gynt, The Pillars of Society, A Doll's House, Ghosts, An Enemy of the People, The Wild Duck, Rosmersholm, The Lady from the Sea, Hedda Gabler, The Master Builder, Little Eyolf, John Gabriel Borkman* and *When We Dead Awaken*, translated by Michael Meyer (London, 1960–66).

MIDBØE, Hans. *Streiflys over Ibsen* (Oslo, 1960).

MOHR, Otto Lous. *Henrik Ibsen som maler* (Oslo, 1953).

MOSFJELD, Oskar. *Henrik Ibsen og Skien* (Oslo, 1949).

NÆRUP, Carl. *Jonas Lie og hans samtidige* (Christiania, 1915).

NAG, Martin. *Ibsen i russisk åndsliv* (Oslo, 1967).

NEIIENDAM, Robert. *Gjennem mange Aar* (Copenhagen, 1933).

NEIIENDAM, Robert. *Mennesker bag Masker* (Copenhagen, 1931).

NIELSEN, L. C. *Frederik V. Hegel: et Mindeskrift*, I, II (Copenhagen, 1909).

NIELSEN, Yngvar. *En Kristianiensers erindringer fra 1850– og 1860–aarene* (Christiania and Copenhagen, 1910).

NYHOLM, Kela. *Henrik Ibsen paa den franske scene*, in *Ibsen-Årbok, 1957–9* (Skien, 1959).

OLLÉN, Gunnar. *Ibsens dramatik* (Stockholm, 1955).

ORDING, Frederik. *Henrik Ibsens vennekreds, Det lærde Holland* (Oslo, 1927).

ØSTVEDT, Einar. *Henrik Ibsen* (Oslo, 1968).

ØSTVEDT, Einar. *Henrik Ibsen og la bella Italia* (Skien, 1965).

PAULI, Georg. *Mina romerska år* (Stockholm, 1924).

PAULSEN, John. *Mine erindringer* (Copenhagen, 1900).

PAULSEN, John. *Nye erindringer* (Copenhagen, 1901).

PAULSEN, John. *Erindringer, Siste samling* (Copenhagen, 1903).

PAULSEN, John. *Samliv med Ibsen* (Copenhagen and Christiania, 1906).

PAULSEN, John. *Samliv med Ibsen, 2den samling* (Copenhagen and Christiania, 1913).

PETTERSEN, Hjalmar. *Henrik Ibsen 1828–1928, bedømt af Samtid og Eftertid* (Oslo, 1928).

ROBINS, Elizabeth. *Theatre and Friendship* (London, 1932).

RUDLER, Roderick. *Scenebilledkunsten i Norge for 100 år siden*, in *Kunst og Kultur* (Oslo, 1960).

SCHINDLER, Peter. *En Ungdom* (Copenhagen, 1942).

SCHNEIDER, J. A. *Fra det gamle Skien*, III (Skien, 1924).

SEIP, Didrik Arup. *Henrik Ibsen og K. Knudsen: Det sproglige gjennembrud hos Ibsen*, in *Edda*, 1914.

SEIP, Didrik Arup. Introductions to *Poems, The Master Builder, Little Eyolf, John Gabriel Borkman* and *When We Dead Awaken*, in **C.E.**

SHAW, George Bernard. *Collected Letters, 1874–97*, ed. Dan H. Laurence (London, 1965).

SHAW, George Bernard. *Our Theatre in the Nineties*, I–III (revised edn., London, 1954).

SHAW, George Bernard. *The Quintessence of Ibsenism* (3rd edn., London, 1922).

SKAVLAN, Einar. *Gunnar Heiberg* (Oslo, 1960).

SONTUM, Bolette. *Personal Recollections of Henrik Ibsen*, in *The Bookman* (New York, 1913).

SPRINCHORN, Evert, ed. *Ibsen, Letters and Speeches* (New York, 1964).

STANISLAVSKY, Konstantin. *My Life in Art*, trans. J. J. Robbins (London, 1924).

STEINER, George. *The Death of Tragedy* (London, 1961).

STRINDBERG, August. *August Strindbergs brev*, I–XI, ed. Torsten Eklund (Stockholm, 1948 ff.).

STRINDBERG, August. *Den litterära reaktionen i Sverige sedan 1865*, in *Tilskueren* (Copenhagen, May, 1886).

STRINDBERG, August. *Konstakadamiens utställning, 1877*, in *Kulturhistoriske Studier* (Stockholm, 1881).

TEDFORD, Ingrid. *Ibsen Bibliography, 1928–57* (Oslo, 1961).

TENNANT, P. F. D. *Ibsen's Dramatic Technique* (Cambridge, 1948).

THORESEN, Magdalene. *Breve, 1855–1901*, ed. J. Clausen and P. F. Rist (Copenhagen, 1919).

THORESEN, Magdalene. *Om Henrik Ibsen og hans hustru*, in *Juleroser* (Copenhagen, 1901).

TYSDAHL, Bjørn. *Ibsen-brev i Brittisk Museum Archer-samling*, in *Edda*, 1966.

VISTED, Kristofer. *Henrik Ibsen i karikaturen*, in *Boken om bøger*, II (Oslo, 1927).

WIESENER, A. M. *Henrik Ibsen og Det Norske Theater i Bergen, 1851–7* (Bergen, 1928).

WIRSEN, C. D. af. *Kritiker* (Stockholm, 1901).
WOLF, Lucie. *Mine livserindringer* (Christiania, 1898).
ZUCKER, A. E. *Ibsen, the Master Builder* (London, 1929).

And the files of:

*Aftenbladet* (Christiania,) *Aftenposten, Aftonbladet* (Stockholm), *Bergenske Blade, Bergens-posten, Bergens Tidende, Christiania-Posten, Dagbladet* (Christiania), *Dagbladet* (Copenhagen), *Dagens Nyheter, Dølen, Edda, Fædrelandet, Folkets Avis, Fortnightly Review, Fremskridt, Illustreret Nyhedsblad, Illustreret Tidende, Illustrated London News, London Figaro, Morgenbladet* (Christiania), *Morgenbladet* (Copenhagen), *Nationen, Nordisk Tidskrift, Ny Illustrerad Tidning, Ny Illustreret Tidende, Nya Dagligt Allehanda, Nyt Tidskrift, Pall Mall Gazette, Politiken, Samtiden, Saturday Review, Scribner's Monthly Magazine, Tilskueren, The Times, Urd, Verdens Gang, Vikingen.*

# Index

(Volume 3 only)

Art, see Painting and Caricature
Arvesen, O., 225–6
Asquith, H. H., 283
*Athenaeum, The*, 167
Atherton, J. S., 315n
Aubernon de Nerville, Mme., 182
Augsburg, 68, 75, 78, 83
Australia, 116, 119, 168, 173
Autobiography, Ibsen's projected, 284–5, 298, 309
Aveling, Dr. Edward, 182
Aveling, Eleanor Marx, see Marx-Aveling


Bach, J. S., 339
Bachke, O. A., 29
Bady, Berthe, 232, 239, 279
Bagge, Magnus, 49
Bahr, Hermann, 105
Bang, Herman, on HEDDA GABLER, 158, 197; Ibsen at Bang's lectures, 197; on THE LADY FROM THE SEA in Paris, 218; advises Lugné-Poe on Ibsen, 232, 235; Réjane's tribute to, 236; takes Lugné-Poe to see Ibsen, 239–40; also 19
*Bankrupt, A*, 103
Bankruptcy, 207, 267
Bardach, Emilie, with Ibsen in Gossensass, 123–7; corresponds with Ibsen, 128–38, 153; Ibsen slanders, 138–9; influence on Ibsen's work, 139–40, 160, 161, 314n; possible part-original of Hedda Gabler, 146, 161; and of Hilde Wangel, 138–9, 216; her subsequent life, 161, 335; her comment on THE MASTER BUILDER, 216n; last message to Ibsen, 138, 282; also 144, 148, 193, 214, 268, 296, 314n, 324
Barnay, Ludwig, 191
Barny, Mlle., 147
Barrie, J. M., 221, 283
Barthel, Alexander, 79
Bastien-Lepage, Jules, 117
Baudelaire, Charles, 109
Bauer, Henri, 233
Beaconsfield, Lord, see Disraeli
Beerbohm, Max, 340
Beerbohm Tree, Herbert, see Tree
Beethoven, Ludwig von, 109, 200, 308, 339
Bell, Clara, 154
Bell, Florence, 222
Bell, Gertrude, 221
Bellew, Kyrle, 33
Benedictsson, Victoria, 94–5, 99n
Benson, F. R., 168
Berchtesgaden, 56, 312
Berg, Leo, 168
Berg, Maria, 79
Bergen, Ibsen revisits, 60–1; performances of Ibsen's plays at, 19, 29, 45, 60, 75, 170, 199;

fees from, 30, 65, 101, 144, 198, 246, 280;*ta passim*
*Bergens Tidende*, 43
Bernhardt, Sarah, 25–6, 76, 77n, 179
Bernini, Giovanni, 145
Besant, Annie, 92
*Beyond Mortal Power*, 88
Bible, The, 100, 213, 298, 303
Bing, Just, 243
Bismarck, Otto von, 213
Bjørnson, Bjørn, artistic director of Christiania Theatre, 40; biographical note on, 46n; 'madness of the young will conquer', 55; directs ROSMERSHOLM, 75; unsuited to play Dr Kroll, 75–6; acts Peer Gynt, 202; on PEER GYNT in Paris, 264; director of National Theatre, 303, 326; also 324n, 325n
Bjørnson, Bjørnstjerne, asks Ibsen to help run theatre, 30–1, 40–1; part-model for Stensgaard, 58n, 139; relations with Strindberg, 31, 38, 40, 99; reconciled with Ibsen in Schwaz, 38–42; assesses Ibsen's intelligence, 40; incompatibility with Ibsen, 42; hates THE WILD DUCK, 43; *Beyond Mortal Power* praised by Ibsen, 88; quarrels with Georg Brandes, 94; admired by Tolstoy, 109; defends Laura Kieler, 148; supposed champion of dilettantism, 187; better than Ibsen at parties, 189; attacked by Hamsun, 193; invites Sigurd to Aulestad, 204–5; angry again with Ibsen, 204–5; on humbug of church weddings, 209–10; supposed model for Solness, 212; Ibsen's need of, 253; bogus interview with, 272; with Ibsen at opening of National Theatre, 303, 307; wins Nobel Prize, 324; insulted by Swedish sentry, 324; part-model for Dr Stockmann, 325; last meeting with Ibsen, 325; 'Ibsen is rich and I poor', 329; dies, 335; Ibsen writes to, 25, 30–1, 41–2, 278, 299; writes to Ibsen, 30, 38, 102, 209; also 23, 54, 55, 110, 148, 170, 274, 293, 299;
Bjørnson, Erling, 39
Bjørnson, Karoline, 242
Blehr, Frøken, 242, 253
Bloch, Felix, 163, 198, 219, 233–4, 246, 250, 261, 270–1, 280, 299, 309, 319, 320
Blumenthal, Oskar, 191
Boer War, Ibsen on, 319
Bøgh, Erik, 45–6, 110, 113
Bonnard, Pierre, 264
Borchsenius, Betty, 29n
Borgström, Hilda, 224
Boström, E. C., 329
Botten Hansen, Paul, 107
Bowen, Crosswell, 340n
Bradley, A. C., 283
Brækstad, H. L., 150–1, 211

Oberammergau, 27, 150, 152
*Observer, The*, 118, 169
Obstfelder, Sigbjørn, 280
O'Casey, Sean, 171
Oedipus complex, 73–4
Oehlenschläger, Adam, 286
Oeuvre, Théâtre de l', 232–3, 235–7, 238–41, 263–4
Olivier, Sydney, 149
Ollén, Gunnar, 52n, 276n
Olrik, Ole H. B., 255
Olsen, Olaus, 261, 310
O'Neill, Eugene, 335, 339–40
Opera, Ibsen and, 91, 92, 230
Orcutt, Mrs. Reginald, 123n, 355
*Ørebladet*, 90n, 284n, 297n, 318, 324
Osborne, John, 19n
Oscar, II, King, dispute with Storthing, 57n; gives Ibsen key to park, 259; bogus interview with, 272; contributes to Ibsen's *Festskrift*, 283; honours Ibsen in Stockholm, 293; has doubts about Sigurd, 293; disapproves of GHOSTS, 293–4; sees LADY INGER, 296; becomes friendly with Sigurd, 302, 328
Oslo, see Christiania
Österling, Hans, 98
*Othello*, 52, 113, 193, 214
Ottersen, Valborg, 318n

Painting, Ibsen's interest in, 49, 54, 68, 103, 130, 131, 151, 192, 195, 203, 245, 253
*Pall Mall Gazette*, 165, 172–3, 222
Paris, 25–6, 31, 38, 52, 84, 108, 115, 141, 147, 166, 171, 181, 182, 197–8, 218–19, 232–3, 235–7, 246, 258, 263–4, 279, 280–1, 295n, 319
Parliament, Norwegian, see Storthing
Passarge, Ludwig, 37
Pasteur, Louis, 170
Paul, Adolf, 168
Paulsen, John, offends Ibsen with *Fru Cecilia*, 107; contributes to *Festskrift*, 284; also 25, 60n, 61n, 110n, 145
Paus, Christian, 207
PEER GYNT, reprints, 65–6, 68, 81, 183, 198, 234, 270, 319; Strindberg refers to, 99; Helene Raff paints Solveig, 146, 203; Pontius Pilate and, 148; Ibsen sees, 202; Ibsen quotes to Hildur, 219; in England, 234, 280–1; in Russia, 259; Ibsen's doubts about Grieg's music, 259; Lugné-Poe's production, 263–4; Shaw on universality of, 263–4; Alfred Jarry in, 264; BORKMAN and, 268, 270; WHEN WE DEAD AWAKEN and, 270; bilingual reading to Ibsen, 279; in *Finnegans Wake*, 315n; also 20, 49, 52, 59, 101, 112, 194, 283, 299, 337
Pekar, Giula, 258

Petersen, Clemens, 98, 110
Petersen, Julius, 65
Petersen, Otto, 30
Petersen, Valdemar, 291n
Petersen, Vilhelm, 190n
Petersen, William, 220, 221
Petterssen, Eilif, 252–3, 255
Philippi, Felix, 68
Photography, Ibsen and, 68, 317, 328
Physical appearance, Ibsen's, 24, 58–9, 65, 66, 80, 85, 88, 93–4, 103–4, 168, 174, 195, 197, 201, 229–31, 254, 257, 259, 304, 315, 317, 320, 322–8, 332
Pigott, W. S., 223
Pilgrim, E. von, 84
PILLARS OF SOCIETY, THE, in England, 32–3, 112, 115, 118, 142n, 227–8; in Germany, 78, 84, 103, 115, 116, 143, 144, 163–4, 198, 234, 261, 319; in Russia, 141, 280, 301, 339; in America, 142n, 372; in France, 263; Ibsen sees, 302; Joyce quotes, 313; in *Finnegans Wake*, 315n; Chekhov wishes to see, 339; also 42, 77, 80, 101, 107, 187, 194, 234, 268, 282, 307, 310, 314n
Pinero, Sir Arthur Wing, 171, 264, 283
Pirandello, Luigi, 167, 284, 339
Pirenne, Henri, 82n
*Playboy of the Western World, The*, 171
Poe, Edgar Allan, 28
Poel, William, 53
POEMS, Ibsen's Collected, reprints of, 81, 198, 219, 318
Poland, 32, 52, 102
Politics, Ibsen and, 23, 34, 55–6, 64, 77, 87, 91, 102, 104, 106–7, 149–52, 155, 187, 191–2, 208, 226
Pollock, Sir Frederick, 221
*Politiken*, 44, 51, 71, 110, 113, 158, 170, 196n, 212, 214, 243, 244, 288, 291n, 306, 308, 309, 319
Pontius Pilate, 148
Pontoppidan, Henrik, 168
Poulsen, Emil, 53, 170, 241, 274, 284
*Power of Darkness, The*, 108, 147
PRETENDERS, THE, reprinted, 21, 30, 115, 143, 246, 270, 310; Bishop Nicholas and Norway, 62; in Sweden, 62, 81, 295, 299; Strindberg's implied respect for, 71n, 100; Henry Irving rejects, 76n; in Germany, 103, 182; in Vienna, 166, 176, 261; Ibsen drunk at, 295; in Denmark, 310, 320; also 49, 58, 243
Proust, Marcel, 182, 218, 324
Prozor, Count Moritz, 115, 141, 144, 146–7, 154, 155, 167, 258, 264, 308, 310, 312
Punctuality, Ibsen's passion for, 67, 323

*Quintessence of Ibsenism, The*, 45, 149, 194, 236, 307n, 312